THE POLITICAL DESCARTES

First published as *Descartes politico: o, della ragionevole ideologia* by
Feltrinelli, Milan 1970 © Feltrinelli 1970
This edition published by Verso 2007
© Verso 2006
Translation © Alberto Toscano and Matteo Mandarini 2006
All rights reserved

3 5 7 9 10 8 6 4 2

Verso
UK: 6 Meard Street, London W1F 0EG
USA: 20 Jay St, Suite 1010, Brooklyn, NY 11201
www.versobooks.com

Verso is the imprint of New Left Books

ISBN-13: 978-1-84467-582-1
ISBN-10: 1-84467-582-3

British Library Cataloguing in Publication Data
A catalogue record for this book is available from the British Library

Library of Congress Cataloging-in-Publication Data
A catalog record for this book is available from the Library of Congress

Typeset in Adobe Garamond by Hewer Text UK Ltd, Edinburgh
Printed in the US

Contents

Antonio Negri and the Antinomies of Bourgeois Thought

The Political Descartes, originally published in Italian in 1970 and only now translated into English, will introduce the reader to the extraordinarily rich Italian tradition of historiography and history of ideas, as well as provide the Anglophone reader with a completely novel insight into Descartes's philosophy. The reader may be surprised to discover the 'father of Modern Philosophy' as a committed political thinker whose metaphysical meditations cannot be divorced from the profound political, economic and social changes that caught seventeenth-century Europe in a spiral of religious and political violence, just as the nascent capitalism was undergoing a profound economic crisis.

All too often Descartes's philosophy is taught within the stark and restricting disciplinary boundaries that characterize the academic compartmentalization formulated centuries after Descartes's epoch. The divorce of the 'History of Modern Philosophy' from the 'History of Political Philosophy' is typically used to delimit the thinking of Modern philosophers and results in the separation of politics and metaphysics by institutional fiat. Antonio Negri's reading of Descartes refuses any such restriction, in the same way as he was to do a decade later with respect to Spinoza in *The Savage Anomaly.* In the latter book, Negri works with the same anti-deterministic, 'biographical' and agonistic concept of historical materialism, and continues to look for Spinoza's politics precisely in his metaphysics. For, as he writes, in a statement that is equally applicable to Descartes: 'how could we not see that metaphysics is the only practicable form of politics, here, in this century, in this country?[1] This insight lies at the heart of what Negri tries to do in his writings on the 1600s, which span fifteen or more years. In *The Political Descartes*, specifically, we find Negri tracing a particularly innovative and prescient ideology for the advance of bourgeois interests at the time of the retreat of its political project in the face of a rising absolutist monarchy and the going into crisis of the progressive impetus of capitalism.

Before considering more closely the connection between Descartes's thought and the epoch to which – as Negri shows – it was so intimately tied, it should be acknowledged that many Anglophone readers of Descartes may, at first, consider this approach to the 'founder of Modern Philosophy' both surprising and misjudged. After all, is not Descartes the rationalist thinker of mind–body dualism and the ontological proof, of the 'I think therefore I am' as the founding moment of modern thought? What has any of this to do with the progressive impetus of capitalism? What has it to do with class or politics at all?[2] Indeed, many readers of Descartes will be completely unaware that he not only wrote many of his most important works in the course of the Thirty Years War but that he fought in many of the bloody battles that scarred the territories of Europe in this period. It is here that we note the striking plasticity of Negri's adoption of the historical

1. A. Negri, *The Savage Anomaly: The Power of Spinoza's Metaphysics and Politics*, Minneapolis 1991, p. 235, note 16.
2. This is not to say that Descartes's political thought has been entirely ignored in the critical literature. For an updated bibliography, see Q. Taylor, 'Descartes's Paradoxical Politics', *Humanitas*, vol. 14, no. 2, 2001, pp. 76–103. Taylor's article is particularly interesting inasmuch as it tries to investigate the paradox between the progressive legacy of Descartes, on the one hand, and his 'reactionary conservatism' in political matters, on the other, and looks at the tension between the utopian and conformist strands in his thought. Taylor's choice of a merely doctrinal (rather than conjunctural and socio-political) treatment of this paradox, however, prevents a real intersection with Negri's work (whom he nevertheless cites).

materialist method with its refusal of strict disciplinary boundaries and its simple separation of problems considered philosophical – in Descartes's case often simply epistemological – from political and social struggles. And so it is to the historical, social and political context that Negri links the development of Descartes's thought. But what is particularly fascinating is the way that the links are made: how metaphysical problems are shown to be immediately political, and political tasks are sustained through the development of a metaphysics. What we find, aside from a provocative reinterpretation of a philosopher who it may be thought had little new to tell us, is the innovative deployment of a concept of ideology, one that refuses the more schematic versions of Marxism concerning the secondary and dependent character of ideology – its relegation to the sphere of reproduction: reproduction cannot be conceived as derived from a primary production, nor can the superstructure be simply reduced to a 'reflection' of the base. Talking about a much later time in French thought, the 1950s and 1960s, when the thematic of 'reproduction' had become central, Negri says that at this time the focus was on 'the ways according to which, passing through the ideological consistency of knowledge, social action and, therefore, social being can be perpetuated or modified, or – rather – interrupted, broken, or overturned'.[3]

Interestingly, this was also central to the 'workerist' reappraisal of the Marxist tradition, as exemplified in Mario Tronti's and Raniero Panzieri's hugely influential studies of book two of *Capital: The Process of Circulation of Capital*.[4] It is no coincidence that in 1968, when work on *The Political Descartes* had already begun, Negri wrote his 'Marx sul ciclo e la crisi' (Marx on the Cycle and the Crisis), in which circulation, or – more broadly –

3. 'Alle origini del biopolitico. Seminario sulla filosofia francese contemporanea', unpublished lecture given on 3 February 1997 at the Collège International de Philosophie, Paris.
4. This second volume of *Capital* was translated by Panzieri for the standard edition of *Capital* for Editori Riuniti in 1956.

reproduction, was the focus.[5] Thus, Negri in the late 1960s was deeply involved in the problem of reproduction, and it is this problem that is the thematic underpinning to the work on Descartes.

This brief introduction will be divided into three sections. The first will attempt to set the book within the context of Negri's other writings on the emergence of the modern state-form prior to *The Savage Anomaly*. This will be followed by a discussion of the debate sparked by *The Political Descartes* between Negri and his erstwhile collaborator, Massimo Cacciari. In conclusion, Negri's discussion of Descartes will be contrasted to the 'return to Descartes' in recent radical political thought.

1

As Antonio Negri points out in the Postface written especially for this translation of *The Political Descartes*, his turn to the study of Descartes in the late 1960s struck many of those who knew him and his work as perplexing. This was not because Negri was considered simply a militant or a strictly political thinker. He was already the author of books on Hegel, German historicism, and Kant. It was, rather, that the late Sixties saw a period of intense political turmoil coinciding with the formation of the group *Potere operaio* – for which Negri and many of his colleagues would pay dearly by the end of the following decade of state-sponsored

5. See A. Negri, *Revolution Retrieved*, London 1988. For a discussion of Negri and the Workerist tradition (*operaismo* in Italian), see M. Mandarini, 'Translator's Introduction', in A. Negri, *Time for Revolution*, London 2003; M. Mandarini, 'Antagonism, Contradiction, Time: Conflict and Organization in Antonio Negri', in *Contemporary Organization Theory*, ed. C. Jones and R. Munro, Oxford 2005, and *The Sociological Review*, vol. 53, no. 1, 2005. See also Y. Moulier, 'Introduction', in A. Negri, *The Politics of Subversion*, London 1989, and S. Wright, *Storming Heaven: Class Composition and Struggle in Italian Autonomist Marxism*, London 2002.

repression in Italy.[6] We will not rehearse here the response that Negri has provided to the very 'reasonable doubt' that struck and may still strike his readers. We shall focus, instead, in this first section of the introduction, on one aspect that connects *The Political Descartes* to the crucial debates concerning the course of capitalist development that in turn provided the background to many of the disputes over the role of bourgeois ideology in the following decade. The debate, which has been central in Marxist discourse since the work of Marx himself, is that surrounding the notion of the 'bourgeois revolution': the supposed progressive function of the bourgeoisie. This debate has been particularly lively amongst Anglophone Marxists over the last thirty years, with historians such as Robert Brenner, Ellen Meiksins Wood and George Comninel – among others – questioning its validity on a variety of grounds.[7] Negri is already questioning this idea in the late Sixties, but from a very different perspective. Whereas Brenner, Meiksins Wood and others are led by the lack of any bourgeois class autonomy on the Continent to question the very existence of capitalism outside England prior to the nineteenth century, Negri argues that it is only the notion of bourgeois class unity that becomes suspect – *not capitalism itself.* Indeed, Negri's principal concern is with what occurs when the capitalist revolution goes into crisis. What happens to bourgeois ideology, to civil society, and to the state? In an article from 1978 in which he reappraises the work of a decade earlier, he writes that he had attempted to show that:

6. For an overview of the repression, as it concerned Negri in particular, see T. S. Murphy, 'Editor's Introduction: Books for Burning', in A. Negri, *Books for Burning*, London 2005. For an internal, militant reckoning of the dynamics of revolt and defeat, see the collective document written from Rebibbia prison by Negri and his comrades, 'Do You Remember Revolution?', in *Radical Thought in Italy*, ed. P. Virno and M. Hardt, Minneapolis 1996.
7. See the two Deutscher Lectures published in *Historical Materialism*, 13.2, 13.3, and 13.4 by Benno Teschke and Neil Davidson for very recent contrasting positions on this debate.

the 'philosophy of manufacture' was anything but a unitary bloc
. . . instead, the structural elements of the transformation of the
world of production, the revolutionary forces that, from the
fourteenth century in Italy and the Low Countries, from the
time of the Renaissance throughout Europe, freed themselves,
encounter . . . a vast field of ideological alternatives . . . These
frequently form the basis of the tendencies of bourgeois ideology
. . . throughout the period of bourgeoisie domination.[8]

The notion of the 'bourgeoisie as a class', Negri insists, is
'extremely ambiguous' – since it lacks the unity and ideological
autonomy demanded by such a notion. Hence, his assertion that,
'generally speaking one cannot speak of bourgeois "revolution"
but one must speak of a *capitalist revolution*'.[9]

At the heart of Negri's account of Descartes is the development
of the notion of 'Reasonable Ideology'. What are we to understand
by this? It gradually becomes evident in the course of *The Political
Descartes* that the idea of ideology is, in conformity with the
Marxist tradition, linked to a class position – in this case that of the
bourgeoisie, although this latter notion is not accepted uncritically. Not least because the unity to be ascribed to the bourgeoisie,
i.e. its class 'identity', such as it is, is something that stems from
without – from the variety of responses to economic crisis and
political subjugation to absolutism. As will become clear, the one
element of ideological continuity is that determined by the
acknowledgement of separation and dualism.[10] Moreover, the
specifically Cartesian twist is given in the specific quality of that
ideology: its 'reasonableness'.

8. A. Negri, 'Manifattura e ideologia', in *Manifattura, società borghese*, ed.
   P. Schiera, Rome 1978, p. 275. Reprinted under the title 'Riflessioni
   su Grossman e Borkenau' as an appendix to *L'anomalia selvaggia*,
   Milan 1981.
9. Ibid.
10. In his 1978 article, Negri adds another element: money as means of
    exchange. More about this later.

To grasp what Negri intends by this, it is worth turning to an article he wrote on the formation of the modern state to which he frequently refers in this book.[11] In this article Negri did much of the historiographical work that sets the scene for the analysis of *The Political Descartes*. He discusses the way that the nascent bourgeoisie, whose emergence he ties to capitalist primitive accumulation – which effectively hastened the collapse of the medieval social relations – as well as to the extraordinary fertile period of Renaissance humanism, attempted to cope with the economic and social crises of the 1600s. Faced with anarchy or tyranny:

> the nascent bourgeoisie discovers in the social order the counterpart guaranteeing the freedom it had won: it is unable to resolve its own crisis without, at the same time, resolving the crisis of the social order. Freedom must now be 'defended' from the general instability that the class struggle produces. The problem is now entirely political: to measure one's own strength in each particular situation, as well as that of one's adversaries; to verify the possibility of forming alliances at the least possible cost, while preserving one's advantage . . . [T]he sun has definitively set on the great hope of being able to unify society as a whole within the design of the development of bourgeois freedom.[12]

The bourgeoisie – Negri argues – chose to renounce (or at least defer) the project of political power in order to maintain a certain autonomy in economic development, aiming to consolidate itself as the capitalist class. The division between civil society and the state stems from this situation – and it marks a tension around which social and political thought and practice will turn for many

11. A. Negri, 'Problemi di storia dello stato moderno. Francia: 1610–1650', *Rivista critica di storia della filosofia*, XXII, 2, April–June 1967.
12. 'Problemi di storia dello stato moderno', pp. 192–3.

years to follow. The bourgeoisie, then, was caught in the complex struggle aiming to maintain its position in the social–cultural–economic hierarchy through mediation with absolutism. The form of the state was that of social order itself, i.e. it maintained a certain class and professional hierarchy. Its content, however, was bourgeois – the bourgeoisie having won a hegemonic position (economically, culturally) within that order. In Negri's terms: 'Order, is the negative form: to each his place. Understood positively, on the other hand, it is: support of industry; pacification in the matter of religion . . .'[13]

Already in this article, published three years prior to *The Political Descartes*, Negri affirms that it is Descartes who grasps the problem of the epoch in its 'deepest essence'[14] whilst refusing to accept that the division between civil society – the bourgeoisie in its relative autonomy – and the absolutist state was final. The reasonable ideology that Descartes formulated affirmed a reformist political ideology, a reformist metaphysics whose task was to operate within the reality of separation. To that extent, the bourgeoisie was never revolutionary other than by default. The dualism between bourgeois class position and political command was reaffirmed but only in so far as the 'infinite metaphysical distance'[15] that divided, the gap between divine–sovereign determination of truths and the human (bourgeois-I), also opened the space for a refounding of the subject's ability to operate within the world. A nostalgia for the monistic universe of Renaissance humanism returned to charge the bourgeois project with the search for the rediscovery of unity within a divided reality. To that extent, Descartes's reasonable ideology was a pragmatic attempt to negotiate the conditions of separation and defeat suffered by the bourgeoisie. The seventeenth century was to be characterized by an 'uninterrupted tension between two formid-

13. 'Problemi di storia dello stato moderno', p. 208.
14. 'Problemi di storia dello stato moderno', p. 209.
15. 'Problemi di storia dello stato moderno', p. 211.

able pressures . . . the one towards the unification of political power, the other towards its social and juridical legitimation. *Machtorganisation* and *Rechtstaat* . . . two forces that, until the great revolution, the French bourgeoisie was unable to unify. And yet, the one is founded upon the other, in the indissoluble dialectical relationship between monarchical absolutism and bourgeois existence, between mechanical consolidation of power and its social legitimation'.[16]

Descartes is by no means the first to note this dualism – as Negri's discussion of the libertines and the mechanists makes clear – but with the notion of the reasonable ideology he opens a novel path out of the impasse that is at once entirely metaphysical and entirely political.

As we have already noted, Negri returns to the themes first tackled in his essay on the modern state and in his Descartes in an essay from 1978. It is, perhaps, here that the precarious position of the bourgeoisie, i.e. its failure to form itself as a class, is most clearly expressed:

Only the fanning out of political alternatives to the solution of the class conflict, which had built up and exploded, in the first half of the 1600s gives a basis for the formation of this social stratum, which is dramatically caught between a nostalgic fantasy of the past as a place of the absence of struggles and an uncertain and dangerous future; between a pressure from above, towards the old dominant classes and towards the state as the element of guarantee [of order], and an insurgency from below, which was the necessary effect of the upsetting of the social structures of development.[17]

16. 'Problemi di storia dello stato moderno', pp. 217–18. With the development of bourgeois culture, *Raison d'état* becomes the ideological support for the autonomy of sovereign will, i.e. of the executive, whereas social contract theory becomes gradually codified into the science of legal positivism.
17. 'Manifattura e ideologia', p. 280.

Negri reasserts his belief that the bourgeoisie never had a progressive function. At best, it engaged in a perpetual negotiation, mediation, between the state, the subaltern classes and the proletariat. Since the time of primitive accumulation, the bourgeois class was always merely the 'result of the dialectical process of class struggle'.[18] Its existence was derivative from the struggle between the other great social actors. Negri goes so far as to write that the only continuity that can be asserted of the bourgeoisie is that of money – as means of exchange, not money as capital. In other words, the realm of the bourgeoisie is the realm of mediation par excellence.[19] Hence, to focus on the bourgeoisie as a class is to draw attention away from the core struggle between capital and proletariat. Indeed, Negri affirms that two great dynamics were at work in this phase of capitalist development. One involved the bourgeoisie's attempt to mediate its existence with that of the absolutist state, so as to maintain its social position and fortunes: 'it is its capacity for mediation that must . . . survive and be reinforced'.[20] The other was the emergent capitalist class that required the state *only* as a political power, i.e. to constitute and police the labour market. As far as everything else was concerned, 'capitalism was self-sufficient'.[21] Negri describes this articulation, between bourgeoisie and capitalist class, both in terms of the dialectic between primitive accumulation and manufacture, and in the dialectic between money as means of exchange and money as measure of average socially necessary labour. It is within this set of material relations that the development of bourgeois ideology would have to insert itself in order to maintain and strengthen its

18. Ibid.
19. The other element of continuity we have mentioned is that of separation. Arguably, these two elements of continuity are interdependent: it is only because reality is divided, fissured, that money is able to form a basis for the bourgeoisie as a class, i.e. as that which connects a divided reality.
20. Negri 1978, p. 281.
21. Ibid.

role of arch-mediator. It reached its height only in the eighteenth and nineteenth centuries in the work of classical political economy and Hegel: 'The concept of the bourgeois class is an apologetic one, which is connected to a particular phase of capitalist development, that where civil society and the state formed a specific alliance. But not even at this time could the bourgeoisie be confused with the class of capitalists'.[22]

The confusion introduced with this 'apologetic' notion has – Negri insists – resulted in serious political and historiographical errors. Among the former are delusions about the defeat of the bourgeoisie coinciding with the defeat of capitalism, and the failure to note that other class actors can adopt the role of exploiters of the proletariat. Among the latter errors, Negri notes particularly how an autonomous existence can be falsely imputed to something that 'exists only in mediation . . . [and] deludes us about the continuity of an ideology that exists, instead, always only as mediation and mystification of the particular interests of the classes in struggle. It is not by chance that the history of the "bourgeoisie" is always a history of ideology, of the "autonomy" of political mediation'.[23]

Eleven years after the publication of *The Political Descartes*, Negri turns to another seventeenth-century thinker, Spinoza. In the preface to *The Savage Anomaly*, Negri indicates that his shift away from considerations of the development of the bourgeois state was undertaken so that he could explore the 'theoretical alternatives and suggestive possibilities offered by the revolution in process':[24] 'Only by going back over the history of metaphysics, only by discriminating within it real alternatives do we have the possibility of contributing to the construction of new models for the refounding of class politics within antagonism'.[25]

22. Negri 1978, p. 284.
23. Ibid.
24. *The Savage Anomaly*, p. xxi.
25. This quotation is drawn from 'Note sulla storia del politico in Tronti', published as an appendix to *L'anomalia selvaggia*, pp. 291–2. Unfortunately the appendices were not reproduced in the English edition of this book.

Thus, in place of the 'idealist dialectic' that Negri uncovers in Descartes, which would be 'developed in the great tradition of metaphysics, and concluded by Hegel',[26] 'Spinoza shows us that the living alternative to this tradition is a material power that resides within the metaphysical bloc of Modern philosophy'.[27] What Negri sought and found in Spinoza was a 'new rationality' entirely different from that of the bourgeoisie: no longer the 'dialectic as generic key' but as 'direct organization of conflict'.[28]

But what is the relation of Spinoza to the bourgeois ideology – defined by Negri as 'in addition to the political forms that have organized it at various points, the foundation and structure of the idea of the market, the efficient mystification of the social organization of production'?[29] Negri's thesis, briefly, is that the early Spinoza and the initial parts of the *Ethics* are, like Descartes's thinking, tied to the 'revolutionary utopia of the bourgeoisie'. The early Spinoza, but, in a far more important sense, Spinozism as a movement of thought, can thus be seen as ideological. Negri links these positions directly to the revolutionary thinking of the bourgeoisie:

> The abrogation of the real world, the duplication of the world in a political and juridical image – this is the effect of this operation, this is the massive and important content of Spinozism as ideology. Without Spinoza, without this ideological reduction of his thought, without the extremist totalitarianism that follows from it, it would be difficult to conceive of the political and juridical dictatorship of Jacobinism, that revolutionary legacy so dear to the bourgeoisie![30]

26. A. Negri, *Insurgencies: Constituent Power and the Modern State*, Minneapolis 1999, p. 324.
27. *The Savage Anomaly*, p. xxi.
28. *The Savage Anomaly*, p. xxii.
29. *The Savage Anomaly*, p. 68.
30. *The Savage Anomaly*, p. 71. This discussion also echoes Nietzsche's characterization of Descartes as 'the grandfather of the Revolution', in *Beyond Good and Evil*, sec. 191.

But the heart of Spinoza's work, after its inner crisis and move beyond the limits of the first parts of the *Ethics*, is – together with the thought of Machiavelli and Marx, depicted by Negri as the core of a radical alternative within political ontology – a definitive break with bourgeois ideology, and ideology *tout court*. In a manner that matches Negri's treatment of contemporary capitalism and real subsumption, Spinoza (rather than Spinozism) breaks with any form of mediation:

> If the metaphysical utopia was a transcription of the ideology of the market, the ethical dystopia is the proposal of the rupture of the market, here transposed and projected in the material and practical dimension of a philosophy of the future. The dystopia is the revelation of the real forces that move behind the rupture of the ideological perfection of the market and within the crisis of the linear development of the Power of the bourgeoisie; it is the vindication of a project that (even with these arduous obstacles) has been able to limit itself and still conserve its power in its entirety. Through this play internal to the *Ethics* a real and enormous historical alternative unfolds, one that we have often and insistently emphasized . . . Either one can submit to the crisis of the market or one can live its crisis, going beyond it through the constitutive tension. The dystopia is the discovery of a real and future revolutionary horizon.

This 'affirmation of an ontological and materialist perspective', writes Negri, 'is free from the order of the development of bourgeois ideology and from the play of the diverse possibilities of capitalistic development'.[31] It is only from the standpoint of Spinoza, then, that Negri, strongly opposing any thesis of the inevitability of ideology or the closure of thought within a capitalist totality, can define the de facto limits of the bourgeois ideology and pose its alternative, not as a distant horizon, but as a present reality of thought and practice. The reasonable ideology is displaced by a revolutionary dystopia.

31. *The Savage Anomaly*, p. 158.

This approach to the history of philosophy has also informed Negri's more recent and better-known work. Marking their difference from any determinist or mechanical understanding of the socio-historical determination of philosophy, Hardt and Negri have very recently returned to Descartes via their attempt to methodologically develop the Marxian notion of the *tendency*, which has been crucial throughout Negri's own philosophical and political trajectory. Commenting, as Negri also does in this volume, on the fact that Descartes dates his vision of intellectual certainly to 10 November 1619 and locates it in his German stay, as a soldier in the Thirty Years War, Hardt and Negri write:

> Certainly, it would be extremely reductive to conceive of Descartes's methodological discovery as merely the reaction of a distraught soldier at war. That would pose too narrow, mechanical, and linear a relation of cause and effect. It would be equally mistaken however, to separate Descartes's revelation from his social reality. Indeed the greatness of Descartes is to have recognized a form and a mode of thought that corresponds to an entire era that was in the process of emergence. The sovereign, individual, thinking self that Descartes discovers has the same *form* as a variety of other figures that would spring up more or less contemporaneously in modern Europe, from the individual economic actor, to the sovereign nation-state. Neither the Thirty Years War nor any other historical event 'causes' Descartes's theory. Rather, the entire set of relations that constitutes the reality of his situation make his theory thinkable. His discovery corresponds in form to the emerging tendency of his social reality.[32]

32. M. Hardt and A. Negri, *Multitude: War and Democracy in the Age of Empire*, New York 2004, pp. 143–4. This treatment is closer to the method of *The Political Descartes* and altogether more adequate than the far too static treatment of Descartes in terms of transcendentalism in M. Hardt and A. Negri, *Empire*, New York 2000, pp. 79–80, where the interpretive schema of Deleuze and Guattari's *What Is Philosophy?* seems to overpower Negri's allegiances to a historical materialist method.

2

Though, as Negri himself indicates in the Postface to this volume, *The Political Descartes* met with a certain incomprehension, it did elicit one reply which shows how the political impetus of ontological speculation was not just a methodological tenet of Negri's, but a reflection of the realities of debate among the Italian Left. Massimo Cacciari, who had worked with Negri agitating at the chemical factories in Porto Marghera from the early Sixties, and whom Negri himself had introduced to works ranging from Marx's *Capital* to Heidegger's *Nietzsche*, published a long review of *The Political Descartes* in a journal they had co-founded, *Contropiano*.[33] However, 'Vita Cartesii est simplicissima' (the ironic title of the review was taken from Valéry's *Monsieur Teste*) did not merely represent a dissenting opinion regarding Descartes's political thought. Rather, it was a case of philosophy as the continuation of politics by other means. After the first issue of *Contropiano*, Cacciari and Negri had in fact broken over a question that tore the radical and intellectual Italian Left apart in the early Seventies: whether to accept the hegemonic force of the PCI (Italian Communist Party) and work within the official workers' movement (the 'entryist' policy adopted by Cacciari, along with the likes of Mario Tronti and Alberto Asor Rosa) or to affirm the separateness and autonomy of the movement, especially in terms of 'irregular' workers and students, and move towards forms of struggle and organization external and alternative to the PCI. How might such concrete matters find reflection in a review of an intricate academic tome such as Negri's?

33. The early relationship between Cacciari and Negri is dealt with in D. Borso, *Il Giovane Cacciari*, Turin 1995, and R. Calimani, *La polenta e la mercanzia*, Rimini 1984 (interview with Cacciari). For the philosophical context, see G. Cantarano, *Immagini del nulla. La filosofia italiana contemporanea*, Milan 1998. For more on the contrasting positions of Negri and Cacciari, see 'Beyond Nihilism: Notes Towards a Critique of Left-Heideggerianism in Italian Philosophy of the 1970s', M. Mandarini, *Diacritics*, 2007.

The crux of Cacciari's review, which was actually presented as a joint review of Negri's text along with Lacan's *Écrits*, Chomsky's *Cartesian Linguistics* and a text by Max Bense, is the systematic rejection of Negri's framing of Descartes's relationship to Renaissance humanism, encapsulated in Negri's discussions of 'memory' and of 'humanist nostalgia'.[34] Where Negri sees Descartes's formulation of the bourgeois project as an attempt to rekindle the Renaissance hope in a possession of the world whilst accepting the reality of defeat and the new conditions this defeat had brought into being (i.e. the situation of absolutism), providing the 'reasonable' parameters for bourgeois autonomy and reconstruction, Cacciari wishes to pose an absolute and irreversible break with the corporeal utopia of Renaissance cosmology. Indeed, he even begins his review by locating a sharp caesura within the Renaissance itself. While accepting the theme of separation – so central to Negri's analysis – Cacciari seeks to evacuate the very 'ambiguity' that Negri discerns in the political Descartes. For Cacciari, while there may be something 'tragic' in departing from the synthetic Renaissance visions of a unified cosmos, there is no forced 'retreat' into the foundation provided by the I, but rather a confident affirmation of a new politics and a new science in a world of disenchanted rationality:

> The problem of overcoming the analogical Renaissance myth is therefore the very problem of the *real* foundation of modern

34. The theme of memory as a key to the logic of political subjectivity recurs in Negri's work. It is a crucial hermeneutic tool in his study on Giacomo Leopardi, *Lenta Ginestra: Saggio su Leopardi*, Milan 2001, ch. 1. However, when Negri turns to an analysis of the formation of political subjects in post-Fordism, his emphasis is on anti-memory, to be understood in terms of the discontinuity of these subjects vis-à-vis the classical workers' movement. As he puts it: 'Dialectics is memory. A black thread of consciousness runs through it.' The 'new' proletariat, on the other hand, is devoid of memory and has broken with any social dialectic. See 'Erkenntnistheorie. Elogio dell'assenza di memoria', in *Fabbriche del Soggetto*, Livorno 1987, pp. 159–60.

science, as a project of the rationalization and domination of the world . . . Abandoning the Renaissance myth does not mean abandoning the hope in possession and domination, but, rather, renewing it, founding it on entirely new logical terms, *more powerful ones* . . . Separation and the *political* domination (through scientific ratio) of the world are no longer in contradiction.[35]

As the rest of Cacciari's review makes clear, his objections to Negri are founded on the contention that the latter, in maintaining the thematic of a humanist nostalgia, does not do justice to Descartes's role in opening up the potent, affirmative movement of a rationalization and disenchantment of the world (the Weberian resonances are of course intended) which is profoundly linked to the imposition of a scientific and political technics in the place of Renaissance sympathies, affinities and analogies. The transcendence of the subject (and of God) in Descartes is 'functional to the domination of ratio over the world. Separation is political, it is the project of a new state' – indeed, Cacciari, explicitly bringing Marx to bear, even goes to the point of making this Cartesian moment responsible for 'the power which creates, *from* separation, the material conditions of *primitive accumulation*'.[36]

This apology of separation and of the annihilation of Renaissance continuity and corporeality, for the sake of modern measurement and domination, is profoundly linked to a theme that would pit Cacciari and his cohorts against Negri throughout the 1970s and onwards, that of the *autonomy of the political*. From an affirmation of the inevitable and irreversible character of the process of rationalization, so prominent in his critique of *The Political Descartes*, Cacciari drew the conclusion that the political task of the working class and its leadership was not that of affirming its own needs and constructing its own world through

35. M. Cacciari, 'Vita Cartesii est simplicissima', *Contropiano*, vol. 2, 1970, p. 377.
36. 'Vita Cartesii est simplicissima', pp. 378, 379.

organization and revolution, but rather that of proving itself more efficacious than capitalists in dominating the process of rationalization, establishing its political command over a process whose technological coordinates and demands were not immediately politicizable. Thus, against Negri's reading of real subsumption as an opportunity to affirm proletarian *potentia*, immanently creating its world (communist social relations, here and now), Cacciari posed the role of the party and the workers' movement as assuming a kind of transcendent *potestas* over the process of rationalization (e.g. around issues of economic productivity).

A political motivation is thus also very much at stake in the methodological choices about how to approach the history of philosophy. Whilst both Negri and Cacciari take their distance from textbook distortions of historical materialism correlating productive base to philosophical superstructure, the 'negative thought' espoused by Cacciari is so resolutely committed to a Heideggerian understanding of the link between metaphysics, technology, mathesis and rationality that it takes on a decidedly determinist or necessitarian hue. Whereas Negri's understanding of political ontology, in a Machiavellian vein, leads to an attempt to diagram the historical force-fields and antagonistic conjunctures wherein a given metaphysics is produced – the reason, incidentally, for the strongly *biographical* character of his historical materialism, as demonstrated in this book and *The Savage Anomaly* – Cacciari's take on the Cartesian caesura treats its political character in massively *epochal* terms. In so doing, he espouses the Heideggerian epic of the metaphysics of modern subjectivity, in which the cogito 'is the first resolute step through which modern machine technology, and along with it the modern world and modern mankind, become metaphysically possible for the first time', in which ' "power" in its correctly understood modern meaning – that is, as will to power – first becomes metaphysically possible as modern history'.[37] Where

37. M. Heidegger, *Nietzsche*, vol. 4, trans. D. F. Krell, San Francisco 1982, pp. 116, 98.

Negri's political ontology is developed in the advances, setbacks, conquests and defeats of metaphysics as a worldly, immanent praxis – whence the idea of Descartes's *Discourse* as a kind of *Bildungsroman* for a bourgeoisie trying to recoup its forces – the Heideggerian approach which was to have such influence on Cacciari and other PCI intellectuals depends on the presupposition of an 'essential *simple line* running through the historical contexts',[38] on a metaphysics of 'the West' which is marked by radical disenchantment and the abandonment of any antagonism to the status quo that could be based on a rich *class autonomy*, a lived experience of struggle. For the likes of Cacciari this was mere nostalgia, a kind of infantile refusal of the metaphysical 'iron cage' in which the *autonomy of the political* needed to operate.

Of particular interest in this respect is the issue of how to place the question of political subjectivity in the reading of Descartes. Cacciari's polemic against Negri is once again based on a familiar Heideggerian line: Descartes, qua philosopher of *representation*, prepares the ground for modern science and its 'rationalized' separation of a measuring subject from a measured object. It is from separation, writes Cacciari, 'that subjectivity can mature, that fundamental reversal of the hypokeimenon into subjectivity that Heidegger has described in such a formidable way'.[39] The subject is thus equated with the subject of science, which is in turn equated with the formal subject that subtends 'the global project of a perfectly rationalized political cosmos'.[40] This is not the local subject of a partisan ideology, but the very metaphysical subject of modernity, hollowed out and calculating. Though this line meshes with much contemporary philosophical common sense, it is worth noting that it has recently been cast into doubt in the works of Étienne Balibar. Regarding the philosophical panorama presented in Heidegger's *Nietzsche*, Balibar writes: 'Though this

38. *Nietzsche*, p. 124.
39. 'Vita Cartesii est simplicissima', p. 379.
40. Ibid.

critique is . . . irreversible, cannot be bypassed, it is itself riddled with strange limitations and lacunae, with historical prerequisites that are extraordinarily fragile . . . This entire tradition [from Kant to Hegel to Husserl to Lukács] considers and repeatedly asserts that it is with *René Descartes* that philosophy became conscious of "subjectivity" and made "the subject" the centre of the universe of representations as well as the signal of the unique value of the individual',[41] thereby inaugurating the properly modern metaphysics of the subject. 'But', Balibar continues, 'this story, however broadly accepted, is materially wrong. It is a mere retrospective illusion, which was forged by the systems, the philosophies of history and the teaching of philosophy in the nineteenth century. Neither in Descartes nor even in Leibniz will you find the category "subject" as an equivalent of autonomous self-consciousness [and] a concentrate of the essence of man'. In its modern sense, 'the "subject" was invented by Kant';[42] while Descartes's thinking of the *cogito* oscillates between the Aristotelian–Scholastic *subjectum*, which he rejected, and an attempt, closely linked to the thinking of sovereignty in the 1600s, to think how man, as *subjectus* to God, could also enjoy freedom.[43]

Without delving into this last point, which resonates with some of Negri's comments on the political metaphors employed by

41. É. Balibar, 'Subjection and Subjectivation', in *Supposing the Subject*, ed. Joan Copjec, London 1994, p. 5.
42. 'Subjection and Subjectivation', p. 6.
43. É. Balibar, 'Citizen Subject', in *Who Comes After the Subject?*, ed. Eduardo Cadava, Peter Connor and Jean-Luc Nancy, New York 1991. According to Balibar, in Descartes, 'freedom can in fact only be thought as the freedom of the *subject*, of the subjected being, that is, as a contradiction in terms' (p. 35). Furthermore, 'Descartes's "subject" is thus still (more than ever) the *subjectus*. But what is the *subjectus*? It is the other name of the *subditus*, according to an equivalence practiced by all of mediaeval political theology and systematically exploited by the theoreticians of absolute monarchy: the individual submitted to the *ditio*, to the sovereign authority of the prince, an authority expressed in his orders and itself legitimated by the Word of another Sovereign (the Lord God)' (p. 36).

Descartes, we can note that, though Negri does touch on the 'epistemological' issue of separation and correlation of 'subject' and 'object', his treatment of political subjectivity in Descartes is both wholly external to the Heideggerian apparatus and transcends Balibar's potent philological rectification. The standpoint of political ontology enacted in these pages by Negri suggests that the primary form of political subjectivity at stake is not that of a formal subject of modernity, *but the political subjectivity of the bourgeoisie.* From Negri's standpoint, the subject of science and of metaphysics which is isolated by Heidegger and Cacciari is in a sense a by-product of the precarious and ambiguous solution that Descartes gives to the problem of a historical and material subject: the bourgeoisie. To understand this crucial point is to understand the distance between the epochal metaphysics of (Western) subjectivity and the conjunctural ideology of (a class) subject as ways of shedding light on the impetus and genesis of Descartes's thinking. In other words, it is to understand the methodological difference between excavating a *reasonable* ideology as a historically specific project, and positing *rationalization* as a trans-historical process founded on 'the teleology of the history of philosophy'.[44]

3

Moving on from the elaborate philosophical mediations of the struggles within the Italian Left, how can we relate Negri's intervention to the contemporary standing of radical political theory? In 1932, Brecht, reading Descartes, had exclaimed, in exasperation: 'This man must live in another time, in another world from mine!'[45] In what sense can we breach this distance and rethink politics with Descartes today? Besides the historiographical and philosophical debates amply reviewed by Negri in the

44. 'Citizen Subject', p. 33.
45. Quoted and commented upon in I. Hacking, *Historical Ontology*, London 2002, p. 32.

Postface, attention should be brought to the 'return to Descartes' which has characterized recent attempts to formulate theories of political subjectivity in Slavoj Žižek and Alain Badiou. In several recent texts, Žižek has polemically identified a broad, if implicit, philosophical front, ranging from feminism to cognitive science, from deconstruction to hermeneutics, which finds its common denominator in anti-Cartesianism, in the relentless critique of the fixity and sovereignty of the subject and its dualistic separation (or transcendence) from the world and its entanglements. He provocatively refers to the Cartesian subject as the 'spectre haunting Western academia'.[46] Indeed, Žižek suggests that this anti-Cartesian consensus is profoundly *ideological*, to the extent that it functions as a (fundamentally uncritical) 'critical' common sense and is surreptitiously linked to the blockage of any militant and anti-systemic affirmation of political subjectivity. Of course, Žižek's retort, and his project of producing 'the philosophical manifesto of Cartesian subjectivity itself',[47] is somewhat oblique, relying as it does on the Lacanian 'return to Descartes' and Lacan's displacement of the *cogito*. It is not the 'substantial' *res cogitans* that Žižek (who explicitly reads Descartes through Kantian lenses) wishes to arm and revive. It is not even the Lacanian–Cartesian subject of science which so attracted Cacciari in his polemic against Negri. Circumventing the Heideggerian narrative, Žižek wishes instead to call on Descartes, via Lacan, for a notion of the subject 'out of joint', '*excluded* from the "order of things", from the positive order of entities'. Relying on psychoanalysis, Žižek identifies here a purely 'excremental subject', which, crucially, he links to a vision of the proletariat as an ontologically evacuated subject:

> For Marx, the emergence of the working-class subjectivity is strictly codependent to the fact that the worker is compelled to

46. S. Žižek, *The Ticklish Subject*, London 1999, p. 1.
47. *The Ticklish Subject*, p. 2.

sell the very substance of his being (his creative power) as a commodity on the market, that is, to reduce the *agalma*, the treasure, the precious kernel of his being, to an object that can be bought for a piece of money – there is no subjectivity without the reduction of the subject's positive-substantial being to a disposable 'piece of shit' . . . if the Cartesian subject is to emerge at the level of the enunciation, he is to be reduced to the 'almost-nothing' of a disposable excrement at the level of the enunciated content.[48]

The function of the subject thus depicted, which links the 'excessive, unacknowledged kernel of the *cogito*'[49] to the possibility of a decision or act taken by a hollowed-out subject of enunci-ation, suggests that Žižek views the unworldly or separated character of the Cartesian cogito as a potent *anti-ideological* element, a point of real dislocation against the imaginary and symbolic fetters of ideology.

Now, while sharing many of Žižek's enmities, and the demand for a theory of political subjectivation that would in a sense return to Descartes via Lacan, Alain Badiou's meta-ontological and metapol-itical project culminates in the idea of a step beyond both (and a definite sidestepping of Kant), so that the void posited by Lacan on the side of the cogito shifts to the side of being (which, following a Cartesian injunction, is of course understood not productively but *mathematically*), and the subject is a rare occurrence which depends on the extra-ontological irruption of events and the production of truths.[50] However, on an ideological plane Badiou's allegiances

---

48. S. Žižek, 'Introduction: Cogito as a Shibboleth', in *Cogito and the Unconscious*, ed. S. Žižek, Durham and London 1998, p. 4. The rest of the volume contains numerous texts elucidating and expanding upon the political and ideological consequences of a Lacanian 'return to the cogito'.

49. *The Ticklish Subject*, p. 2.

50. A. Badiou, *Being and Event*, trans. O. Feltham, London 2005, 'Meditation 37: Descartes/Lacan', pp. 431–5.

remain firmly Cartesian.[51] Polemicizing in a recent text against what he sees as a 'democratic materialism' exemplified by Negri himself, Badiou turns to Descartes, and to the *Principles of Philosophy* in particular, to argue that Descartes 'acknowledges the wholly exceptional ontological and logical status of truths. Truths are without existence. Is that to say they do not exist at all? On the contrary. Truths have no *substantial* existence. That is what must be understood by they "are nothing outside of our thought"'. From Descartes, Badiou thus draws the notion that 'a truth is an exception to what there is', and the slogan of his 'materialist dialectic': 'There are only bodies and languages, except that there are truths'.[52]

Now, if we briefly contrast this recent attempt to reinvent a radical political Cartesianism with Negri's assessment of *The Political Descartes*, we encounter two drastically different appraisals of the very question of political ontology. For Negri, the 'separation' of Descartes's subject is born of conjunctural pressure on the emergent bourgeoisie, and represents an ideological solution to the effect of defeat and the attempt to maintain the possibility of the reconstruction of the world as a philosophical and political project. For Badiou and Žižek, on the contrary, a politics of subjective decision and separation, loosely modelled on the principles of Cartesianism, is the only opening to perform an anti-ideological operation against the current political order.[53] What transpires

51. It is worth nothing that Badiou, in an uncharacteristic usage, terms this struggle between democratic materialism and the materialist dialectic 'ideological'.

52. A. Badiou, 'Democratic Materialism and the Materialist Dialectic', trans. A. Toscano, *Radical Philosophy*, vol. 130, 2005, pp. 22, 23. This text is a translation of some of the Preface in A. Badiou, *Logiques des Mondes*, Paris 2006.

53. Taking one's cue from the kind of standpoint formulated in *The Political Descartes*, it would be possible to read the Cartesianism of Badiou and Žižek as an ideological separation which is itself based on the defeat, not of the bourgeoisie, but of the working class. On Badiou's relation to Marxist politics and the theme of separation, see A. Toscano, 'Communism as Separation', in *Think Again: Alain Badiou and the Future of Philosophy*, London 2004.

from such a comparison is the acute difference between a political ontology (Negri's) which develops from the idea of a *class* subject, and an attention to its mnemonic and productive experience, on the one hand, and a political ontology (Badiou and Žižek's, broadly speaking) whose figure of militant subjectivity is based on an evacuation of experience and a formal decision or act, on the other. If nothing else this profound contrast testifies to the contemporary relevance of an investigation into the link between Cartesianism and the political subject.

The translators would like to thank Kamini Vellodi for her comments on the introduction.

Metaphor and Memory

There is a single active power in things: love, charity, harmony.

PWD I 5

1

To join Descartes[1] on the 'path' of inquiry, to set about establishing the 'foundations' of truth with him, to inspect by means of reason the

1. References to Descartes's works in the original French and Latin are to the Adam–Tannery edition of the *Œuvres complètes*, Paris 1964–71, from here on marked 'AT', followed by the Roman numeral indicating the volume and the page number. [TN: For the translation of the quoted passages, we shall refer to *The Philosophical Works of Descartes*, vols I and II, translated by J. Cottingham, R. Stoothoff and D. Murdoch, Cambridge 1984–5, and vol. III, translated by J. Cottingham, R. Stoothoff, D. Murdoch and A. Kenny, Cambridge 1991. From here on these are marked 'PWD I', 'PWD II' and 'PWD III'. For the passages cited and not contained in *The Philosophical Works of Descartes*, and other texts, all translations from the French are by Alberto Toscano, from Latin by Clover Peake and Francesco Montares. All quoted passages for which English versions could not be located have been translated directly from Negri's text.] We have also made use of Gregor Sebba's *Bibliographia Cartesiana: A Critical Guide to the Descartes Literature 1880–1960*, The Hague 1964. This will enable us to avoid copious and unnecessary references. One should also bear in mind N. Edelmann, 'The Seventeenth Century', in D. C. Cabeen and J. Brody (eds), *A Critical Bibliography of French Literature*, vol. III, Syracuse 1961.

'factory', the 'machine' of the world[2] – these and countless other metaphorical themes strike his reader. They appear insistently and repetitively. At first sight, their meaning is uncertain. The only certainty is that the singularity and persistence of these motifs reveals their non-accidental quality and their complex role throughout Descartes's oeuvre. Many interpretations have been offered to account for this. Some say that this is a baroque mode of arguing, a sign of the times. Let us begin with an analytical approach, setting aside all the 'dead metaphors' that Descartes draws from common usage.[3] If we pursue our investigation into the 'living metaphors' in Descartes's work, we discover that their use differs from that of the baroque. Descartes lacks the poetic metaphor, the image that becomes myth, the word that becomes divine. For him, metaphor is the means of discursive and rational comparison. It is the manifestation 'of the idea of a coherent construction'. It is not the revelation of 'a star-studded space'. In Descartes's use of metaphor we find continuity and solidity, not vertigo.[4] Discovering the straight and

2. On the theme of the 'right path', see, for example, AT IV 636; PWD I 111, 112, 118, 119, 122–3, 141, 152–3 and *passim*; PWD II 6, 15 and 176; PWD I 9; PWD II 401, 408 and 419; PWD I 328 and 380–1. On the theme of the 'safe house', see, for example, PWD III 21; AT II 83; PWD III 282, 289 and 292; PWD I 116, 117, 117–18, 122, 125 and *passim*; PWD I 189; PWD II 404, 407 and 408. On the theme of the 'machine', see, for example, AT II 268; PWD I 136, 139 and 141; AT VI 148, 269; PWD II 20–1; Descartes, *The World and Other Writings*, ed. S. Gaukroger, Cambridge 1998, pp. 106–7, 108 and 171ff; PWD I 329–30 and 333–4.

3. See, for example, AT II 274, 280; AT III 390–1 [extracts at PWD III 184–7], 523 [extracts at PWD III 209–10]; AT IV 548, 549, 551, 595; PWD I 112, 119, 131–2 and 147; PWD II 407–8; *The World and Other Writings*, pp. 131, 142–3, 146; PWD I 381, 390. We could cite countless other passages. Almost invariably, we are dealing with literary metaphors of a classical or chivalrous nature, or with metaphors in common usage.

4. This is what T. Spoerri argues in 'La puissance métaphorique de Descartes', in *Descartes. Cahiers de Royaumont, Philosophie II*, New York 1987, pp. 273–87. E. Gilson, in his commentary to the *Discourse on the Method (Texte et commentaire*, 3rd edn, Paris 1962, p. 85), seeks the origin of Cartesian metaphor in supposed Stoic sources, in particular Seneca's *De vita beata*. In this case, metaphor would point to a kind of 'theoretical stoicism' – something that seems to us to be extremely doubtful.

narrow path through the hazards of a tortuous trail or an inhospitable forest; reassuring oneself that the house is built upon rock and not sand; seeing the world in the functional interdependence of constructive elements, like a watchmaker beholding his product, or a hydraulic engineer conceiving the fantastical devices in a sixteenth-century garden – all this relies on a measured argumentative order, which bears no relation to that rupture of existential mediation that the baroque imagination always demands. The distinction between Cartesian and baroque metaphor has been represented as follows: the former is explanatory, it wants A to stand in the same relation to B as C does to B. The latter, which is regarded as the genuine metaphor, requires two denominators and demands that A stands in the same relation to B as C does to D. Those who have underlined this distinction add that in the second case a dualistic, analogical conception of being is at play, whereas in the first case we find a univocal conception of being.[5]

So, are we to surmise that a univocal conception of being underpins the Cartesian use of metaphor? Does this specific argumentative and literary form lead directly to a metaphysical position? It is too early to say, especially since such a reading would raise far-reaching doubts about the entire traditional interpretation of Descartes's philosophy. It would reveal – as a counterpoint to the system and held together by metaphor alone – an originary metaphysical thread that is irreducible to the system itself, as irreducible as univocity is to equivocity, as monism is to dualism. For now, all that seems certain is that the Cartesian metaphor alludes directly to an ideal of science whose necessary elements are the certainty of the path, the security of the foundations and a rigid interlinking of reasons.

And yet – lending further weight to our hypothesis – the univocal Cartesian metaphor seems, at times, to play a decisive role and to possess an intensity that is not just simply methodological.

5. As indicated by C. Perelman in the discussion that followed T. Spoerri's paper at Royaumont.

Let us consider another metaphorical theme in addition to those of the path, the house and the machine, namely, the theme of the 'tree' and the botanical metaphors that accompany it. Certainty, security and cohesion in the order of reasons are all led back towards a horizon constituted by the circulation of truth. The mechanical order of reasons is replaced by the flux of nature – the living order. The truth is a fertile realm, a soil rich in fruit and brooks that nourish those who investigate it in an orderly manner. Arid deserts and uninhabitable mountains are the abode of those who inquire without method.[6] Order becomes overabundance, a living productiveness internal to the reality of things. Despite its mechanical motion, the world bursts with natural force, like a tub of boiling must or fermenting hay, like an infinite number of small streams flowing violently, in a full and continuous movement, 'just as grains of sand and pebbles do when they roll with the water of a river'.[7] Thus the order of science itself is represented as a 'tree', and the unity and circulation of life are projected into the unity and circulation of knowledge: 'Thus the whole of philosophy is like a tree. The roots are metaphysics, the trunk is physics, and the branches emerging from the trunk are all the other sciences, which may be reduced to three principal ones, namely medicine, mechanics and morals. By "morals" I understand the highest and most perfect moral system, which presupposes a complete knowledge of the other sciences and is the ultimate level of wisdom.'[8] What fullness of being and truth! It seems inevitable that a reading of this passage should exclude another set of interpretations of metaphor in Descartes, specifically, those that attribute to it an emblematic, allusive and instrumental function. If indeed a baroque interpretation of Cartesian metaphor is impossible, it is also frankly inadequate to give this image a purely literary value,

6. PWD II 402–3.
7. *The World and Other Writings*, p. 34. For the other metaphors cited here see PWD I 134 and 154ff; PWD I 319–20, 320–1, 322, AT XI 271, 274 and *passim*.
8. PWD I 186.

that is, to insist on the 'Ignatian' limits of the Cartesian procedure and thereby endow it with a purely instrumental utility.[9] For here the image truly does follow and express the rhythm of being. Not only does it appear to require the discovery of the truth that it epitomizes, it seems itself to be the truth. In other words, the image would appear as an objective order of truth, since according to that order, truth organizes itself within reason; and as a subjective order of truth, since the search for wisdom is articulated in accordance with that order. On the basis of this first approach, it follows that, on the one hand, Cartesian metaphor seems irreducible to the baroque analogical procedure, and, on the other, that at least in one case it manifests a real content and serves to interpret a specific metaphysical horizon.

This first hypothesis regarding the metaphysical horizon implied by the development of Cartesian metaphor is enriched by another set of motifs. If truth is indeed picked from the leafy tree of science like a ripe fruit, it is nevertheless endowed with

9. This is the second line of interpretation concerning the Cartesian use of metaphor, which is defended principally in M. Gueroult, *Descartes' Philosophy Interpreted According to the Order of Reasons*, translated by R. Ariew, Minneapolis 1985. According to Gueroult, Cartesian imaginism, which is based on the parallelism between concrete images (distinct impressions, in the language of Ignatius of Loyola, whose *Exercises* – particularly week 3, day 1 – Descartes would have come across at La Flèche) and the functions of understanding, would play a purely explicative, literary and psychologically suggestive role, while it would be excluded in principle from metaphysical reasoning. Much more perceptive in this respect is M. Mesnard (see his 'L'arbre de la sagesse' in *Descartes. Cahiers de Royaumont*, pp. 336–49), who, while insisting on the analogies between Descartes and Ignatius in terms of the use of metaphor, and thus accepting the emblematic interpretation of Cartesian metaphor, also recognizes that this use of metaphor – in particular the metaphor of the tree of science or of wisdom – achieves a real determination. It is no longer simply a veil behind which hides a purely allusive truth but rather the outline of the real circuit of truth. According to Mesnard, the second phase of Descartes's thought, which is dominated by ethical reflection, is correctly represented by this imaginative concretization of the system.

something akin to a germinal existence: 'For the human mind has within it a sort of spark of the divine, in which the first seeds [*semina*] of useful ways of thinking are sown, seeds which, however neglected and stifled by studies which impede them, often bear fruit of their own [*spontaneam frugem producant*]'.[10] A seed spontaneously bearing fruit! The *humana mens* rooted in a productive being from which truth emanates! Is it possible to glimpse, from this angle, the horizon within which the Cartesian metaphor is implanted? Does metaphor really present itself as the univocal predication of being because it presupposes a univocal conception of being? Indeed, it seems we are operating entirely within the language of humanism and are confronted with a creative, radical symbolism that is immediately expressive of being.[11] The impression is even stronger once we factor in that incontrovertibly humanist themes are evident from the very outset. Starting from a germinal existence, truth spreads through the tree of science and articulates itself in a concatenation that is simultaneously an order of reasons and a methodological sequence. Moreover, the vital order of truth's development is also constructed in the rational order of argument.[12] It has been said

10. PWD I 17.
11. On the features of humanist symbolism, see E. Cassirer, *The Individual and the Cosmos in Renaissance Philosophy*, Mineola 2000; P. O. Kristeller, *The Philosophy of Marsilio Ficino*, New York 1943; E. Garin, *Italian Humanism: Philosophy and Civic Life in the Renaissance*, Oxford 1965. But we should bear in mind that prior to the rise of the new science, the positivity of humanist symbolism is given a negative inflection: 'Humanism operates in the direction of a demobilization of all those symbols that tended to project the terms of a worldly, historical experience onto the planes of the divine and the eternal' (E. Garin, 'La dialettica del secolo XII ai principi dell'età moderna', *Rivista di filosofia*, vol. 2, 1958, p. 253). With the onset of the new science, this positivity is forcefully emancipated.
12. PWD I 14–15, 20–1; PWD II 400–1; PWD I 120. In his *Commentaire*, pp. 210ff and 370, E. Gilson believes he can relate this Cartesian concept of the circulation of truth back to the deductive method of its procedure – something which to us appears absolutely insufficient.

that this shows the influence of Renaissance exemplarism, of Lullian themes,[13] which is true enough. But there is more: an experience, an allegiance. This kind of metaphor is not a means but rather the proper form of an experience, not an allusion but an effective guide. It is Ariadne's thread, and not Minerva leaping from Jupiter's head. This metaphor leads us into being at the same time as it expresses being's structure. It is a univocal metaphor: the univocal horizon of being and truth.

If this is true, will it not also be possible to grasp the memory, at least, of a much denser, much more significant primordial thread, in that cluster of metaphors which seemed more adequate to the merely methodological and systematic discourse of Descartes's maturity? Certainly. The terms 'path', 'house' and 'machine' point again to an order where the concatenation of reasons provides the process of inquiry with security and a real foundation. But in these themes, it seems possible to discover something more than the reference to the inquiry's methodological development, something more than that same reference to the Renaissance image of the world and to the univocal order of being that this image sustains. It seems possible to discover in those themes the memory of the humanist experience of the world. This memory has become body and lived experience. It is distributed throughout the materiality of this actual existence as the art of the flautist is embodied in the nervation of the hand:[14]

I am convinced that certain primary seeds of truth naturally implanted in human minds thrived vigorously in that un-sophisticated and innocent age – seeds which have been stifled in us through our constantly reading and hearing all sorts of errors. So the same light of the mind which enabled them to see (albeit without knowing why) that virtue is preferable to

13. P. Rossi, *Logic and the Art of Memory: The Quest for a Universal Language*, London 2000.
14. AT III. But see also AT X 201.

pleasure, the good preferable to the useful, also enables them to grasp true ideas in philosophy and mathematics, although they were not yet able fully to master such sciences. Indeed, one can even see some traces of this true mathematics, I think, in Pappus and Diophantus who, though not of that earliest antiquity, lived many centuries before our time.[15]

Many centuries ago? No, that experience is not remote, that 'ancient wisdom' is the transfiguration of a recent hope.[16] In fact, the metaphorical themes we have encountered so far assume a form and meaning whose cultural novelty it is hard to overlook. Let us consider them again.

First of all, the 'machine'. It constitutes a structure of comprehension and a subterranean articulation of reality. But it is also a schema of the reproduction and the technical possession of the world. The tree is mechanized. First, as a mechanical garden, a Renaissance magician's sleight of hand,[17] then, as a structure for the comprehension of reality, and finally, as an operational and productive schema.[18] An unbroken thread links these different experiences, such that the necessity to emancipate science from

15. PWD I 18–19. See also PWD I 15–16.
16. See the remarks by E. Garin on the passage at PWD I 18–19 in his introduction to *Opere*, vol. I, p. xv.
17. AT X 120, 130–1 (with extensive comments by Adam–Tannery at pp. 212–15 and 669, indicating a series of earlier and contemporary texts enthusiastically preoccupied with the description of artificial fountains. Probably, according to Adam–Tannery, the fountains 'in the gardens of our Kings' are those at Saint-Germain-en-Laye rather than those at Fontainebleau).
18. On this theme see the works already cited in note 2 above. For more on the theme of the 'clock' see also, for example, PWD III 208, 306; PWD I 141; PWD II 58–9; PWD I 288; AT X 229; PWD I 99, 108, 315 and 335; on the theme of 'automata' see, for example, AT I 24; II 39–41; PWD III 208; PWD III 366; PWD I 139–40 (and the extended commentary in E. Gilson, *Commentaire*, pp. 420–6), and AT VI 165; PWD II 17 and 21–2; PWD I 288–9; AT X 216–19, 231–2; PWD I 99, 330, 333–4, 334–5, 341 and XI 669.

magic is born from within the experience of magic itself.[19] This is perhaps a contradictory experience but nevertheless one that is both full and complex, providing an almost immediate, physical contact with the world – an enthusiastic and heroic hope of possession and transformation of the world.

The theme of the 'house' should be considered next. Here too, the metaphor unfolds, acquiring an ever more distinctively humanist connotation. It indicates the necessity of a basis, of a method that will guarantee the inquiry and prevent it from collapsing. However, alongside this need for security and at one with it, the Cartesian metaphor is also involved in the critical process of reason. When one notices that all received knowledge is insufficient, as with 'a badly built house, whose foundations are not secure', then 'I do not know a better way to fix it than to throw it all to the ground and build a new one . . . and whilst we work on this demolition, we shall be able, with the same instruments, to dig the foundations necessary for our task, and prepare the new and more solid material to fill them . . .'[20] The analytical process of foundation opens onto the critical process of construction and the metaphor unfolds within this horizon of reconstruction: from the search for security to the search for a new order in its substantive aspect; from the security of the house to the design of the new city, to the utopian daydream of its realization in the imagistic form of the procedure. The metaphor presents an overwhelming passion for renewal and, bit by bit, it expresses not so much a generic need for security but rather the myth of a new order – with all the wealth of contents that may be attributed to such an order.[21]

19. There is a very significant passage, in this regard, at PWD II 404–5.
20. AT X 59.
21. See texts mentioned in note 2 above. The extent to which the metaphorical theme of the 'house' – and, in Descartes, of the 'city' – depends on a specifically humanist procedure might well be confirmed by a reading of E. Garin's 'Città ideale', in *Scienza e vita civile nel Rinascimento italiano*, Bari 1965, pp. 33ff. [TN: English translation in *Science and Civic Life in the Italian Renaissance*,   *cont'd over/*

However, it is around the theme of the 'path' that the metaphor is freed from any limit whatsoever, to the point of being able to take up the humanist call. The path is certain if its certainty is won, that is, if one dares to traverse the world and ground the security of knowledge in this traversal. Security is not a reductive ideal. It affirms itself to the extent that knowledge grasps its own foundation in the world. A number of images provide the sense of this certainty that is achieved in the world and all of them express the sense of participation in the world: immersion in the deepest waters; the conquest of a safe ford across a fast-flowing river . . .[22]; until the security of the path, finally attained, is experienced happily and the possession of the true returns like a refrain.[23] Thus, the possibility of attaining certainty is achieved only through a profound and persistent adherence to the world. That is because the world is a *grand livre* to be leafed through, an experience to be lived fully, the demand for and foundation of a limitless knowledge.[24] Descartes takes this theme – which is

21. *cont'd*   Garden City 1969.] Consider, for instance, the following eloquent observation: 'Anyone who, looking beyond urbanism and architecture in general, were to examine the philosophical conception of nature present in Alberti and Leonardo would discover numerous analogies between the works of these two artists, precisely in their shared idea of "*logoi*", of "seminal reasons" and immanent mathematical laws that man discovers at the very base of being. Here, amongst natural beings, man is able to situate his works, which although new and original must nevertheless find a foothold in natural "necessities" and obey the rational web of the whole . . . the ideal city is, at one and the same time, the natural city and the rational city. In other words, it is the city rationally constructed in accordance to a human scale, but it must also correspond perfectly to the nature of man' (p. 36). Could we not say that Descartes's metaphor of the 'home' refers to just such a context?

22. PWD II 16 and 408. Other nautical images can be found at PWD III 264, 317; PWD I 141 and VI 237. But these are more interesting as observations than as metaphors.

23. PWD II 419–20.

24. PWD I 115 (see E. Gilson, *Commentaire*, p. 142), but also throughout Descartes's œuvre, especially in *The Search for Truth*, PWD II 399ff.

humanist *par excellence* – from Montaigne, but it can be encountered everywhere, in the 'new science', in Bacon and Galileo, in the 'revolutionary' Turquet as in the 'geographer' Popelinière.[25] In fact, more than with a metaphor, we are dealing here with a watchword of the century, with a defining aspect of its mentality and with the object of a collective task. In relation to this theme, Cartesian metaphor resolutely reveals its cultural referent, the humanist world, the new hope of possessing the world *iuxta sua propria principia* (according to its own principles).[26]

The instrument of metaphor is now declared to be, in itself, the key to scientific inquiry. It is such a scientific instrument in so far as it establishes a situation of complete adherence of knowledge to the world and vice versa. If the world presents itself as '*fable*', then metaphor delves into a homogeneous terrain and adheres to the

25. Montaigne, *The Complete Essays*, vol. I, ch. XXVI; Bacon, *Novum Organum*, vol. I, p. 89; *De dignitate et augmentis scientiarum*, vol. I, p. 469; *Advt.*, vol. III, ed. Spedding, Ellis and Heath, London 1887, p. 301; Galilei, *Opere*, vol. VI, p. 232, Florence 1929–39: 'Philosophy is written in that enormous book that is perpetually open before our eyes (I call it the universe) . . .'; in addition *Opere*, vol. III, book 1, pp. 138ff and *passim* (see also E. Garin, *Scienza e vita civile*, pp. 149 and 153, who cites various passages from Galileo, as well as other authors, to demonstrate the ubiquity and importance of metaphor). On Louis Turquet de Mayerne, see *La monarchie aristodémocratique, ou le gouvernement composé et meslé des trois formes de légitimes Républiques, <<dédié aux Etats-Généraux des Provinces confédérées des Pays-Bas>>*, Paris 1611, p. 5. According to him, we arrive at the truth 'above all by reading this great but unwritten and unprinted book called the Course of the World [*Train du Monde*]' (see R. Mousnier, 'L'opposition politique bourgeoise à la fin du XVIe siècle et au début du XVIIe: l'œuvre de Louis Turquet de Mayerne', *Revue historique*, vol. 213, 1955, pp. 1–20). On Henri de la Popelinière, his writings and the spirit of his œuvre see C. Vivant, 'Alle origini dell'idea di civiltà: le scoperte geographiche e gli scritti di Henri de la Popelinière', *Rivista storica italiana*, vol. 74, 1962, pp. 225–49; M. Yardeni, 'La conception de l'histoire dans l'œuvre de la Popelinière', *Revue d'histoire moderne et contemporaine*, vol. 11, 1964, pp. 109–26.

26. The meaning of this humanist slogan in the political field will need to be fully elucidated in the course of our investigation.

real, inasmuch as it uncovers it in its truth. Assuming *falsa pro veris*, inventing the hypothesis whilst trusting in the correspondence between thought and reality, 'with philosophical honesty' – in this way the investigation reaches *ad veritatem illustrandam.*[27] This method progresses to the point that Descartes lays claim to its validity even with regard to the most delicate matter that his inquiry touches upon, i.e. theology, in relation to which Descartes wants his metaphor to be full-bodied, superior to any other exemplification, and able to represent the effects of divine action upon the world.[28] The aim is to discover truth, to unmask it, yet always to proceed masked, on the basis of the hypothesis of the world, covering up one's own role in this sublime *fable* or *comédie* which the world and the inquiry into truth together constitute. Descartes wants to reach that point where the dramatic relationship that extends from *fable* to reality configures the inner movement of philosophy, which ceaselessly implicates those elements that appear to be opposites but in reality are not.[29]

To sum up, Cartesian metaphor is not a sign of the times, because it is not baroque, not open to the vertigo of analogy, being instead constructed in terms of a univocal logic. Neither is it an emblem, a mere literary suggestion, since it is pervaded by the revelation of a metaphysical continuum, by the experience of the vital circulation of truth. Thus, Descartes's metaphor is a substantive one, the index of an immediate relation with the world. It is a metaphor that seems to turn into the experience of science in the humanist sense,

27. PWD II 242. We shall have to return to this question in order to underline how the opposition between Descartes and the mechanicists, specifically in relation to the use of metaphor and hypothesis (at PWD II 180, we find Descartes in dispute with Gassendi), typifies two different attitudes to the problem of the relationship between investigator and world. See also PWD I 112 (E. Gilson, *Commentaire*, pp. 98–100), although here the fable-hypothesis is much more ambiguous.
28. AT IV 593–4.
29. See the very useful comments on this issue in R. Champigny, 'The Theatrical Aspect of the Cogito', *Review of Metaphysics*, vol. 12, 1959, pp. 370–7.

apparently alluding to and carrying within it the entire passion of Renaissance man. But does this not take us away from the outlook of the mature, systematic Descartes, for whom the methodological proposal of metaphysical discontinuity is essential? Does it not represent a scandal? It is beyond doubt that a strange speculative thread is revealed by this first approach, by this initial analysis of Descartes's metaphoric universe. The Renaissance world, which the mature Descartes escapes and against which he battles, appears instead throughout his oeuvre in a series of linguistic metaphorical usages that create – in their continuity – something like an auto-signifying, systematic network. Let us then raise the following questions: Is there a real experience behind these appearances? Is there a Cartesian tale behind the metaphor? Is there a Cartesian memory within the metaphor? More generally: what is the significance of the clash – if clash there is – between the memory of the humanist world and Descartes's systematic development? Finally: does this clash illustrate one of the century's decisive concerns?

2

We have argued that the metaphysical thread uncovered in Descartes's use of metaphor reveals his memory of the humanist world. We must now ask whether Descartes lived in the world of his metaphor before his mature works fixed its distance in memory and subjected the latter to critique. That is, before the memory of that world appeared to force the system in order to preserve itself, by putting its trust in metaphor. In other words, we must establish whether Descartes underwent a humanist experience.

'This young man from Poitou has had contacts with a number of Jesuits and educated men. And yet he declares he has never found anyone, besides myself, who uses the method of study that I employ and who carefully brings together physics with mathematics. On the other hand, I have spoken to no one except him about these studies'[30]

30. AT X 52.

– this is Isaac Beeckman's description of his encounter with Descartes in Breda in 1618.[31] The relationship between the two young scientists develops through what we may assume are daily meetings for about two months. Their common programme of study is defined precisely: *accurate cum Mathematica Physicam jungere.* We will return shortly to the texts that have come down to us from this period.[32] An essential question arises at once concerning this first documented example of the scientific activity of the young Descartes: within what horizon does his 'physico-mathematical' activity develop? It is not enough to note the pre-eminence of Descartes's interest in mathematics, or the already unambiguous outline of the geometrical work,[33] to reach a decision on the scope and character of the project. At the close of the Renaissance, such studies are not homogeneous with one another in the methodology applied and even less in the philosophical substrate upon which they rest. This is all the more true in that Nordic world where Descartes lived at the time, in which the relative tardiness of the humanist explosion was accompanied by a

31. In AT X one can find the interesting passages of the *Journal tenu par Isaac Beeckman de 1604 à 1634* (see also the 4-volume edition by Cornelis De Waard, The Hague 1939–53). For the history of the relationship between Beeckman and Descartes see: AT X 17ff; XII 45–6; G. Cohen, *Ecrivains français en Hollande dans la première moitié du XVIIe siècle*, Paris 1920, pp. 374–91, 429–35, 454–7; H. Gouhier, *Les Premières pensées de Descartes. Contribution à l'histoire de l'anti-renaissance*, Paris 1958, pp. 21ff; E. Gilson, *Commentaire*, pp. 151–2; E. Garin, *Opere*, vol. I, pp. xxiiff. Descartes and Beeckman met on 10 November 1618 and remained together in Bremen until 2 January 1619. They then exchanged a series of letters (also in AT X) from 24 January 1619 to 6 May 1619. In 1628–9, the relationship between Descartes and Beeckman has its second phase (see again AT X).
32. In section 3 of this chapter.
33. AT X 162–3. In particular: 'regarding the other discoveries I boasted of in my previous letters, I really made them with the aid of new compasses and am not mistaken. But I will not present my results to you in a fragmentary way: one day I will compose a work on this question; and I believe it will be new and by no means worthless'.

radical and intense revolutionary development that made visible the accumulation of heterogeneous methodological and philosophical strata, while nevertheless allowing their positive coexistence.[34] One finds here the 'physico-mathematical' Descartes discussing Lull and Agrippa in the taverns and – although the old Lullist of Dordrecht with whom he conversed seemed a swindling chatterbox – he nonetheless asked Beeckman for information concerning the keys to Lull's dialectic.[35] At the same time, however, the abstractions of the new mechanics were well known to Descartes. He worked on them with Beeckman and pondered over them in the course of his travels. As he wrote to Beeckman: 'If I should stop somewhere, as I hope I shall, I promise to see that my *Mechanics* or *Geometry* is put in order, and I will salute you as the promoter and prime author of my studies'.[36] It suffices to look at the *Compendium musicae*, dedicated by Descartes to Beeckman *pridie Calendas Januarias 1618*, to see what an entanglement of heterogeneous cultural elements can exist in such a situation: a quantitative and a qualitative mechanics, a naturalistic and a subjectivist aesthetics are superimposed and coexist to

34. 'Humanism, in a typically Nordic and characteristically different form, in the Low Countries has always been the ground upon which civilisation has developed', Johan Huizinga, *Dutch Civilisation in the Seventeenth Century, and other essays*, ed. P. Geyl and F. W. N. Hugenholtz, New York 1968. This study also contains some comments on the complex set of cultural motifs that constitute this form of humanism.

35. AT X 164–5. Beeckman's reply can be found at AT X 167–8; see AT X 63–5 for some preparatory notes for the reply. We should also keep in mind a passage from Beeckman's notes for the period 1628–9, 'Whether moons or letters to be read could be inscribed on the absent' (AT X 347), which reveals Descartes's knowledge of Gianbattista Della Porta's *Magia naturalis*. See note 51 below. See E. Garin, *Opere*, vol. I, pp. xxviii–xxx.

36. PWD III 4. To grasp the extremely advanced level that Beeckman had already reached we should bear in mind (as one can glean from AT X 58–61) that already in 1613 he had formulated the principle that 'Once things have been moved they never rest, unless they are obstructed'.

the point that their respective traits are thrown into confusion and become indistinguishable.[37] On the one hand, we have the correct study of the mathematical relations of consonance: 'If you look carefully at what I wrote on discords and the rest of my treatise on music, you will find that all the points I made on the intervals of harmonies, scales and discords were demonstrated mathematically'.[38] On the other hand, Descartes writes: 'The human voice

37. One can find the *Compendium musicae* in AT X 89–141. [TN: English translation in *Compendium of Music*, trans. W. Roberts, American Institute of Musicology, 1961. Unfortunately the text does not include page references to the AT *Œuvres de Descartes.*] Information on the text can be found in AT X 79–88. In 'Descartes et le problème de l'expression musicale' (*Descartes, Cahiers de Royaumont*, pp. 438–48), Roland-Manuel correctly and acutely grasps the complexity and contradictoriness of the themes developed in that work. This ambiguity can also be found in later texts on musical subjects. It seems that Descartes never freed himself from it. See, for example, AT I 132–3 [TN: partly in PWD III 19–20] and, in particular, the pages in *The Treatise on Man* on the relation between sensation and the geometric structure of sound (for example, *The World and Other Writings*, pp. 122–4 and, especially, 131): 'amongst the colours, green, which consists in the most moderate action (which by analogy one can speak of as the ratio 1:2), is like the octave among musical consonances, or like bread among the food that one eats, that is, it is the most universally agreeable. And finally, all the different fashionable colours which are more refreshing than green are like the chords and passages of a new tune, performed by an excellent lute-player, or the stews of a good cook, which stimulate the senses and first make them feel pleasure but then become tedious faster than simple and ordinary objects'. In contrast to this interpretation, see B. Augst, 'Descartes' Compendium on Music', *Journal of the History of Ideas*, vol. 26, 1965, pp. 119–32. Augst finds in this work a sufficiently complete methodological attempt, a broadly developed mechanicist project, and even a very well-defined metaphysical approach. This thesis is unquestionably a courageous one.
38. PWD III 1. See also the study of relations in *Compendium of Music*, pp. 16ff, as well as the pages relative to mathematic-musical themes in Descartes's exchanges with Beeckman: AT X 52, 53, 54, 56–8, 61–2, 63 and then – in 1629 – AT X 337, 348.

seems most pleasing to us because it is most directly attuned to our souls. By the same token, the voice of a close friend is more agreeable than the voice of an enemy because of sympathy or antipathy of feelings – just as it is said that a sheep-skin stretched over a drum will not give forth any sound when struck if a wolf's hide on another drum is sounding at the same time.'[39] Nevertheless, behind and through this assortment of heterogeneous elements, of ingenuousness and 'hearsay', there is a project that unifies Descartes's position and makes it original. It is Descartes himself who, in the midst of his mathematical investigations, declares as much to Beeckman: 'Let me now be quite open with you about my project. What I want to produce is not something like Lull's *Ars Brevis*, but rather a completely new science [*scientiam penitus novam*], which would provide a general solution of all possible equations involving any sort of quantity, whether continuous or discrete, each according to its nature [*unaquaeque iuxta suam naturam*].' And he adds:

> I am hoping to demonstrate what sorts of problems can be solved exclusively in this or that way, so that almost nothing in geometry will remain to be discovered [*adeo ut pene nihil in Geometria supersit inveniendum*]. This is of course a gigantic task, and one hardly suitable for one person [*Infinitum quidem opus est, nec unius*]; indeed it is an incredibly ambitious project. But through the dark chaos of science I have caught a glimpse of some sort of light, and with the aid of this I think I shall be able to dispel even the thickest obscurities [*nescio quid luminis per obscuram huius scientiae*

39. *Compendium of Music*, p. 11. According to R. Lenoble, *Mersenne ou la naissance du mécanisme*, Paris 1943, p. 430, n. 3, this example (which is certainly a curious one) can already be found in Ambroise Paré and in Mersenne. In Descartes it seems to be second-hand (as suggested by the expression *ut aiunt*, 'as they say'). We should also note that Lenoble strongly downplays the importance of Descartes's musical studies for the development of mechanism.

chaos aspexi, cuius auxilio densissimas tenebras discuti posse existimo].[40]

Let us pose the question again. What is the content of this 'completely new science'? What is the project of the 'mathematician-physicist'? Is it perhaps a specialist project that is as abstract in its motivations as it is determinate in its specific contents? The context of the statement, tightly bound to the aims of the mechanical and geometrical works, to those arithmetical examples proposed from the outset whose origins can be traced back to the specialist discussions with Beeckman, would seem to confirm it. We will indeed see how the central axis of Descartes's positive inquiry is constituted around this nucleus.[41] However, it would be seriously limiting to stop at this, since the extent to which the general scope of the project surpasses the determinateness of its mathematical character will become immediately evident. To throw light upon 'the dark chaos of science' through this radically new science does not indicate a specific problem but rather alludes to a much vaster problematic. More precisely, it represents the identification of the world, in its obscurity and complexity, as the object of the inquiry. The enthusiasm that accompanies the determination of the project is more eloquent than its literal definition. It shows that Descartes is inside that world and entirely caught up in it. This is a world characterized by lack of distinction between the vital and the metaphysical that the scientific project wishes to match. The *scientia penitus nove* is a science that traverses the world and nature *iuxta sua propria principia*. It is a science in which the humanist faith in discovery

40. PWD III 2 and 3 [TN: Translation modified].
41. See our comments to *Parnassus* in the third section of this chapter. Taken in this attenuated form, we can accept Augst's standpoint, according to which the writings of this period already evince the mechanicist and methodological direction of Descartes's thought. Augst bases his interpretation especially on the conclusions of J.-P. Weber's dissertation, *La constitution du texte des Regulae*, Paris 1960.

and reconstruction, in the radical renewal of the world, is fully unfolded. This science wants to reorder the cosmos.

The so-called *Private Thoughts* (*Cogitationes Privatae*) were elaborated in the very midst of the travails that followed the definition of the project and, perhaps, constitute the best commentary to it.[42] They thematize the scientific project, firstly, by clarifying its heroic character, secondly, by emphasizing the 'marvellous' place of the inquirer within the world and within science, and, moreover, affirming the possibility of reconstruction. Finally, they qualify the metaphysical character of the inquiry. *Preliminaries, Observations, Olympian Matters*: three degrees – not successive, but historically contemporary – of the argument's progression, of the sharpening of Descartes's urge to fix the content of his vocation and, at the same time, to define the content and scope of the ideal of wisdom.

'*Initium sapientiae timor Domini*': the *Preliminaries* open with the repetition of the psalm.[43] The stress falls on the theme of the *initium*, which is consecrated in the religious relationship which engages the inquirer and marks his solitude. The *initium* is also privileged by the radicality that, within this framework, the inquiry assigns to the definition of the foundation of wisdom and science. Here the theme of the foundation is immediately shaped as the tension between the solitude of the inquirer and the radicality of the object of his investigation. The chapters of the *Preliminaries* are all marked by this tension. 'Actors, who are taught not to let any embarrassment show on their faces, put on a

---

42. These texts can be found in AT X. *Cogitationes Privatae* is the title attributed to them by Leibniz and by Foucher de Careil, who first published them. On the many questions raised by these writings see, above all, J. Sirven, *Les années d'apprentissage de Descartes (1596–1628)*, New York 1987, reprint. Although it represents a fundamental philological contribution, Gouhier's more recent *Les premières pensées de Descartes* is, as far as its basic theses are concerned, very much open to discussion (see, for example, E. Garin, *Opere*, vol. I, pp. xxxivff).

43. AT X 8. For the identification of the psalm (no. 110, according to the Vulgate), see H. Gouhier, *Les premières pensées*, pp. 66–7.

mask. I will do the same. So far, I have been a spectator in this theatre which is the world, but I am now about to mount the stage, and I come forward masked.' 'In my youth, when I was shown an ingenious invention, I used to wonder whether I could work it out for myself before reading the inventor's account. This practice gradually led me to realize that I was making use of definite rules.' 'Science is like a woman: if she stays faithful to her husband she is respected; if she becomes common property she grows to be despised.'[44] Scientific investigation is a heroic conquest, the function of a tension that the inquirer discovers and that he carries with himself as he traverses the world. This tension is never placated, never mollified, but rather is intensified when the world reveals itself: 'The sciences are at present masked [*larvatae nunc scientiae sunt*], but if the masks were taken off, they would be revealed in all their beauty. If we could see how the sciences are linked together [*catenam scientiarum*], we would find them no harder to retain in our minds than the series of numbers.'[45] This is what *invenire* is: the affirmation of the possibility of attaining the coincidence of individual and cosmos; the exacerbation of *virtus* through a method that possesses the key to the complete comprehension of the universe and which is itself homogeneous with this universe. There is no place within this horizon for doubt, scepticism, the sense of crisis or dualism. If the sceptical motif appears at all,[46] if there is any expression of mistrust in the universal capacity of humanity to lay hold of truth,[47] it is not in order to demonstrate the vanity of the Renaissance ideal of

44. PWD I 2.
45. PWD I 3.
46. 'In the case of most books, once we have read a few lines and looked at a few of the diagrams, the entire message is perfectly obvious. The rest is added on to fill up the paper' (PWD I 2).
47. 'For each of us there is a limit to our intellectual powers which we cannot pass. Those who, through lack of intelligence, cannot make discoveries by employing first principles, will still be able to recognize the true worth of sciences, and this will enable them to arrive at a correct judgement of the value of things' (PWD I 3).

science but rather to better discern the heroic and individual quality of the process of achieving wisdom.

Nor do the *Observations* show the tension of the investigation being placated. Instead, they show it transfigured, opening again to a higher level, one not already defined by the relationship between individual and totality. This is a tension within the totality, when the 'diseases of the mind' (*morbos animi*),[48] the burden of the relationship with individuality, have been overcome and a kind of youthful joy (*laetitia*) becomes operative in the full adherence to being.[49] The tension stems from a possession of the world that knows how to become a creative reproduction of natural effects, an urge which is proper to the marvellous. The Renaissance magi possessed an *ars mirabilis* able to *singulare ac mirabile artificium.*[50] Descartes is himself a Renaissance magician who has resolved the first problem of the relationship with the world in substantive self-awareness. Now this relationship issues into the reconstruction of the world. The marvellous shows itself to be the expression of the heroic Prometheanism of one who has seized the rules of *invenire.* We find Descartes trying out illusionist tricks.[51] At other times we discover him intent on or absorbed by the construction of automated machines.[52] The theme *mira machina, merveilleux artifice* will persist in Descartes's early thinking and it will be possible to follow its transformation

48. PWD I 3. See also PWD I 4: 'In the minds of all of us there are certain elements . . .'
49. '. . . if I am full of joy [*laetitia*], I do not eat or sleep' (PWD I 3).
50. See P. Rossi, *Logic and the Art of Memory.* Thus, *scientia admirabilis* is a common expression, employed by Magism as well as Lullism.
51. PWD I 3. The passages describing illusionist techniques are directly inserted in French into the Latin *Observations (Experimenta).* On the sources (Cardano, Della Porta), see G. Rodis-Lewis, 'Machineries et perspectives curieuses dans leurs rapports avec le cartésianisme', *XVIIe siècle*, vol. 32, 1954, pp. 461–74.
52. See AT X 231–2, where Descartes discusses automatic machines in the form of tightrope walkers, Archita's doves, and so on.

into metaphor.[53] The marvellous reconstruction of the world is thus both the conclusion and the overcoming of the problem of the relation between individual and cosmos. Here, the problem of 1619 ('What road in life shall I follow?') finds a solution: 'In the year 1620, I began to understand the fundamental principles of a wonderful discovery [*inventi mirabilis*].'[54]

In the pages of the *Olympian Matters, invenire* acquires a further and final qualification. The enthusiastic nexus takes on an entirely metaphysical scope, first, in terms of a heroic subjectivism and, second, in terms of the cosmic and universalizing force of the marvellous. The *scientia penitus nova* flows back into the metaphysical order that we are already acquainted with, repeating the motifs of Renaissance exemplarism. Here this metaphysical order forcefully reasserts itself. Having been formulated in the *Preliminaries*, the hypothesis that *invenire* re-establishes a total relationship with the cosmos was verified in a positive manner in the *Observations*. Descartes moves with the highest degree of metaphysical awareness. Science becomes *sapientia*; *invenire* has penetrated being. Now consciousness works to reconstruct from within the significant links of an ordered world. And it is a world that is as dense and corporeal as the dense and full-bodied microcosm from which the force of *invenire* set out.

53. As we shall see below, the key locus of this transformation is to be found in Descartes's *The World*. See, for example, *The World and Other Writings*, pp. 139, 168 and *passim*. On this cluster of problems, one should bear in mind F. Alquié's interpretation in *La découverte métaphysique de l'homme chez Descartes*, Paris 1950, pp. 38–55.
54. PWD I 3. For issues of dating and various interpretations of the '*inventum*' of 1620, see H. Gouhier, *Les premières pensées*, pp. 74–8, and E. Garin, *Opere*, vol. I, pp. xlvii–xlix. We can concur with Garin's suggestion that the *inventum* is a first definition of geometrical algebra, as long as this intuition is given all the philosophical and cultural substance that transpires from reading Descartes's texts from this period. The other interpretations of the *inventum* (according to Liard: a solution of problems concerning third and fourth degree solids using parabolas and circumferences; according to Milhaud: the invention of an astronomical telescope) seem to fail precisely because of their excessive particularity.

The things which are perceivable by the senses are helpful in enabling us to conceive of Olympian matters [*Sensibilia apta concipiendis Olympicis*]. The wind signifies spirit; movement with the passage of time signifies life; light signifies knowledge; heat signifies love; and instantaneous activity signifies creation. Every corporeal form acts through harmony [*omnis forma corporea agit per harmonium*]. There are more wet things than dry things, and more cold things than hot, because if this were not so, the active elements would have won the battle too quickly and the world would not have lasted long.[55]

All the elements that would otherwise be separate and in tension with one another are brought back together: sensibility and imagination,[56] imagination and intelligence,[57] enthusiasm and reason[58] can harmoniously traverse the universe. The microcosm is repeated in the macrocosm: 'There is a single active power in things: love, charity, harmony [*Una est in rebus active vis, amor, charitas, harmonia*].'[59] We also witness the projection of the

55. PWD I 5.
56. 'Man has knowledge of natural things only through their resemblance to the things which come under the senses. Indeed, our estimate of how much truth a person has achieved in his philosophizing will increase the more he is able to propose some similarity between what he is investigating and the other things known by the senses' (PWD I 5).
57. 'Just as the imagination employs figures in order to conceive of bodies, so, in order to frame ideas of spiritual things, the intellect makes use of certain bodies which are perceived through the senses, such as wind and light. By this means we may philosophize in a more exalted way, and develop the knowledge to raise our minds to lofty heights' (PWD I 4).
58. 'It may seem surprising to find weighty judgements in the writings of the poets rather than the philosophers. The reason is that the poets were driven to write by enthusiasm and the force of the imagination. We have within us the sparks of knowledge, as in a flint: philosophers extract them through reason, but poets force them out through sharp blows of the imagination, so that they shine more brightly' (PWD I 4).
59. PWD I 5.

natural order directly into the divine: 'The Lord has made three marvels [*tria mirabilia*]: something out of nothing; free will; and God in Man.'[60] The circulation and commutation of the constitutive elements of the universe is given in full. We observe the apotheosis of a Renaissance conception of the world in which the youthful vigour of the philosopher is exalted: '10 November 1619, when, full of enthusiasm, I was discovering the foundations of a marvellous science . . .'[61]

Those who have denied Descartes's participation in the Renaissance world cannot sustain their thesis in light of his early philosophical experiences. Moreover, one cannot attenuate the intensity

---

60. PWD I 5.
61. AT X 179. The severity of H. Gouhier's attack (*Les premières pensées, passim*) against the identification of the first phase of Descartes's philosophical development with Renaissance thinking is well known. According to him, this phase should instead be linked to the historical category of the 'anti-Renaissance'. Amongst the numerous criticisms of Gouhier's work on the young Descartes it suffices to recall the following: 'M. Gouhier seems to us to be untrue to his method when he rejects as "pre-Cartesian" the most original and stimulating texts of the *Olympian Matters*. A note such as the one that had enthralled Foucher de Careil and Adam: "There is a single active power in things: love, charity, harmony", cannot be considered "a youthful thought cast aside in the years of maturity" . . . but should rather be understood as a proposition that could, better than any other, account for the "wisdom" to which Descartes's philosophy has always remained faithful' (P. Mesnard, 'Les débuts du Cartésianisme et la fin de la Renaissance', *Les Etudes philosophiques*, vol. 13, 1958, pp. 191–5); '. . . Gouhier's otherwise invaluable investigation has two limitations: an insufficient knowledge of Renaissance literature and the idea of the anti-Renaissance. These limits make their presence felt especially in the interpretation of the *Olympian Matters*' (E. Garin, *Opere*, vol. I, p. xliv). In general, on the idea of 'anti-Renaissance' see H. Haydn's *The Counter-Renaissance*, New York 1950, and, above all, D. Cantimori's powerful critique, 'L'Antirinascimento', now in *Studi di Storia*, Turin 1959, pp. 455–60. It should be pointed out, however, that the concepts of anti-Renaissance in Gouhier and Haydn feature substantial differences. The only thing they share is their denial of the centrality and modern radicalism of the phenomenon of the Renaissance.

of Descartes's participation in that world by recalling the polemic against his supposed affiliation with the Rosicrucians.[62] It seems correct that the 'dreams'[63] of the night in Ulm, on 10 November, should be interpreted through the reduction to the philosophical nucleus expressed in the fragments collected by Leibniz, and that the formal features of the narration of the 'dreams' should be understood in terms of a broader cultural framework, rather than in relation to Rosicrucian discipline. But that is a long way away from severing Descartes's experience in the course of these years from contact with humanist and Renaissance culture. In fact, it confirms and deepens his relationship to that culture, at least in so far as Descartes shows that this relationship is an internal one, not mediated by extrinsic, sectarian affiliations. But, one may reply, Descartes's development is not only independent of, but in open conflict with, and refutes, that of the Rosicrucians. That might be true. The philosopher of the *mirabilia* is engaged in a polemic with the *miracula*. But in what sense? And to what end?

The mathematical treasure trove of Polybius, citizen of the world. This work lays down the true meaning of solving all the

---

62. See especially, in this regard, H. Gouhier, *Les premières pensées*, pp. 117–41, 150–7. The thesis of Descartes's affiliation to the Rosicrucian sect has been defended, above all, by G. Cohen, *Ecrivains français*, pp. 388–90, 399–400, 402–7; G. Persigout, 'L'illumination de René Descartes rosi-crucien (Contribution à l'étude de l'imagination créatrice)', in *Congrès Descartes. Etudes cartésiennes*, vol. II, Paris 1937, pp. 123–30; Paul Arnold, *Histoire des Rose-Croix et les origines de la Franc-maçonnerie*, Paris 1955, 'Appendice I' (which argues not in terms of affiliation but of an extremely profound literary influence). See also F. A. Yates, *Giordano Bruno and the Hermetic Tradition*, Chicago 1964, p. 452: '[on the night of 10 November 1619] we are completely in the atmosphere of the hermetic trance, of that sleep of the senses in which truth is revealed. The atmosphere is maintained on the following pages . . .' More generally, on the Rosicrucians, see S. Hutin, *Histoire des Rose-Croix*, Paris 1955, which also features some curious details.
63. AT X 179–88.

difficulties in the science of mathematics, and demonstrates that all human intellect can achieve nothing further on these questions. The work is aimed at certain people who promise to show us miraculous discoveries in all the sciences, its purpose being to chide them for their sluggishness and to expose the emptiness of their boasts. A further aim is to lighten the agonizing toil of those who struggle night and day with the Gordian knots of this science, and who squander their intellectual resources to no avail. The work is offered afresh to learned men throughout the world and especially to the brothers of the Rose Croix in Germany.[64]

If this is the passage on which the belief in Descartes's polemical attitude toward the Rosicrucians is based, one must acknowledge that this polemic has precise limits that do not concern his actual adherence to humanist culture but instead confirm it. For in this text Descartes reaffirms nothing less than the necessity of overcoming the split between *invenire* and cosmos. Not the promise of new miracles, not perennial foolhardiness, not the useless ensnaring of the investigation by worthless objects, but the serene adequation of *invenire* to being, the exaltation of the *vera media* as the indispensable treasure of man open to the experience of the world. What is opposed to the *miracula* is still the humanist ideal, the security and liberty of Polibio Cosmopolita and his admirable skill in reconstructing the world. There is nothing ironic in this move. Descartes renews his benevolent, fraternal attack on the Rosicrucians: not *miracula* but science! And we already know what kind of science we are dealing with. We find there a passionate reminder of a common destiny, of a positive science rooted in the totality of being and, because of this, *mirabilis*, universal and revolutionary. The alternative posed – Rosicrucianism or anti-Renaissance – collapses on itself inasmuch as it merely shows the fundamental incapacity, on the part of those who advocate it, of

64. PWD I 2.

grasping in full the positivity and complexity of the humanist ideal of science. That is because the Prometheanism of Renaissance man consists in conquering the cosmos, in reconstructing order, and not in eccentricity or madness.[65]

This then is the content of the mature Descartes's memory. It is a content that is revealed in the form of metaphor because it is the memory of a relationship and of the myth of a humanity that discovers and projects itself as free in the conquest of the world. That world is itself metaphorical, the exposition of a human plan.[66] However, the rational sense of the world is not lost in this enthusiastic blurring of distinctions. All *invenire* follows the thing

65. See P. Mesnard's apposite comments in 'Les débuts du cartésianisme'. It will never be sufficiently emphasized that H. Gouhier's polemical interpretation, which rejects any possible link between Descartes's thought and that of the Renaissance, has as its sole aim to establish the religious authenticity of Descartes's thought (in accordance with the thesis already sustained by him in *La pensée religieuse de Descartes*, Paris 1924). We should also underline how the exclusion of every mystical moment from Descartes's youthful experience is also in the service of the religious interpretation, of the need to turn the religious 'datum' into a moment proper to 'philosophical reasoning'. Note how Gouhier applies his methodological demand in general; for instance, in *Blaise Pascal. Commentaires*, Paris 1966, in the analysis of the *Mémorial* (pp. 11–65). In this case too the extraordinary character of religious experience is denied. Pascal's 'memoir' involves 'rethinking' his life 'through the schemata of model situations illustrated by biblical scenes' (p. 64). The normality of mysticism for reason, this non-specificity of mysticism, is thus a basic theme in Gouhier, the stopping-point for his historicism. This is an evident mystification as regards both Descartes and Pascal.

66. On the prominence of the mythical function in Renaissance thought see G. Weise, *L'ideale eroico del Rinascimento e le sue premesse umanistiche*, Naples 1961; and *L'ideale eroico del Rinascimento. Diffusione europea e tramonto*, Naples 1965 (we will consider these works more fully below). See also some of the comments on the importance of the Hegelian definition of the Renaissance (in which the mythical function is given a broad treatment) in M. Biscione, *Neo-umanesimo e rinascimento. L'immagine del Rinascimento nella storia della cultura dell'ottocento*, Rome 1962.

iuxta sua propria principia, both substantively and rationally. At the apex of enthusiasm one also finds the apex of clarity: '10 November 1619, when, full of enthusiasm, I was discovering the foundations of a marvellous science . . .' The entire sense of the humanist *renovatio* of the world, which traverses all aspects of the experience of Renaissance man, flows back into the *mirabilis*, which is both enthusiasm and science. For Descartes, as for the humanists, 'the age in which we live seemed to me to be flourishing, and as rich in good minds, as any before it.'[67] This is not only true for Descartes. The sentiment is a common one. 'Our century is the father of a universal shift . . .', it is widely argued.[68] Now that man has made himself master of the world, destroying the fetters of metaphysical subjugation that the medieval world had imposed upon him, affirming control over the nature to which he had hitherto been subjected, how can one imagine that traditional elements, heterogeneous moments, will not continue to survive in the midst of this new passion? The old horizon of man's existence is broken by a new feeling of his relation to the world. What does it matter if the scientific impetus

67. PWD I 113. Descartes's biographer, Baillet, thinks that the origin of this statement is to be found in the earlier *Studium bonae mentis* (AT X 192).

68. From Mersenne's letter to Rivet (12 March 1644, *Correspondance du P. Marin Mersenne*, ed. Mme P. Tannery, Paris 1932–88). However, one should note a further, bitter observation by Mersenne: 'What do you think of these innovations? Don't they presage the end of the world?' We will see the extent to which this contrast constitutes an extremely important element in defining the cultural themes of the epoch. To complete the positive moment in the definition of the self-consciousness of the time, we may turn to E. Garin (*Scienza e vita civile*, p. 148), who stresses that the mark of the new philosophy, between 1500 and 1600, 'is the idea of a progress in time in which the achievements of the speculative devices [*gl'ingegni speculativi*] unfold. The motto *veritas filia temporis*, which in 1536 decorated the typographic imprint of Marcolino da Forlí's Venetian editions, opens, with altogether different gravity, the *Narratio* of 1611 (published in Frankfurt), where Kepler expounds his observations on Jupiter's satellites.'

is still unable to completely free itself and indeed continues to be subjected to the old forms? What does it matter if it is confined within Neo-Platonic, hermetic, astrological schemata which in fact appear to increase their influence in this inaugural phase of the new scientific consciousness?[69] The old forms do not belittle the new content but are swept away by it.[70] So if the new content does not spurn the form of myth – whether philosophical, scientific or political – and instead recovers and remoulds many elements of the tradition, it is because it is fully rooted and the faith in the immediate correspondence between the proposal and the realization of the project of the world is acute. By expressing itself in the form of myth, the new consciousness transfigures the past and exalts its current existence.[71]

The question we posed at the start – whether Descartes had a

69. J. Dagens, 'Hermétisme et cabale en France de Lefèvre d'Etalpes à Bossuet', *Revue de littérature comparée*, vol. 1, 1961, p. 6: 'The end of the sixteenth century and the beginning of the seventeenth were the golden ages of religious hermeticism.' In 'Magia e astrologia nella cultura del Rinascimento' and 'Considerazioni sulla magia' (in *Medioevo e Rinascimento. Studi e ricerche*, Bari 1954, pp. 150–69 and 170–91), E. Garin warns against the distinction between the natural aspects and scientific aspects of equivocal disciplines such as astrology or alchemy, observing that 'the continual interweaving of the two themes, which for the sake of ease and according to custom we shall call mathematical and astrological, is incredible. Not only is mathematical knowledge sought after for its application, that is, in order to allow one to operate by making use of celestial forces rather than being subjected to them, but the calculus itself is continually entangled with numerous demands and motifs that are by no means mathematical.'
70. It is beyond doubt, in our eyes, that this is the fundamental result of the historiography on the Renaissance. It clearly transpires from critical reviews about the historiography, such as Ferguson's.
71. F. A. Yates has elucidated this in exemplary fashion in her numerous works on the subject. Simply to introduce themes to which we shall return later, it is important to underline how, at the start of the 1600s, myth acquires a directly political function in the process of the legitimation of national monarchies. See C. Vivanti, *Lotta politica e pace religiosa in Francia fra Cinque e Seicento*, Turin 1963, pp. 74ff, where he cites Yates's writings on the subject.

direct experience of the world of Renaissance humanism – is answered in the affirmative. In the *poêle* (the theme is itself humanist,)[72] Descartes submits enthusiastically, spellbound, to the urgency of a Renaissance project that demands to be realized. *Scientia penitus nova* as *scientia mirabilis*; the science of the foundation as the science of the worldly *renovatio*. This is how, in the mature Descartes, memory is constituted. It is a theme that he persistently confronts, whether as a symbol of division or of reconstruction.

3

It is not just the broad horizon of Descartes's early estimation of the world – and thus the horizon within which the mnemonic relation of the mature Descartes is framed – that is humanist. The specific themes that characterize the positive investigation of the 'mathematician-physicist' are also rooted in the world of humanism. The new science sees its first light within the world of metaphor, from which it draws nourishment but in which it also encounters barriers to its growth. In the early Descartes, however, it finds above all nourishment.

'. . . I want to produce . . . a completely new science, which would provide a general solution of all possible equations . . .'[73] It has been correctly noted that this arena is still analogous to that of Lullism.[74] At this time, Descartes's investigation is indeed focused not simply on discovering – through the *scientia penitus nova* – the

---

72. G. Cohen, *Ecrivains français*, pp. 393–4, 718–19, who refers back, for the theme of the *poêle* [TN: the stove or stove-heated room in which Descartes experienced his dreams on 10 November 1619] to Montaigne's *Journal de voyage*, in *Œuvres complètes*, pp. 1137–8; *The Complete Essays*, London 1991, vol. III, ch. XIII. See also E. Gilson, *Commentaire*, p. 157.

73. PWD III 2.

74. P. Rossi, *Logic and the Art of Memory*; P. Zambelli, 'Intorno al lullismo, alle arti mnemoniche e occulte e al metodo del loro studio', *Studi storici*, vol. 3, 1962, pp. 527–41.

formal links for the unification of knowledge and the rule of universal mathematization, but on identifying a science at the origin of all others, the unitary root of every branch of the tree of knowledge. It is not just the theme of the *scientia penitus nova* that places the young Descartes in the same cultural climate as Lullism. We will see other such themes emerge, aside from those already considered, in the *Rules*,[75] in the *Studium bonae mentis*,[76] as well as here and there in the mature works.[77] Thus, the urge to move through the real connections in the universe, which arose from the humanist intuition, reappears and expands within the Cartesian outlook. And yet, at the same time that Descartes breathes this cultural atmosphere, he appears to separate himself from it. The

75. See especially PWD I 13ff (*Rule Three*) and 454ff (*Rule Sixteen*). See also the important commentary by P. Rossi, *Logic and the Art of Memory*.

76. AT X 201–2. Especially noteworthy for its Lullian resonances is the distinction between local and intellectual memory, in which the most general principles of a cardinal science are established.

77. In particular PWD I 119, 120, 131 (see E. Gilson, *Commentaire*, pp. 185–6, 370) and PWD II 400–1. To grasp the degree of opacity that not so much Descartes's thought but his form of exposition can reach, it is enough to recall – in addition to AT X 347 (from Beeckman's *Journal* of 1629), which attests to Descartes's interest for Della Porta – the following fragment: 'The use of these is trigonometric' (AT X 289–97). Having established the formula for the relationship of the base and the sides of the inscribed polygon, Descartes states that from this 'theorems about infinity can be worked out, and one can easily explain those arithmetical progressions which include the bases or sides of triangles of such kind, in imitation of the Cabala of the Germans' (297). One should also recall Descartes's letters concerning the thought of Comenius. One can find three, written in 1639–40, in the *Correspondence*: PWD III 119–20, AT *Supplement* 97–102 and 1–6. In a note to his *Descartes, Œuvres philosophiques*, vol. II, Paris 1967, p. 154, F. Alquié has raised grave doubts as to the authenticity of the second letter. Though he refutes Comenius's project, Descartes appears, in these writings as well, to accept the idea of a parallelism between nature and language – such that the latter presents itself as a 'painting' or 'mirror' of the former – which is certainly not far from the general framework of the mnemonic and Lullian arts.

requests for information directed at Beeckman,[78] as well as Descartes's references to Lullism, contain ever more explicit polemical hints. These are made explicit in the definition of the *scientia penitus nova* – in opposition to Lull's *Ars brevis* – and especially in a note on Schenkel's mnemonic arts.[79]

What is the significance of this separation? The texts we have just referred to show us what Descartes refuses straight away, namely the ostentatious display of method and the charlatanry that accompanies its propaganda. Later, he will qualify this stance, saying that those techniques 'are less use for learning things than for . . . speaking without judgement about matters of which one is ignorant'.[80] In these cases, the universal symbolism of nature is grasped merely in its external aspects. A bookish culture has succeeded in usurping the place otherwise taken by the reading of the great book of the world. Science has been replaced by extravagance, or even magic. Out of this has emerged a static, alienated world in contradiction with the very presuppositions of humanist feeling, with the dictates of the humanist *scientia mirabilis*. Is this the first forewarning of the exhaustion and crisis of Renaissance thought? Perhaps, but not to the point of undermining the entire frame of reference, of implicating the critique of the humanist impetus of the inquiry. On the contrary, this

78. AT X 63–4 (here is a note from Beeckman's *Journal*, with regard to requests for information from Descartes: 'Lull's *Ars Brevis* (from what I could gather from one hour or at most two reading Agrippa's *Commentaries*) could be considered to have this use, that it teaches briefly the sum total of all things: that is, it divides all things in such a way that there is nothing of a thing that cannot be reduced to some part of his classification. And thus things are first divided into six or seven parts . . . And he divides the single parts for a second time . . .') PWD III 4–5, AT X 167–8.

79. AT X 230. Descartes's discussion of Schenkel's 'profitable trifles [*lucrosas nugas*]', with its emphasis on the opposition between the Lullian art of memory and the '*vera ars*' (true art) that he himself proposes, is used by P. Rossi (in *Logic and the Art of Memory*) as the pivotal point for a severe but absolutely correct critique of Gouhier's theses.

80. PWD I 119. See E. Gilson, *Commentaire*, pp. 185–6.

impetus emerges reinvigorated from the critique. Behind the immediate reasons for Descartes's rejection of the more extravagant Lullist claims, we discover a vocation and a demarcation: a vocation to traverse the true order of the universe and a demarcation of his own scientific work from Lullist extravagance. As had already been affirmed in the polemic with Schenkel, Descartes's *vera ars* will be clearly contrary to the theories of that worthless man.[81] And if, for example, the *ars nova* (new art) that Descartes opposes to the Lullian techniques is to form the basis of a universal language: 'all the thoughts which can come into the human mind must be arranged in an order like the natural order of numbers'; the 'discovery of such a language depends upon the true philosophy', i.e. on the capacity to re-examine the world starting from its complexity and moving to the simplicity of its constitutive moments, and to renew it marvellously in the new language; it does not depend on the sterile games and self-advertising of the Lullists: 'as soon as I see the word *arcanum* [mystery] in any proposition I begin to suspect it'.[82] So the rejection or negation of Lullism involves Descartes in the assertion of an even more radical faith in human reason and saves the humanist moment from Lull's extravagances.

However, it would be a mistake to consider Descartes's relation to Lullism itself without a broader reference to the humanist and Renaissance thematic of method. That is because in the ambiguous relationship with Lullism Descartes actually formulates his first confrontation with that entire cultural milieu. Once again, this confrontation involves the discovery of a vocation and the exclusion of spurious elements. The vocation involves the trust in a general rational method for the solution of the problems of knowledge. It is

81. AT X 230.
82. PWD III 10–12. One should note, however, that Descartes opposes the practical impossibility of artificial languages to their theoretical possibility. Only *l'usage* can allow the construction of a language. See, in this regard, the conclusion of the cited letter, as well as AT I 106 and, especially, 125–6.

here perhaps that one finds the deepest, most essential form of the revolutionary, humanist moment that had become sedimented in European culture in the 1400s and 1500s.[83] But the moment of demarcation – the separation from the merely rhetorical, abstractly philological aspects that the Renaissance form of philosophical development had imposed on the subject of method – is no less important.[84] In Descartes, as in the 'new science', once it has separated itself from the spurious elements of philosophical development, the trust in method attains an almost mythical status and takes on a Promethean force, defining itself – along with its commitment to scientific verification – as a sort of heroic, originary ingenuity: 'Descartes is considered to be the founder of modern philosophy not because he gives precedence to the idea of method, but because he sees in it a new task. Not only the formal structure, but also the entire content of "pure" consciousness must be extracted and deduced in an uninterrupted sequence from an originary methodological principle.'[85] Hence the theme of method arises not from the refusal but from the (discriminating) acceptance, the deepening and extolling of the motifs that inspire and characterize the world of metaphor.

There is as little question regarding Descartes's humanist inspiration as there is about what enabled him to expound the theme of method, namely, his activity as 'mathematician-physicist': 'Before a few days went by I was fortunate to enjoy the company of a most clever man . . .' And so we come back to the meeting with Beeckman,[86] a decisive turning-point in Descartes's life: 'For it was you alone who roused me from my state of

83. N. W. Gilbert, *Renaissance Concepts of Method*, 2nd edn, New York 1963, pp. 224ff in particular. See also, as proof of the extraordinary currency of the theme of method in the late Renaissance, the bibliography, pp. 233–5.

84. N. W. Gilbert, *Renaissance Concepts of Method*, pp. 221–2, 224ff.

85. E. Cassirer, *Das Erkenntnisproblem in der Philosophie und Wissenschaft der neueren Zeit*, Hamburg 2000. However, one should immediately note the deficiency of Cassirer's interpretation when he insists exclusively on the 'purity' of both the speculative content and the method in Descartes.

86. AT X 219.

indolence.'[87] The topics discussed by the two thinkers are well known: the problem of the free fall of weights,[88] musical themes,[89] questions regarding the physics of liquids,[90] geometrical arguments,[91] and so on. Descartes's first idea of method is positively constituted in the excavation and discussion of these topics. This idea is precisely the refinement of the general humanist model of the construction of knowledge, a refinement elicited by the need to render the model workable, to make it confront the world and to verify it in this relation. This project could be realized only by winning back humanist heroism in all its mythical originality. In Descartes's years of peregrination,[92] in the inextricable tangle of metaphysical and scientific studies documented in our reading of the *Private Thoughts* this desire becomes stronger and more definite. How then is Descartes's first idea of method configured?

It is to the *Rules*[93] that we must turn in order for the idea of

87. PWD III 4.
88. AT X 219–20, 58–61, 75–8.
89. AT X 224, 227, 51, 52, 53, 54, 56–8.
90. AT X 225–6, 228, 67–74.
91. AT X 229, 232, 233, 234–40, 240, 246, 247, 46–51, 54–6.
92. Between 1621 and 1629, between the texts that make up the *Private Thoughts* and the *Rules* – that is to say, in the years of Descartes's peregrination, prior to definitively settling in Holland – one can find a number of fragments of a scientific character. Of particular interest are: *De solidorum elementis* (AT X 265–77), which is an attempt to put the elements of solids in algebraic form; some *Excerpta mathematica* and, above all, the three texts (AT X 310–24) on the nature of ovals. These are all problems that will reappear prominently in the *Geometry*. Finally, we should recall the various writings referred to or reproduced by Beeckman in his *Journal*, starting from 8 October 1628 (AT X 331–48).
93. See *Rules for the Direction of the Mind*, in PWD I 9–15, as well as the critical edition by G. Crapulli, The Hague 1966. AT X 486–8 establishes 1628 as the date of composition of the *Rules*; a date upon which the critical literature is generally in agreement. On the question of the composition of this text, see E. Garin, *Opere*, vol. I, pp. lviii–lxi. Garin concludes by identifying numerous strata of composition that would correspond to various strata of thought. We believe that this conclusion is acceptable only if this multiplicity of strata of composition is considered as a function of the strong and substantive unity of the work's motivation.

method – which has nonetheless been an element of Descartes's thought throughout – to be completely constituted and for it to present in systematic form the elements developed hitherto. The first, privileged moment stemming from Descartes's speculative work relates to the mathematical foundations of the method. We can turn to geometry and mathematics alone for certain and indubitable knowledge: 'Therefore, concerning all such matters of probable opinion we can, I think, acquire no perfect knowledge, for it would be presumptuous to hope that we could gain more knowledge than others have managed to achieve. Accordingly, if my reckoning is correct, out of all the sciences so far devised [*ex scientijs iam inventis*] we are restricted to just arithmetic and geometry if we stick to this rule.'[94] And, negatively, 'in seeking the right path of truth we ought to concern ourselves only with objects that admit of as much certainty as the demonstrations of arithmetic and geometry.'[95] But why, among all the disciplines, can these alone guarantee us certainty and hence lead us along the correct path of knowledge? Why is it here that we find the full expression and development of the two fundamental means that the mind has at its disposal to secure, in itself, the foundation: intuition, as rational light *in actu*, and deduction, as the capture of the articulated movement of reality? Descartes answers as follows:

> By 'intuition' I do not mean the fluctuating testimony of the senses, or the deceptive judgement of the imagination as it botches things together, but the conception of a clear and attentive mind, which is so easy and distinct that there can be no room for doubt about what we are understanding. Alternatively, and this comes to the same thing, intuition is the indubitable conception of a clear and attentive mind which proceeds solely from the light of reason [*a sola rationis luce*].[96]

94. PWD I 11. On this theme in general, see *Rule Two*.
95. PWD I 12–13.
96. PWD I 14. On this theme in general, see *Rule Three*.

Furthermore:

> [D]eduction, by which we mean the inference of something as
> following necessarily from some other propositions which are
> known with certainty . . . very many facts which are not self-
> evident are known with certainty, provided they are inferred from
> true and known principles through a continuous and uninter-
> rupted movement of thought [*per continuum et nullibi interruptem
> cogitationis motum*] in which each individual proposition is clearly
> intuited. This is similar to the way in which we know that the last
> link in a long chain is connected to the first: even if we cannot take
> in at one glance all the intermediate links on which the connection
> depends, we can have knowledge of the connection provided we
> survey the links one after the other, and keep in mind that each
> link from first to last is attached to its neighbour.[97]

Does the mathematical basis not appear here merely as the
occasion for a far more solid and profound metaphysical foundation? Certainly.[98] From the mathematical standpoint, the order of
being and the order of truth, the ontological and epistemological
horizons, are unified in this summa of Descartes's youthful
investigations. Intuition, the epistemological tool, repeats – with
its proper intensity – the unity of reality and being. The vision of

97. PWD I 15.
98. F. Alquié, *La découverte métaphysique*, pp. 56–83, and *Descartes.
L'homme et l'œuvre*, Paris 1956, pp. 23–36. After having correctly
and elegantly underlined the complexity and universality of the methodological and technical position developed in the *Rules*, Alquié denies
its 'metaphysical' character. Alquié says that it is a case of a 'technical'
standpoint, not a metaphysical one. But why exclude the possibility of a
metaphysics *of* the technical? It is precisely the existence of such a
metaphysics that appears to characterize these pages of Descartes. This
attitude is certainly irreducible to the metaphysics of the *Meditations*, but
is not for that less metaphysical. For it is a different, Renaissance,
humanist metaphysics that Descartes will be obliged to critique so as to
achieve the unique development of his thinking.

the world determined by intuition implies universal interpenetration, whereas deduction repeats intuitive certainty within space and time, grasping the order of truth in the concatenation of reality. In the relation between epistemological tool and metaphysical order, the very project of the *Rules* becomes clearer: to define the productive core of science and to express the truth of its relation to being. Thus, Descartes writes: 'It must be acknowledged that all the sciences are so closely interconnected that it is much easier to learn them all together than to separate one from the other. If, therefore, someone seriously wishes to investigate the truth of things, he ought not to select one science in particular, for they are all interconnected and interdependent. He should, rather, consider simply how to increase the natural light of reason'.[99] It should be noted that in the *Rules* this relationship to being is considered as an intimately structured one, as the full correspondence of reason and reality. Science traverses being in its order and complexity. At the very moment when it presents itself as the sublime art of *invenire*, science is therefore also a norm internal to the structure of being, the awareness of a movement and possibly of a limit determined by that same order of being. Thus, when one follows the proper method and arrives at an insoluble difficulty, it will be evident that this occurs 'not because of any defect of his intelligence, but because of the obstacle which the nature of the problem itself or the human condition presents [*obstat*]. His recognition of this point is just as much knowledge as that which reveals the nature of the thing itself [*quae cognitio non minor scientia est, quam illa quae rei ipsius naturam exhibit*]; and it would, I think, be quite irrational if he were to stretch his curiosity any further.'[100] Therefore *invenire* is the science of being, the retracing of the structure of being in certainty (which the relation formally grounds) and in limitation (which is materially imposed by its adequacy to the order of being). There is no possible extrapolation

99. PWD I 10. On this theme in general, see *Rule One.*
100. PWD I 28. On this theme in general, see *Rule Eight.*

from the awareness of the limit of cognition, or from other intimations of doubt, to the assertion of a different and higher degree of maturity in Descartes's thinking. Here the limit is the obverse of certainty, it is the cognitive counterpart of the nature of the object, of the placement of the object in its proper order of reality. Not a sense of crisis, then, but the essential confirmation of Descartes's humanist inspiration, as well as a verification of his first fundamental problem: the relationship with the 'cosmos'.[101]

Another element of Descartes's discourse is reorganized on these grounds. This is the polemic against extravagance, in other words, the distinction between the first, heroic humanist demand for knowledge and the later, unproductive form that this demand develops into. The polemic proceeds on two levels. First, against the unreality of a logic that is not anchored in being (in this regard the polemic implicates Scholasticism as fully as later disciplines or arts). Second, against the unproductive character of a philosophy unable to reconstruct being.

101. The neo-Kantian interpreters of Descartes do not consider the methodological position elaborated in the *Rules* to be metaphysical, but merely formal and/or transcendental. The importance of these neo-Kantian interpretations should not be underestimated. The significance of their philological and substantive contributions to the understanding of the *Rules* – the truly privileged work for neo-Kantianism, especially in some passages such as those in *Rule Six* (to which we shall return) – is indisputable. For the overall framework of the neo-Kantian interpretation see E. Cassirer's *Das Erkenntnisproblem*, as well as the introductory chapter on Descartes in his *Leibniz' System in seinen wissenschaftlichen Grundlagen*, Hamburg 1998. See also L. J. Beck, 'L'unité de la pensée et la méthode', in *Descartes. Cahiers de Royaumont*, pp. 393–411. The interpretation of the neo-Kantians is certainly contestable – as far as we are concerned it is completely unacceptable. But this is not to say that we can accept the kind of criticisms – inspired by the historiography of Italian idealism – that are expressed in the otherwise very useful paper by A. Corsano, 'Misticismo e volontarismo nelle cartesiane *Regulae ad directionem ingenii'*, *Giornale critico della filosofia italiana*, vol. 11, 1930, pp. 337–62. This reading of the *Rules* is almost exclusively directed to tracing its Neo-Platonic motifs and, through them, a determinate conception of spirit ('in its actuality' [*attuosità*], even) that would be developed within it.

The first polemic, to which we will return, aims to expunge any kind of rhetoric from philosophy. As for the polemic against the *miracula*, the lauding of the ordered correspondence between science and being reinforces the conception of the *mirabilis* and the function that it attributes to science. The sense of the ontological limit and the definition of the order of being tend to be overturned and reconfigured as the meaning and definition of the technically possible. The reaffirmation of the order of the world is accompanied by the championing of the *hominum artificia*, precisely as both the repetition and remaking of that order. 'In order to acquire discernment we should exercise our intelligence by investigating what others have already discovered, and methodically survey even the most significant products of human skill, especially those which display or presuppose order.'[102] We should not be fooled by the modesty of this prescription. In its simplicity it expresses an enormously innovative project. Not only is the genetic impetus of humanist culture opposed to its contradictory outcomes but it is reproposed in all its creative intensity, and the method itself is tailored to this end. A mythical ingenuity – which recurs ever since the pages of the *Olympian Matters* – is won back within this framework: 'to penetrate the inner truth of things almost in a playful way'. Descartes affirms that the world is order, albeit veiled. One must penetrate this sanctuary to joyfully discover the 'writing concealed in unknown characters' and the order that lies behind it, precisely so as to reproduce that order.

In this phase of Descartes's thinking, method is therefore inseparable from the metaphysical horizon in which it is situated. It possesses both a heuristic and a reproductive function, and these functions are articulated with being. The *universalis mathesis* proposed by the development of method is a real cosmos. The path of method is ordered because it traces the order of being: 'We need a method if we are to investigate the truth of things [*Necessaria est Methodus ad rerum veritatem investigandam*]'.[103]

102. PWD I 34–5. On this theme in general, see *Rule Ten.*
103. PWD I 15.

This is a method that follows and gradually unveils the order of things and that, in unveiling this order, identifies the relationship between the subject and object of knowledge in the 'almost divine' unity of the *semina veritatis* ('seeds of truth')[104] which grounds science, the source of all knowledge, in the universal *mathesis*.[105]

Besides, if there is to be an articulation of method, it will have to be an articulation of reality. To the relationship of intuition and deduction there will correspond the relationship of the absolute to the series of apparent things. According to Descartes, the 'secret of this method consists entirely in our attentively noting in all things that which is absolute in the highest degree'.[106] It is of course true that here Descartes interpolates a series of considerations which make a clear appreciation of the relationship and an explicit identification of the ontological nexus very difficult. He explicitly declares that 'what we are contemplating here is the series of things to be discovered, and not the nature of each of them',[107] for 'it instructs us that all things can be arranged serially in various groups, not in so far as they can be referred to some ontological genus (such as the categories into which philosophers divide things), but in so far as some things can be known on the basis of others.'[108] And yet the relation of appearance to the founding absolute, to the real simplicity that corresponds to intuitive immediacy, is not thereby removed. It coexists with the phenomenalist and epistemological appreciation that is here proposed in isolation, perhaps more in a polemical, anti-Scholastic function than for any other reason.[109] It soon exceeds it however, putting

104. PWD I 17, 18.
105. PWD I 15–20: *Rule Four*; and 20–1: *Rule Five*.
106. PWD I 22 [TN: translation slightly modified]. On this theme in general, see *Rule Six*.
107. PWD I 22.
108. PWD I 21.
109. This takes nothing away from the fact that *Rule Six* is deeply contradictory. In this case, an interpretation that would take the *Rules* to be a composite work would be entirely appropriate. Nevertheless, it seems to us that the general outlook of humanist discourse　　*cont'd over/*

back in play the full-bodied and indistinct totality of the humanist viewpoint. It is the order of the *scientia mirabilis*, the function of the *invenire*, that hurtles over appearances to arrive at truth. The relationship established by method makes itself internal to the nexus between appearance and reality, revealing itself as the effective tension between the multiplicity and unity of the real. It is no coincidence that precisely at this point Descartes also incorporates induction and enumeration into the rhythm of *invenire*, gathering and organizing them under the direction of intuition.[110] Intuition becomes transcendental imagination as it traverses the series of known things, working to identify and validate their connections and establishing the general character of the relationship within a unifying intuition. One could conclude that this relationship between intuition and induction is even privileged with respect to that between intuition and deduction, since what was static in the latter is here overcome. Placed between intuition and induction (enumeration), the imagination reveals the productivity of the *humana mens*. In its continuous and uninterrupted movement it shows the power of the ontological foundation already uncovered by intuition.

Let us return then to intuition. It is the foundation for the validity of mathematics. It makes it possible to draw on the internal armature of the world: *universalis mathesis*. With respect to deduction and its justification, it is simultaneous, universal *mathesis (rem totam simul intueri)*.[111] With respect to induction, enumeration and their justification, it is an ontologically articu-

---

109. *cont'd*   clearly prevails over the indisputable ambivalence of the motifs. This is also true of *Rule Six*, where the distinction between cognitive order and ontological order appears to hold, above all, with reference to the deductive procedure – '*pro tempore*', that is – until the connection is brought back to the unity of intuition, the real indissoluble link between epistemological and ontological truth.

110. PWD I 25–8: *Rule Seven, Rule Fourteen* and *passim*.

111. PWD I 38. On this theme in general, see *Rule Eleven*.

lated and spatially distributed universal *mathesis*.[112] Lastly, intuition is the radical possibility of possession of the world, a human
power that ventures forth into the totality of being so as to possess
and create it anew – a power capable of multiplying the world in
order to unify it, to simulate it in order to realize it.[113] Later
Descartes will add, to negate the world in order to recreate it. This
is the most creative moment in his thought. Now, within the
positive horizon of his humanist method, he summarizes the
determination of intuition as follows: 'the whole of human
knowledge consists uniquely in our achieving a distinct perception
of how all these simple natures contribute to the composition of
other things.'[114]

Having examined the content and general form of Cartesian
method in this early formulation, we must now return to considering its cultural milieu and revisiting the ideal circuits within which it
was elaborated. This milieu was that of the 'new science', and the
relationship of the 'mathematician-physicist' Descartes with 'many
Jesuits, scholars, and educated men'. We must return to this
question in order to clarify some aspects of the situation in which
the method – the frame of reference and approach of the new science
– finds itself. This situation is at once stimulating and somewhat
awkward, inasmuch as the method is caught up in a complex tangle
of metaphysical themes. And yet Descartes's position does not
appear particularly original in this respect. The mediation between
the knowledge of the world and its technical realization can be and
must be metaphysical. The horizon to which the whole method of
investigation should be related cannot but be that of metaphysics.
This position, at least in the initial phase of the genesis of the new
science and among its principal instigators, is extremely widespread.

112. 'We must concentrate our mind's eye totally upon the most insig-
     nificant and easiest of matters, and dwell on them long enough to
     acquire the habit of intuiting the truth distinctly and clearly' (PWD I
     33). On this theme in general, see *Rule Nine*.
113. PWD I 39–51. On this theme in general, see *Rule Twelve*.
114. PWD I 49.

What unifies the often contradictory aspects of the two sources from which the new science is built – that of the progress of technical work and of the highest mathematical abstraction – is precisely the heroic metaphysical project that envisages the possession and transformation of the world through mathematization.[115] The mathematical schema is reality itself in so far as it is possessed. Vice versa, reality as technically possessed is dominated in the contemplation of the necessity that has thereby been uncovered and exalted.[116] The

115. The following commentators are in fundamental agreement with this point: A. Carugo, 'Sui rapporti tra progresso tecnico e pensiero scientifico (Cronaca bibliografica)', *Studi storici*, vol. I, 1959–60, pp. 835–47; P. Rossi, *I filosofi e le macchine, 1400–1700*, Milan 1962, pp. 105ff; P. Zimbelli, 'Rinnovamento umanistico e teorie filosofiche alle origini della rivoluzione scientifica', *Studi storici*, vol. VI, 1965, pp. 507–46. On the other hand, the deep and reciprocal inherence of the theoretical and technical moments is dealt with in a particularly inadequate way by those theses that derive from the otherwise remarkable studies by R. Hall (e.g. 'The Scholar and the Craftsman in the Scientific Revolution', in L. Marsak, ed., *The Rise of Science in Relation to Society*, New York 1964, pp. 21–41); A. C. Crombie (e.g. *Augustine to Galileo: The History of Science* AD *400–1650*, London 1952, vol. II, p. 122: 'In its initial stages, the scientific revolution came about rather by a systematic change in intellectual outlook, than by an increase in technical equipment. Why such a revolution in methods of thought should have taken place is obscure'); R. Mousnier (e.g. *Progrès scientifique et technique au XVIII siècle*, Paris 1958); and by G. Sarton (e.g. *The Appreciation of Ancient and Mediaeval Science During the Renaissance: 1450–1600*, Philadelphia 1955). In the work of each of these scholars the reciprocal inherence of the single moments is forgotten, either because the theoretical moment is privileged over the technical, or because the connection between the two is identified outside (and in advance) of the framework of the Renaissance conception of the world.
116. We take up here and in the following passages the theses expressed by A. Koyré (see, for example, the essays collected in *Etudes d'histoire de la pensée scientifique*, Paris 1966, in particular the attack on Crombie's position on pp. 48–72). However, we wish to correct his marked propensity to depict Renaissance Platonism in a manner that is sometimes very strictly theoretical (see in this regard the amendments suggested by P. Zambelli in his introduction to A. Koyré, *Dal mondo del pressapoco al mondo della precisione*, Turin 1967).

specificity of the Cartesian position as it presents itself in this phase can thus be related to a significant general cultural horizon. This is not to be understood in a merely generic manner. Consider, for instance, Descartes's dialogue with other 'authors' of the scientific Renaissance, such as Bacon and, especially, Galileo. From Bacon Descartes draws a large number of themes that he will employ within his own discourse, and the two converge on that terrain of method that posits itself as the mediation between scientific knowledge and technical practice, understood as the science of the possession of the world.[117]

However, it is above all the Galileo–Descartes relationship which, in the phase of Descartes's oeuvre prior to the condemnation of the Florentine thinker, enables us to grasp and underline some absolutely distinctive moments in the initial development of Descartes's thought. Both these authors, Galileo as well as Descartes, experience at the time the same humanist passion of *invenire*, the same metaphysical confidence in the ontological correlate of the *scientia penitus nova*, and the same heroic technical project of the *scientia mirabilis*. It is not improbable that, from 1611 onwards, Descartes

117. On the dissemination of Bacon's thought in France, see R. Lenoble's *Mersenne, passim* and H. Butterfield, *The Origins of Modern Science*, New York 1997. Descartes appears to have had a profound knowledge of Bacon's thought. In the first years of Descartes's scientific activity there are frequent references to him (AT I 109, 195, 251, 318; and then in the *Dioptrics*, AT VI 82 and in the *Discourse*, PWD I 111, 112, 115–16, 117, 125–6, 142–3, 142–4, 146–7). We should also underline the compatibility of Descartes's and Bacon's discussions of the mnemonic arts, as P. Rossi has done in his *Logic and the Art of Memory*. However, we do not think it is legitimate to move from a recognition of Descartes's knowledge of Bacon's thought to the assertion of a broad influence of the latter on the former, in contrast to E. Gilson, *Commentaire*, pp. 84–5, 90, 146, 169, 276, 444–6, 449–57, 462; L. Roth, *Descartes' Discourse on Method*, Oxford 1937; and, finally, E. Denissoff, 'Les étapes de la redaction du *Discourse de la Méthode*', *Revue philosophique de Louvain*, vol. 54, 1956, pp. 254–82. It is a general discursive atmosphere that Descartes and Bacon share. It is not possible to establish a direct relationship between the two thinkers at the thematic level.

was stimulated by the great excitement that affected all cultured circles in the wake of the publication of the *Sidereus Nuncius*. It is also likely that, in the course of his peregrinations, he would have heard of the *Saggiatore*. What cannot be disputed is that the horizon to which Descartes's scientific methodology refers is fundamentally characterized by Galileo's mathematical characterization of the structure of reality. Both authors, albeit with slightly differing philosophical motivations (the Platonism of the one is matched by the vaguer humanism and innatism of the other), take the path of the self-legitimization of the mathematical definition of the universe. This is the path that leads to the metaphysical and ontological foundation of the universal scope of *mathesis*, to the privileging of intuition and deduction as fundamental instruments of knowledge, and to the reduction of induction within the schema of the primary necessity of thought's intuitive development.[118] As a proof *ad absurdum*, but no less efficacious for all that, of the profound closeness or even contiguity of Descartes's and Galileo's paths, let us recall that, within this cultural and intellectual milieu, we find the same knot of metaphysical, methodological and scientific themes in Galileo that we had encountered in Descartes – further evidence, if any were needed, of the density and complexity of this kind of metaphysics. We also discover more subterranean themes: a metaphysics of light and a mystical naturalism, traditional themes that renew themselves by changing guises, placing themselves in a mythical and operational perspective and yet conserving the full-bodied character of their early definition.[119] But it suffices to refer back to the fundamental node in the constitution of Cartesian thought represented by the encounter and collaboration with

---

118. A. Koyré, 'Galilée et Descartes', in *Congrès Descartes. Etudes cartésiennes*, vol. II, pp. 41–6. See also, with some circumspection, A. Banfi, 'Galilée, Descartes et Vico', in *Descartes. Cahiers de Royaumont*, pp. 376–92.
119. E. Garin, *Scienza e vita civile*, pp. 126, 129, 154, 156, and so on. The weight of Galileo's thought is revealed in these pages. Moreover, Garin's observations are valid for the entire development of the new science. It is truly everywhere that one can register 'the   *cont'd over/*

Beeckman in order to see to what extent, ironically, it is Descartes's very metaphysical trust in the mathematical structure of reality which enables him to go further in the explantion of fundamental physical laws than Beeckman's more correct and positive approach.[120]

What can we say about all this? That what is at work in the new science, in Galileo as well as Descartes, is a general philosophical horizon, the renewal of the essentially humanist inspiration and vision of the world. We have previously called this horizon 'metaphorical'. We can reaffirm this now, giving the concept greater precision.[121] If we are indeed dealing with metaphor, its role is not so much that

119. *cont'd*   stark refusal of logical procedures; we are dealing with the assertion that the new cosmological doctrines are *real*, not hypothetical; with the awareness that the vision of the physical universe that is being delineated in the mathematical experiences and demonstrations is total and exhaustive in its scope . . .' Also very important, in my view, is Garin's polemic against Koyré's distinction (in *Etudes galiléennes*, vol. III, Paris 1939) between Platonism understood as mathematicism and Platonism understood as mysticism. The two moments are instead absolutely interwoven in Galileo (p. 139) as well as, generally speaking, in the new science.

120. A Koyré, 'La loi de la chute des corps. Galilée et Descartes', *Revue philosophique de la France et de l'étranger*, vol. 62, 1937, pp. 149–204, commenting on AT X 219–20 – that is, on the passage of the *Parnassus* that includes Descartes's explanation of the law of falling bodies – underlines the singular accord between Descartes's error of definition and Galileo's (initial) one. On the basis of this observation, Koyré is led to refine his investigation and to discover the reason for this common position in the profound agreement of Descartes's and Galileo's methods. In both cases this is due to an overestimation of the mathematical conception of reality which leads to the hypostasis of the explanation in spatial rather than temporal terms. Conversely, in Beeckman, it is precisely the lack of this metaphysical tension that hinders the general, albeit partially mistaken, formulation of a law that is already experimentally known.

121. Lucien Febvre has written some beautiful passages on this metaphorical world, within which the new science develops – a world that it tries to overcome but also to recover. See *Au cœur religieux du XVIe siècle*, Paris 1957, in particular pp. 293–300; and *Pour une histoire à part entière*, Paris 1962, pp. 730–5.

of exhibiting a symbolic ordering in which all parts of the universe must be situated (if anything this definition merely marked the starting point of the discussion), as of showing the general equivalence of these parts, the totality of cognitive and operational implications that this horizon entails. We can now begin to suggest an interpretive hypothesis for this ideological world. The hypothesis that will forcefully emerge in the course of our investigation envisages this cultural horizon as the ideological horizon that presides over the conquest of the world by a new class. This class regards general equivalence as the precondition for its own advance, for the general interchangeableness of roles, and for the possibility of the destruction of all obstacles to its own growth. Moreover, it sees the reality of its new social existence and efficacy reflected in the mathematical form of this universe. Finally, it puts forward the revolutionary absoluteness of its own task in the totalitarian form of the project.[122] Thus, the cultural world in which the investigation and definition of the new Cartesian method takes shape becomes immediately functional to an ideal of universal efficacy which is principally scientific but also political and generically civic. So it is that Beeckman feels his deep affinity with the Venetian Servite friar Paul.[123] And Turquet de Mayerne says of the education of the sons of the new class:

122. Edgar Zilsel's indications ('Problems of Empiricism', in G. De Santillana and E. Zilsel, *The Development of Rationalism and Empiricism*, International Encyclopaedia of Unified Science, vol. II, no. 8, 2nd edn, Chicago 1947, pp. 53–94) are as valid for rationalism as they are for empiricism. Certainly, Zilsel's article is only a summary but we think it worth referring to, in preference to other relevant works, because of the radicalism of the theses it advocates. Concerning the incessantly repeated polemic against these positions (which are also our own), see H. F. Kearney, 'Puritanism, Capitalism and the Scientific Revolution', *Past and Present*, vol. 28, 1964, pp. 81–101.

123. AT X 348 (from Beeckman's *Journal*): 'He told me today, on 11 October 1629, that a Father Paulus of the Venetian Servites holds the same opinion as I do, as is clear from what is said above about motion, viz. "that whatever is moved once will always move unless a hinderance should occur [to stop it]", and that in this way they   *cont'd over/*

And to aid in raising them by opportune degrees to this divine knowledge, on which the capacity to rule well depends, it is important to instruct them in the mathematical disciplines – not superficially, in order to attach them to the earth and to materials, but to immerse them into their intimate secrets, which are great. For in the contemplation of these disciplines are found the foundations and roots of justice and temperance which consist of number, measure, proportion and harmony, the proper subjects of these noble and liberal sciences, which have always paired, ever since the beginning, Theory with Practice.[124]

Is there a more explicit anticipation or profound elucidation of the implications and presuppositions of the Cartesian discourse in the *Rules*? Is there a more manifest application of a method that, before being employed and monopolized by the scientific procedure, is grasped as politically adequate to the existence of the new class?

Once again and, with particular intensity, Descartes's initial participation in the humanist world is confirmed. This participation constitutes a kind of originary intellectual ground on which the philosophy of the mature Descartes will develop (depending on the circumstances) through critique, refusal or the attempt at sublimation.

4

If what has been said so far were deemed insufficient to demonstrate the deep-rooted Renaissance metaphysical content of

123. *cont'd*   have proven the eternity of motion in the heavens, which have been moved by God once. D. Colvius told me this, as I say, who had made a note of this from the writings of this Venetian Father.'

124. *La monarchie aristodémocratique*, p. 510. On the revolutionary character of the reference to arithmetic (in particular in Turquet), see N. Zemon Davis, 'Sixteenth-Century French Arithmetics on the Business Life', *Journal of the History of Ideas*, vol. 21, 1960, pp. 18–48, in particular p. 45.

Descartes's thinking, one can provide other proofs *ad abundantiam*. Even after the Cartesian system has turned to other objectives, that is, once the entire thematic horizon has mutated, we still find some of Descartes's youthful themes surviving, resisting within the changed reality of the system. And this is not just in limited areas, marginal to the scientific interests of the mature Descartes. Indeed, the most interesting example of the survival of the *scientia mirabilis* in the meshes of the mature system is to be found in the anatomical and medical investigations – not least because the underlying motives of these investigations are reverberations from, and will reverberate upon, other fields of inquiry.

It is widely known that throughout his life Descartes was engaged in anatomical investigations and entertained a general interest in the problems of medicine. The insistence on this aspect of his activity has also led some commentators to consider him as a Rosicrucian. Indeed, if the hope in a victory over death was – as it seems – an essential theme in that sect's propaganda, it certainly was in Cartesian medicine too: 'I have never taken more care to preserve myself than now, and while I used to think that death could only take thirty or forty years from me, it would no longer surprise me if it could take from me the hope of more than a century'.[125] To vanquish death and prolong life – what extraordinary significance this project must have had for seventeenth-century man, immersed as he was in the terrible precariousness of the time.[126] Why should he who promises this not appear as a 'magus'? Why should he not sense the extraordinary character of this work? All the more so since as soon as he discovers his object, the author finds himself, within his *fabrica* (workshop), face to face with the marvellous spectacle of life. His science is caught up in

125. AT I 507. With regard to the affinity between the Cartesian and the Rosicrucian conceptions of medicine, see G. Cohen, *Ecrivains français*, pp. 404–5.

126. F. Braudel, *The Mediterranean and the Mediterranean World in the Age of Philip II*, Berkeley 1953; R. Mandrou, *Introduction to Modern France, 1500–1640: An Essay in Historical Psychology*, London 1975.

this spectacle and, from the order of connections it reveals, draws its confidence that great results must be at hand. In 1630, Descartes writes this to Mersenne: 'Please look after yourself, at least until I know whether it is possible to discover a system of medicine which is founded on infallible demonstrations, which is what I am investigating at present.'[127] Descartes speaks of infallible proofs, which can become operative at once, restoring life. Ever since its inception, the medical project is a *scientia mirabilis*, because it partakes in the absoluteness of the full-bodied metaphysics of the young Descartes, drawing from it hope that the world can be reproduced.

Let us see how the metaphysical foundation of Descartes's medical research is delineated. In the years around 1630, Descartes begins his anatomical studies: 'I am now studying chemistry and anatomy simultaneously; every day I learn something that I cannot find in any book.'[128] Studying anatomy means, first of all, sectioning, anatomizing ('almost every day in the house of a butcher . . .').[129] Secondly, it means reconstructing the general design of animal life within the framework of the general principles that support the universe. Again, we encounter the two sides of the *scientia penitus nova*, where the investigation into the thing *iuxta suum principium* is accompanied by a general solution (*generaliter solvi*). The originality of Descartes's thought in these early stages (which also closely ties it to Renaissance themes) is that far from separating the two poles he makes them act upon one another, thus concretizing and individualizing the moment of generality so that it may live in things and be recognized as the

127. PWD III 17.
128. PWD III 21.
129. Descartes will continue his anatomical exercises throughout his life. See, for example, AT I 263, PWD III 58–9 [TN: this second letter is dated early June 1637 in PWD III and 25 May in AT I]; PWD III 134–5; AT II 621; AT IV 555 and *passim*. We should also recall the great anatomical work carried out in the winter of 1629–30. The lines cited in the text refer to that work.

principium within them. Tracking down the general in the simple, the *principium* in the *proprium*, this is the key that lets us follow Descartes's continuous path from descriptive anatomy to mechanistic physiology, and from mechanistic physiology to embryology. This path almost gives one the impression that Descartes is moving on a slippery surface. The explanation ends up resting on genesis, and the problem of the *generatio animalium* is both founding and fundamental.[130] Here at last the process of reduc-

130. This can also be confirmed by a few observations of a philological character. Amongst Descartes's medical writings there is a work called *Generatio animalium* (AT XI 505–38). The editors of this work (*Opuscula posthuma*, Amsterdam 1701) entitled it *Primae cogitationes circa generationem animalium.* This title is inaccurate since, following the discovery of Leibniz's manuscripts in Hanover, part of the *Generatio* undoubtedly turns out to have been composed at a very late date (1648). It is nevertheless a significant title because it underlines the composite character of this work. What we have here, in our view, are the working notes for the development of Descartes's thought on the problem of generation, the outline of Descartes's medical thinking throughout his experimental investigations into generation. In particular, the *Generatio animalium* appears to include texts that can be referred to three periods of his anatomical studies: around 1630, around 1637 and around 1648. With respect to the period around 1630, one can certainly include the passage (AT XI 538) of the *Generatio* that is also included (and explicitly dated 1631) in Leibniz's Hanover manuscripts (AT XI 601–7). We should also bear in mind Descartes's statement, in a letter to the Marquess of Newcastle dated October 1645, in which he declares that he has been working on a *Traité des animals* for over fifteen years (see PWD III 274–6). The question remains: is it possible to find any other fragments of the activity of the 1630s amongst Descartes's medical-anatomical writings? Certain internal motifs of a thematic character (the reprise of the anthropogonic fable, naturalistic finalism, the stress on the theory of cardiac heat, etc.) would lead one to believe that the fourth and fifth part (*The World and Other Writings*, pp. 186–205) of Descartes's second great medical work, *La description du corps humain*, were also composed in the 1630s (the first three parts of which were composed in the second half of the 1640s, see *The World and Other Writings*, pp. 170–86). The fourth and fifth parts, which even in stylistic terms differ markedly from the first three parts, are published with   *cont'd over/*

tion is halted by the discovery of a motor, of an originary dynamism that is as general as it is concrete. We are speaking of the heart, the originary heat, the cardiac fire. It should be immediately noted that even though the centre of this biological dynamism produces mechanical movements, successive dilations or contractions whose rhythm lends its shape to the organic and physiological functions, this core of life never loses either its undeniable qualitative character or its sharp naturalistic definition. Three fires are set alight in man; the first one in his heart from air and fire; the second in the brain from the same two elements, but in a more tenuous form; the third in the stomach, set alight from foods and the substance of the stomach itself. In the heart the fire is as if from dry and dense matter; in the brain it is like fire from the exhalation of wine; in the stomach it is like fire from green wood. There they are able, even without the aid of food itself, to spontaneously grow rotten and become warm, just like humid hay.[131] The metaphor is explicitly corporeal and the metaphysical significance of fire is inseparable from the thematic articulation of the scientific analysis. Despite the recurrent polemic against the extravagant sciences, curious motifs can be encountered in the

130. *cont'd*   the separate title *Digression, dans laquelle il est traité de la formation de l'Animal.* Nevertheless, against this dating of the *Digression* stands the fact that in it we find a series of references to the *Dioptrics* (PWD I 323 and *The World and Other Writings*, p. 188) and, above all, to the French translation of the *Principles* (PWD I 322 and *The World and Other Writings*, p. 188). Furthermore, Descartes's correspondence also bears testimony to the study of the 'formation of the animal in general' as work of 1648 (PWD III 329; and also 170–1, 260–1). Perhaps the only solution would be to consider the *Digression* the fruit of a 1648 reworking of materials from the 1630s. See also the fundamental and brilliant article by H. Dreyfus-Le Foyer, 'Les conceptions médicales de Descartes', *Revue de Métaphysique et de Morale*, vol. 44, 1937, pp. 237–86, in particular, with reference to the *Digression*, pp. 248ff. See also the Avertissement in AT XI 219–22. In both of these cases, the dating of the *Digression* is, in contrast to our estimation, unquestionably 1648.

131. This passage is certainly from 1631. It appears in AT XI 603 (from the Hanover manuscripts) and AT XI 538 (from the *Generatio*).

writings on medicine.[132] The fact is that the magical conception of the universal analogy survives in Cartesian embryology, sustained by the metaphysics of fire: But blood and soul [*spiritus*] mingle in the heart, and there they start that continuous fight, of which human life is consists, just like the life of fire in a lamp. . . . And at that point he begins to be an animate being, because the fire of life has been set alight in his heart[133] From this *incipit* the anthropogonic fable is set in motion. In the same way that heat lies at the centre in the system of the universe, so it is in the system of animals;[134] from this point – that is, once the analysis has descended from descriptive anatomy to physiology, and from physiology to embryology – the fable takes the inverse path.

Evidently, the atmosphere is still that of the *Private Thoughts*. Yet there are those who have considered this foundation less as a triumph of Renaissance cosmogony than as a reminder of Scholasticism.[135] It is doubtful whether such an interpretation possesses any validity, because, although it is true that certain Aristotelian motifs (above all the insistence on cardiac fire) are present, these motifs are transfigured in Descartes's standpoint.[136]

132. AT X 519 (on the soul of the brute), 524 (on the hermaphrodite), 525ff (on the beardlessness of the castrato). These passages from the *Generatio* can probably be dated to around 1630.
133. AT XI 509, from the *Generatio*.
134. *The World and Other Writings*, pp. 192ff and 202ff, from the *Digression*.
135. E. Gilson, *Etudes sur le rôle de la pensée médiévale dans la formation du système cartésien*, Paris 1951, reprint, pp. 51–101; *Index scolastico-cartésien*, Paris 1913, *passim*.
136. H. Dreyfus-Le Foyer (*Les conceptions*, in particular, pp. 244–5) underlines with particular vigour the reversal of the Scholastic standpoint by the Cartesian one – even where influences remain. However, the article exaggerates the presence of strictly mechanistic models in Descartes's medical work. On the nexus between Cartesian thought and Scholastic thought with respect to physiological matter, see P. Specht, *Commercium mentis et corporis. Ueber Kausalvorstellungen im Cartesianismus*, Stuttgart 1966. Whether intentionally or otherwise, it elucidates to what extent the Aristotelianism that Descartes could perhaps have laid claim to had been corrupted, having become complicit with, and implicated in, the great themes of Renaissance philosophy.

In Cartesian naturalism, the mechanism that underlies reasoning is entirely new. The qualitative form of the life-process becomes a function of the comprehension of the universe's quantitative harmony, operating within it as the dynamic rule of its composition. Besides, quantity and quality are congruent and concurrent: they are the functions of a totality that only science is able to distinguish so as to contemplate them again within unity, once the productive links of the living articulation have been re-examined. Consequently, the metaphysical horizon of Descartes's early years is to be found intact in these scientific essays, where it is simply augmented by the naturalistic glorification of fire.

Having arrived at this point and verified the importance of the metaphysical approach of the early anatomical and medical studies around the 1630s, we still have to ask ourselves the most interesting question: whether (and if so, to what extent) Descartes's anatomical studies are able to extricate themselves from the significant influence of these metaphysical motifs once the general outlook of the system is profoundly transformed in the mid-1630s.[137] Only if we are able to answer this question in the negative will our hypothesis about the survival of the *scientia mirabilis*, of the metaphysical presuppositions

137. By way of an overall hypothesis, the whole of Descartes's medical writings could be classified as follows:
   - 1631: AT XI 601–7, as well as the parts of the *Generatio* that literally (AT XI 538) or otherwise refer to these themes.
   - First draft of the *Digression* (part IV and V of the *Description?*).
   - 1633: *Treatise on Man.*
   - *Dioptrics.*
   - 1637: *Discourse on the Method,* part V.
   - AT XI 583–600 (and perhaps also 549–83), as well as the parts of the *Generatio* that literally (AT XI 534–7) or otherwise refer to these themes. All this material should be related back to the project, articulated in AT I 507, of a medical *Abrége.*
   - 1644: *Principles.*
   - 1648: *Description,* parts I, II, and III; and the reworking of parts IV and V (*Digression?*).
   - AT XI 608–21, as well as the parts of the *Generatio* that literally (AT XI 537–8) or otherwise refer to these themes.

of the young Descartes, throughout his speculative undertaking be verified (albeit only in specific, but not for that matter marginal, domains). And indeed, things stand exactly as we have suggested. Of course, the mechanistic moment will become increasingly important in the subsequent anatomical writings, but the exposition will never conceal the predominant role played by the metaphysics of natural harmony, rendered dynamic by the metaphysical fire of the universe.

That is what happens in the *Treatise on Man*, where the privileging of fire as the motor and vivifying element of the human machine is expressed with the greatest clarity.[138] The animal spirits are 'like a wind or a very fine flame', ubiquitously active and putting their mark on movement.[139] Witness the Fifth Part of the *Discourse*: 'there is always more heat in the heart than in any other place in the body.'[140] And it is this heat which, by expanding the blood, initiates movement. Here, Descartes's metaphysical presupposition means he is unable to assent to Harvey's more correct and widely known analysis.[141] The same may be said of the writings that remain of a planned *Abrégé* of medicine and of the parts of the *Generatio animalium* that were compiled during the same period of medico-anatomical work, following the publication of the *Discourse*.[142] This is so despite the fact that in the latter writings, perhaps owing to the polemic instigated by Froimodus and Plempius,[143] Descartes attempts to reformulate the theory of the for-

138. For example, *The World and Other Writings*, pp. 101, 161–3, 168–9.
139. *The World and Other Writings*, pp. 109 and 112–14.
140. PWD I 135.
141. Aside from Gilson's invariably hostile interpretation, and whatever some others may say, one should (following Dreyfus-Le Foyer, *Les conceptions*, p. 265) recall that the Cartesian doctrine of circulation is not fundamentally erroneous. For the relationship between Descartes and Harvey in general, see the texts mentioned by E. Gilson, *Commentaire*, pp. 407–8.
142. See note 137 above.
143. AT I 402–31 [TN: partly in PWD III 61–6], PWD III 76–7, AT I 496–9, 521–36 [TN: partly in PWD III 79–85]; AT II 52–4, PWD III 92–6, AT II 343–5.

mation of the animal foetus by starting with the liver and the lung and moving up towards the heart.[144] Having said that, even in these writings where the metaphysical conception of the source of movement seems to wane, Descartes arrives at the following conclusion: 'The formation of plants and that of animals are comparable in this respect, that they can be created from parts of a substance which has been shaped into a sphere by the force of fire . . .'[145] At most, Descartes will forsake the reduction 'heart: centre of heat and life', but he will not be able to reject the metaphysical image of a world sustained and set in motion by this impalpable, dynamic and omnipresent element.

Finally, even in the writings of the 1640s,[146] which operate on the basis of an extreme dualism of soul and body, and propose the struggle against all forms of animism as one of the fundamental polemical aims of the analysis,[147] one comes across statements such as these: 'fire or heat – the strongest agent that we know of in nature'.[148] Descartes dedicates the entire Second Part of the *Description* to the theory of circulation and the heart, reprising and sharpening the polemic with Harvey.[149] He prolongs this in the Third Part, where he studies the phenomena of nutrition. There, the animal spirits, excited by the glandular system but vivified by cardiac heat, flow – like *ruisseaux* (streams) – through and within the entire vital mechanism.[150]

We are presented, then, with a radical metaphysical foundation, and we have seen what shape it takes.[151] But does this radical

---

144. AT XI 505–6, 511ff, 526ff from the *Generatio*.
145. AT XI 595; the same passage can be found in *Generatio*, AT XI 534–5.
146. See note 137 above.
147. PWD I 314 and *The World and Other Writings*, pp. 170–1, 314–15, from the *Description*, part I.
148. PWD I 318 and *The World and Other Writings*, p. 182.
149. *The World and Other Writings*, pp. 172–82.
150. PWD I 319–21 and *The World and Other Writings*, pp. 182–6.
151. It might be objected that, in the second part of the *Description*, precisely in the context of the harshest polemic against Harvey's theory, Descartes makes an explicit reference to the cont'd over/

metaphysical foundation of the anatomical theory represent the persistence of at least one fundamental metaphysical motif throughout Descartes's scientific enterprise? Yes. However, we should add that the anatomical studies are merely one facet of Descartes's scientific discourse, and that our analysis of them was intended simply as an exemplification. Having said that, it would not be difficult to follow the development of themes which are consistent with that original metaphysical intuition in other parts of Descartes's thought, and to observe analogous effects in the dialectic that begins with the more mature, mechanistic approach. Such an analysis could, for instance, consider the various formulations of Descartes's physics from *The World* to the 1637 *Essays* and the later *Principles*,[152] underlining both the privileging and the persistence of those themes. Equally significant, and more profitable, could be the study of the development of themes explicitly, and to some extent completely, elucidated by Descartes ever since his early years – the musical ones, for example. Here we find Descartes unable to free himself from the naturalistic presupposition that connects the definition of a natural geometry to a solidly naturalist aesthetic, even when such a move ends up being in total contradiction with his own latest scientific and systematic findings.[153] Further examples could be adduced.

Having affirmed that there persists in the mature Descartes a nostalgia for a solar and Renaissance metaphysics, we must consider whether the other aspect of the *scientia mirabilis* – the humanist faith in the worldly *renovatio* – also extends from his

151. *cont'd*   Aristotelian theory of the cardiac fire, as it is expressed in chapter 20 of his book *On Breathing* (PWD I 319). But the spurious and merely polemical character of this reference is immediately evident. However, let us say so again, the literal influence – if there is one – is not sufficient to demonstrate dependence or allegiance. In general, on the 'solar' metaphysics, see the collection *Le soleil à la Renaissance: Sciences et mythes*, Brussels and Paris 1965.

152. We will return to these themes below, in section 3 of chapter 2 and section 3 of chapter 4.

153. See the passages from the *Treatise on Man* cited in note 137 above.

youth to the work of his maturity. In the following chapters we shall return to this problem at length, and on more than one occasion, since it represents the crucial node and the real critical crucible of the Cartesian experience. Here it is simply a case of asking whether the *mirabilis* moment of his *scientia* is sometimes reproduced in an unmediated and in some sense uncritical manner. That is to say, whether in some restricted, albeit relevant areas of Descartes's experience, one may observe the persistence of his youthful ideal – with all the confidence and enthusiasm, all the metaphysical and operative force that such an ideal entails. For instance when, in a crucial moment within the development of Descartes's physics, and of his optics in particular, we discover that: 'There is a part of Mathematics, which I call the Science of Miracles, because it teaches one to use air and light in such a way as to show by means of them all the same illusions which it is said the Magicians make appear with the help of Demons. As far as I know, this Science has yet to be practiced . . . but I am convinced it could do such things . . .'[154]

Even easier to verify is the relationship, in the medical studies, between a metaphysical theory and a praxis of radical *renovatio*. In this instance, the reversal of the theoretical anatomical schema into a practical project takes place directly – the one constitutes the counterpart and complement of the other. The tension of the *scientia mirabilis* is at its unmediated maximum: 'The preservation of health has always been the principal end of my studies, and I do not doubt that it is possible to acquire much information about medicine which has hitherto been unknown.'[155] This project is such a fundamental moment of Cartesianism that Descartes appears, at times, to attempt to organize the entirety of his system, in its practical aspect, on the basis of his medical research. Without much success, we might add. There are times in his work at which mechanicism is at its peak, to the point that Descartes proposes that

154. AT I 20–1.
155. PWD III 275.

morality itself be constituted as an extension of rigorous medical science.[156] Nevertheless, this takes place only in very particular instances. This scientistic illusion enjoys only a very brief existence and is soon plunged into crisis.[157] Neither the anatomical studies as such, nor the therapeutic exercises that Descartes occasionally attempts,[158] prove capable of sustaining the project in the comprehensive scientistic terms in which it was proposed. The result of these travails is expressed in the following, critical, form, by Descartes: 'instead of finding ways to preserve life, I have found another, much easier and surer way, which is not to fear death.'[159] Beware, this conclusion critically implicates the mechanistic project and not the *scientia mirabilis*. This demand 'not to fear death' is not the resigned pronouncement of someone unable to uncover a path to acquit himself of the task he took on and who must therefore fall back on the merely stoic declaration of a strength of spirit. On the contrary, it is precisely here – and we are at the heart of the crisis within the development of Descartes's mature system – that there reappears that profound moment in the Cartesian experience, which memory perpetually renews: *scientia mirabilis* as the science of man. 'Not to fear death' therefore means still thinking that life is indomitable and that this awareness can get the better of death. The full-bodied, solar soul of Renaissance man can conquer the body.[160] The primitive Cartesian conception of man's natural

156. PWD I 142–3.
157. This particular moment of crisis is superbly elucidated by P. Mesnard, *Essai sur la morale de Descartes*, Paris 1936, in particular pp. 139, 143, 161; and M. Gueroult, *Descartes' Philosophy Interpreted According to the Order of Reasons*, vol. II.
158. Evidence of Descartes's therapeutic activity can be found in AT III 90–3; PWD III 300–1, 304, AT IV 698–9; AT V 233.
159. PWD III 289.
160. AT IV 201, PWD III 249, 275, 289; PWD III 329, and AT V 178–9. According to Dreyfus-Le Foyer (*Les conceptions*, p. 275), medicine in Descartes 'gradually turns towards a sort of partial and indirect animism'. P. Mesnard *Essai*, p. 224) arrives at an analogous and, to our mind, equally correct conclusion.

Prometheanism reappears in integral form precisely where science or the system fall short. Once again we discover this unknown Descartes, this 'magus' and priest of the religion of man.[161]

It is here that an entire ideological horizon reappears, revealing itself as an originary thread in Descartes's thought. Medicine is conceived as the index of the relation between microcosm and macrocosm, between soul, body and world; as the interpretation and possibility of transformation of this nexus, as well as the revelation of the harmonious interchangeableness of the parts of the universe. This is among the highest conceptions of humanism, which we find in Coluccio Salutati as well as in Pico della Mirandola, in Paracelsus as well as in Grotius.[162] However, this

161. In an elegant article, 'Un souvenir cartésien dans les *Pensées* de la reine Christine', *Revue philosophique de la France et de l'étranger*, vol. 62, 1937, pp. 368–9, Pierre Maxime Schuhl provides convincing evidence that Descartes arrived at the court of Christina with a reputation as a doctor, whose difference from the 'mage' is only slight. Certainly, Descartes did not fulfil expectations. In Christina's *Pensées*, Schuhl finds hints of this disappointment. Sumaise's testimony (now in AT V 461) also points in this direction. But that reputation came from somewhere; we have seen the reasons for it and the forms that it took. Now Descartes, having reached the final phase of his thinking, the (largely radical) critique of his great youthful hopes, is nevertheless unable to free himself from it.

162. This is not the place for it, but it would be very interesting to pursue further this Renaissance conception of medicine. It suffices, just to restrict ourselves to the thinkers closest to the period in which Descartes's own thought develops, to look through the writings of Paracelsus (for example, in the collection *Sozialethische und sozial-politische Schriften*, ed. Kurt Goldammer, Tübingen 1952) or Grotius's *De Imperio Summarum Potestatum circa Sacra*. In these cases, the concept of medicine is strictly linked to that of religious jurisdiction, thereby taking on some of its qualities – both positively, in the sense that it reconstitutes the body as a divine thing, and negatively, in the sense that it must submit to the supreme authority of the state as the force by which human unity is recomposed (see Joseph Lecler, *Toleration and the Reformation*, vol. II, London 1960). On the tendencies in medicine that fall under the purview of the solar metaphysics see, in general, *Le soleil à la Renaissance*, pp. 279ff.

is also the revolutionary moment par excellence. It shows us man rising up against an otherwise intolerable natural destiny. It praises man absolutely as he rises up against death. As we shall see, the tension that this motif frees up in Descartes's thinking will become visible even in the most refined and exhausting speculative labours of his mature years, as he persistently strained the classical tranquillity of the analysis and the completeness of its literary form. For now it is sufficient to note how essential this theme is in the framework of Descartes's philosophical experience, despite the fact that it appears masked or remains hidden. When the Encyclopedists, and later the revolutionaries of 1789, celebrated Descartes primarily as the 'doctor' – the man who set the task of eliminating 'an infinite number of illnesses and perhaps also of infirmity and death'[163] as the ultimate goal of his scientific programme – and saw his thinking unfold the ideal 'of the subjection of nature to Man',[164] they celebrated, in reality, Descartes as humanist. Is this interpretation one-sided, tendentious? Of course. But that does not make it any less true, because, in rediscovering a frequently unrecognized aspect, they found in Descartes the link between humanism and bourgeois revolution.

5

We have spoken of metaphor and memory. The memory of an experience of the world of metaphor which, as we have seen, is a world with specific, culturally defined contents. To immerse Descartes's thought in this horizon, to guarantee him this 'precedent' – which is actually a real root and a continuous tension within the whole development of the system, even for the mature Descartes – this appears to be the task set for a historiographical

---

163. See the entry 'Cartésianisme' in the *Encyclopédie* (vol. II, 1752, p. 719), written by the Abbé Pestré, cited in A. Vartanian, *Diderot and Descartes*, Princeton 1956.

164. A. L. Thomas, *Eloge de Descartes*, Yverdon 1765, p. 11, cited in A. Vartanian, *Diderot and Descartes*.

confrontation with Descartes's philosophy.[165] We shall try to verify the hypothesis that Descartes's mature thought is constituted in its discussion of this mnemonic content. What are the results of this discussion? Is it the radical and definitive removal of this content? Or is it the attempt – critically meditated and culturally gauged – to renovate this content within the new historic situation?

Before we confront these questions directly, before we retrace the critical development of Descartes's thinking, we must note another crucial element to which we have alluded frequently: the resoluteness of the critical commitment to the humanist conception of the world in Descartes's youth. We are unable to call this total, critical adherence and this general dimension of the appreciation of the surrounding reality by any other name than 'political', especially if we consider the intimate dialectic between theoretical moment and practical perspective which it involves. We must underscore here the 'political' nature of Descartes's

165. See E. Garin's hypotheses in 'Descartes e l'Italia', *Giornale critico della filosofia italiana*, vol. 29, 1950, particularly pp. 391–94. 'Now, I believe that this is the sense of Descartes's itinerary: a total separation of man and a rediscovery within oneself of the foundation of the world, to which one may return as agent and subjugator. If that is the case, it is clear that the relationship with the Renaissance takes on a precise hue. In this way we can free ourselves from the vain search for a single dependence upon Campanella (Blanchet); and we can also refute the tight link to the Middle Ages via post-Tridentine Scholasticism (Gilson) . . . the ideal time of Descartes cannot be grasped other than through those two centuries of thought, the 1400s and 1500s, that completely transformed the horizon of philosophizing and even gave the ancient sounds another timbre . . . we do not wish to establish direct dependences or textual rapprochements, we simply wish to say that Descartes's metaphysics is not born from the trunk of post-Tridentine Scholasticism, but rather is entirely immersed in the atmosphere of Renaissance philosophies, from which it borrows tones and motifs, in a manner that is sometimes even too obvious . . . perhaps Descartes's greatest merit is to have consciously brought together again the legacy of Renaissance philosophy with the results of Galilean science . . .'

discourse, the 'politicality' of a thought that adheres to the overall vicissitudes of his society and that puts in question the entire image of civic man from the Renaissance to the seventeenth century. Descartes is a philosophical, religious, scientific and political man. Or rather, he is 'political' above all because in these years – from the 1500s to the 1600s and in France in particular – in a situation of radical alternatives and of profound reflection on the historical events of the time, it is the moment of politics which internally tends to confer meaning upon all others.

Let us not forget that Descartes appears on the scene wearing the *robe*. The family of magistrates, the Jesuitical and juridical education, and his environment all conspire to turn the *sieur du Perron* into a magistrate, a parliamentarian.[166] It is only in 1625, after much hesitation, that Descartes appears to free himself from being destined to this world of *officiers*, definitively deciding not to enter the *profession de robe*.[167] But the alternatives chosen are equally significant: soldier, traveller, *rentier* and philosopher. First, the soldier: this was still a *profession* of *robin*, which had recently become the mark of a new dignified status and thereby came to represent an ideal of glory and adventure through which the bourgeois excitement at the recent revolutionary events was both exalted and renewed.[168] This was all the more true in the Low

---

166. There is some information in this regard at AT I 1–5. Adrien Baillet's *La vie de Monsieur Des-Cartes*, Paris 1691 (from here on indicated as *Baillet*), nonetheless remains fundamental. H. Gouhier expands on Baillet and puts the information in order, in his *Essais sur Descartes*, Paris 1937, pp. 253ff.

167. *Baillet*, vol. I, p. 129.

168. On the ideal of the 'soldier' in the first part of the 1600s, see C. Vivanti, *Lotta politica e pace religiosa in Francia fra Cinque e Seicento*, pp. 102ff, with regard to France; in a far more general vein, see the writings of G. Oestreich, for example, 'Der römische Stoizismus und die organische Heeresreform', *Historische Zeitschrift*, vol. 176, 1953, pp. 17–43; and 'Justus Lipsius als Theoretiker des neuzeitlichen Machstaates', *Historische Zeitschrift*, vol. 181, 1956, pp. 31–78. Oestreich gives an extensive description of the figure of the seventeenth-century soldier, of the bourgeois soldier whose *cont'd over/*

Countries, whose very existence was conceived as the triumph of freedom and which were seen to be 'giving a memorable example to all peoples of what they can do against their sovereigns'.[169] Second, within this military experience we find the traveller, the new clergyman, since travelling for Descartes means 'learning about business, gaining some experience of the world, and forming habits he did not yet have; adding that if he did not come back richer, at least he would return more capable'.[170] Is this an example of the humanist anxiety for new knowledge, a first,

168. *cont'd*   military 'profession' is tied to virtue and not nobility, to '*constantia*' and not mere heroism. This description takes the form of an extremely rich analysis of cultural influences, namely Stoic ones. A sort of intra-worldly ascesis is realized in the bourgeois soldier, especially in Holland. For the bourgeois polemic against the nobility qua hereditary military class, see also Turquet de Mayerne, discussed in R. Mousnier, 'L'opposition politique bourgeoise', pp. 7–9. It should not be forgotten however that, alongside this embourgeoisement of the ideal of soldier, it is still a fact that 'the soldier must not be of the people'. See G. Procacci, *Studi sulla fortuna di Machiavelli*, Rome 1965, p. 129.

169. This is what Jean Louis Guez de Balzac declares in his youthful 'Discours politique sur l'estat des Provinces-Unies des Pays-Bas', in G. Cohen, *Ecrivains français*, pp. 713–15. In general, on the appearance of Holland to the *jeunesse française* at the beginning of the 1600s, see also, from the same volume, part 1, and pp. 357ff and 424ff. As far as Descartes is concerned, he will insist frequently on the contribution of young Frenchmen to the struggle for Dutch freedom: 'the usefulness of the public, and the calm of these Provinces, which has always been desired and procured with greater care by the French than by many of the natives of this Country . . .' (AT VIII B 212); and in the course of the polemic of 1647 against the theologians he will write to the Prince of Orange so as to avoid the possibility that 'after all the blood the French have spilled to help them chase away the Spanish Inquisition, a Frenchman, who had also at one point borne arms for the same cause, should today be subjected to the Inquisition of the Ministers of Holland' (AT V 26). In the latter case, the biographical detail is doubtful, to say the least. See also PWD I 126 (from the *Discourse*), where Descartes praises the Netherlands as a country that has constituted itself through the discipline of war.

170. *Baillet*, vol. I, p. 118.

captivating opening of the great book of the world? Immediately the picture grows more complex. Recalling his youth and the love of weapons, Descartes alludes ironically to his restlessness at the time (to 'that warmth of the liver which in earlier years attracted me to the army').[171] In truth, the anxiety for knowledge is soon complicated and charged with disquiet. It reflects the leaden shadows of the terrifying European war and the itinerary of the voyage itself becomes uncertain and insecure.[172] Thus, external events introduce doubts into the inner clarity of the project. In addition to the humanist anxiety for new knowledge, is there also the disquiet of the *robin*? In addition to the bourgeois vocation to free oneself in the world, is there not also an attempt to escape the new and impending sense of frustration that affects everyone in that dramatic historical situation? We shall return to these problems at length. For the time being, it suffices to observe how these motifs are all, indistinguishably, at play here. The precondition for approaching them is the immersion in experience, the discovery of this new reality. Every experience is instructive for life. In battles, 'experience and natural prudence, joined to the presence of spirit'[173] are worth more than precepts. But each experience also instructs science. Paradoxically, the discourses of worldly men about fencing express an inexhaustible scientific curiosity, because *l'Art d'escrime* may be considered mathematically, if you hypothesize 'two men of equal size, equal strength and with the same

171. PWD III 131.
172. AT X 158–9: 'And not the sudden movements of Gaul . . .' This is the warning of the German war (although we find here the well-known error whereby *Germaniae* has been replaced with *Galliae*). See also PWD III 4: 'The preparations for war have not yet led to my being summoned to Germany, but I suspect that many men will be called to arms, though there will be no outright fighting'. It would be interesting to consider whether the projected voyage through central Europe, as far as Bohemia, follows a 'Rosicrucian' itinerary.
173. AT I 458–60.

weapons'.[174] Science, weapons and philosophy – that gossip Voetius may divert himself with this concoction and malign Descartes for founding '*novam philosophiam*' in order to traverse 'a new path to glory . . . despairing (after brief military training) of the command of the Marshall or the Legate.'[175] And yet how significant is this interlacing of interests, this tireless implication of all experiences with one another. Here we encounter a kind of Renaissance man. There is nothing astonishing in finding out that his philosophy is that of the *Private Thoughts*; that the *physico-mathematicus* lives alongside the soldier, the clergyman and the man of the world; or that musical interests coexist with painterly and architectural ones.[176] Moreover, it is no coincidence that one can suspect him of being a Rosicrucian who consecrates the whole of this experience in hermeticism, and who thereby exalts the indistinct form of his own existence.[177] Surely, from whatever angle one looks at it, this man and this world belong to the *robins*.

Who are these *robins*? Or rather, first of all, who were they? A historian[178] tells us that they were the 'offensive vanguard of the bourgeoisie', that is, the social group that emerged from the first wave of mercantile and capitalist development of the 1400s and 1500s, which, in the sixteenth century, consolidated its power through the parliaments and the law courts, in other words, through the professions of the *robe*.[179] This is already a historical

---

174. *Art d'escrime* is a brief work that was perhaps composed in 1628–9 and was lost very early on. See the various indications at AT X 535–8. *Baillet*, vol. II, p. 407, provides an outline of the text; the phrase quoted above is his.

175. AT VIII B 23.

176. See the letter dated 24 January 1619 to Beeckman, PWD III 1.

177. See, once again, F. A. Yates, *Giordano Bruno*, on the Renaissance character of Rosicrucian hermeticism.

178. R. Mandrou, *Classes et luttes de classes en France au début du XVII siècle*, Messina 1965, p. 49.

179. F. Braudel, *The Mediterranean*; G. Procacci, *Classi sociali e monarchia assoluta nella Francia della prima metà del secolo XVI*, Turin 1955; and C. Vivanti, *Lotta politica*, p. 26 and *passim*.

development of considerable importance, a political and cultural
development determined by the revolution in which the old, fixed,
medieval world is shattered and the social order renewed. A new
class comes to recognize itself in the discovery of freedom and, in
so doing, is emancipated. The *robins* interpret, for France, the
general significance of the bourgeois revolution which, having its
roots in the humanism of the Italian city states, will affect the
whole of Europe.[180] Their culture is at once individualist and
rationalist. It expresses freedom, revolutionary impetus, and reveals the civic passion subtending the political urgency of their
demands. Furthermore, the *robins* operate in such a way as to
bring together 'the contents of a tendentially cosmopolitan humanist culture into a process of national and state formation'.[181]
In France, this entails specifying, politically and institutionally, the
civic passion that characterizes their culture. Thus, the entire
cultural intervention which is demanded by the revolutionary
situation is organized as a system whose peak is constituted by
political will. This will passes in turn through all the intervening
links and qualifies the component parts of the system. Thus, a
system of values, of interests and of cultural and material needs –
perceived in their immediacy – is opposed to the old way of life.
This accounts for the essentially political character of the *robins'*
experience, which is honed further in the hard-won opportunity to
allow these values to work through the institutions. In this
framework, the conflict between civil society and the state reaches
its climax. The *robins* see it in terms of the need to subordiante the
latter to the former, where civil society is regarded as the space in
which bourgeois liberties are extended and in which the relationship with the state can be renewed in line with civic aims. This is a

180. As well as the work already cited by Georg Weise, see also Robert P.
      Adams, *The Better Part of Valor: Erasmus, More, Colet and Vives on
      Humanism, War and Peace, 1496–1535*, Seattle 1962, which gives an
      excellent portrayal of the mechanisms of expansion of humanist
      ideology in a different but not dissimilar cultural area.
181. C. Vivanti, *Lotta politica*, p. 139.

radical revolution that conceives bourgeois freedom as the supreme value, the productive key to history and the organizer of the
social totality.[182]

Some will say that this is not the situation of the world of the
robins in Descartes's time. This is true and we shall discuss below
what its circumstances were.[183] Nevertheless, what we have just
laid out is the memory that the *robin* has of the development of his
class. This memory tends to become idealized amid all the new
difficulties that are placed in the way of the realization of its
contents. This mnemonic content is an emblem of class self-
identification and, at the same time, an operative utopia that takes
on the lineaments of myth to the extent that its effectiveness is put
into doubt.[184] Descartes's memory, which we have reconstructed
here in its general philosophical terms, inheres in this class
memory. The idealized reading of the past fixed within bourgeois
memory is nothing other than the operation which Descartes
repeated in the period that leads from the *Private Thoughts* to the
Rules. In the *Thoughts*, this takes the guise of a description of the
marvellous interconnection and circularity among the parts of the

---

182. See my 'Problemi di storia dello stato moderno. Francia 1610–1650',
     Rivista critica di storia della filosofia, vol. 2, 1967, pp. 182–220.
183. See section 2 of chapter 2 below.
184. Therefore, it is no coincidence that in the same period and in the same
     authors we discover both the first attempts at a historical knowledge of
     the recent past (the consciousness of the necessity of the birth of a
     national historiography) and the first operative mythical ideologiza-
     tions of that same recent past. See especially C. Vivanti's comments in
     his *Lotta politica* concerning Jean de Serres and Jacques-Auguste de
     Thou (pp. 246ff and 292ff respectively). In both cases, historiography
     is born of the immediate need to discover the political vocation of the
     bourgeoisie. This is even truer for the following period, as F.-E.
     Sutcliffe correctly notes when considering the historical works of
     Naudé, Faret, Silhon, Meré, Chapelain and, obviously, Balzac (*Guez
     de Balzac et son temps. Littérature et politique*, Paris 1959, in particular
     pp. 176–83). See also the aforementioned articles by Yardeni and
     Oestreich, concerning the contribution of Stoicism to the foundation
     of a historiographical consciousness, always for a political function or,
     rather, for the sake of political prudence.

universe. In the *Rules*, there is an exaltation of the reproductive nexus that stems from the link between *invenire* and *universalis mathesis*, between freedom and its real possibility. The wonder and enthusiasm that fill those pages are the sign of the youthful rediscovery of a general class dimension, of an extremely pure renewal (within the span of his own, young generation) of the humanist discovery of freedom and the new reality of a world to be won.

We must add that if we have been able to identify the overall significance of the young Descartes's path by referring to the general meaning of bourgeois memory, it is also true to say that Descartes was able to uncover other, equally fundamental, connotations of bourgeois memory that characterized it during this period. The birth of the bourgeoisie as a class is in fact accompanied by the birth of the modern, manufacturing mode of production. The two dimensions are concomitant and concurrent, since the elevation of man above the world requires the discovery of practical means for dominating it and the former is only possible to the extent that the latter are successful. Now, Descartes's *Rules* provide us with a reading of the ideological horizon of the bourgeois revolution in which these features can be seen to unfold. The manufacturing form of production is championed and translated into a philosophical context. This context is as important in its ideological significance as it is comprehensive vis-à-vis the determinate definition of the new mode of production.[185] How is this context expressed? First, in the proposal of a new project of possession of the world that begins with the dissociation of its elements, and which, at the end of its reconstruction, gives us back the world in an enriched form. Second, by accounting for the

185. Aside from Karl Marx's brief discussion (*Capital*, vol. I, London 1976, pp. 455–8), see also Franz Borkenau's fundamental *Der Übergang vom feudalen zum bürgerlichen Weltbild. Studien zur Geschichte der Philosophie der Manufakturperiode*, Paris 1934, 'Descartes', pp. 268–383. On Borkenau's work, see the very positive judgement given by L. Febvre in *Au cœur religieux*, pp. 345–6.

division of labour, discovering its multiplying function in the redefinition of the unity of the world's design. The *Rules* pose this problem from the start, problematizing the antonymic (and yet necessary) nature of the separation of the applied sciences, and postulating the methodical reconstruction of unity. *Qua* method – i.e. as the possibility of understanding reality as a process of analytical division and productive reconstruction – scientific knowledge and human wisdom become labour.[186] Thus, the frequent allusions to artisan work in the *Rules* are no longer metaphors, not even in the improper sense that Descartes accorded to metaphorical language. In reality, artisan techniques directly assist and advance knowledge,[187] inasmuch as they directly reconstruct the articulations of the world:

> Still, since not all minds have such a natural disposition to puzzle things out by their own exertions, the message of this Rule is that we must not take up the more difficult and arduous issues immediately, but must first tackle the simplest and least exalted arts, and especially those in which order prevails – such as weaving and carpet-making, or the more feminine arts of embroidery, in which threads are interwoven in an infinitely varied pattern. Number-games and any games involving arithmetic, and the like, belong here. It is surprising how much all these activities exercise our minds, provided of course we discover them for ourselves and not from others. For, since nothing in these activities remains hidden and they are totally adapted to our cognitive capacities, they present us in the most distinct way with innumerable instances of order, each one different from the other, yet all regular. Human discernment consists almost entirely in the proper observance of such order.[188]

186. PWD I 359, i.e. the opening to *Rule One*.
187. PWD I 33.
188. PWD I 35.

But this is not enough. The reconstruction is not merely the recomposition of the sundered elements, but their proportionately accelerated recomposition. It is a productive recomposition, a technical, manufacturing-centred explanation of production, a delineation of the enigmatic (but mathematically and metaphysically intuitive, as well as astonishingly visual) process of accumulation. Reproduction is greater than the mere sum of the analytic elements whose dissociation originally made it possible. Reproduction itself is precisely this additional something, the acceleration, the proportional expansion . . . The mechanical art constitutes and reproduces its own technical basis:

> Our method . . . resembles the procedures in the mechanical crafts, which have no need of methods other than their own, and which supply their own instructions for making their own tools. If, for example, someone wanted to practice one of these crafts – to become a blacksmith say – but did not possess any of the tools, he would be forced at first to use a hard stone (or a rough lump of iron) as an anvil, to make a rock do as a hammer, to make a pair of tongs out of wood, and to put together other such tools as the need arose. Thus prepared, he would not immediately attempt to forge swords, helmets, or other iron implements for others to use; rather he would first of all make hammers, an anvil, tongs and other tools for his own use.[189]

The reconstructed cosmos is thus greater than the given cosmos.

We have reached the core of Cartesian memory: the memory of the revolutionary growth of the bourgeoisie, the lived experience of this first class *essor*. It is a political memory, inasmuch as it spans the whole arc of the social activities of the bourgeoisie and the values that sustain it. The world of metaphor, once again, is shown to be founded on a real experience. All the elements that constitute it end up relating back to and fixing themselves in an overall

189. PWD I 31.

framework of meaning that is homogeneous with Descartes's intuition of and participation in that historical world. The hypothesis which we set out from, that of the existence of an originary thread in Descartes's thought, which is specified metaphysically to the extent that it is founded historically, seems to have been verified. This originary thread is both the background against which Descartes's mature works should be read and the moment that dramatizes his entire philosophical venture. Indeed, Descartes's thinking achieves its own autonomy and uniqueness, its radical and innovative speculative force, only to the extent that this mnemonic content is problematized. What matters here is not opening a debate on the causes and results of this problematization of memory. This is a question to which we shall return. What needs instead to be underscored is its fundamental importance. This problematization lends the development of Descartes's thought both meaning and direction. When he feels abandoned by it, it takes the form of a persistent nostalgia for that mythical and heroic horizon. Whenever he feels implicated in it, on the other hand, his thinking is subject to repeated and strenuous problematization. In any case, Descartes's mature thought is always intuitively and elementally rooted in this mnemonic dimension in which (as well as in contrast to and against) it develops and acquires meaning.

It is significant that it is precisely from the moment of this problematization, from an initial effort in this direction, that we must date the launch of Descartes's mature thought. When, sure of his vocation, Descartes finally arrives in Holland at the end of the 1620s, he is soon reached by a letter from Guez de Balzac:

> Remember, I beseech you, the history of your spirit [*de l'histoire de votre esprit*]. All our friends await it and you promised it to me in the presence of Father Clitofon, commonly known as Lord Gersan. It will be a pleasure to read of your various adventures in the median and supreme regions of the air, and to consider your feats against the Giants of the School, the path

that you have followed, the progress that you have made in the truth of things, and so on [*le chemin que vous avez tenu, le progrès que vous avez fait dans la vérité des choses*].[190]

L'histoire de votre esprit. Here it is not essential to uncover the content of this *histoire* (students of the *Discourse* have speculated that it is a first draft of the first part).[191] Rather, we should underline the form taken by this first meditation of the mature Descartes. It is a historical form and it takes the guise of a direct confrontation with memory. In this relation to memory, which is deliberately assumed as central reference point, Descartes the *robin* will rediscover his world, its reality of development and crisis, seeking a response to his problem there. Returning to subjective memory, he will problematize the memory of a class. Who, after all, demands this history from Descartes? Guez de Balzac. He is the author who, perhaps more effectively than any other, expresses in a refined albeit naïve form the nostalgia for the world of freedom and revolution of the Renaissance.[192] In the letters between Descartes and Balzac, which evince significant agreement, the praise for Holland is repeated interminably. Balzac writes, 'I am as Dutch as you, and the Lords of the Estates will have no better citizen than I, nor one with a greater passion for liberty';[193] and Descartes responds: 'Where else on earth could you find, as easily as you do here, all the conveniences of life and all the curiosities

190. AT I 570–1.
191. See G. Gadoffre, 'Sur la chronologie du *Discours de la méthode*', *Revue d'histoire de la philosophie*, January–March 1943, pp. 45–70 (and in the 'Introduction' to Descartes, *Discours de la méthode*, Manchester 1947); and Élie Denissoff, 'Les étapes'.
192. G. Cohen, *Ecrivains français*, pp. 243–74. On the Guez de Balzac family and its recently gained nobility, see the remarks by Jean Pierre Labatut, 'Cahier des remonstrances de la Noblesse de la Province d'Angoumois', in R. Mousnier, J. P. Labatut, Y. Durand, *Problèmes de stratification sociale. Deux cahiers de la noblesse pour les états généraux de 1649–1651*, Paris 1965, pp. 70–2.
193. AT I 201.

you could hope to see? In what other country could you find such complete freedom, or sleep with less anxiety, or find armies at the ready to protect you, or find fewer poisonings, or acts of treason or slander? Where else do you still find the innocence of a bygone age?'[194] Both see in this effective freedom of the moderns the model for the new arts, for style, for language.[195]

L'histoire de votre esprit: the quality of Descartes's response will match the intensity and tone of Balzac's entreaty. They both live at the heart of the dramatic cultural and political turmoil of the time, and they ground their thinking in it. They live within this atmosphere as do all the *robins* – Bérulle, for instance, whom the hagiographical Cartesian tradition deems responsible for Descartes's compulsion to philosophize. In fact, the *entretien* with the 'great and learned company assembled at the Nuncio's palace' represents something more than an encounter between educated men.[196] The diarist naïvely emphasizes this when, in order to signal the remarkable nature of the occurrence, he goes so far as to situate it in concurrence with the assault on La Rochelle: 'In that siege of Rupella he performed a deed worthy of being remembered . . .'[197] In actual fact, the

194. PWD III 32 Holland is to be preferred to Italy – this is the gist of Descartes's tirade, in which we can sense the reference to the 'Machiavellian' image of the Italian and of Italian customs. Indeed, Descartes strongly advises Guez de Balzac against the trip. On the 'peaceful' image of seventeenth-century Holland, see J. Huizinga, *Dutch Civilisation*.

195. Extremely important in this regard is the letter (AT I 5–13) in which Descartes intervenes directly in literary questions, siding with Guez de Balzac. On this matter, see F.-E. Sutcliffe, *Guez de Balzac*, pp. 31–2. G. Gadoffre, 'Le *Discours de la méthode* et l'histoire littéraire', *French Studies*, vol. 2, 1948, p. 310, argues that Descartes was enormously influenced by the style of Guez and that, in particular, Descartes inherited from Guez the literary form of the *essai*. On the subsequent relations between Descartes and Guez de Balzac, see AT I 132, PWD III 2–31, AT I 322, 380–2; AT II 283, 349; AT III 257. See also *Baillet*, vol. I, pp. 139–40.

196. PWD III 32. But for an account of the entire episode, see *Baillet*, vol. I, pp. 163ff.

197. Pierre Borel, *Vitae Cartesii Compendium*, 1653, p. 4.

entretien provides us, once again, with a measure of the depth of Descartes's participation in the world of the *robins*, a world that renews the memory of metaphor within its own culture. In the same manner as Bérulle, he takes it up, criticizes it and reproposes it, drawing into this project, along with nostalgia, the best intellectual energies of the time.[198]

Metaphor, memory, saturated in cultural and political contents, and Descartes's participation in the humanist experience in its totality – these are the results of the first part of our investigation. From here we must set out again while bearing in mind Descartes's radical allegiance to this world. It is only this allegiance that gives meaning to everything else, that lends substance to the *raison* that will here on guide us.

198. We will return to this theme at length. For the time being we can note that doubtlessly the relationship between Descartes and Bérulle can only be considered in very general terms (see Garin, *Opere*, vol. I, pp. lxxiii–lxxv). But it cannot be denied that it is precisely around the theme of metaphor, of the relationship between Renaissance metaphor and the experience of the baroque, that a large part of Bérulle's ascetic thought develops; and that it is this side of Bérulle's thought which, above all, is widely influential in Descartes's intellectual milieu. See in particular Jean Orcibal, *Le Cardinal de Bérulle. Evolution d'une spiritualité*, Paris 1965, pp. 18, 85ff, 129ff and *passim.*

2

Philosophy and Conjuncture

It will be said that if God had established these truths he could change them as a king changes his laws. To this the answer is: Yes . . .

PWD III 23

1

1629. Descartes has definitively settled in the Low Countries. He leads a solitary existence, '*dans le desert*'.[1] He protects this prized solitude, repeatedly asking his friends not to reveal his whereabouts. The beginning of maturity and the definitive choice of the philosophical vocation mark an act of separation from the world. Why?[2]

As we have seen, the first sign of this new intellectual experience appears to be his commitment to retrace 'the history of himself'.

---

1. AT I 14.
2. There was a debate between G. Cohen (in *Ecrivains français*) and E. Gilson (in *Etudes sur le rôle*) over the reasons for the move to Holland. But the reasons respectively adduced by the two authors do not seem convincing. Cohen contends that Descartes was forced to flee Paris by the fear of persecution for his reputation as an anti-Aristotelian; whereas Gilson is able easily to underline (p. 271) that many anti-Aristotelians lived peacefully in Paris during that period. But if that is the case, then why see a Descartes in search of 'tranquillity' in Holland as Gilson does? The move to Holland is, in fact, a search for 'separation' . . .

However, this commitment already appears as a problem and the transformation reveals itself as a break. First, the 'history of himself' is problematic inasmuch as it concerns the problem of memory and tries to isolate its discriminating feature. Is the problem of memory a problem of separation? The task that Descartes sets himself in the *Studium bonae mentis* – a brief tract that was probably composed at this time[3] – is that of grounding the radical integrity of an intellectual power to judge freed from and opposed to the encumbrance of past, unproductive and alienated knowledge (whence the new polemic against Lullist and Rosicrucian follies).[4] Descartes at once resolves this problem by distinguishing the soul and the intellect from mnemonic materiality and habit:

> In him there was a great imbalance between memory and spirit. He had no great need of what they call *local* memory. Perhaps, in his isolation, he had failed to cultivate *corporeal* memory through exercises that need to be frequently repeated so as to consolidate habits. But he had no reason to complain of what he called *intellectual* memory, and which depends only on the soul . . .[5]

Thus is formed the problematic framework of a radical separation of the pure mind and its science from the science of memory and experience:

> He divided the sciences into three classes . . . the first, which he called *cardinal* sciences, are the most general and may be

3. It seems that the work could be seen as a product of this period, if for no other reason than because the problem is fundamentally attuned to it. But against this position see E. Gilson, *Commentaire*, p. 180, who dates the composition of the *Studium* as early as 1620; and J. Sirven, *Les années*, pp. 292–3, who dates it instead to 1623. See, however, what remains of the text – a series of passages collected together by Baillet – in AT X 191–203. In general, see also E. Garin, *Opere*, vol. I, pp. livff.
4. AT X 191, 191–2, 193–7, 198–200.
5. AT X 201.

deduced from the simplest and best-known principles. The second, which he called *experimental,* are those whose principles are not clear and certain for everyone, but only for those who have learnt them from experience and observation, although some know them in demonstrative form. The third are those which he called *liberal.* These require, in addition to the knowledge of truth, a disposition of the soul or at least a habit acquired through exercise . . .[6]

The sequence runs as follows: (1) solitude, (2) the encounter with himself, (3) the problem of memory, and (4) the clash with memory. But the theoretical problem of memory cannot be divorced from that of its historical consistency, from the totality of experience which it registers. Therefore, if memory is the habit of a lived experience, the bodily sign of participation in the humanist adventure, the clash with memory immediately implies a general horizon. In other words, the problem at once evinces metaphysical implications. In separating itself, the *bona mens* demands a global elucidation of its own separation. Wisdom can no longer be founded on a secure possession of the world, on an immediate relation to the world. Only the demand to *abducere mentem a sensibus* ('withdraw their minds from their senses') makes possible the new philosophical proposal of a path toward wisdom.[7] The situation is one of separation and it is from within separation that the problematizing thrust must come. The *Treatise on the Divinity (Traité de la Divinité)*, 'which I began

6. AT X 202.
7. PWD I 129; PWD III 53. See also E. Gilson, *Commentaire*, pp. 81–3; *Etudes sur le rôle*, pp. 265–6. In both cases Gilson insists on the Stoic origins of the term '*bona mens*'. This might be entirely true but it cannot, I believe, be introduced here to clarify the problems that preoccupy us. Indeed, the critical position with respect to Stoicism is already completely resolved. The use of the term is already entirely subordinated to a completely new perspective. We shall return to these themes, but it is already necessary at this juncture to exclude these merely philological filiations.

whilst in Frisia, and whose main points are to prove the existence of God and our souls, when they are separated from the body',[8] seems to develop within this atmosphere. Descartes devotes the first nine months of his Dutch exile to this text,[9] which is precisely a metaphysical investigation tied to the discovery of the fundamental role of the critique of memory. So it is in the metaphysical dimension that separation situates itself – or better, that it must situate itself.

A metaphysics of separation, then. We know very little about the *Treatise on the Divinity*.[10] Yet, from the little that we know, it

8. PWD III 29.
9. One can find indications of the work around the metaphysical themes which are usually discerned in the *Traité de la Divinité*, in AT I 17, 23, 137, 144, 350.
10. *Baillet*, vol. I, pp. 170–1. In *Etudes sur le rôle*, pp. 17–20 and 151–2, E. Gilson advances the hypothesis that Descartes's metaphysics is born from an already precise elucidation of the fundamental principles of physics, i.e. of mechanism, and is therefore based on the need to establish the metaphysical foundations of the separation of the soul from the body. Descartes's metaphysics would thus constitute a *continuum* that attains its greatest clarity in the Sixth Meditation. Frankly, this thesis is unacceptable. H. Gouhier, 'Pour une histoire des *Meditations métaphysiques*', *Revue des sciences humaines*, vol. 61, 1951, pp. 5–29, is far more cognizant of the distance that separates the Latin tract of 1629 from the metaphysics of the *Discourse* and the *Meditations*. Gouhier insists on the properly metaphysical development of the theme, pointing out – in particular – the absence in this text of the essential moment of Descartes's mature metaphysics, i.e. the discourse of doubt and the *cogito* interpreted according to the metaphysical density that distinguishes it, and not simply in accordance with the tradition of 'learned ignorance' (p. 11). Having said this (and assuming, as is generally done, that the Latin tract is the one the letters to Mersenne from 1630 refer to), we still have to elucidate the truly metaphysical significance of this text. It appears to us – and we shall return to this repeatedly – that F. Alquié's interpretation in *La découverte métaphysique* (in particular pp. 87–109) is closer to the truth than other readings. On Alquié's reading, Descartes does not develop an argument which complements physical investigation, but rather fixes at the metaphysical level a particular and absolutely characteristic experience of separation (which will   *cont'd over/*

emerges that what the *Treatise* demands is above all the critique of immediacy and the complementary affirmation of the radical precariousness of the world. The Renaissance world is shattered. Universal discontinuity takes the place of universal continuity. Radical contingency takes the place of the ubiquitous necessity of the Renaissance world. The reversal could not be more complete. As Descartes writes to Mersenne: 'The mathematical truths which you call eternal have been laid down by God and depend on him entirely no less than the rest of his creatures'.[11] Reason, which had found itself to be in absolute conformity with and adequate to the cosmos, now discovers that it is entirely subject to a totally external and totally transcendent will. Truth is not cosmos but power [*potere*], divine power [*potenza*]. It is the seal of an absolute separation. In a subsequent letter, Descartes says to Mersenne:

> You ask me by what kind of causality God established the eternal truths. I reply: by the same kind of causality as he created all things, that is to say, as their efficient and total cause. For it is certain that he is the author of the essence of created things no less than of their existence; and this essence is nothing other than the eternal truths. I do not conceive them as emanating from God like rays from the sun; but I know that God is the author of everything and that these truths are something and consequently that he is their author. I say that I know this, not that I conceive it or grasp it; because it is possible to know that God is infinite and all powerful although our soul, being finite, cannot grasp or conceive him. In the same way we

10. *cont'd*   have repercussions at the level of physics, but only in a subordinate manner). The theory of eternal truths does not stem from the necessity of physical-mathematical work, it breaks with it. E. Brehier emphasizes the singular nature of this metaphysical experience and its ontological significance (an ontology of separation); see his 'La creation des vérités éternelles dans le système de Descartes', *Revue philosophique de la France et de l'étranger*, vol. 62, 1937, pp. 15–29.
11. PWD III 23.

can touch a mountain with our hands but we cannot put our arms around it as we could put them around a tree or something else not too large for them. To grasp something is to embrace it in one's thought; to know something, it is sufficient to touch it with one's thought. You ask also what necessitated God to create these truths; and I reply that he was free to make it not true that all the radii of the circle are equal – just as free as he was not to create the world. And it is certain that these truths are no more necessarily attached to his essence than are other created things. You ask what God did in order to produce them. I reply that from all eternity he willed and understood them to be, and by that very fact he created them. Or, if you reserve the word created for the existence of things, then he established them and made them. In God, willing, understanding and creating are all the same thing without one being prior to the other even conceptually.[12]

The separation is as radical in its intensity as it is global in its extension. The affirmation of the contingency of essences with respect to the divine will appears to deprive the world of all reality.[13] We shall return to this later. What we need to emphasize here is that the relation between subject and reality is deprived of all reality. Were such a relationship to be given, it could only be momentary, perilously poised over the radical discontinuity of reality.[14] What is taken away is above all the relationship with the past as memory, with the past as the substantive experience of contact with reality which was given in the prospect of a humanist possession of the world. Memory itself is thereby transformed

12. PWD III 25–6. See also, in general, PWD III 24–5.
13. In this regard, F. Alquié's interpretation in *La découverte métaphysique* represents an essential commentary and reading aid; see in particular pp. 87–109.
14. J. Wahl has illustrated this situation very elegantly in his dissertation, *Du rôle de l'idée d'instant dans la philosophie de Descartes*, 2nd edn (1st edn: 1920), Paris 1953.

from being a sign of reality into an eminently precarious condition.[15] The critique of the passivity of memory, elaborated in the *Studium bonae mentis*, has come to rest on ontological bases that transform its meaning. They destroy its innermost structure of continuity and expose subjectivity to all the risks of a solitary relationship with the separated world. But the perspective indicated by reason, *abducere mentem a sensibus*, cannot provide a solution, nor does it intend to. On the contrary, Descartes's suggestion in these pages simply concerns a new viewpoint which does not overcome separation but allows it to be appreciated more fully. From this perspective, both the dualistic condition and separation appear inexorable. At the same time, the perspective indicated by reason arises from an immediate awareness of this situation. It is as if Descartes both inserts and aggravates, within the mechanism of reason, the form of the mystical procedure of abstraction from the world. It is clear then why Descartes claims to side with Bérulle and Gibieuf on this question. Indeed, the themes of the *Treatise on the Divinity* arise from an affinity with a spiritual situation wherein we can discern the problem of the century as a whole. We can thus say that the *Treatise* emerges from a discussion which seeks to endure, advance and find resolution in a confrontation with these authors: 'but I expect to put you to some trouble when I complete a little treatise that I am starting';[16] 'As for the liberty of God, I completely share the view which you tell me was expounded by Father Gibieuf'.[17] But it does not end there. Both Bérulle and Gibieuf deny the possibility of comprehending

15. On memory as fundamental element in the precariousness of judgement see, for example, PWD III 6, AT I 44; PWD III 233, 234; PWD II 4–5, 16–17, 48, 104; PWD I 25, 37–8; PWD II 409–41, and so on.
16. PWD III 5.
17. PWD III 26. See also AT I 220. On the problem of Bérullean influences and, more generally, of the Oratorio on Descartes [TN: this sacerdotal order, the *Congregatio Oratorii Sancti Philippi Nerii*, was introduced by Bérulle into France], see E. Gilson, *La liberté chez Descartes et la théologie*, Paris 1913, pp. 27–50; H. Gouhier, *La pensée religieuse*, pp. 57ff; E. Gilson, *Etudes sur le rôle*, pp. 33–6, 289.

the absolute, of embracing it through reason.[18] This denial represents at once a mystical tension, a metaphysical affirmation and a historical confrontation with Renaissance memory.[19] It is a separation that traverses all levels, summing up the totality of a situation. Perhaps nothing can provide a sense of the effect of the crisis within which Descartes's thought operates better than this religious connotation. Especially if we consider that in the seventeenth century the generalization of a lived experience was most often entrusted to the tyrannical impact of religious sentiment.

The self-criticism of memory comes to define a situation of general precariousness, universal contingency and global separation. This is the particular predicament of Descartes's thought at the end of the 1620s. The horizon of the *scientia mirabilis*, the Promethean hope of *invenire* and the enthusiasm of the *renovatio* appear to have vanished into an indefinable distance: 'as soon as I see the word *arcanum* [mystery] in any proposition I begin to suspect it'.[20] Nor can these themes be revived by memory, since memory has gone astray in an interrupted and extremely fragile dimension of temporality. The reversal is total, precise and stark.

Recognizing this is necessary but not sufficient. The question is why this reversal? Our task in the following pages will be to answer this question. But before clarifying this point, it is still worth underlining the richness of its implications. We have spoken of the move from the critique of memory to the reversal of the

18. On the distinction between understanding (*intendere*) and comprehending (*comprendere*) in Bérulle, see J. Dagens, *Bérulle et les origines de la Restauration catholique (1575–1611)*, Bruges 1952. On p. 257, he concludes as follows: 'this distinction is fundamental; we encounter here one of the closest links between Bérulle's and Descartes's thought.' The point is also clearly grasped by J. Orcibal, *Le Cardinal de Bérulle*, particularly in relation to the theory of continuous creation (pp. 99ff).

19. The first part (pp. 1–77) of the aforementioned work by J. Dagens shows just how deeply rooted in the culture of the Renaissance is Bérulle's critical thinking and that of his school.

20. PWD III 11.

metaphysical standpoint. But the inverse path is also travelled: from the separation fixed in the metaphysical order to the separation in the historical order. The radical contingency discovered in the theological domain impinges immediately on the historical domain. The fundamental characteristics of that contingency are repeated in the social world. This should not come as a surprise. We saw how in the world of metaphor there is a sort of unitary compactness and a convergence of all the aspects of experience. Now the crisis becomes general to the precise degree to which that universe was compact. The separation is established with equal intensity in the world and in social relations. Consider how the theory of the creation of eternal truths, which grounds the radical effort to make the world contingent, is immediately exemplified. Truth is posited by God as the law of the absolute sovereign, the validity of the law is entrusted to the power that sustains it and this power is incomprehensible in both its origin and motivation:

> Please do not hesitate to assert and proclaim everywhere that it is God who has laid down these laws in nature just as a king lays down laws in his kingdom. There is no single one that we cannot grasp if our mind turns to consider it. They are all inborn in our minds just as a king would imprint his laws on the hearts of all his subjects if he had enough power to do so. The greatness of God, on the other hand, is something which we cannot grasp even though we know it. But the very fact that we judge it beyond our grasp makes us esteem it more greatly; just as a king has more majesty when he is less familiarly known by his subjects, provided of course that they do not get the idea that they have no king – they must know him enough to be in no doubt about that. It will be said that if God has established these truths he could change them as a king changes his laws. To this the answer is: Yes he can, if his will can change. 'But I understand them to be eternal and unchangeable.' – I make the same judgment about God. 'But his will is free.' – Yes, but his

> power is beyond our grasp. In general we can assert that God
> can do everything that is within our grasp but not that he
> cannot do what is beyond our grasp. It would be rash to think
> that our imagination reaches as far as his power.[21]

But if this is the case, everything that unifies is also an element of
separation. Transcendence qualifies every relationship between
subject and world in the same way. What is the world then? A
phantom over which looms the incomprehensible will of the
sovereign. This is indeed the upside-down image that Descartes
arrives at. Where has the *laetitia* of an achieved relationship with
the real gone, the faith in the correspondence of the real with the
subject or in the originary, necessary convergence of subject and
world? 'Nature', wrote Galileo, 'mocks the constitutions and
decrees of princes, of emperors and monarchs, whose commands
cannot alter its laws or statutes one jot . . .'[22] Here, human virtue
finds its universal realization without any kind of mediation. Not
so long before, Descartes could have endorsed this statement.
Now, however, the free will of the sovereign extends over things
and power makes a mockery of nature.

Why is the bourgeois hope of a happy conquest of the world
criticized and abandoned? Why is the humanist faith in the
possession of the world destroyed? Why this reversal?

2

Because of its radicality, intensity and the all-encompassing scope
of its implications, the reversal of Descartes's position at the end of
the 1620s leaves us perplexed. In light of the development of
Descartes's thinking up to that moment, such a change seems
devoid of a rationale. In the first phase of his work, there was no
lack of criticisms regarding the more excessive Renaissance pos-

21. PWD III 23.
22. Quoted by E. Garin in *Scienza e vita civile*, p. 155.

itions. But, as we have seen, these criticisms aimed at discriminating in the service of renewal, so as to champion the humanist moment that inspired those very same excessive conclusions. Descartes opposed the *scientia mirabilis* to the *miracula*. He did so because philosophical intuition rested upon the solid possession of the world and wisdom rested upon faith in the correspondence of science and reality, upon the confident acquisition of the experience of the Renaissance. But if there is no theoretical motive for this change, can we say it is historically justifiable? Its formal character may already make us think that it is: a sudden and profound crisis, the almost unforeseen impact of a calamity that is not caused by the subjects it affects but which involves them nonetheless. It would appear that only a collective, individually binding crisis could account for the transformation. Descartes's crisis is truly the crisis of the century, the individual facet of a collective drama.

For some time now, the 'great century' has ceased to be presented by historiography in the golden fixity accorded to it by a certain apologetic tradition. It is a century marked, instead, by a host of dramatic events and enormously momentous struggles in which all political and cultural equilibriums are thrown into crisis and are only gradually reconstructed.[23] But it is not enough to underline the precariousness of the century. Historical research has also identified the most specific moments of the crisis, the most characteristic and defining conjunctures of the century. And it is without doubt on the decade following 1619 that the attention of the most recent historians has dwelt, indicating it as one of the most significant conjunctural moments. Indeed, historians have identified this decade as the central point of a conjuncture that represents not just the 'caesura of the century' (the true beginning of the 1600s as an epoch in the history of European man) but,

23. We refer the reader, once again, to our article 'Problemi dello stato moderno. Francia: 1610–1650'. In that text we collect, discuss and organize the rich bibliography on this subject (particularly with reference to what we may refer to as the 'revisionist' strand).

above all, as the decade that sees the emergence of the characteristic 'style' of that century. In the economic crisis of 1619–22, the
historians tell us, the great capitalist hopes of the sixteenth century
were exhausted. The long period that witnessed the economic and
civic growth of the Renaissance merchant comes to a close and the
tendency begins to reverse.[24] So the decade is marked by an
unfavourable economic conjuncture, but not by that alone. We
also witness the full-blown crisis of the development that had
marked the 1400s and 1500s, in its most profound, inspirational
elements, in the impetus that moved from economic activity
towards the heroic reconstruction of the world. But that humanist
hope had already become historical substance, an indelible in-
gredient in the development of European consciousness. It could
never be forgotten. So the crisis develops within the structure and
continuity of humanism.[25] But that does not mean it is in any
sense less burdensome or harsh. Indeed, it is the very style of the
epoch that changes. It is marked by the sense of defeat, by the state
of separation in which the new man is forced to live, immersed in
the nostalgia for the revolutionary plenitude of humanist and
Renaissance development but caught up in the necessity of the

24. R. Romano, 'Tra XVI e XVII secolo: una crisi economica, 1619–
1622', *Rivista storica italiana*, vol. 74, 1962, pp. 480–531. More in
general, see *Crisis in Europe: 1560–1660: Essays from 'Past and Present'*,
ed. Trevor Aston, London 1965. See in particular the articles by E. J.
Hobsbawm (pp. 5–58) and H. R. Trevor-Roper (pp. 59–95).

25. 'The humanist age' is the one that 'in literature goes from Petrarch to
Goethe; in the history of the Church from the Western schism to
secularization; in economic and social history from the city-states and
pre-capitalist mercantilism to the industrial revolution; and in political
history from the death of Emperor Charles IV to the French Revolution', Delio Cantimori, 'La periodizzazione dell'età del Rinascimento',
in *Studi di storia*, p. 361. (See also 'Il problema rinascimentale proposto
da Armando Sapori', ibid., pp. 366–78). What should be clearly
underlined, therefore, is that the 1600s are to be defined in continuity
with what precedes and what follows them. They do not mark a break
but, rather, a developmental crisis, a reorganization of problems that
had already arisen.

crisis. The 'baroque' seems to consist in the tension between the awareness of the severe, implacable defeat of the Renaissance, on the one hand, and the always re-emerging nostalgia for that experience, on the other. Some have correctly defined the mentality that takes hold and spreads in this situation as 'pathetic'. Just as legitimately, others have insisted on the extraordinary influence that this crisis has on all aspects of cultural and civic life.[26] In any case, it is the continuity-break relationship that should be borne in mind. This break is all the more painful the more the continuity is felt and the past nostalgically recalled.[27]

But what are the reasons for the crisis and, specifically, for its upsurge in the conjuncture of the 1620s? We have already gestured towards the answer. It is to be found in the crisis of the first capitalist development (an eminently mercantile form of capitalism, of course) and of all the political and cultural elements linked to that development. That is to say, the crisis of bourgeois freedom, in so far as this freedom was regarded as the agent of the reconstruction of the world, of the economic as well as the religious and political worlds, all brought back to the human dimension and viewed as macrocosms that are qualitatively continuous with the human microcosm. It is the crisis of individual freedom, of the first heroic and historically significant emergence of individuality. In it, society as a whole hoped to be comprehended and globally renewed, with individual freedom as its standard and measure. This sublime hope is expressed in varying guises – from philosophical exemplarism to the exemplarism of the mystics of the *renovatio*, scientific universalism and technical Prometheanism. Mathematism itself is inscribed within this theoretical and practical

---

26. See F. Braudel, *The Mediterranean*. But above all, see R. Mandrou, 'Le baroque européen. Mentalité pathétique et révolution sociale', *Annales ESC*, vol. 14, 1960, pp. 898–914.
27. A. Adam, 'Baroque et préciosité', *Revue des sciences humaines*, 1949, pp. 208–24; M. Bonfantini, *La letteratura francese del XVII secolo. Nuovi problemi e orientamenti*, 2nd edn, Naples 1964, in particular, pp. 17ff, 89ff, 105ff.

horizon. Even as it reads it theoretically, mathematism also aims to reproduce this horizon – thereby signalling the emergence of the manufacturing mode of production.[28] All these elements enter into crisis, not so much – and certainly not in a decisive manner – because they clash with the ancient image of the world and with the forces that organize themselves around it, but because freedom comes up against the effects and results of its own development on the cultural, religious and civic planes. Paradoxically, the unifying moment of the humanist proposal everywhere results in division. But it is above all on the economic plane, where the development of the monetary economy (the necessary form of the socialization of individual action within the market) reveals itself through mechanisms that upset all equilibria and display the utopian character of the project of ascending, seamlessly, from the individual to the collective. Once this terrible precariousness has been registered, it is above all on the economic plane that the reflection on the generality of the crisis makes itself felt. This is the crisis of a bourgeoisie that must relinquish – as though its illusions had been definitively dispelled – the attempt to comprehend the general social interest within itself. The bourgeoisie must step back and abandon the demand for power over society as a whole. We shall see what forms this retreat will take. For now, it is sufficient to note that the crisis which begins in 1619 represents the concluding moment of the process of increasing critical awareness of development. The moment is characterized by weariness in the face of repeated monetary crises and by preoccupation with the new European war that is then in its first stages. Above all, it is so characterized because, at this time, the bourgeoisie feels decisively threatened by the struggles of the new classes that its very own development had formed and given a new prominence to. Peasant

28. On all the aspects of this theme, see Alfred von Martin, 'Die bürgerlich-kapitalistische Dynamik der Neuzeit seit Renaissance und Reformation', *Historische Zeitschrift*, vol. 172, 1951, pp. 37–64. See also the aforementioned work by Borkenau, and von Martin's *Sociology of the Renaissance*, New York 1963.

and proletarian revolts follow closely upon one another,[29] revealing the breadth of the consequences determined by development and its crisis, by the general restructuring of the relations between classes and by the collapse of the bourgeois project of drawing these classes together into a new order. The situation is on the brink of reversal. The new order that the bourgeoisie had been unable to provide, or which had been demonstrated to lie on the other side of a far more severe crisis, now demands other and new revolutionary forces. In the new situation, those same early bourgeois achievements risk being destroyed or compromised. Should we be surprised then that for the bourgeoisie the search for security takes the place of the earlier hopes? That, confronted with the crisis provoked by its own development, the bourgeoisie responds by disavowing the more extreme consequences of what it had hoped for, demanding instead assurances about what it had already achieved?[30] This is the grave and definitive crisis of the third

29. On this very important issue allow me to refer once again to 'Problemi dello stato moderno. Francia: 1610–1650' and to the relevant works mentioned therein. Particularly: B. Porchnev, *Les soulèvements populaires en France de 1623 à 1648*, Paris 1963; R. Mousnier, 'Recherches sur les soulèvements populaires en France avant la Fronde', *Revue d'histoire moderne et contemporaine*, vol. 5, 1958, pp. 81–113; R. Mandrou, 'Les soulèvements populaires et la société française du XVII siècle', *Annales ESC*, vol. 14, 1959, pp. 756–65; and C. Vivanti, 'Le rivolte popolari in Francia prima della Fronda e la crisi del secolo XVII', *Rivista storica italiana*, vol. 76, 1964, pp. 957–81.

30. Regarding this question we refer the reader to our comments and to the works discussed in our critical review, 'Problemi dello stato moderno. Francia: 1610–1650'. A useful illustration of the internal character of the crisis could be garnered by following the dialectic of *virtù* and fortune (and its insolubility) first in humanist thought and then in that of the European Renaissance. Let me quote a beautiful passage by E. Garin on this question (*Scienza e vita civile*, p. 53): 'In all this, the humanist faith in man, his reason, and his capacity for edification prevailed: homo faber as the maker of his own self and fortune. And yet, if one follows the writings of the 1400s, one will be struck by the alteration in the theme of fortune, by the expansion of its realm, by a growing mistrust in the forces of man and   *cont'd over/*

decade of the 1600s – the recognition of the end of a revolutionary epoch, the inversion of the tendency, and a conjuncture that cumulatively gathers together each moment of the crisis so as to fix it in the very structure of the century.

The summary and cumulative character of the crisis of the 1620s can also be registered in its cultural dimensions, in particular in the sceptical and libertine motifs which, ever since the rupture of the cultural and religious unanimity of Europe, had repeatedly signalled a recognition of the critical situation. These motifs are now reconfigured and take on a radical intensity. If there is a moment in the history of thought in which it is possible to recognize the qualitative leap over and above traditions, this is it.[31] Here the experience of the end of the Renaissance world is realized in collective terms as a sense of separation which is experienced and borne as historical destiny. Libertinism, with its sceptical, sacrilegious motifs, is the first significant expression of this new situation.[32] Here the sense of

30. *cont'd*   by the sense that even those perfect cities of antiquity were ultimately undone by fortune. It is the *tuche* that also destroys Plato's republic; the only task left to the wise man is to reflect on the causes of Rome's downfall . . .' *Virtù* and fortune then – but the fortune that previously registered the assertion of *virtù*, of realized freedom, later reveals itself to be an external power standing against freedom . . . This dialectic is characteristic of the birth of capitalism, and we shall find it writ large over the whole of its existence. Here, in the genetic moment of bourgeois culture, it can be beheld in its utmost clarity.

31. A. Tenenti, 'Milieu XVI siècle, début XVII siècle. Libertinisme et hérésie', *Annales ESC*, vol. 18, 1963, pp. 1–19.

32. H. Busson, *La pensée religieuse française de Charron à Pascal*, Paris 1933; R. Pintard, *Le libertinage érudit dans la première moitié du XVII siècle*, Paris 1943, 2 vols; A. Adam, *Théophile de Viau et la libre pensée française en 1620*, Geneva 2000; but also *Les libertins au XVIIe siècle*, ed. Antoine Adam, Paris 1964; J. S. Spink, *French Free-Thought from Gassendi to Voltaire*, London 1960; R. H. Popkin, *The History of Scepticism from Erasmus to Descartes*, New York 1964 [TN: recently revised and expanded as *The History of Scepticism: From Savonarola to Bayle*, Oxford 2003]. Concerning the position of the libertines in the crisis of Renaissance thought, see L. Febvre, 'Libertinisme, Naturalisme, Mécanisme', in *Au cœur religieux*, pp. 337–58.

separation reaches its zenith. The life of the Renaissance, human-ism's political and civic hopes, the scientific preoccupation with comprehending the world as a totality – they all break down and are subjected to radical criticism. But the longing for those ideals remains alive amongst the libertines, who experience the separa-tion as a drama that affects the internal process by means of which every ideal is realized, rendering the process irrational and the ideals unattainable. Once the Renaissance hopes are taken away, the world becomes extremely precarious and it is countered by the longing for those old ideals – a conscious longing that underlines this precariousness. In this situation, it will certainly not be difficult to pass from longing to utopia. And the outcome of the libertine movement will, in fact, explicitly reveal what was always implicit in the movement.[33] But now, in the initial phase of the development of libertinism, it is above all the sense of separation that imposes itself on the movement; a separation of the full-bodied density of the Renaissance conception of life and science, but also the psychological and subjective isolation of civic life. Better still, it might even be possible to immerse oneself in such a life, but judgement is suspended, and passion is isolated by contrasting it with participation and communication. The ideal is freed from the temptation of becoming collective. It will be lived in separation as an unrealizable utopia. Were it to become such a collective ideal, it could only, once again, develop that destructive power which manifested itself elsewhere. One does not come back from defeat, it is best not even to try.[34] Wisdom becomes social conformism and mere inner freedom. In the words of the libertine motto: *intus ut libet, foris ut moris* (within as you please, without according to custom). The remarkable success of Charron is

33. A. Adam insists specifically on this passage to utopia in his preface to *Les libertins*. See also C. Vivanti, *Lotta politica e pace religiosa, passim.* However, it is principally in the second half of the century that utopian demands will express themselves most widely.
34. For more on this, see again our 'Problemi dello stato moderno. Francia: 1610–1650'.

entirely due to the fashion in which he promotes the separation of wisdom from all universalizing projects (in the theoretical field), and all revolutionary projects (in the practical one).[35]

The themes of libertine thought and practice are finally organized and revealed with particular intensity in the political reflection on the crisis. Once again, the general motif of separation comes to the fore. It is viewed from within the political development of French society and fixed in a particular situation. In other domains and other experiences, the refusal or the negative choice can be contained within negativity. But this is not the case in politics, where a negative choice remains a choice, an unavoidable determination vis-à-vis social being. Therefore, the libertine sense of separation and the calling to isolation must manifest themselves here with extreme intensity and in an emblematic form vis-à-vis the other motifs of reflection, uncovering their genetic motif. The separation here is the one of civil society from the state, a separation that registers the failure of the humanist project of the recomposition of the state within civil society. The libertine acceptance of the new political and state structure (the new

35. On the fortunes of Charron, see R. Lenoble, *Mersenne*, pp. xliv–xlv; H. Busson, *De Charron à Pascal*, pp. 47ff, 73ff and 181ff. More recently (besides A. Tenenti, *Libertinisme et hérésie*, pp. 12–18), Hans Baron, 'Secularisation of Wisdom and Political Humanism in the Renaissance,' *Journal of the History of Ideas*, vol. 21, 1960, pp. 131–50, has brilliantly underlined the critical substance of Charron's ideal of wisdom against the theses defended in what remains an important work by E. J. Rice, *The Renaissance Idea of Wisdom*, Cambridge 1958, in particular pp. 214ff. Baron defends (as does Garin in *Scienza e vita civile*, pp. 117–18) the negativity of the critical content of the concept of wisdom – as it is elucidated by Charron and developed by the libertines – against those who regard the essential critical moment in positive terms (that is, as shaping the continuity between libertinism and the age of Enlightenment). There is no need to stress our complete agreement with this interpretation. Nevertheless, despite its negativity, the concept of wisdom that is identified herein maintains a fundamentally *social* tonality: 'French free-thinking was always essentially *social*' (J. S. Spink, *French Free-Thought*, p. v).

absolutism) as the positive determination of refusal stems from the awareness of such a separation. That is because absolutism is now the only arrangement wherein the renunciation of political participation guarantees a limited but safe social space in which the isolated enjoyment of freedom is permitted. We encounter here the nostalgia for the Renaissance dream, cultivated in solitude by restricted groups of the elect, finally freed from the possibility that the dream could become once again a collective instrument of subversion. The ideological lesson of the wars of religion, which had found in Bodin its precise formulation, is here taken up again. Theory becomes life, the wisdom of living within separation.[36]

This is the environment and atmosphere to which one must relate the sense of desperate separation that characterizes Descartes's thought at the threshold of the 1630s. The mutation of Descartes's philosophical horizon is decisively tied to this historical conjuncture. Are we in the presence of a baroque Descartes? Certainly, if we take the terms 'baroque' and 'baroque era' in their broadest sense, denoting a period of reflection, of extreme tension

36. On the fortunes of Bodin at the beginning of the seventeenth century, see R. Lenoble, *Mersenne*, p. xliii; J. Lecler, *Tolerance and the Reformation*, vol. II (which documents in particular the circulation, during this period, of handwritten copies of the *Heptaplomeres*); R. von Albertini, *Das politische Denken in Frankreich zur Zeit Richelieus*, Marburg 1951, pp. 35–7; W. F. Church, *Constitutional Thought in Sixteenth-Century France: A Study in the Evolution of Ideas*, Cambridge 1941; G. Picot, *Cardin Le Bret (1558–1655) et la doctrine de la Souveraineté*, Nancy 1948. A. Tenenti, in *Libertinisme et hérésie*, pp. 9–11, underlines in exemplary fashion the relationship between political thought and theological rationalism in Bodin against the background of the crisis imposed by the wars of religion. See also Busson, *Le rationalisme dans la littérature française de la Renaissance (1533–1601)*, Paris 1957, pp. 540ff. However, the move towards political absolutism in the context of the cultural crisis that begins with the wars of religion and concludes in the economic conjuncture of the seventeenth century is documented in other sources as well. For example, see the texts and commentaries in C. Bontems, L. P. Raybaud, and J. P. Braucourt, *Le Prince dans la France des XVIe et XVIIe siècles*, Paris 1965, particularly the article by Bontems.

arising from the awareness of the defeat of the Renaissance myth.[37] A libertine Descartes, then? Here the argument becomes more complex. On the one hand, it is precisely in the years around 1630 that we find in Descartes a series of motifs and, above all, a lifestyle which appear perfectly to reproduce the secular asceticism of the libertine: 'I fear fame more than I desire it; I think that those who acquire it always lose some degree of liberty and leisure, which are two things I possess so perfectly and value so highly that there is no monarch in the world rich enough to buy them away from me'.[38] We also discover sceptical motifs of Pyrrhonian origin that are profoundly anti-humanist. Indeed, it is precisely to his comrade in humanist militancy, Beeckman, that Descartes feels the need to speak of his mistrust of philosophy, thereby definitively marking his distance from him: 'Plato says one thing, Aristotle another, Epicurus another, Telesio, Campanella, Bruno, Basson, Vanini, and the innovators all say something different.' This is true not only in classical and traditional philosophy but also in the new philosophy: 'I have never learnt anything but idle fancies from your *Mathematical Physics*, any more than I have learnt anything from the *Batrachomyomachia*.'[39] Last but not least, we find in the

37. See the reflections and bibliography on this theme by Moritz Hag- mann, *Descartes in der Auffassung durch die Historiker der Philosophie. Zur Geschichte der neuzeitlichen Philosophiegeschichte*, Winterthur 1955, pp. 17–25: 'Descartes als Philosoph des Barock'.

38. PWD III 21.

39. These passages can be read in the letter that marks the break between Descartes and Beeckman, 17 October 1630, AT I 156–70 [TN: partly in PWD III 26–8]. On this last phase of the dispute between these two old collaborators, see also AT I 154–6, 170ff, 177ff. We are undoubtedly dealing with sceptical arguments: Descartes himself confesses that he 'had [many years ago] seen many ancient writings by the Academics and sceptics' (PWD II 94, Second Set of Replies). Conversely, one should note that, in contrast to Descartes's stand- point, Beeckman discerns with mounting clarity an original mechan- istic content (with all the atomistic, Epicurean and partly sceptical resonances that frequently accompany this doctrine). See T. Gregory, *Scetticismo ed empirismo: studio su Gassendi*, Bari 1961, pp. 133–4.

Descartes of this period that *mélange* of critical radicalism and mystical as well as positivistic tendencies through which the Renaissance world is attacked and reduced to a precarious horizon stripped of all necessity, where only social conformism and a sort of brute ethics anchored in the positivity of the normative universe are permitted. This is the same attitude one finds in Charron, to whom Descartes refers explicitly, as well as in Guy Patin, Gabriel Naudé and other libertines.[40] And yet, thanks to a not entirely fortuitous coincidence, it is precisely in those letters where the sense of separation is stressed and the dramatic situation of precariousness is made explicit that we find an initial attack on the libertine positions. In the letters of 15 April and 6 May 1630 we are confronted with the critical moment in Descartes's defin-ition of the doctrine of eternal truths. Indeed, it is in these letters in which Descartes replies to Mersenne's invitation that he accepts to enter the fray against a 'bad book' (*un méchant livre*) – of which, moreover, only thirty-five copies were in circulation and which Descartes himself would have to wait for more than a year to see.[41] A 'bad book' (perhaps the dialogue *Sur la divinité* by Mothe le

40. The references to Charron's political conformism can be found in PWD I 117–18, 119, 122 (see E. Gilson, *Commentaire*, pp. 173–4, 179, 235). Other allusions may be found in Descartes to Charron's theory of beasts, PWD I 140–1 and 303. On this whole question, see J. Sirven, *Les années*, pp. 259–73. Moreover, the conformist position is decidedly a libertine one. There is an embarrassment of riches as regards texts on this issue. See *Les libertins*, ed. A. Adam, particularly the considerations on Guy Patin (and the celebrated letter of Patin to his son: *audi, vide, tace, si vis vivere in pace*; 'listen, look, keep quiet, if you wish to live in peace'). One can find analogous attitudes in Naudé, see J. S. Spink, *French Free-Thought*, pp. 20–1. In this regard, one should also look at the relation between Descartes's thought and that of Sanchez and Cherbury, or at their influence on him, in relation to what has been termed the constructive scepticism of Sanchez and the dogmatism of faith of Cherbury. There are some (often excessively fanciful) annotations on this question in R. H. Popkin, *History of Scepticism*, pp. 38–43, 155–65.
41. PWD III 22–3, 24, 29, AT I 220.

Vayer)[42] that denies the possibility of a logical demonstration of the existence of the divinity. Descartes's attack on libertine thought does not stop here, it continues throughout the rest of his oeuvre, even once libertine doctrines are pretty much out of circulation and the attack appears misplaced.[43]

How should we interpret this state of affairs? The suspicion arises that, at least with regard to the polemic against the book by La Mothe, we are dealing with a very superficial adherence on the part of Descartes to the programme of anti-libertine polemic advocated by Mersenne[44] which is perhaps aimed at hiding a much deeper involvement with the crucial themes of libertinism. This is what is suggested by the ironic metaphor of combat that Descartes feels compelled to adopt, the sardonic polemical cynicism that leads Descartes, first, to argue for the necessity of handing the author of the 'bad book' directly over to the police and, second, to propose compelling the author himself to include the objections in his text.[45]

---

42. The identification of the *méchant livre* with La Mothe's dialogue is defended by R. Pintard, 'Descartes et Gassendi', in *Congrès Descartes. Etudes cartésiennes*, vol. II, pp. 120–2. For a general treatment of the standpoint of La Mothe and the theses of *De la divinité* (see the Tisserand edition, Paris 1922, pp. 94ff), see A. Adam, in *Les libertins*, pp. 121ff; J. S. Spink, *French Free-Thought*, p. 18.

43. PWD III 104; AT III 207; PWD III 248, 278, and so on. What's more, we should recall that in the letter of presentation to the Sorbonne, the *Meditations* are depicted as a work aimed against the libertine standpoint (PWD II 3 and 6). See also the indignation with which Descartes responds to Voët's insinuation that he is 'a new Vanini' (AT VIII B 169, 207, 210 and 254).

44. The polemic against libertinism is one of the fundamental components of Mersenne's work. See R. Lenoble, *Mersenne*, pp. 168–99. On the positions of other anti-libertine apologists, in particular Garasse, see A. Adam, *Les libertins*, pp. 33–50.

45. PWD III 24. Needless to say, we do not wish here to espouse the image of 'Descartes, the masked philosopher', which was proposed, very suggestively but also very adventurously, by Maxime Leroy, *Descartes, le philosophe au masque*, 2 vols, Paris 1920. The association between Descartes and the libertines is for us an objective fact, an endured consequence, rather than a subjective fact. For Leroy the contrary is true.

Nevertheless, the contradiction exists and it has a particular place in the development of Descartes's thought, which must be understood in this light. Descartes effectively accepts the libertine denunciation of the crisis of the Renaissance world, the assertion of the state of radical separation in which man finds himself today. And yet he also problematizes this situation. The entire further development of his thought will be focused on identifying the negative conditions of separation, as well as the positive conditions of reconstruction. So Descartes does accept the libertine denunciation of the situation and, around 1630, he is truly a libertine in the aforementioned sense. That is the extent to which the conjuncture affects him, marking his thought in an entirely determinate manner. However, Descartes refuses – spontaneously at this stage, then with increasing awareness and efficacy – to accept the freezing of this situation, to consider it as definitive.[46] This is because in the situation of separation described through the theory of the creation of eternal truths, the humanist nostalgia is trying to open itself up to hope again, in contrast to what may be found amongst the libertines. Although it is true that within the metaphysical horizon all necessity is removed, every universal correspondence denied, and man is suspended over the radical contingency of everything, the divinity nevertheless rules the world as the image of freedom and of production, as the allusion to and solicitation of other horizons of freedom. Despite being transferred to and fixed in the unknowable, the free being is given. At this time of immensely severe crisis its separate existence is extremely clear. Where the crisis is deepest, there the reverberations of divine power are at their peak.[47]

46. What characterizes libertinism is not the assessment of separation so much as the static and definitive character of this assessment. In *The History of Scepticism*, particularly pp. 89–112, Popkin has explained this with great elegance by analysing the overall sceptical impact of libertine thought vis-à-vis its antecedents and consequents.
47. J.-P. Sartre has insisted widely on the hypostasis of human freedom in the divinity, see 'Cartesian Freedom', in *Literary and Philosophical Essays*, New York 1955. We will return to this article in some depth below.

So, Descartes the libertine. Both moments of libertine consciousness can be discovered in his thinking: the awareness of the crisis of the Renaissance and the nostalgia for those freedoms. And, just as for the libertines, these moments are separate for Descartes. Only the conjuncture of the 1620s can explain the sudden mutation in his thought. But the tension between these elements is stronger in Descartes, the hope is present, and the possibility of reopening the circuit is called for. The long travails of the later path are presaged here. The problem, however, will be to repropose a new nexus based on the definitive achievement of the dualist horizon.

3

The situation is one of separation and of radical tension between the extremes of a divided world. There is an extremely dense interplay between the awareness of this new reality – a world of reflection, of abandonment of the Renaissance ideal – and a burning nostalgia. We should note that, within this separation, the tension develops powerlessly. Alongside the conjunctural recognition of the new situation there is the awareness of the inability to overcome it. In the development of Descartes's thought, the beginning of the 1630s represents a period of critical retreat into the impossibility of putting forward reconstructive hypotheses. Whatever the suggestions and conjectures made in some erudite Cartesian apologetics (of confessional origin, in this instance), the pure and simple reversal of the humanist perspective through the derealization of the world cannot constitute a reconstructive standpoint. Rather, it represents nothing but reversal and negation.[48] The sundered moments are unable to rediscover a correct relationship that would once again set in motion

48. In this regard it is necessary to tackle, above all, the theses of Lenoble and Popkin. In their already cited works, which remain exemplary from several points of view, the originary and fundamental dualism of sixteenth-century thought – whether it takes a sceptical form or not – presents the grounds for the possible reconstruction   *cont'd over/*

the possible reconstruction of the world. On the contrary, through this division, sceptical thought proceeds not only to derealize the natural world but above all to devalue the human world. Everything is called into question, hollowed out from within. Every legal form is eradicated from the world. Divine law and human law have no foundation, if not in mystical intuition (or in positivist acceptance) which still, in the only relationship remaining, links the separated terms. As Montaigne writes: 'Now laws remain respected not because they are just but because they are laws. That is the mystical basis of their authority.'[49] The true is doubtful, religion is only valid through faith, or, when faith is missing, through individual or collective utility. The legislators, when they realised that there are evil men who would no doubt abstain openly from doing wrong out of fear of punishment, but would not secretly abstain from doing so, fostered this belief that Divine Nature could penetrate all the most secret things and that it could see even hidden crimes which it would punish through the Furies, if not in this life, at least in Hell, and that punishments would be meted out thereby.[50] For one must, indeed, live. What we find here, in the collapse of every criterion of truth, is therefore an appeal to pragmatic and empirical themes that might enable life to endure: 'Scepticism corrodes the ideality of prevailing norms, but strengthens their factual validity'.[51] Without doubt,

48. *cont'd*   of a meaningful universe; or rather, in the majority of cases it determines it directly. The denominational origin of such a thesis is obvious: only on the basis of dualism is a meaningful world possible. And, we could add, only on the basis of the anti-Renaissance. The partiality and the ideologically unilateral character of this thesis seems to us to be sufficiently evident. See also H. Busson, *De Charron à Pascal*, pp. 297ff, 303ff, where the thesis is generalized and where the compatibility of the Catholic counter-Reformation and the genesis of the new science is also upheld. In partial support of this thesis, see T. Gregory, *Scetticismo ed empirismo*, pp. 121–8.

49. Montaigne, *Essays*, III, ch. XIII. See also Charron, *Sagesse*, vol. I, p. 5.

50. Gassendi, *Instantiae*, p. 327 (quoted by T. Gregory, p. 103).

51. H. Friedrich, *Montaigne*, Bern 1949, p. 241 [TN: Thanks to Armin Beverungen for his translation from the German]. R. Popkin defends analogous theses in *The History of Scepticism*, pp. 113–31, 132–54.

when it is impossible to get a grip on reality, it is by relying on a pragmatic logic of appearance that elements emerge which are proper to the new science and positively included in its genetic process.[52] But we must be careful. To assume this position absolutely, qualifying scepticism as *tout court* reconstructive, is to mistake some effects for the totality of the causes. It is to forget that, in the specificity of the crisis, scepticism constitutes a moment of profound disorientation, an element that as such is constitutive of the crisis of the epoch. In other words, to rely on the pragmatic criterion is not to reconstruct but to survive. And how could it be otherwise, for men to whom the humanist hope in the totalitarian affirmation of truth had seemed so close at hand? To men roused by revolutionary will? As we have seen, though we can now understand it more forcefully, in the political world too scepticism does not present itself as a reconstructive moment but instead reveals the inevitable. Absolutism is born of the lack of pursuable alternatives for men who had set their sights on revolution.[53]

But let us turn once again to the scientific field and consider some examples. What form does Descartes's scientific thinking

52. R. Popkin, *The History of Scepticism,* pp. 133–43; T. Gregory, *Scetticismo ed empirismo,* pp. 121–8.

53. L. I. Bredvold, *The Intellectual Tendencies of John Dryden,* Ann Arbor 1934, p. 130: 'Pyrrhonism, though it often lent itself to disruptive and libertine tendencies has, by and large, and since the time of its founder, been the doctrine of traditionalists and conformists rather than of reformers. It stimulated fear of change and distrust of novelty far more than dissatisfaction with things as they are. Such a connection between scepticism and conservative politics was almost a commonplace of thought in the seventeenth century, when every man who pretended to reading was familiar with his Montaigne' (quoted by R. Schnur, *Individualismus and Absolutismus. Zur politischen Theorie vor Thomas Hobbes (1600–1640),* Berlin 1963, p. 57). For similar positions see also J. S. Spink, *French Free-Thought,* pp. 23–6; and A. Tenenti, *Libertinisme et hérésie,* p. 11, who engages in a similar consideration when he recognizes libertinism as the fruit of a 'movement of moral retreat after the defeat of Anabaptism', rediscovering in this the sixteenth-century origin of the phenomenon.

take in this phase? How, and to what extent, is Descartes able to operate scientifically within this situation of severe crisis? We re-encounter, here, in the scientific perspective, the motifs that we had already identified as the constituents of the metaphysical horizon of the crisis. From the start, we witness a decisive attack on every conception that exalts the unity and necessity of nature. Here the attack is turned, first of all, against the Scholastic theory of quality: 'I did not originally intend to give an account of particular bodies on the earth but only to treat of their various qualities. In fact, I am now discussing in addition some of their substantial forms, and trying to show the way to discover them all in time by supplementing my reasoning with observations'.[54] In this way that there opens up the path leading to the exclusion of substantial forms and the replacement of the qualitative principles of Scholastic physics with mechanical principles opens up. The consequences of this move are clear: the physical world is emptied of that intimate reality, that specific necessity that the medieval and Renaissance images attributed to it. The operation is analogous and contiguous, albeit less radical, to the one carried out with regard to the concept of truth. Eternal truth is divine creation, whereas natural truth is a pragmatic criterion of cognition, a human product.

It is more than evident that this position is anti-Scholastic. But what needs to be emphasized is that this operation is also, and above all, anti-Renaissance. In Descartes's discourse, the destruction of real qualities initiates an attack on the general conception of the relation between reason and cosmos which underlay his humanism and youthful hopes. The real correspondence between the subject and the object is here criticized: the world is separated from the subject. It is separated from the possibility of functioning as the projection and continuity of man, of grounding his desire

54. PWD III 37. See also AT I 109 [TN: partly in PWD III 17–18], 228 [TN: partly in PWD III 33] and PWD III 39. On this entire question, see E. Gilson's *Etudes sur le rôle*, p. 174, where he identifies the fundamental moment in the genesis of Descartes's metaphysics.

and constituting his terrain and his dominion. The world is configured instead as obstacle or limit. Human power has fallen in the face of the world.

However – and this is the second moment characterizing the situation – there must be a relationship between the terms of this separation. What marks out Descartes's work in this period from every other proposal is the desperate search for a relationship. There must be such a relationship and Descartes seeks it with unrelenting resolve. This is a bitter but unavoidable task for one who knows that the pragmatic reference point, which only now is he in possession of, will nevertheless not suffice to realize the project: 'I think that the science I describe is beyond the reach of any human mind; and yet I am so foolish that I cannot help dreaming of it though I know that this will only make me waste my time . . .'[55] It is impossible to overemphasize the insistence on the search for relation in a divided world. The originality of Descartes's discourse and the importance of his contribution stem from this search, from the painful participation in the historical world that such a search represents, and from nothing else. Descartes offers an original solution to a real problem and a forceful attempt to shatter reality so as to ground a true judgement in it. The beginnings of the Cartesian ideology can be found precisely in this intensity and in this separation.

At the beginning of the 1630s – years of extremely intense activity for Descartes – his scientific thinking develops on the basis of these presuppositions. There is now a complete recognition of reality's lack of necessity but also an extremely potent need to reconstruct a scientific horizon. Yet there is also an awareness of the complete insufficiency of the pragmatic demand on which such an operation should be founded. We thus observe endless uncertainties and ambiguities. The technical–pragmatic mechanism that should constitute the fundamental nucleus of the reconstruction is forever in crisis. There are countless slippages back

55. PWD III 38.

into the assumptions of the recent naturalist and Renaissance experiences, and relapses into a Scholastic-inspired finalism become prominent.[56] How could this surprise us? It is a sign and a consequence of the powerlessness of the pragmatic criterion to sustain the work of reconstruction. Lacking a valid criterion, Descartes repeatedly entrusts himself, in a rash and precarious manner, to terms drawn from the cultural tradition.

As we have said, the years around 1630 were years of intense activity. The *Treatise on Light*,[57] the *Treatise on Man*[58] and substantial parts of *Meteors* and *Dioptrics*[59] were produced during this period, which is to say in the first months of Descartes's stay in Holland, once he had outlined the terms of the new metaphysical situation of separation.[60] And it is under the impact of this situation that the introduction to the inquiry is set out:

56. F. Alquié, *La découverte métaphysique*, pp. 110–33, 'La fable du monde'. This chapter contains, I believe, the best account of the tensions and contradictions of Descartes's thinking of this period.

57. The *Treatise on Light*, in AT XI 3–118 [an extract from which can be found in PWD I 81–98]. On the composition see, aside from the 'Avertissement' at AT XI I–VII, the note at AT XI 698–706.

58. The *Treatise on Man* can be found in *The World and Other Writings*, pp. 99–169.

59. The *Dioptrics* (AT VI 81–228, Latin text 584–650 [extracts in *The World and Other Writings*, pp. 76–84, and PWD I 152–175]) is the oldest of the essays collected together with the *Discourse*. G. Gadoffre, 'Sur la chronologie', considers Discourse 10 of the *Dioptrics*, concerning the cutting of lenses, to have already been composed by 1629, and Discourses 1 and 2 to have been composed in 1632; by 1633, the work should be considered complete. E. Denissoff, 'Les étapes', believes the *Dioptrics* to have been finished in 1635. Generally speaking, the essay should be considered to have formed a part of the *Treatise on Light*. The *Meteors*, suggests Gadoffre, was composed between 1633 and 1635. Despite the differences in dating (in general, we are persuaded by Gadoffre's commentary), both the *Dioptrics* and the *Meteors* should certainly be regarded as closely linked to the work on *The World*. The *Meteors* can be found in AT VI 231–366 (Latin text, 651–720) [extract in *The World and Other Writings*, pp. 85–98].

60. PWD III 7ff and 13ff.

The subject I propose to deal with in this treatise is light, and the first point I want to draw to your attention is that there may be a difference between the sensation we have of light (i.e. the idea of light which is formed in our imagination by the mediation of our eyes) and what it is in the objects that produces this sensation within us (i.e. what it is in a flame or the sun that we call by the name 'light'). For although everyone is commonly convinced that the ideas we have in our mind are wholly similar to the objects from which they proceed, nevertheless I cannot see any reason which assures us that this is so. On the contrary, I note many observations which should make us doubt it.[61]

But the definition of the difference between the sensation of the object and the objects that such a sensation produces is only an aspect – merely a propaedeutic, elementary aspect – of the radical critique of quality. Thus the analysis develops by drawing separation into the world. The attack on quality is radical and involves not only the complex Scholastic apparatus of the 'natural places' but the substantive Renaissance concept of movement itself. It does so by uncoupling *mobile et mouvement*, thereby emptying movement of all internal power. What remains is the image of a world constituted by an infinity of movements, the purely geometric seat of their eternal duration: 'I believe that countless different motions go on perpetually in the world.'[62] The denial of the vacuum (*vuoto*) is the consequence, as well as the condition, of this conception of movement and reality.[63] It is futile therefore to seek the Scholastic origins of this theory:[64] the denial of the

61. PWD I 81 and AT I 126.
62. PWD I 84.
63. PWD I 85–8.
64. This is what E. Gilson contends throughout the vast philological work he has dedicated to the study of the thought and, in particular, the physics of Descartes. It is worth declaring, once again, our total and persistent opposition to Gilson's interpretation of   *cont'd over/*

vacuum does not derive here from the championing of the qualitative plenitude of the world; it is, rather, the correlate of its lack (*vuotezza*) of reality. It is a purely geometric and intellectual plenitude.

The *fable* of a new world, the mental history of its constitution, unfolds on this basis.[65] Cosmology becomes cosmogony – but only in thought. In the 'imaginary spaces', adopted ironically from the Scholastic tradition, God creates a 'plenitude' that extends indefinitely: 'so much matter around us that in whatever direction our imagination may extend, it no longer perceives any place which is empty.'[66] And this is a real extended body, without either elements or qualities but perfectly solid, an infinitely divisible pure extension. All the differences in this full universe derive solely from the diversity of movement that the parts assume in the creative act. This diversity of movement is prolonged into the laws of nature, which 'are sufficient to cause the parts of this chaos to disentangle themselves and arrange themselves in such a good order that they will have the form of a quite perfect world – a world in which we shall be able to see not only light but also other things, general as well as particular, which appear in the real world.[67]

There is no need to continue this narration of the *fable*. It suffices to observe how it completely realizes separation within the physical world, determining an image of the world which is merely functional to practical and technical ends. It is no coincidence that in the same period Descartes worked on specifically technical

64. *cont'd*   Descartes's thought, whose basic thesis is that Descartes's metaphysics depends on the physics and is thus built in polemical contrast with Thomist and Scholastic metaphysics, to the very extent that it polemicizes with Aristotelian physics. Whereas, as this argument implies, modern (i.e. mechanistic) physics is compatible or even congruent with classical metaphysics. For an effective critique of Gilson's interpretation, see A. Del Noce, *Riforma cattolica e filosofia moderna*, vol. I: *Cartesio*, Bologna 1965, pp. 53ff, 255, 307–20.
65. PWD I 90. The *fable* is first announced at PWD III 28.
66. PWD I 90.
67. PWD I 91.

themes. Discourse 10 of the *Dioptrics, On the way of grinding lenses*, was composed as far back as 1629.[68] So if we ask ourselves, 'What is the truth of this world?' there can only be one answer. None, by definition. The world is supported only by a pragmatic hypothesis. We encounter here the most symptomatic and dramatic paradox of this phase of Descartes's discourse: the more the hypothesis appears coherent, the greater Descartes's dissatisfaction with the development of the project. In Descartes there is always, despite everything, a powerful impetus to give a human meaning to the scientific reconstruction, to bring this reconstruction back to the definition of the human situation. Thanks to the insufficiency of the pragmatic criterion, and in the absence of any other reconstructive horizon, we witness what we have called slippages into old positions inherited from the tradition. It is as though, by relying on such positions, Descartes were seeking a renewed meaningful universe. I call them slippages and not options, because when they intervene in the new scientific framework these elements of the Scholastic and humanist traditions are always loaded with ambiguity. Descartes takes them up and, at the same time, rejects them.

That is what happens in the *Treatise on Light*, for instance, where Descartes, albeit in a simplified guise, reproposes the Scholastic theory of the natural elements,[69] a theory that is directly and immediately in contradiction with that unity of matter affirmed only a few pages before. Of course, Descartes intends to critique and reconfigure the conception of the single elements within the framework of the mechanistic hypothesis: fire, air and earth are composed of more or less subtle matter and that subtleness is in turn movement.[70] But why then privilege these elements? Why reintroduce, even if only surreptitiously, a sign and

68. AT VI 211–17. As we have already said, Discourse 10 of the *Dioptrics* seems to be contemporaneous with the collaboration with Ferrier. See AT I 13–16, 32–8, 38–52, 53–69 and 183–7.
69. AT XI 23–31 [TN: partly in PWD I 88–90].
70. PWD I 89.

a memory of natural places?[71] These ambiguities derive from the inability to sustain the rhythm of pure geometrism, from an intolerance of that fleeting world.[72] In the *Treatise on Man*, the recourse to the Scholastic world acquires greater breadth. It represents an attempt to give meaning to the human world through the recovery of Scholastic finalism. The soul, penetrating the body, tends to reveal itself as the perfection of the mechanism of the passions and sensations. Significantly, its emergence as a finalistic structure is contemporaneous with the analysis of passion, *doleur*:

> Suppose, firstly, that the tiny fibres which make up the marrow of the nerves are pulled with such force that they are broken and separated from the part of the body to which they are joined, with the result that the structure of the whole machine becomes somehow less perfect. Being pulled in this way, the fibres cause a movement in the brain which gives occasion for the soul (whose place of residence must remain constant) to have the sensation of *pain [doleur]*.[73]

Here nostalgia clashes with separated reality. Pain is the sign of the one and the other. But even elsewhere, and in a manner less encumbered by anthropomorphic resonances, the appeal to

71. *The World and Other Writings*, p. 19.
72. There is no question that the decision not to publish *The World* stems from Descartes's crisis following the condemnation of Galileo (see the next section in this chapter). And yet we believe that there are other, internal reasons that prevented its publication, such as the ones we have already intimated, i.e. the sense of the profound precariousness of the world as it is defined in the work. As proof of this one could adduce Descartes's continued refusal to publish *The World* even once the reasons for the initial decision were no longer pertinent and his friends were incessantly pressing him to publish it. See AT I 368, 518; AT II 547, 549ff, 551ff; AT III 520ff [TN: partly in PWD III 209–10] and *passim*.
73. PWD I 102–3.

finalism makes itself heard. This is above all the case with regard to the relation between the senses and the passions.[74] Are these elements in contradiction with the main thrust of the investigation? Certainly, but they are nevertheless present and they amount to signs of a profound crisis. The same happens in the *Meteors*, which is, among the *Essays*, the work where the coexistence and antagonism between Scholastic reminiscences and the new scientific model is at its strongest.[75] Turning to Discourses 2 and 7 of the *Meteors*, for example, we can observe, in the ambiguity deriving from the traditional arrangement of the inquiry's material, a continual reflux of the mechanistic explanation towards the theory of natural places.[76] Even in Discourse 8: *On the Rainbow*, which Descartes quite rightly considers methodologically exemplary,[77] the exacerbation of mechanistic modes of analysis – among them the possibility of a technical repetition of the investigated phenomena[78] – is accompanied by the illusion of a natural order

74. *The World and Other Writings*, pp. 139–40. See also pp. 104, 107, 116, 118–19.
75. Gilson concludes his article on the *Meteors* (in *Etudes sur le rôle*, pp. 102–37) in the following manner: '. . . the influence exerted by the Scholastic Meteors on Descartes's thinking is not in doubt. He let the School impose upon him both the choice of subject-matters and the order of reasoning – even when he wished to refute them; lastly, he remained completely prisoner to the doctrines that he was content to merely interpret and transpose' (p. 126). The fact that this conclusion is unacceptable is correctly underlined by E. Denissoff, 'Les étapes', pp. 256–7. While noting the weight of the Scholastic influence, Denissoff emphasizes the originality of Descartes's overall framework and the diversity of his influences, such as, for example, that of Bacon, which is for Denissoff the predominant one. Indeed, the very appropriation of the Scholastic heading for the subject matter ('Meteors') could, in Baconian fashion, signal the polemical character of Descartes's stance. It is no coincidence that Bacon's polemic was entitled *Novum Organon*.
76. AT VI 239ff and 312ff.
77. PWD III 85, in a letter to P. Vatier from 1638. Descartes also notes the excellence of the method at the start of the discourse, *The World and Other Writings*, p. 85.
78. AT VI 343–4.

which inheres regardless, as the intimate finality of the phenomena under consideration.[79]

While in his search for a comprehensive meaning that would lead beyond the pragmatic horizon, Descartes finds himself relying, in a contradictory albeit effective fashion, on Scholastic reminiscences, the motifs and attitudes of the Renaissance natural philosophy towards which he turns remain very powerful. Of course, this too is equivocal, oscillating between acceptance and rejection. And yet how powerful is the temptation to discover a foundation of absoluteness and necessity within the mechanical concatenation of the reasons of the world. There are moments[80] when Descartes is forced to warn of this danger: 'Note, in the first place, that by "nature" here I do not mean some goddess or any other sort of imaginary power.'[81] He is forced to say this because the World that the *fable* offered us is so substantial – in the totality of movement which it envelops and in the intensity of the inertia which it harbours – that all dualism of *mobile* and *mouvement* seems to have vanished, and so too every dualism with regard to the deity. It seems that the theory of continuous creation (originating in the Platonist tradition) is still being rehearsed here. At this point the *fable* even manages to be staged, once again, in one of the thousands of *theatra* of the Renaissance tradition as the '*fable de*

79. The persistent ambiguity that Descartes's discourse presents between naturalism and mechanism, or, better still, the ambiguity in the naturalistic image of the mechanical whole, has been effectively underlined by A. Rivaud, 'Remarques sur le mécanisme cartésien', *Revue philosophique de la France et de l'étranger*, vol. 62, 1937, pp. 290–306, as well as by Laporte. See also the comments by E. J. Dijksterhuis, 'La *Méthode* et les *Essais* de Descartes', in *Descartes et le cartésianisme hollandais. Etudes et documents*, The Hague 1950, pp. 21–44, concerning the substantial discontinuity between the method and the essays; on the *Meteors*, see particularly p. 43.

80. Chapter VII of the *Treatise on Light* is the one that most extensively develops the attempted interpretation '*iuxta sua propria principia*' of the natural world – although in the fictional form determined by the *fable*. See *The World and Other Writings*, pp. 24–32.

81. *The World and Other Writings*, p. 25.

mon Monde, the desire for possession that prolongs the recon-struction.[82] The naturalistic temptation is also extremely strong in the *Treatise on Man*. From the privileging of the element of fire in forms representing the solar metaphysics,[83] to the various for-mulations of the theory of vital spirits, Descartes comes very close to a naturalistic vitalism, an approximation of the unveiling of nature *iuxta sua propria principia*.[84] Furthermore, we witness the reappearance of youthful themes: natural geometry,[85] the topic of *scientia mirabilis*,[86] physico-metaphysical indistinction,[87] and so on. The same can be said of the *Meteors*[88] and of Discourses 1 and 2 of the *Dioptrics*[89] at least, where, alongside the overall pre-dominance of mechanical explanations, the metaphysical demand for the self-comprehension of the world resurfaces.

We have now documented Descartes's uneasy reliance on traditional themes in his attempt to discover a real sense, a comprehensive human meaning for scientific research. But such a recourse to tradition resolves nothing. Descartes is fully aware of this. The fact is that behind these vicissitudes there still remains the heterogeneity between the scientific outlook and the meta-physical horizon. The metaphysically separated world could not be unified by science. The investigations are carried out on distinct

82. PWD III 28.
83. *The World and Other Writings*, pp. 101, 162–3 and 168–9. Once again, we refer the reader to the collection *Le soleil à la Renaissance*.
84. *The World and Other Writings*, pp. 109, 112–13 and *passim*.
85. *The World and Other Writings*, pp. 133–4.
86. *The World and Other Writings*, pp. 139 and 168–9.
87. *The World and Other Writings*, pp. 143–5, 148–9 and 149–50.
88. Beside the facts already mentioned in note 59 of this chapter, the persistence of Descartes's interest in the phenomena which were then collected in this work is confirmed in AT I 23ff [TN: partly in PWD III 6–7].
89. Once again, see note 59 in this chapter. On the composition of the *Dioptrics*, see also PWD III 28, AT I 189ff, 192ff, 235, 315, 322 and 325. That the *Dioptrics* preceded the *Treatise on Light* is confirmed by the fact that, in this last treatise, the former work is said to have been concluded. See *The World and Other Writings*, pp. 7 and 125.

planes, which sometimes even appear to be opposed to one another. To begin his work in physics Descartes must abandon the one in metaphysics: 'I had to interrupt my current work . . .'[90] For its part, science was incapable of attaining rigour in its method until the separation was somehow dealt with, until a completed meaning had been given to its trajectory, until one had arrived once again at 'the discovery [*connoissance*] of this order' which 'is the key and foundation of the highest and most perfect science of material things which men can ever attain. For if we possessed it, we could discover *a priori* all the different forms and essences of terrestrial bodies, whereas without it we have to content ourselves with guessing them *a posteriori* and from their effects'.[91] No flights were possible, whether backward or forward, whether towards dogmatism or towards the Scholastic and humanist traditions: 'I do not think there is any need to entertain you any more with these matters; for I hope that in future those who will have understood all that has been said in this treatise will find nothing in the skies whose cause they cannot easily grasp, or which still gives them opportunity for admiration.'[92] So the solution, if there was to be one, had to bear in mind these elements, in other words, this metaphysical separation and this new way of doing science.

So, under what conditions would it be possible to achieve a specific solution of the crisis?

90. PWD III 6. See also AT II 396 and AT III 166–7.
91. PWD III 38. See also AT III 648–55 [TN: partly in PWD III 216–17].
92. AT VI 366. In the Cartesian horizon, the flight ended up becoming a flight towards magic, astrology and also (once again) towards the indeterminacy of Descartes's earliest scientific experience, which now appears purely and simply as a negative digression precisely towards magic. For Descartes's critique of astrology see, for example, PWD I 16–17, 20, 31, 34, 113–15 (and E. Gilson's *Commentaire*, pp. 109, 120–1, 141); AT III 15; AT V 65–6, PWD III 370 and AT V 338. In these last cited passages from the correspondence, the polemic is particularly harsh: astrology is defined as a science which, rather than letting one live, 'leads to the deaths of people who without it would not have been ill'.

4

It was necessary to begin by defining the specificity of the crisis. It had been represented as the condition of the scientific undertaking around 1630, as a crisis that was given but not resolved. Only by digging into its meaning – by assuming it entirely and exacerbating the tension in which the crisis was taking shape – was it possible to find some indication as to how it could be overcome. The context of the crisis that was projected by the historical horizon – with all the density that horizon lent to it – showed itself in the philosophical horizon of the theory of the creation of eternal truths. What emerged here was the metaphysical precariousness of the world and of truth itself. The situation was the following: the crisis was irresolvable to the extent that it was founded metaphysically; the only possibility was to rely on the pragmatic, the technical, in other words, on the will to survive. But what had provoked all this? The question presented itself urgently, again, within the philosophical horizon: what is the specificity of the crisis? What is its genesis?

There is an episode of great historical weight and immense importance for the development of Descartes's thought: the condemnation of Galileo. Descartes reconfigures his philosophical reflection in the light of this event. The entire metaphysical substratum of the critical rethinking that had occupied Descartes during these years finds a way to confront history directly, to clarify itself in relation to the Galileo affair. For such an event expresses, in exemplary fashion, the meaning of the century's conjunctural crisis. Hence Descartes historicizes, dramatizes and deepens his thinking. It is no coincidence that the ambiguities within which Descartes's thought had hitherto unfolded now dissolve. Not because the crisis has been overcome but because, in relation to its new intensity, in the inexorable awareness of its insolubility, those ambiguities are no longer possible.

But let us examine the whole question in all its different aspects. In the summer of 1632 Descartes maintained an arrogant, although rather ambiguous, attitude towards the theological disputes on the question of heliocentrism. As he writes to Mersenne: 'I too pity this author who employs astrological reasons to prove the immobility of the earth; but I would pity the century even more, if I thought that those who wanted to make this opinion into an article of faith did not have stronger reasons to uphold it'.[93] And he perseveres in his work: 'my *treatise is practically complete*'.[94] By chance, in November 1633, Descartes learns of the condemnation of Galileo. After fifteen days of fraught reflection he decides not to publish *The World*, so as not to adopt an attitude contrary to that of the Church:

I had intended to send you my *The World* as a New Year gift, and only two weeks ago I was quite determined to send you at least a part of it, if the whole work could not be copied in time. But I have to say that in the meantime I took the trouble to inquire in Leiden and Amsterdam whether Galileo's *World System* was available, for I thought I had heard it was published in Italy last year. I was told that it had indeed been published but that all the copies had immediately been burnt at Rome, and that Galileo had been convicted and fined. I was so astonished at this that I almost decided to burn all my papers or at least to let no one see them. For I could not imagine that he – an Italian and, as I understand, in the good graces of the Pope – could have been made a criminal for any other reason than that he tried, as he no doubt did, to establish that the earth moves. I know that some Cardinals already have censured this view, but I thought I had heard it said that all the same it was being taught publicly even in Rome. I must admit that if the view is false, so too are the entire foundations of my philosophy, for it can be demonstrated from them quite clearly. And it is so

93. AT I 258. The 'author' to whom Descartes refers is Jean-Baptiste Morin.
94. AT I 268. The passage is quoted from a letter dated 22 July 1633.

closely interwoven in every part of my treatise that I could not remove it without rendering the whole work defective. But for all the world I did not want to publish a discourse in which a single word could be found that the Church would have disapproved of; so I preferred to suppress it rather than to publish it in a mutilated form.[95]

The decision is reiterated in February and April of 1634[96] and it is irrevocable.[97] Yet Descartes is certain of the truth of Copernicanism and he is theologically aware of the dubious validity of the Vatican's decision, which lacks ratification by the Council. He knows, moreover, that the scientific milieu – universally, but particularly in France and Holland – affirms the truth of Copernicanism and has decisively distanced itself from the attitude of the Roman Church.[98] Why does Descartes in practice end up accepting the condemnation? He seems to suggest the reasons for it himself: 'But I am not so fond of my own opinions as to want to use such quibbles to be able to maintain them. I desire to live in peace and to continue the life I have begun under the motto 'to live well you must live unseen' [*bene vixit, bene qui latuit*]. And so I am more happy to be delivered from the fear

95. PWD III 40–1.
96. PWD III 41–3.
97. PWD III 43–4, AT I 298 and PWD III 45. See also the way Descartes returns to the question in PWD I 131–2 and 141–2 (as well as E. Gilson's *Commentaire*, respectively, pp. 379–83 and 439–42). On Descartes's attitude to the Galileo affair, one should consult the general summaries in *Baillet*, vol. I, chs 11 and 12; C. Adam, *Descartes, sa vie et son œuvre*, Paris 1937 (but also AT XII–XIII); H. Gouhier, *La pensée religieuse*, pp. 84–7 and *Essais*, pp. 70ff; and F. Alquié, *La découverte métaphysique*, pp. 117ff.
98. On the reaction to the condemnation of Galileo in France and Holland, especially in the scientific milieu – and on the general attitude of refusal, disapproval and solidarity with Galileo (revealing, at bottom, a less worried attitude than the one we discover in Descartes) – see AT I 290–1 and 324; R. Lenoble, *Mersenne*, pp. 391–408; R. Pintard, *Le libertinage érudit*, vol. I, pp. 288–9, 298–302; and T. Gregory, *Scetticismo ed empirismo*, pp. 170–2.

of my work's making unwanted acquaintances than I am unhappy at having lost the time and trouble which I spent on its composition'.[99] But is this persuasive?

The frame of reference should be broadened because we touch here upon the decisive point of the crisis. In effect Descartes appears to accept Rome's harsh decision not only for pragmatic reasons, as he too easily suggests, but rather for philosophical and scientific reasons – the former follow from the latter. The picture of the world – of his *The World* – that has been reconstructed so far is, in truth, insufficient. It is not fuelled by scientific necessity but rather, as we have seen, by a reliance on the practical, within a technical horizon. And Descartes's discovery, in this moment of conflict, is that reliance on the practical is not only insufficient to overcome the crisis but does not even represent a first step towards its solution. On the contrary, it is contradictory, since it is itself the result of the crisis. Reliance on the practical is heteronomous not only because it does not lead to any hope in renewal but because in practice one is forced into defeat. 'To live well you must live unseen' is now the only possible resolution within the practical horizon. It is the only solution adequate to a situation in which the terms for a scientific response are lacking. In Descartes's eyes, then, the problem is not whether Galileo is wrong or right. The problem is how truth can live in the world. That is, how we may recognize the real relation that underlies this demand.[100] But now truth cannot live in this world – and we have seen how Descartes suffered from this – because the

99. PWD III 43.
100. In his *Essais* (p. 70), H. Gouhier writes: 'in Descartes's eyes, Galileo is not a philosopher', because his principal interest does not concern method. This might turn out to be true over the course of the development of Descartes's thinking. Doubtless, Descartes increasingly tended to underscore (and not simply for reasons of convenience) his distance from Galileo's thought (for example, PWD III 127–8). (In this regard, see the ironic comment by Henry More, cited by John Laird, 'L'influence de Descartes sur la philosophie anglaise du XVIIe siècle', *Revue philosophique de la France et de l'étranger*, vol. 123, 1937, p. 244: 'terrified by the imprisonment of Galileo', *cont'd over/*

strength to make it live is lacking; because the relationship that the humanist hope of renewal demanded no longer exists, having been undermined. Of course, the possibility for truth to live in the world had existed. Descartes's memory is directly turned to the humanist experience through which he had lived. Descartes had seen the world in the same way as Galileo: the wondrous unfolding of divine laws immediately comprehensible to man, the macrocosm homogeneous with the microcosm – this was a scientific fabric that practical hope latched on to. Practical hope was then immediately revolutionary. It was certain of its strength and happy to contemplate its own triumph. A memory of freedom, of its heroic development.[101] No longer. This stirring of freedom in history met its contradiction in its own development. The drama of the bourgeois revolution delineates itself in this predicament, when the development of freedom becomes, in the eyes of the bourgeois, a heteronomous development. The force of the free man has been hobbled by the aporiae of historically realized freedom. Reason comprehends its opposite, finding it within itself, indestructible.[102] This awareness of the intrinsically dramatic character of the development of freedom is not to be found just in Descartes, but characterizes the period as a

100. *cont'd*   Descartes had supposedly 'defined movement in such a bizarre way that no human reason could make sense of it'). But that Descartes should now, at the time of the condemnation, feel that there is an essential difference between his own kind of work and Galileo's – this we cannot at all concede. It is precisely by confronting the controversy around Galileo that Descartes will be led to revise his position and thus to discover the conditions for his philosophical relationship to the world, contrasting it with Galileo's. It is in terms of the determinate quality of the confrontation with the world that the two positions become substantially differentiated.

101. In this regard, see the already cited works by E. Garin, as well as A. Koyré's general frame of interpretation.

102. R. Michéa, 'Les variations de la raison au XVIIe siècle. Essai sur la valeur du langage employé en histoire littéraire', *Revue philosophique de la France et de l'étranger*, vol. 126, 1938, pp. 183–201, notes how, in the 1600s, the term *raison* constitutes an 'umbrella term', a word of 'extraordinary complexity', 'a term whose borders   *cont'd over/*

whole. It is there especially in Corneille, where the humanist memory of freedom and the acrid awareness of its contradictory development reach the pinnacle of clarity and crisis. Once the magical virtue of the I clashes with reality, once the spontaneous immediacy of the development of freedom is forced to turn back upon itself, the entire framework of development comes apart in the insoluble conflict between the tragic hubris of the subject – the last irrational surge of the emergent individual – and an opaque world that is impermeable to freedom.[103]

Truth, therefore, can no longer live in the world. Reflecting on the condemnation of Galileo leads Descartes to deepen his concern with

102. *cont'd*   are imprecise and wavering'; adding that 'moreover, the imprecision of the term is the condition for its success'. It is precisely this essential duplicity, the problematic nature of the term 'reason', that should be emphasized. 'Reason' appears, also in Descartes, as a markedly collective term, capable of expressing the fundamental antinomies of the bourgeois thinking of the epoch. We will see further that, in the intellectual arc that goes from Descartes to Pascal, 'reason' is far more a problem than a solution.

103. We will have opportunity to return to the relationship between Descartes and Corneille, especially when studying the *Treatise on the Passions*. We must, however, underline already that not only were the two thinkers probably aware of one another's work (see AT XII 505–6, as well as AT *supplement* 103ff; the intermediary between the two, aside from the common Parisian milieu, can no doubt be identified in Huygens, a friend and admirer of Corneille. We remain unconvinced, however, by the suggestion that the relationship is a polemical one – see, for example, G. Gadoffre, 'Corneille et Descartes', in *Traditions de notre culture*, Paris 1941, pp. 76–91), but there were also unquestionable affinities in their general considerations on the crisis of the time. This means it is possible to situate Corneille's thinking too in the context of the crisis of bourgeois expansion. This is the thesis (which we support) advocated in J. Starobinski, 'Sur Corneille', *Temps modernes*, vol. 10, 1954, pp. 713–29: the magical exaltation of individual virtue takes Corneille's conception of the I decisively beyond the limits of its initial aristocratic, noble and ancestral definition, thereby fully revealing its irrepressible dialectic within the inevitable crisis. Close to Starobinski's position (though less clearly defined) are the theses of R. Schneider, *Grandeur de Corneille*, Baden Baden 1948; H. C. Ault, 'The Tragic   *cont'd over/*

the historical precariousness of truth. Contingency descends from the metaphysical horizon to the human world. The meaning of the Renaissance defeat of freedom is entirely unfolded. So? 'To live well you must live unseen' – this suggests that Descartes is still a libertine.[104]

103. *cont'd*   Genius of Corneille', *Modern Language Review*, vol. 45, 1950, pp. 164–76; and B. Dort, *Pierre Corneille dramaturge*, Paris 1957. But all these authors repeat the mistake of typifying in too abstract a manner the historical referents of the crisis interpreted by Corneille. Having traced, in exemplary fashion, the historical context of Corneille's dramatic work, S. Doubrovski, *Corneille et la dialectique du héros*, Paris 1963, takes to an extreme this abstract typological method: the *échec du héros* (failure of the hero) that each of Corneille's tragedies registers (and necessarily so: 'the theatre of Corneille represents the incessant demonstration of the same theorem: the recognition of the *Maîtrise* is, by its very nature, destructive of the order that it claims to establish', p. 476) cannot be referred to the *échec* of the parliamentary bourgeoisie but is the sign of the *échec* of the *Maîtrise* project in general (the Hegelian dialectic of master and slave) (in particular, see pp. 494ff). Certainly, it cannot be denied that the form of Corneille's drama is aristocratic, but there is a substantial difference between considering this aristocratic form as the envelope of a 'feudal morality' (P. Bénichou, *Morales du Grand Siècle*, Paris 1948, particularly pp. 13–76) and, more accurately, judging it to be the external configuration of a very different content, to wit, of the new, heroic sensibility of European humanism (this is the angle persuasively taken by G. Weise, *L'ideale eroico dal Rinascimento. Diffusione europea e tramonto*, pp. 118–42, in explicit contrast to Bénichou's thesis). This attitude is analogous to that which we encountered in the young Descartes and which we will rediscover, transformed but not disfigured, in Descartes's discussion of the morality of the passions.

104. The motto '*Bene vixit, bene qui latuit*' is libertine not merely in an episodic sense. On the contrary, it appeared continuously in the works of libertines as an element characterizing an exhaustive morality – one born of the crisis that followed the misfortune of Théophile de Viau. Sorel's 'to live like gods' (from the *Histoire comique de Francion*, 1623) exalts human dignity in isolation against the shabbiness of worldly life (A. Adam, *Les libertins au XVIIe siècle*, pp. 63ff); the same goes for the theorization of the 'honest voluptuousness' in Vauquelin des Yveteaux's sonnets and Sarasin's discourses. Much the same can be said regarding the other recurring motto, *Foris ut moris, intus ut lubet* ('Within as you please, without according to custom'), which is very widespread, both in the minor writers as well as in La Mothe or in Naudé.

Abducere mentem a sensibus – within a secular asceticism that is renewed with every passing day. Galileo was perhaps rightly condemned because he put his trust in a real horizon that was already drained of metaphysical validity. He wanted to assume its practical validity. But even reliance on the practical can no longer be accepted uncritically. At this stage, the imperative is to break away from this *vulgaire* who lives practically.[105] For it is here that the crisis appears in all its historical radicality. The world is represented as *malin*, as inverted truth, as a *fable* of a power that does not want truth to live in the world.[106] The appreciation of the

105. We should note, however, that although up to this point the term *'vulgaire'* represented the negative residue of the *abducere mentem a sensibus* (one could say, *a vulgaire* or, as it often appears, *a vulgi sensu* – PWD II 102, but also 8, 21, 44, 244, etc.), it did not do so exclusively. Indeed, *vulgaire* appears in the early Descartes as an evaluative term (and, in this sense, always pejorative), as well as a term descriptive of the material reality of life, of everyone's lived experience and, thus, as necessary and even as a source of knowledge (for example in AT II 554). Sometimes it is even charged with a positive sociological meaning as, for example, when Mersenne says that the merit of Cartesian philosophy is that it can be also understood by the *'vulgaire'*, whereas Scholastic philosophy cannot (AT II 287); or when Descartes speaks of his decision to write the *Discourse* in French (PWD III 51, as well as AT I 350, 353 and PWD III 85). But in the present situation, there is a break with the ambiguity of the linguistic use of *vulgaire*. Here it is used only in pejorative evaluative terms – and it will continue to be in relation to moral themes (for example, in the letters to Elizabeth in AT IV 2, 159, 202, PWD III 256, AT IV 269, etc.). Finally, one should recall that *'vulgaire'*, when united with the term *'philosophie'*, will become the definition of Scholastic philosophy.

106. It is necessary to insist on the plasticity of Descartes's image of the *malin*, the *malin génie*. The image is both historically and ideologically rich, and it is by this richness that it is possible to measure the radicalism and intensity of Descartes's interpretation of the crisis. An initial semantic analysis of the terms *'malin'* and *'génie'* can already demonstrate it. *'Malin'* appears in Descartes as both noun and adjective: *'les malins'*, *'les esprits malins'* are all those who, out of pure wickedness, are opposed to the communication of truth (e.g. AT II 83, 220, III 521, PWD III 326–7). Therefore, they are subjects or powers characterized by their wickedness. A similar semantic   *cont'd over/*

historic structure of separation is thus the theme that comes to provide the specificity that had been lacking up to this point in Descartes's philosophical awareness. Here philosophy is philosophy of the conjuncture in the full sense of the term: the definition of the real as separation, the definition of the world as an inverted world – as the magical and fabulous dominion of the *malin*.

Thus, through the image of the *malin*, Descartes's critique of the Renaissance does not simply expose the radicality of the crisis it is undergoing – it also discloses the necessity and current insolubility of that crisis. In the same way that the metaphysical hypothesis which sustained the theory of the creation of eternal truths opened itself to history, historical awareness now becomes, once again, a metaphysical thesis. The conversion of history into metaphysics, the rupture of the metaphysical world of the Renaissance through the consciousness of the historical crisis of freedom's process of realization – these are fundamental motifs of Descartes's philosophy of the conjuncture. Historical discontinuity is hypostasized as metaphysi-

---

106. *cont'd* analysis can be carried out on the term '*génie*': from the *génie* of the *Olympian Matters* (AT X 182, 185 and 186) to the deceitful God of *The Search for Truth* (PWD II 407–8) and, finally, to the projected *Génie de Socrate* (*De Deo Socratis*, concerning which see AT IV 530 and comments on 532–3, as well as *Baillet*, vol. II, p. 408), the *génie* is always a personified being (see H. Gouhier, *La pensée religieuse de Descartes*, p. i; J. Sirven, *Les années d'apprentissage*, p. 131; J. Maritain, *Le songe de Descartes*, Paris 1932, p. 31; the attempt to downplay the thesis in H. Gouhier, *Les premières pensées*, pp. 57–8, is not particularly convincing). In addition to a semantic analysis of the term, we would also need to carry out a historical and cultural analysis of the (extraordinarily broad) dissemination and the (incredibly complex) meaning of demonism in the seventeenth century. Since that is obviously not possible here, we refer the reader to the indications in L. Febvre, 'Sorcellerie, sottise ou revolution mentale?', in *Au cœur religieux*, pp. 301–9, and *Le problème de l'incroyance au XVIe siècle. La religion de Rabelais*, new edn, 1962, pp. 455ff. Febvre correctly explains the dissemination of demonism (and witchcraft) in terms of the crisis of the epoch, that is, in terms of the collapse of the positive mythology of humanism: 'the platonic demons have become devils', myth becomes torment.

cal discontinuity, drawing the weight of historical experience into this arena of abstraction. Separation and the metaphysical power of the *malin* will become definitive, irremovable facts.[107] Of course, the conjuncture passes. Doubt and the desperate accentuation of dualism may also diminish, at least in the most paradoxical and extreme formulations (and in the specific literary representation) that they assume here. But they will never be taken away, because Descartes's metaphysical world has itself been formed through the very assumption of the dualistic tension in its extreme guise.[108]

107. The manner whereby doubt comes to impress itself on being is taken up – in variously nuanced ways – by the existentialist and phenomenological schools. See K. Jaspers, 'La pensée de Descartes et la philosophie', *Revue philosophique de la France et de l'étranger*, vol. 123, 1937, pp. 39–148 (however, Jaspers considers his own assessment of Descartes to be more allusive than substantial, more basic than detailed) [in English see K. Jaspers, *Three Essays: Leonardo, Descartes, Max Weber*, New York 1964]; J.-P. Sartre, 'Cartesian Freedom' (although Sartre reproaches Descartes for not having been able to ascend from negation as the condition of the autonomy of the subject to the concept of autonomous production qua negation); and, finally, many pages in E. Husserl, *Cartesian Meditations: An Introduction to Phenomenology*, The Hague 1977; and *The Crisis of European Sciences and Transcendental Phenomenology*, Bloomington 1970 (on Husserl's interpretation of Descartes, see G. D. Neri, *Prassi e conoscenza*, Milan 1966, pp. 30ff). The definitive character of this attack by doubt on being is grasped by all these thinkers.

108. According to H. Gouhier, *Essais*, pp. 143–96, the question of the *malin génie* is entirely artificial. Having acted as a kind of agent provocateur, the *malin* 'is as though absorbed by his own nothingness'. It does not escape Gouhier that there is 'an ontological situation that demands epistemological desperation', but he then (inexplicably) depicts the *cogito* as an uncontaminated certainty. At this point, the *malin* is reduced to a 'mocking analogy' of divine omnipotence. Also according to M. Gueroult, *Descartes' Philosophy Interpreted According to the Order of Reasons*, the idea and use of the *malin génie* are purely 'provisional'. This perfectly suits his interpretation, which argues that Descartes's (historical) order of argumentation is entirely different from his (metaphysical) order of reasons. As usual, Gueroult's reasoning is extremely elegant: the *malin* is an opinion that has nothing to do with the metaphysical order, 'a false idea we have of our creator and his omnipotence'. We hope to have implicitly emphasized in the body of the text just how inadequate these interpretations are.

Descartes's dualistic statements, as they reappear in the later works, will sometimes allow a pale likeness of real intensity to resonate. At other times they will amount to mere functions, instrumental to the unitary reconstruction of the world, or even appear as an opportunistic homage to the religious tradition.[109] And yet, if we look closely, the pacification will always be external, and the meaning of the conjunctural revelation will never be erased from the metaphysical structure of Descartes's thought.

Let us insist then on the importance of the conjunctural moment understood as the historical moment of the revelation and maximum accentuation of the recognition of the crisis, as what we might call the 'motor element' of the metaphysical hypostasis of separation. Indeed, it is the force of the conjuncture's impact that determines the mutation of the Cartesian horizon and affects its orientation. Deep down, the theme of doubt was an element that was already present in the earlier period of Descartes's work.[110] Socratic doubt – I know that I know nothing – acts as the launch pad for the innovation of knowledge and the excavation of truth.[111] But what has happened to the assumption of Socratic doubt? Or, if you like, where is the intense speculative faith of the Socratic question? Here, in the historical conjuncture of Cartesian thought, man does not live doubt but is lived by it. He is

109. Beginning with the *Discourse on the Method*, PWD I 111–12 and 126–31 (see E. Gilson, *Commentaire*, pp. 285–369), doubt then reappears in the *Meditations*, PWD II 15; in *The Search for Truth*, PWD II 407–8; in the *Principles*, PWD I 193–5, AT IX B 25–7; and in the *Preface*, PWD I 183–4. Little by little, the function of doubt appears (but only appears) to be extinguished.

110. In the *Rules* (PWD I 46 and 53), *The World* (*The World and Other Writings*, pp. 3–5) and the *Treatise on Man* (*The World and Other Writings*, pp. 146 and 165).

111. 'Concerning the Socratic problem, which is essential for every philosophy, the *Rules* argue that the consciousness of non-knowledge contains and guarantees the guaranteed certainty of a difference between the true and the false'. This is E. Cassirer's commentary to Rule XII, where he defends the purely epistemological character of Cartesian doubt (in *Storia della filosofia moderna*, vol. I, p. 531).

overwhelmed by the malicious demon.[112] The entire Christian tradition, which had handed down the Socratic standpoint in its more acceptable Augustinian form – which would ultimately take the shape of humanist hope – is itself radically overturned, despite effectively having been registered within Descartes's discourse.[113]

112. E. Gilson, *Etudes sur le rôle*, particularly pp. 236–40, has lucidly grasped this hyperbolic and tragic inherence of doubt, of the *malin*, in the metaphysical structure of existence.

113. After the quantity of evidence that has been brought to bear on the matter, this seems certain. Numerous references to patristics and the works of St Augustine can be found in Descartes. See, for example, AT I 376; PWD III 129, 159, 160, 161, 168, 169; AT III 358–9; PWD III 179; AT III 543–4 and 507; PWD III 232, 235 and 331–2; AT V 147 and 186. There are also copious references to Augustine's texts in the discussion surrounding the *Meditations*. In terms of the theme of doubt, Augustine's main texts are: *Soliloq.*, bk. II, ch. I; *The City of God*, bk. XI, ch. 26; *De libero arbitrio*, bk. II, chs 3 and 5; *De Trinitate*, bk. X, ch. 10; *De vera Religione*, ch. XXXVII (see E. Gilson, *Commentaire*, 295–98 and *passim*). Besides these very specific references, however, there is another reason for believing that Descartes was aware of patristic philosophy, which is that at the beginning of the seventeenth century it was enormously widespread in France (J. Dagens, *Bérulle*, pp. 28ff). Its dissemination was linked to the apologetic Catholic need to contrast the radical evangelism of certain Protestant sectors. The influence will continue to grow, especially in the wake of the affirmation of Jansenist doctrine (in the *Logique de Port-Royal* – which can now be read in the excellent critical edition by P. Clair and F. Girbal, Paris 1965 – the reference to St Augustine is essential). On the whole question of the Augustine–Descartes relationship, see L. Blanchet, *Les antécédentes historiques du 'Je pense, donc je suis'*, Paris 1920; E. Gilson, *Etudes sur le rôle*, in particular pp. 27–50, 191–201, 215–23 and 289–94; C. Boyer, *Filosofia e storia nell'interpretazione del Cogito*, Padua 1935. Among these authors, it is Gilson who, displaying his usual elegance of argument, insists on the strong dependence of Descartes's thinking on patristic philosophy. Generally more open to the Scholastic influences on Descartes is A. Koyré, *Essais sur l'idée de Dieu et les preuves de son existence chez Descartes*, Paris 1922. Nevertheless, we believe that the standpoint expressed in this text requires corroboration, for even when a cultural tie exists between the patristic tradition and Descartes's thinking, that tie is radically altered by the new Cartesian standpoint. For a similar opinion, see G. Kruger's admirable 'Die Herkunft des philosophischen Selbstbewusstein', *Logos*, vol. 22, 1933, pp. 225–72; and even Pascal, in his *De l'esprit géometrique* (*Œuvres complètes*, ed. J. Chevalier, Paris 1954, p. 600).

Besides, where are the Reformation's critical capacity and doubt, as well as its apostolic tension, which, when all is said and done, result in hope?[114] How Bérulle's teaching – which led through doubt towards faith – has melted away![115] Where is the sceptical elegance that exalts the practical capacity of man against the uncertain advance of reason?[116] All these are different cultural elements that perhaps influence Descartes's development, but that

114. In this regard, we may consider the relationship between Descartes's tract *De Methodo* and the *Stratagemata Satanae* by Giacomo Aconcio. We shall return to the *De Methodo* shortly, when analysing the proximate sources of Descartes's methodological text. Here it is instead worth insisting on the meaning of a theory of inquiry that sets out from methodological doubt in the civic and religious dispute of the Reformation. As may be ascertained from the *Stratagemata*, its effect is to dissolve some of the knots of theological contention in the name of the essentiality of faith and religious practice, which find their basis in the certainty of consciousness. In this way, Aconcio goes to the extent of outlining a universally valid Christian confession. It is clear that such a conception and function, entrusted to doubt and methodological inquiry, have nothing in common with Descartes's argument. One should bear in mind that, like the *De Methodo*, the *Stratagemata* were also widely circulated in Holland, precisely in the years of Descartes's stay. The work was used above all by Arminians, Remonstrants and Irenics (particularly by Comenius) for their polemics (see C. D. O'Malley, *Jacopo Aconcio*, Rome 1955, in particular pp. 199ff). On the entire question, see the very balanced judgements of G. Radetti, 'Introduzione' to the critical edition of Giacomo Aconcio's *De Methodo e opuscoli religiosi e filosofici*, Florence 1944, and to *Stratagematum Satanae libri VIII*, Florence 1946.

115. On the trajectory of Bérulle's thought, in particular in the *Discours sur l'abnégation*, from the hyperbole of mystical doubt into critical doubt to the positivity of the ascetic procedure, see J. Dagens, *Bérulle*, pp. 133–49.

116. See in particular Popkin, *The History of Scepticism*, pp. 175–96 and 192–217. Popkin considers Descartes as the 'conqueror of scepticism', in so far as, by denying the validity of a pragmatic exit from the critique of reason, he aims instead at a new metaphysical dogmatics; whereas scepticism presses on with the pragmatic perspective which in this case is seen to ground the possibility of science.

this development – in the intensity of the crisis which it both registers and interprets – modifies and reshapes substantially.

Let us return to the initial question. We can now say that the specificity of the Cartesian crisis consists in its radicalism, in the desperate conviction of the metaphysical insolubility of the problem. Here, the historical substance of the failure of the bourgeois revolution mutates and is fixed in the philosophical form of separation. And yet one must live! 'To live well you must live unseen' – as the libertines teach. But this saying counts only for a day, not a whole lifetime. Here one must live. The one speaking is the bourgeois who bases his fortune on labour, on accumulated wealth. He might indeed acknowledge his defeat, recognize his separation from the hope of possessing the world, as well as the inanity of the humanist project of totality. But live he must. As a bourgeois, he is condemned to. Though the separation is metaphysical and cannot be overcome by freedom's revolutionary urge, it is a separation within which one must live. Should one rebuild within separation? What world will bourgeois virtue glimpse, amid the ghosts of the malicious demon's power? What space will it be able to occupy? Of course, not everything has been destroyed. The bourgeois retains the social form of his existence – an existence based on manufacture and methodologically articulated. Up until yesterday, the conquest of truth inhered in the method. Method was a way to read the articulations of reality, the structure of the world. But what will method achieve today? Will it rend the veil of mystified being so as to grasp that fragment of truth which, despite everything, is constituted by the indubitable social existence of the bourgeoisie? This is what method must do.

From the *Rules* to the *Discourse* method changes both in form and substance. Without doubt, it is turned upside down. In the *Rules* the world is continuous and the method follows its order. In the *Rules* the method is freedom and possession of the world. Conversely, in the *Discourse* the method concerns those antinomies determined by the development of the power of the *malin* and organized by it.[117] If we wish to speak of the continuity between these two works, the only one we can refer to is biographical[118] – a psychological intensity, the appreciation of reversal within the continuity of the personal history. It might even be the case that Descartes takes the name of his *Discourse* from the Renaissance tradition[119] – but really just the name, since

117. Therefore, it is not extrinsic causes that prevent Descartes from publishing the writings preceding the *Discourse*, as he would sometimes have us believe (e.g. for the period around 1637, see the letters now published in AT I 368 and 370).

118. The insistence on the continuity between the *Rules* and the *Discourse* is typical particularly of the neo-Kantians, as well as other interpretive currents linked to the epistemological problematic. This position is best encapsulated in E. Cassirer, *Leibniz's System, passim.*

119. There has been particular emphasis on the extraordinary similarity between the title of Aconcio's *De Methodo* and Descartes's *Discourse on the Method.* Note:
    – Aconcio: *On Method, or, On the correct reasoning in investigating and transmitting the arts and the sciences*;
    – Descartes: *Dissertatio de Methodo recte regendae rationis et veritatis in scientiis investigandae* (Discourse on the Method of rightly conducting one's reason and seeking the truth in the sciences).
    E. Denissoff, in 'Les étapes', concludes his comparison of the two titles by declaring that 'the analogy between the two formulas is striking. No doubt is permitted: the title of the *Discourse* is taken from Aconcio's (p. 271). In agreement, although more cautious, are J. Laird, 'L'influence de Descartes sur la philosophie anglaise du XVIIe siècle', pp. 229–30, and R. Jacquin, 'Le titre du *Discours de la méthode* est-il emprunté?', *Recherches de science religieuse*, vol. 26, 1952, pp. 142–5. The titles of the two methodological discourses had already been linked in a letter from Hübner to Mersenne, from August 1641 (AT III 438–9). Another reason in favour of the influence of Aconcio's tract on Descartes is that the text comes back into circulation in Holland – alongside the better-known *Stratagemata* – in Jean Maire's new edition of 1617. Even if we grant this, our impression is that the influence of Aconcio's text on Descartes's *Discourse* is restricted to the title. As G. Radetti notes, 'Introduction', pp. 38ff, the *recta ratio* to which Aconcio entrusts the process of knowledge does not express anything more than a demand – whose relation to the Scholastic tradition remains ambiguous. (In contrast to this position, see C. D. O'Malley, *Jacopo Aconcio*, pp. 120ff, who does not exclude some more concrete influence, specifically in relation to the rules for the certification of truth.)

here, in this new world, the humanist cannot exist. The very conditions for his existence are absent.

Galileo cannot be. So it is not merely a pretext to take Galileo's condemnation as the proximate cause of Descartes's specification of the individual and collective crisis. Indeed, Galileo's succumbing to the *malin* is a sign whose importance we could hardly overstate. Along with Galileo, the *malin* sweeps away the revolutionary illusion, the humanist hope. Descartes takes note of all this, accepting the setback but refusing to abandon hope. One must live. Once the revolution is over, the war of position begins.

5

The *Discourse on the Method* is the work of an epoch. It is the judgement of an epoch formulated in the course of the most unfavourable but most formative conjuncture. It both registers and reacts to a crisis which the individual suffers but which is collective and collectively meaningful. From this point of view, its literary form is exemplary. Written in the vernacular, the *Discourse* tells 'a history or, if you prefer, a fable'.[120] In other words, it posits a subjective experience as the narrative thread for the analysis of the epoch and, on that basis, it exemplifies, in a hypothetical manner, both a method and a metaphysics. This literary figure should be referred back to Montaigne: it constitutes a reflection upon the events of the epoch as a whole, filtered through 'this account of [his] life',[121] a reflection upon the crisis of an epoch which – as it relives its motifs, one by one – controls them and seeks to positively sublimate them.[122] Indeed, it seems probable that the idea of writing a *Discourse* – although not the project that sustains it – had been inspired by

120. PWD I 112.
121. Montaigne, *Essais*, III, ch. IX, p. 1108.
122. R. H. Popkin, *The History of Scepticism*, pp. 44–56.

Montaigne.[123] For whereas Montaigne keeps the subjective experience at the centre of analysis – alternately sublimating it and proposing pacification – in Descartes the core of the proposal is located in the metaphysical dimension. The more one delves into the individual story, the more it appears as exemplary. The course of historical events is thrown back upon a speculative nucleus of universal significance. In this privileged sense, then, the *Discourse* is *une histoire, une fable* – today one would call it a 'historical novel'. In effect, the *Discourse* is perhaps the first *Bildungsroman* of bourgeois thought.[124] This is true from a formal standpoint. Descartes's autobiography is the subject of a problematic relationship with the world, with an external world that must be authenticated while through this relationship the problematicity of the subject is sublimated. But it is also true from a substantive standpoint. The tension between subject and world concludes with a conscious, subjective self-limitation. This will be considered in more detail below. For now, it suffices to emphasize that at the centre of this matter, and constituting its specificity – the individual discovery of the possible, the individual will to adhere to it ('realistically', as one will later say) – is the subjective recognition of the historical crisis of the bourgeois world in its originary definition,

123. G. Cohen, *Ecrivains français en Hollande*, pp. 417–18; E. Gilson, *Commentaire*, p. 98; H. Gouhier, *Essais*, pp. 13, 20–2 and 25. One should bear in mind, for the period we are concerned with, the extraordinary success of the *Essais*. See H. Busson, *De Charron à Pascal*, pp. 177ff. (Busson considers 1635 to be the moment when Montaigne's success takes off; but between 1600 and 1630 the *Essais* had already gone through around thirty-five editions – see H. Gouhier, *La pensée religieuse de Descartes*, p. 281); A. M. Boase, *The Fortunes of Montaigne: A History of the Essays in France, 1580–1669*, London 1935; M. Dreano, *La pensée religieuse de Montaigne*, Paris 1936; and E. Marcu, *Répertoire des idées de Montaigne*, Geneva 1965.

124. We speak of the novel, of the *Bildungsroman*, in the sense that G. Lukács already spoke of it in his 1920 *Theory of the Novel*. See also L. Goldmann, *Towards a Sociology of the Novel*, New York 1975. We draw our hypothetical definitions from Goldmann's text.

a definition that by this stage has become the negation of the revolution. We need not remind ourselves again of the countless paths that led to this final collapse of the first emergence of bourgeois hope: the internal crisis and tension between the bourgeois project and its impossible realization; the separation of the bourgeoisie as a social body after having conceived the dream of a free dominance of totality. All this becomes secondary when one grasps, in the conjuncture (as Descartes eventually does), the central moment in the affair, when all the components of the event are organized in a unified manner and both the continuity of the genesis and the severity of the crisis reveal themselves in the irreducible novelty of the definition, in what has become a qualitative emergence, the sign of a new period.

Thus the *Discourse* exemplifies a substantive recovery of historical experience and a distillation of the entire meaning of the epoch. History both precedes theory and wants to constitute it. Theory wants to bow to history and, at the same time, to wrest its entire meaning away from it. In this relationship there is a perennial instability, a deep, reiterated and wilful precariousness. It is enough to look at the title of the little treatise and consider the vicissitudes of its development. In March 1636, Descartes writes to Mersenne:

> So that you may know what it is that I want to have printed, there will be four treatises, all in French, and the general title will be as follows: 'The Plan of a Universal Science which is capable of raising our Nature to its Highest Degree of Perfection, together with the Optics, the Meteorology and the Geometry, in which the Author, in order to give proof of his universal Science, explains the most abstruse Topics he could choose, and does so in such a way that even persons who have never studied can understand them'.[125]

125. PWD III 51.

The title has been regarded as Baconian[126] in its proclamation of a new science. But in February 1637 the new title appears, quickly followed by a crucial specification: 'for I have not put *Treatise on the Method* but *Discourse on the Method*, which means *Preface* or *Notice on the Method*, in order to show that I do not intend to teach the method but only to discuss it. As can be seen from what I say, it is concerned more with practice than with theory.'[127] The definitive title is even more explicit: 'Discourse on the Method of rightly conducting one's reason and seeking the truth in the sciences'.[128] So we are not dealing with a universal science but with the definition of a practical task in a provisional situation. That takes nothing away from the radicalism of the approach. Here, the explicitly provisional character of the project is not opposed to the decision to do metaphysics. The subjective and practical filter of historical experience does not close but rather opens the way to a discourse on being. In fact, the path chosen by Descartes is that of stabilizing the provisional character of the crisis – however profound its significance – while projecting its figure metaphysically. The tension between theory and history is not placated, instead it is elevated in the course of the analysis.

So we should not be fooled by the paradoxical and ironic opening of the *Discourse*. For, though it is true that 'Good sense is the best distributed thing in the world',[129] nevertheless 'it is not enough to have a good mind; the main thing is to apply it well'.[130] Do not be fooled, because the irony whereby good sense is equally distributed amongst men – following different paths and being applied to different objects to the point of confusion and error –

126. E. Denissoff, 'Les étapes', p. 261, shows that the title, *Projet d'une science universelle*, is drawn directly from Bacon's *De dignitate et augmentis*.
127. PWD III 53.
128. PWD I 111.
129. PWD I 111.
130. PWD I 111. An analogous argument can be found in the *Testament politique du Cardinal Richelieu*, ed. L. André, Paris 1947, p. 249.

alludes in fact to a tragic situation. To apply good sense, to identify the secure path (it matters not if it is the longest) in order to move about in the world,[131] is therefore the indication of a task but also implies a historical judgement. The trials of the reasonable individual, of the bourgeois man, have, so far, ended in failure. This is the failure of a unitary ideal of reason that has collapsed into the most irreducible diversity, as well as the failure of immediacy as the form of realization of the ideal of reason. The story that Descartes tells about himself is itself a historical judgement amounting to an ever-renewed introduction to the definition of the metaphysical situation.[132] Through his own history, Descartes exemplifies the defeat of Renaissance man. He follows the path leading from the joyous, spontaneous participation in the life of science and the world to one's separation from the world; from the lucky wandering in truth to the discovery of the necessity of method; and from the exaltation of spontaneity to the recognition of organization.

'From my childhood I have been nourished upon letters, and because I was persuaded that by their means one could acquire a clear and certain knowledge of all that is useful in life, I was extremely eager to learn them. But as soon as I had completed the course of study at the end of which one is normally admitted to the ranks of the learned, I completely changed my opinion.'[133] The judgement is radical and uncompromising: Everything I learnt is

131. PWD I 111: 'The greatest souls are capable of the greatest vices as well as the greatest virtues; and those who proceed but very slowly can make much greater progress, if they always follow the right path, than those who hurry and stray from it.'
132. The lengthy dispute that has developed around the truthfulness of Descartes's story is undoubtedly of notable philological interest, but its philosophical interest, if any, is slight. On the question of the truthfulness of the account, see E. Gilson's extensive comments in *Commentaire, passim*, as well as the notes by G. Sebba in *Bibliographia cartesiana*.
133. PWD I 112–13. On this passage see E. Gilson, *Commentaire*, pp. 101–3.

nothing but a heap of errors and doubts, a veil or membrane that conceals reality. It is not the foundation of clarity and security for the conduct of life. Which are the sciences that Descartes criticizes? They are the human sciences, the entire culture of humanism. Nothing is immune. Certainly, the polemic is not only directed against Scholasticism. In fact, Scholasticism is already far behind and Descartes, despite what might be expected, is fairly indifferent to it. The attack here is against the humanist conception of the relationship between science and the world, against erudition and the arts. It contests their human meaning. Descartes had spontaneously adhered to that model, he had profitably travelled certain paths. But what certainty is there in the foundation of knowledge? When spontaneity and the immediacy of the relation to the world wane, so does the certainty of the foundation.

Nevertheless, humanist science is still attacked from the standpoint of humanism. Indeed, Descartes's first option is to seek a higher level of immediacy. This is demonstrated in the second passage, which is entirely internal to the humanist conception of science:

> That is why, as soon as I was old enough to emerge from the control of my teachers, I entirely abandoned the study of letters. Resolving to seek no knowledge other than that which could be found in myself or else in the great book of the world, I spent the rest of my youth travelling, visiting courts and armies, mixing with people of diverse temperaments and ranks, gathering various experiences, testing myself in the situations which fortune offered me, and at all times reflecting upon whatever came my way so as to derive some profit from it. For it seemed to me that much more truth could be found in the reasonings which a man makes concerning matters that concern him than those which some scholar makes in his study about speculative matters. For the consequences of the former will soon punish the man if he judges wrongly, whereas the latter have no practical consequences and no importance for the scholar

except that perhaps the further they are from common sense the more pride he will take in them, since he will have had to use so much more skill and ingenuity in trying to render them plausible. And it was always my most earnest desire to learn to distinguish the true from the false in order to see clearly into my own actions and proceed with confidence in this life.[134]

The decision to seek in oneself and in the great book of the world is precisely humanist. The practical world, with its wealth of truth and danger, stands in opposition to the knowledge that the scientist has 'in his cabinet'. It stands opposed to it because the relationship to the world is 'more' immediate and contains within itself the prize – or the price – of its achievement. The full-bodied bourgeois hope of these pages cannot be ignored. The revolutionary enthusiasm that courses through them bears a fervent relationship to memory.

But it is precisely here, in this bourgeois world turned towards the dominance of the cosmos and the universal exaltation of the experience of freedom, that the definitive crisis explodes: 'It is true that, so long as I merely considered the customs of other men, I found hardly any reason for confidence, for I observed in them almost as much diversity as I had found previously among the opinions of philosophers.'[135] That then is the third passage. In this experience too there is no logic, no order and no meaning. Here the unity of experience also explodes into irreducible difference. We are on the edge of the sceptical crisis. Unquestionably, scepticism has its advantages. It can free us from illusions and received errors, and it can play the salutary mental role of a restorative bath. But with what result? That of leaving us alone, to rethink, and perhaps to rebuild. As Descartes writes: '. . . after I had spent some years pursuing these studies in the book of the world and trying to gain some experience, I resolved one day to

134. PWD I 115.
135. PWD I 115.

undertake studies within myself too and to use all the powers of my mind in choosing the paths I should follow.'[136]

The process that leads to the discovery of the solitude of the I in this first part of the *Discourse* is like an internal erosion of the world of humanism, which is to say a reductive process, neither uplifting nor reconstructive. Historically, it is marked by nostalgia, by the experience of the complete failure of humanism's radical hope. The situation it describes is thus one of maximum tension. The rediscovery of the I takes place as the discovery of a final basis of resistance in the face of a world emptied of reality, of a world that has seen the motif which inspired its unity explode, a world refracted into a diversity that is crisis itself. The I emerges as a problematic essence in the face of a world that has become estranged from it. It is on the basis of these presuppositions that, in the second part of the *Discourse*, the confrontation between I and world becomes more acute, directly implicating the historical reasons of the crisis. Moving beyond the psychological and particularistic horizon of the first part, the confrontation here reaches a fundamental level. It is fundamental for two reasons. First, in so far as Descartes travels the reductive path from the world to the I over again, further specifying and qualifying its contents in a more general and historically significant manner. Second, to the extent that, having reaffirmed the reasons for the crisis and the problematic emergence of the I, Descartes seeks an initial form of authentication for the world that stands before him, through the definition and application of a method. Was this not the scientific experience of the early 1630s, the attempt to overcome the precariousness of being through the use of pragmatic criteria? This level is fundamental, finally, because here thought does not reconstruct the path that leads to the crisis but is already fully internal to the conjunctural situation.

Besides, had it not placed itself within the conjuncture, as marked by crisis, the thinking of the *Discourse* would have played a

136. PWD I 115.

very different game. Descartes acknowledges this in the second part. Had it not been for the conjuncture, the I would in fact have rediscovered its immediate, productive reality and the destruction of the existent would have aimed at a liberating individual *renovatio*. That is because 'there is not usually so much perfection in works composed of several parts and produced by various different craftsman as in the works of one man'.[137] To reconstruct radically – that should be the work of the new man; that had been his hope. All the examples used by Descartes derive from the Renaissance: the urban planning utopia of the ideal city,[138] the utopia of the political city,[139] and then the polemic juxtaposing classical simplicity to Scholastic dialecticism and educational fragmentation.[140] But this is not possible. The lengthy conformist and sceptical considerations that follow work to re-establish the conjunctural situation.[141] All that is left is to descend again to the

137. PWD I 116.
138. PWD I 116–17. We have already insisted on the Renaissance meaning of this metaphor in the first chapter, where we also directed the reader to the relevant bibliography. Here it is simply worth underlining that the Renaissance motif is so explicit as to be specified further in a series of linguistic uses: this architectonic art is virtue against fortune (PWD I 116 [AT VI 12, line 1]); it is '*fantaisie*' (AT VI 11, line 26; in the Latin text: '*libere*', AT VI 546); it is individual creative work in contrast to centuries-old work of others (AT VI 12, line 7) – one could even speak of free enterprise. But the effect produced by this creative work is also typical of the Renaissance: beauty and order (AT VI 11, line 19), regularity (line 26) . . . as is the indistinctness and the totality into which all these elements flow. Aesthetic ideal and social ideology, individual freedom and collective growth, all come together and sustain one another.
139. PWD I 116–17. In this regard, we could repeat some of the points made in the preceding note. But we shall return to this question when considering Descartes's political thought more directly.
140. PWD I 116–17. With respect to the humanist polemic on the theme of school, see E. Garin, *L'educazione in Europa (1400–1600)*, Bari 1957.
141. PWD I 117–18. The process whereby the humanist hypothesis is refused is extremely sharp and brutal. Descartes takes up again the examples from urbanism and architecture, jurisprudence   *cont'd over/*

I, the point of extreme reduction, of extreme defence: 'and I found myself as it were forced to become my own guide'.

Marked precisely by this defeat, there arises the proposition of 'true method'.[142] That is, not the organization of a universal yearning for knowledge but a limitation to individuality and, at the same time, its guarantee: 'like a man who walks alone in the dark, I resolved to proceed so slowly, and to use such circumspection in all things, that even if I made but little progress I should at least be sure not to fall.'[143] In contrast to the *Rules*, what is lacking is the hope in a truthful relationship to the world – but this is everything and it suffices to overturn the whole framework of the

141. *cont'd*   and the state, philosophy and culture which had been proposed up to this point in order to attack them comprehensively, noting that 'there would really be no sense' in wanting to proceed to radical reforms (ones in accordance with the humanist model) in these fields. The humanist hypothesis is pure utopia. Moreover, concerning politics in particular, the humanist hypothesis is not only an unrealizable utopia but a ruinous project. Here the experience of the crisis, in its political specificity, is declared loud and clear: in the 'reformation of the smallest matters that concern the public' the difficulties are 'without remedy'. 'These large bodies are too difficult to lift up once they have been knocked down, or even to prop up once they have begun to totter, and their fall cannot but be a hard one.' There is nothing to be done then. The entire experience of the *robin* that Descartes underwent through his family and class, the French tragedy of the late 1500s, is given full expression here. Descartes's reasoning is that of the *politique*. It is better, therefore, to adjust oneself to circumstances, to trust in the use and practice which blunts defects. In other words, better the injustice of traditional order than the risk we run by modifying it. The passage concludes with a veritable curse: 'That is why I cannot by any means approve of those meddlesome and restless characters who, called neither by birth nor by fortune to the management of public affairs, are yet forever thinking up some new reform.' On this question in general, we shall return in chapter 3, section 1, confirming the profound analogies and the occasional terminological identity between Descartes's critique and that of Montaigne, Charron and the *politiques* of the 1600s – among the latter, above all, Richelieu.

142. PWD I 119.

143. PWD I 119.

investigation. Both the denunciation of the insufficiencies of philosophical logic, geometric analysis and the algebra of the moderns,[144] and the subsequent definition of the four methodological rules,[145] operate entirely within the compass of a world emptied of reality and necessity. The *universalis mathesis*, which had already emerged as the model for ontological penetration, is here adopted in the guise of a general science of proportions.[146] That is how it appears in the *Geometry*, composed, according to Descartes, as the *Discourse* was being printed, and repeatedly declared by him to be the model for the method.[147] That is also

144. PWD I 119–20. See E. Gilson's lengthy explanation in the *Commentaire*, pp. 187–96.
145. PWD I 120–1. In contrast, see E. Gilson, *Commentaire*, pp. 197–214.
146. See the commentary on these pages by Descartes himself in his *Entretien avec Burman. Manuscrit de Göttingen*, ed. C. Adam, Paris 1937, pp. 120–5.
147. The French text of the *Geometry* is published in AT VI 367–485 [TN: English translation in *Geometry of Descartes*, trans. D. E. Smith and M. L. Latham, New York 1954]. For Descartes's declarations on the excellence of the method in the *Geometry*, see PWD III 51, AT I 458 and PWD III 77–9. Concerning the composition of the text, E. Denissoff, 'Les étapes', p. 262, has doubts regarding the truth of Descartes's statements on the matter ('it is a treatise that I more or less only composed while my *Meteors* was being printed, and I even invented part of it during that time'). Denissoff argues that the statement instead expresses a typically arrogant attitude on the part of Descartes towards the Parisian geometers. The question would be somewhat otiose were it not for the fact that it touches upon a much deeper problem, that of the nature of the geometrical conception expressed in that text. Indeed, the backdating of the *Geometry* would make it easier to attribute to it that metaphysical approach which E. Gilson, for example (see note 145 above), is not averse to according it. In truth, as G. Gadoffre rightly maintains ('Sur la chronologie'), a later dating of the text seems more suited to the internal features of the text. Certainly, there converge in this text a number of geometrical problems that Descartes had treated from the beginning of his activity in a very different metaphysical framework (it suffices to recall the solution to Pappus's problem, AT VI 380ff) – but now these problems are reconfigured in the light of the 'true Method'. Conversely, if the second part of the *Discourse* counts as an introduction   *cont'd over/*

how it appears in the *Excerpta mathematica* of those years.[148] The true method leaves as its residue a bewitched world, a world of pure relations between disembodied magnitudes, a world of mere extension – a hypothesis put forward in place of a true comprehension. This is a world in which the mark of the bourgeoisie's Renaissance defeat goes very deep, a world that allows the bourgeoisie to maintain its productive, manufacturing hypothesis but suspends it over the void of the historical failure.

The third, fifth and sixth parts of the *Discourse* do not escape this framework, nor do they modify the general direction of Descartes's analysis. In part three, the elaboration of a 'provisional' morality presupposes the situation of crisis in its entirety, and this project stands opposed by definition to the foundation of a morality that is both scientific and triumphalist – of the kind that had already been announced in the youthful works.[149] Furthermore, the complaints about the exasperating conformism of a 'provisional' morality are useless. As has been rightly noted,[150] it is certainly not 'derived from this method', but rather precedes the composition of the *Discourse*, if not chronologically, certainly logically.[151] In fact, it is the direct consequence of the crisis.

147. *cont'd*   to the *Geometry* (and on this both Gadoffre and Denissoff are in agreement), the *Geometry* and Part Three of the *Discourse* should be read together, for the philosophical horizon that frames their project is the same. It is in terms of this horizon that the composite reality of the *Discourse* and the treatises that accompany it forms a single response to the problem that is *now* Descartes's.

148. AT X 297–308.

149. See chapter 1 above and the mention in the *Rules*, PWD I 18–19, of the possibility of a scientific morality based upon the uncontaminated idea of virtue.

150. E. Gilson, *Commentaire*, p. 81. The intention to found morality on method is expressed by Descartes in the summary at the start of the *Discourse* (PWD I 111).

151. PWD I 111. Indeed, the hypothesis has been set forth – with great elegance by Gadoffre, somewhat simplistically by Denissoff – that Part Three of the *Discourse* was written around February 1637, as a treatise conveniently composed in order to reassure the censors.

What's more, it is already the active effect of the crisis, the separation from libertine hesitation and sceptical nihilism, the desire to live in the world come what may.[152] Besides, if this morality had been deduced from the method, what scope and form could it have ever adopted? Would a substantive foundation ever have corresponded to the more precise logical entailment of arguments? It does not look like it. In the bewitched world left behind by the method, only the will to live could have hoped to attain the result; only the formal positing of life as inquiry could have found support at the heart of the catastrophe of meanings: 'Finally, to conclude this moral code . . . I thought I could do no better than to . . . devote my whole life to cultivating my reason, and advancing as far as I could in the knowledge of the truth, following the method I had prescribed for myself.'[153]

Indeed, it is still only the pragmatic will to survive that sustains the fifth and sixth parts of the *Discourse*. In the fifth part, the discourse retreats to the scientific experience of the preceding years and, as in that phase, it rests on substantive ambiguities. The general climate is that of the hypothesis of the derealization of the world through the renewed critique of substantial forms,[154] and the entire series of motifs linked to it.[155] Contemporaneously,

152. We shall return to these themes, and to the content of the rule of morals *par provision*, in chapter 3, section 1. See, however, PWD I 122 and 125–6.
153. PWD I 124.
154. PWD I 132. See Gilson's *Commentaire*, p. 384, for a reminder of the precedents for Descartes's attack on the substantial forms and places of *The World*.
155. For example, PWD I 133–4, on the doctrine of continuous creation (see E. Gilson, *Commentaire*, pp. 390–3). It is worth underlining that the paradox of doubt in nature is actualized, so to speak, with regard to the doctrine of continuous creation. Thus, nature simultaneously is and is not, it is certain and it is nothing – its absolute contingency is brought back to necessity only by the actuality of the will. The derealization is at its height, the bewitched image of the world is fulfilled. Moreover, it should be emphasized that this doctrine also works when turned against the Scholastic conception   *cont'd over/*

however, we find elements and passages that, in a contradictory fashion, give new life to positions typical of the Renaissance universalism of Descartes's earlier writings.[156] Perhaps never so much as in this case does the structure of the text reveal the arduous, gradual and stratified process of composition of the *Discourse*.[157]

155. *cont'd*   and, better still, against the Renaissance one. For another example, see PWD I 139 (Gilson's *Commentaire*, pp. 420ff), where the precariousness of nature turns into a kind of automatic existence. Nature is not given but made. Its reality is artificial. These are only two limit-examples of the derealized image of nature from Part Five of the *Discourse* – limit-examples which form the extremes of a long series of phenomena that can be coherently interpreted in this manner.

156. In this sense, the opening of Part Five of the *Discourse* is, to say the least, ambiguous, if not downright contradictory: 'I would gladly go on and reveal the whole chain of truths that I deduced from these first ones' (PWD I 131). In effect, this renewed call for an order of truth and being chained to necessity, this renewal of the compact Renaissance conception of being, appears somewhat strange after having passed through the discovery of the ontological structure of doubt and having indicated the process of derealization of the world. And it is not merely a question of linguistic usage. A series of elements reveal the survival of the Renaissance conception in Part Five of the *Discourse* too. Merely to give a few examples, this is the case with the reappearance, in a new form, of the theory of the *semina* (PWD I 131: 'certain laws . . . established in nature . . .' – an extremely full-bodied image; very good in this regard is also Gilson, *Commentaire*, pp. 372–4); of another enhancement of the theory of light (PWD I 132: the thematic of light is nothing less than the Trojan horse of the naturalistic conception within Descartes's mechanism; see also *Commentaire*, pp. 375–6); and once again of an attack – which we know to be completely mistaken – on Harvey's theory of the circulation of the blood in favour of the metaphysics of heat (PWD I 135; *Commentaire*, pp. 400ff).

157. This is the essential result to which Gilbert Gadoffre's crucial research has led, independently of Denissoff's challenges and/or complements on matters of detail. F. Alquié, *La découverte métaphysique*, pp. 134–58, has insisted, demonstrating an extraordinary capacity for synthesis, on both the composite character and the ambiguity of the *Discourse*. For Gouhier (*Essais*, p. 56), on the other hand, 'the *DM* is the work of a contented philosopher: content with his philosophy and his method, which is continuously verified by his philosophy . . .';   *cont'd over/*

Finally, in the sixth part, the meaning of the epochal and personal crises is given its fullest expression. By this point, the discourse is wholly historical and is founded on the project of 'master[ing] . . . nature'.[158] This project had already been intimated in the *Discourse* (and earlier in the midst of full-bodied humanist hope), but it reveals itself to be impracticable at the very moment it is put forward. On the one hand, it is indeed 'the law which obliges us to do all in our power to secure the general welfare of mankind', and not so much in an individual, speculative form, as in a collective, practical form – in the same way that artisans' trades are formed. This is in order to 'thus make ourselves, as it were, the lords and masters of nature. This is desirable not only for the invention of innumerable devices which would facilitate our enjoyment of the fruits of the earth and all the goods we find there, but also, and most importantly, for the maintenance of health, which is undoubtedly the chief good and the foundation of all the other goods in this life.'[159] We are on the plane of the humanist *renovatio*, still possessed by a hope that takes itself to be reality ('There ought to be no doubt that human life could be prolonged, if we were to know its workings . . .'[160]) and by the collective construction of a common destiny ('by combining the lives and labours of many, we might make much greater progress working together than anyone could make on his own').[161] But, on the other hand, we have the effectiveness of the inquirer's solitude – faced with the infinite field of experience that must be traversed – and the inability, the

---

157. *cont'd*   all this without mentioning just how much the work of the '*philosophe sans masque*' is in every respect unitary and consistent. Lastly, see C. Láscaris Comneno, 'Analisis del *Discurso del método*', *Revista de filosofía*, vol. 14, 1955, pp. 293–351.
158. PWD I 142–3.
159. PWD I 142–3.
160. *Entretien avec Burman*, p. 127.
161. PWD I 143.

political impossibility, of promoting such a civic and scientific programme.[162] Here, the extreme tension between, on the one side, the reductive and unifying intensity of the scientific and practical project and, on the other, the extension, inexhaustibility and irreducibility of experience, together with the lack of collective means of organization, makes the opposition between I and world, between certainty and progress, explode. In reality, it is the possibility of science as wisdom, as control and possession of the world, as collective growth and revolutionary conquest, which does not exist. Of course, this need cannot be suppressed, but now, in the world, between the I and reality there is an indefinite space. The more Descartes wants to overcome this distance the more he suffers from it. In effect, every attempt at overcoming wavers between a necessarily unfinished path and the repetition of the utopian hope.[163] Why then should one wish to see, precisely in these extreme moments of Descartes's crisis – as has been done all too often – a positive moment instead of the declaration of an impotent hope, the awareness of a collective destiny of defeat that Descartes takes on his shoulders? The indefinite or the utopian do

---

162. PWD I 143–4.
163. A. Koyré saw this clearly in 'Entretiens sur Descartes', in *Introduction à la lecture de Platon*, Paris 1962, particularly pp. 184ff. It is precisely in this acknowledgement of Descartes's situation, of this profound crisis experienced by Descartes, that Koyré sees the conditions for the subsequent turnaround: from the oppression exerted by the infinite on the intellect to the 'intellectual discovery of the infinite'. This moment of crisis is thus essential. Only through it can there be a real possibility of rediscovering the world. The interpretations that have failed to grasp this moment of crisis and its necessity for the development of Descartes's thought have shut themselves off from any possibility of attaining a correct interpretation. The elevation of Part Six of the *Discourse*, so common in the literature on Descartes – both on the right (Gouhier) and the left (Leroy) – flattens what is perhaps one of the most dramatic moments of Descartes's thinking. Part Six expresses a hope and declares a crisis – were it anything else it would be mere rhetoric. Part Six functions as a critical introduction to Part Four – were it anything else it would be merely an invocation *de vita beata*.

not bring the crisis to an end. Rather, they constitute one of its most profound moments. In the face of a world that demands authentication there is only the I in its solitude.

Nevertheless, in this situation, with the failure of the Renaissance experience behind him – when the world of the senses, philosophy and experience is internally separated, completely derealized, and appears (or is) nothing but a dream – Descartes declares that: 'I resolved to pretend that all things that had ever entered my mind were no more true than the illusions of my dreams.'[164] It is here that the solitude of the I reveals itself to be something that, although implicated in the crisis, is superior to it: 'I think, therefore I am.' This is the first and only contact with being. The principle is indubitable because it is real. The I is alone but its solitude is in reality, not in a dream. The paradox of the '*je pense*' is all here, in the idea that the self-limitation of the subject constructed in the course of the investigation – that moment of dramatic reduction and resistance – should become the only positive moment. Not mere resistance but ontological foundation, reduction to being, destruction in its intensity of every possible appearance. But the paradox unfolds and is further specified. If the 'I think, therefore I am' emerges 'while I was trying thus to think everything false',[165] then the qualification of oneself as thinking substance also develops in accordance with the

164. PWD I 127. See E. Gilson, *Commentaire*, pp. 287–92. F. Alquié, in his commentary to Descartes's *Œuvres philosophiques*, vol. I, pp. 602–3, insists – perhaps even more so than in his *La découverte métaphysique de l'homme* – on the fact that Cartesian doubt develops more on the scientific plane than on the ontological one. This leads him to regard the *Discourse* almost as an introduction to the finally radically metaphysical themes of the *Meditations*. Frankly, this position appears to us untenable when confronted with the letter of Descartes's texts.

165. The full sentence reads: 'But immediately I noticed that while I was trying thus to think everything false, it was necessary that I, who was thinking this, was something' (PWD I 127; E. Gilson, *Commentaire*, pp. 292–301). It is important to quote it in full, for in saying 'thing', 'something', the I expresses an organic, determinate, unequivocal link with being. Positions such as those of Alquié, which only look to the developed ontological consciousness that the I   *cont'd over/*

paradoxical rhythm of the negation of the reality of the body.[166] In defining itself as real, the I promotes a function internal to the process of derealization of the world. Furthermore, within the paradox, within the painful awareness of separation, the proof of certain knowledge – that is, the proof of the existence of the divinity – emerges. Note that it is not only the proof of perfection[167]

165. *cont'd*   expresses in the *Meditations*, collapse in the face of this single word. Of course, we still do not have here an ideological conception of the I completely separated from the ontological discovery of the I. In sociological terms we could say that here the consciousness of the bourgeois I still expresses the consciousness of autonomy and not the full-blown consciousness of organization – and this would be true. Nevertheless, the qualitative leap has been accomplished, the mature philosophy and the ideological path are opened up. This affirmation of the I still forms part of an elementary assessment which, although it is still (with respect to the *Meditations*) an undeveloped moment, nevertheless represents an indisputably original and innovative force in the history of bourgeois thought.

166. PWD I 127. See E. Gilson, *Commentaire*, pp. 301–12. If the world is unreal, so is the body. The being that thinking discovers as its support is a totally autonomous being. It would be worthwhile to delve further into the dispute with those who hold that the 'I think, I am' of the *Discourse* is a function of the discourse on science (against scepticism), rather than of the reflection on being, and who take advantage of this exclusion of the body, of the corporeality of the affirmation of existence, to advance their position. But isn't the very ontological dignity of Descartes's approach to be found precisely in this affirmation of the autonomy of thought? Thinking is being, it is ontological reality precisely to the extent that it does not need any support other than itself.

167. PWD I 127–9. E. Gilson, *Commentaire*, pp. 314–42. It is obvious that we are working on a plane that has nothing to do with the traditional one of the proofs for the existence of God. The entire procedure – in the case of this first proof as in the case of the ontological proof – operates within a conception of being as spiritual autonomy, as independence and foundation of reality that has little to do with the tradition. In this regard at least, the interpretation of Descartes carried out by classical idealism was on target. It is well known that the analysis of the passage from doubt to the proofs of the existence of God was one of that tradition's pivotal points. See M. Hagmann, *Descartes in der Auffassung*, pp. 82–110. See also the articles by F. Medicus, J. Schwarz and A. Gehlen in *Congrès Descartes. Etudes cartésiennes*, vol. III.

('reflecting upon the fact that I was doubting and that consequently my being was not wholly perfect . . .')[168] that is born from the paradox, but also the so-called ontological proof,[169] itself articulated on the basis of doubt, that is to say, not in terms of essence and the consequent couple of perfection and privation, but in terms of existence and its alternative, inexistence. What opens up here is a path that is entirely internal to the autonomy of being, of this new being that the '*je pense, je suis*' has discovered. This thinking essence alludes to the absolute. The radicalism of doubt opens onto that of the absolute.

Let us explain this further. We have said that, in this manner, the solitude of the I reveals itself to be something which – although implicated in the crisis – is irreducible to it. To be more precise, the solitude of the I is irreducible to the crisis in so far as it is different, autonomous and superior. The certainty of the I, the soul, God, and the world which is recaptured here is not a peaceful possession of the universe, the guarantee of a heroic reconstruction of the cosmos. It is not the overcoming of the crisis. It is, instead, the first hint of a different horizon, one that is paradoxically, ironically uncovered by the deepening and definitive acceptance of the crisis. The crisis does not result in a pacification with the world, but in the proposal of a world adequate to the self-limitation and autonomy of the subject. The first problem that had triggered the crisis, the problem of the conquest of existence, is now set aside. The distance from existence and reality is definitive and insoluble. If we wish to speak of reconstruction, we can do so in the sense of a particular definition of existence – not as absolute but as relative to the particular form taken by the subject's essential self-limitation. The 'I think' does not eliminate separation, rather, it deepens it and makes it metaphysically definitive. So it is that in the *Discourse* the rupture of the happy Renaissance existence is

168. PWD I 127.
169. PWD I 129. E. Gilson's comments on this point are superb, *Commentaire*, pp. 342–54.

specified and accomplished. The historical conjuncture of the 1630s finds its definitive systematization in this text. From this point of view, the *Discourse* is really a bourgeois novel. In it, Descartes ironically takes his distance from the revolutionary experience of his youth, in order 'realistically' to accept the call to reconstruct the world on the basis of isolation, defeat and the establishment of the self-limitation of the subject.[170] The *Discourse* does not represent the reconstruction of the possibility to do science, the human science of the reconstruction of the world. Rather, it signals the impossibility of science as the actual possession of the world. At the same time, it is the project of a different world, the exclusive valorization of the I as the basis for the (distant but not impossible) reconstruction of a hope (untimely but active) of domination.

170. At this point, in order not to leave the question up in the air, it is perhaps worth returning to the Montaigne–Descartes relationship, from which we took our cue, to attempt a final clarification concerning the distinctive theoretical nucleus that this relationship presides over. There are some who establish a rigid separation between the two authors precisely on the basis of an assessment of the ontological radicalism of the Cartesian I. For example, see the positions defended by L. Brunschvicg, *Descartes et Pascal lecteurs de Montaigne*, Neuchâtel 1945, pp. 95ff (Pyrrhonism is Montaigne's proper terrain; although Descartes passes through it, it is only in order to oppose it); A. Koyré, 'Entretiens', pp. 175ff ('The *Essais* are . . . a treatise of renunciation' . . . 'To the story of a defeat, Descartes opposes a story of a victory'); and G. Weise, *L'ideale eroico*, vol. II, pp. 66–70. This seems to us mistaken because, as M. Gueroult underscores (*Descartes' Philosophy Interpreted in Accordance with the Order of Reasons*, vol. II, pp. 190 and *passim*), what separates Montaigne from Descartes is not so much the different inflection given to the same problem that is present in both thinkers – defeat or victory as an attempt to positively qualify the humanist ideal of science–wisdom – so much as the different terrain upon which they carry out their respective investigations. One should not then speak of Montaigne as a precursor, however dialectical, of Descartes. The latter's innovation is not superior but heterogeneous.

Political Science or Reasonable Ideology?

> For I do not wish to be one of those jobbing builders who
> devote themselves solely to refurbishing old buildings because
> they consider themselves incapable of undertaking the con-
> struction of new ones.
>
> PWD II 407

1

It has been said that Cartesian philosophy constitutes 'a metaphysical accident in the history of mechanicism'.[1] Keeping in
mind the findings of the *Discourse on the Method* it would be
tempting to accept this definition. Cartesian philosophy would be
marked by an exasperated dualism, a world bewitched by relations
of mere proportion, a universe reduced to extension, which the
emergence of the I as thinking substance only counters as if by
accident. Moreover, even this emergence cannot determine the
conditions needed effectively to enter into relation with the world.
The sense of indefinite distance is not mediated in any way:
thought stretches towards that lunar world without comprehending it, without possessing it. As we have seen, in the *Geometry*[2] the
image of a world bewitched appears with the greatest clarity. This
is no accident: the *Geometry* reveals the level of scientific analysis

---

1. R. Lenoble, *Mersenne*, p. 614.
2. See above, chapter 2, section 5.

that Descartes had attained at the time of the *Discourse*. Paradoxically, it also exhibits the starkest opposition to the fourth metaphysical part of the *Discourse*, which is contemporaneous but appears accidental, a pure sign of contradiction in the overall framework. The order of reasons that the intellect deploys with regard to the geometric world is in fact entirely formal: the mathematical horizon excludes the metaphysical one, just as imagination excludes intellection.[3] It is indeed true that the validity of the mathematical order of reasons is founded on divine veracity. But it is so founded once and for all, as a metaphysical accident, as a foundation that cannot unfold in the articulation of reasons. It turns out, instead, to be a ground transcendent to

3. At least as regards the *Discourse*, this thesis was put forward and very persuasively argued by Pierre Léon Boutroux in his now classic investigation, *L'imagination et les mathématiques selon Descartes*, Paris 1900. Against Boutroux's approach see, on the one hand, J. O. Fleckenstein, 'Descartes und die exakten Wissenschaften der Barock', *Forschungen und Fortschritte*, vol. 30, 1956, pp. 116–21, which argues for the immediate ontological significance of Cartesian geometry; on the other, J. Vuillemin, *Mathématiques et métaphysique chez Descartes*, Paris 1960, which, following in Gueroult's footsteps, strongly supports the subsumption of the order of reality by the order of theoretical reasons, thereby reifying (*entificando*) the geometric horizon. It is worth adding that, as we shall see, in Descartes we often witness the attempt to geometricize nature or to reify intellectual formality. But in our view the error consists in considering these horizons as exclusive to one another, which is to say in the inability to see them as pieces of a mutating mosaic, aimed at continually reinventing the terms of the problem of the I–world relation. By this I mean that what is mistaken is not so much the fact of considering as effective certain tensions towards the realization of the scientific or formal horizons, but the fact of considering these tensions as closed, not seeing them instead as variables of a perpetually open problematic process. Ultimately, it is the I–world problem that most interests Descartes. In support of our approach see N. K. Smith, *New Studies in the Philosophy of Descartes*, London and New York 1952, a volume which, albeit questionable in many respects, is very attractive on account of its harsh 'historiographical' assault on every monolithic or non-problematic conception of Descartes's thought.

reasons, which moreover is deprived of any possibility of being related to them. Separation is the form of this world. The accidental character of the I rises, without any mediation whatsoever, over the mechanical order that science imagines for nature.[4]

The picture becomes more precise – and the incidental features of the emergence of the metaphysical moment gain in depth – if we look at some of the findings of the *Discourse*. Relevant and crucially significant themes, such as morality or politics, seem to develop in that same bewitched atmosphere of a mechanical world to which any directly human meaning is alien. Let us reconsider, for example, the third part of the *Discourse* and the rules for provisional morality prescribed therein. It is not particularly important for now to underline its conformist and retrograde aspects; it is far more relevant to reveal its fundamental character, its essential formalism: 'The first [maxim] was to obey the laws and customs of my country, holding constantly to the religion in which by God's grace I had been instructed from my childhood, and governing myself in all other matters according to the most moderate and least extreme opinions – the opinions commonly accepted in practice by the most sensible of those with whom I

---

4. In contrast, and expanding on Gueroult's thesis, J. Vuillemin argues that the Cartesian order of reasons distinguishes itself from the formal ordering (defined as 'an interlinked set of propositions deduced from a given number of primitive propositions'), since the first order is 'essentially *irreversible* and, despite the fact that the primitive propositions are posited as necessarily true, the relation of entailment which they give rise to does not allow one to consider the derived propositions as equivalent to them, or to invert their order. This order is therefore regarded by Descartes as *absolute*.' It will suffice here to note that even if this were to be correct, which is not altogether certain (at least in this absolutely rigid form), it is not conclusive. The irreversibility in the order of reasons does not in any sense prove its ontological substantiveness. The world may yet be a dream, though one founded on certain truths! In sum, Vuillemin's hypothesis might collapse when confronted with the *Dieu trompeur*. See 'Sur les propriétés formelles et matérielles de l'ordre cartésien des raisons', in *Études d'histoire de la philosophie en hommage à M. Gueroult*, Paris 1964, pp. 43–58.

should have to live';[5] 'My second maxim was to be as firm and decisive in my actions as I could, and to follow even the most doubtful opinions, once I had adopted them, with no less constancy than if they had been quite certain';[6] 'My third maxim was to try always to master myself rather than fortune, and change my desires rather than the order of the world. In general I would become accustomed to believing that nothing lies entirely within our power except our thoughts, so that after doing our best in dealing with matters external to us, whatever we fail to achieve is absolutely impossible so far as we are concerned'.[7]

There is no valorizing grasp of the world here; rather, what we have is the exclusion of all content, the exacerbation of the formal characteristics of decision. Of course, this formalism is ambiguous to the very extent that it wishes to be provisional – but is it really provisional? At the very least we can say that we are dealing with a 'provisionality' radicalized by the lack of desire for an alternative. In fact, no other path is indicated once the thinking I has emerged in its full-bodied metaphysical reality. This emergence stands opposed, purely and simply, to ethical rules, thereby excluding the possibility of actually intervening in them or modifying them. And it does not suffice to argue, despite what we have already said, that this framing of the moral problem is political, born from the call to respond to urgent requests deriving from the defeat suffered by the bourgeoisie, from the impossibility of drafting any kind of alternative.[8] What all this leads to is the further establishment,

5. PWD I 122.
6. PWD I 123.
7. PWD I 123. As regards the so-called 'fourth' rule of provisional morality, see the remarks by Ferdinand Alquié who, in his edition of Descartes's *Œuvres philosophiques* (vol. I, p. 587, n. 1), characterizes it in terms of a particular, rather than general, application, thereby expunging it.
8. It is typical in this regard that the rules are replete with observations relevant for tactics. This is the case, for instance, in the first rule, with its tactical function of refusal–acceptance of religious vows and civil contracts as immobilizing conditions in a situation   *cont'd over/*

rather than attenuation, of the provisional character of said morality – especially once we recall that the historical situation registered herein is precisely characterized by the social juxtaposition of bourgeois autonomy on the one hand, and of a repressive apparatus that does not desire its expansion on the other. Here lies the specificity of this morality, the ground of its metaphysical essentiality.

When the argument, having been moral, becomes expressly political, the marks of separation are intensified: if the individual is compelled to moral choices that in some sense affect being, he is so to a lesser degree in that social and political world which now represents itself as bewitched, as the true second nature standing before the I. Here there are fewer hindrances to the I separating itself than there are vis-à-vis the world in general. The attitude we already encountered in provisional morality is accentuated: do not change the order of the world, follow the more moderate ideas, obey. The sense of the present impossibility of an alternative becomes more pressing. Prescription follows the judgement of fact, and the latter presents, to the subject, a separation that tends to repeat in the political world the rigidity encountered in the natural world. Descartes describes the political world in the vocabulary of absolutism: a fully sovereign will, inscrutable in its majesty, which simply owes its capacity to legislate to its arbitrary power ('*Si veut le Roi, si veut la Loi*');[9] and this will is

8. *cont'd*   where nothing remains 'always in the same state'; and in the second rule with its praise of probability and its polemic against the 'weak and wobbling minds', all of which takes place within the framework of a firm assumption of the political responsibility of the moment, as corroborated by the original reprise of stoic motifs in the third rule.

9. See PWD III 23: '. . . it is God who has laid down these laws in nature just as a king lays down laws in his kingdom. There is no single one that we cannot grasp if our mind turns to consider it. They are all inborn in our minds just as a king would imprint his laws on the hearts of all his subjects if he had enough power to do so. The greatness of God, on the other hand, is something which we   *cont'd over/*

binding, we cannot avoid subordinating all social obligation to it.[10] The analogy between natural world and political world is so total in this phase that the two dimensions continuously exhibit their interchangeableness – in the form of metaphor.[11] After all, what can we juxtapose to that reality void of human meaning which is the political world, propped up as it is by the arbitrary will of the sovereign? Nothing, if we agree that the individual discovers his own true reality only through isolation. Every spontaneous

9. *cont'd*   cannot grasp even though we know it. But the very fact that we judge it beyond our grasp makes us esteem it the more greatly; just as a king has more majesty when he is less familiarly known by his subjects, provided of course that they do not get the idea that they have no king – they must know him enough to be in no doubt about that. It will be said that if God had established these truths he could change them as a king changes his laws . . .' Or again, just to pick one example among many: '. . . only sovereigns, or those authorized by them, have the right to concern themselves with regulating the morals of other people' (PWD III 326).

10. This is also the case for religious questions which, as is well known, represented a *punctum dolens* within the casuistry of civil obedience. There is no doubt that this is the case in Descartes: just as it is criminal to deem that one must be faithful to the Catholic king in countries not ruled by him, and seditious, even when clerics do so, to preach this (AT II 584), so it is legitimate to have contacts with persons of other religions when legitimate sovereigns allow it (AT VIII B 206). In any case, the principle of obedience to the absolute sovereign is for Descartes beyond dispute. For the seventeenth-century *robin* any doubt in this regard has been dispelled. (It is curious, and quite significant, to note how in the course of the *Entretien avec Burman*, p. 16, while speaking of the intellection–memory–meaning relation, Descartes proposes this immediate exemplification: '. . . hearing that the sound [*vocem*] R-E-X signifies supreme authority, I commit it to memory . . .'). See also PWD III 293–4.

11. For example, see AT I 45, AT III 353, PWD I 116–18. It is worth recalling that if the other side of the absolutist royal metaphor functions as a definition of divinity, nevertheless we are certainly not faced here with that 'constitutionalist god' (commanding on the basis of pre-given laws) discussed by B. Groethuysen, in *The Bourgeois: Catholicism vs. Capitalism in Eighteenth-Century France*, London 1968, and whose image is revisited by T. Gregory, *Gassendi*, pp. 64–5.

expression of freedom that impinges on and configures the world, that issues from the individual, is here excluded. *Usage* alone makes history, and this *usage*, together with its codification, falls under the exclusive consideration of the sovereign and represents his direct duty.[12] The themes of the science of the *politiques* are assumed and recur constantly in this phase of Descartes's work: a few comparisons[13] would suffice to prove how Descartes assumes not only the terminology but also the ideological referent of the discourse of the *politiques*. Even when we find ourselves confronted with assertions that seem to express an overt and optimistic natural law perspective, we should not be fooled. In the usage of the *politiques*, the rhetorical allusion to justice amounts to a legitimation of constituted power, the precise assertion that in politics value is a formal element: order versus mutiny and rebellion; legality (as some today would say instead of justice) against disorder.[14]

12. Only *usage* makes history (PWD I 116ff), perfects language (AT I 125–6) and science (PWD I 188–9). Only the sovereign can codify on the basis of *usage*: PWD I 117–18, 142; and PWD III 326 [TN: *usage* is in French in the original].

13. AT IV 78: this use is ironic but faithful to the tradition of '*coup d'État*'; AT V 232–3: the splendid metaphor of maritime life, of its dangers (including shipwrecks) in order to illustrate the life of sovereigns, and the great majesty of their risk . . . All of this simply by way of a very brief exemplification. We shall return to it. It is also worth noting the curious justification of the usage of Machiavellianism at AT VIII B 367.

14. In the *Lettre apologétique* (AT VIII B 224), we read the following: 'For there is nothing but Justice, which maintains States and Empires; and it is for love of her that the first men left the caves and the forests to build cities; and it is her alone which gives and maintains freedom; while, on the contrary, it is from the impunity of the guilty and the condemnation of the innocents that licence stems, which, as all politicians have observed, has always been the ruin of the Republic . . .' The rhetoric is justified: Descartes asks for absolution in the trial initiated by Voetius. It is interesting to note the thematic, worthy of a '*politique*': the reference to the passage from the state of nature to the civic state, the discussion of the ruin of republics (on which see also the nice passage at AT IV 438), and especially the precise conception of justice as a function of power with the aim of maintaining peace (see also the passage on the Utrecht '*mutination*' and the '*esprit rebelle de Voetius*', AT IV 27).

If we look at passages in which Descartes expresses opinions of a juridical or juridical–philosophical kind, the impression elicited by his political reflections is confirmed. Let us leave aside those assertions that represent simple remembrances of his past juridical studies[15] or rekindle memories of his career – and of social promotion through that career: 'I knew . . . that jurisprudence, medicine, and other sciences bring honours and riches to those who cultivate them'.[16] Wherever the consideration of juridical experience is deepened, we find the same acute pessimism that is also expressed by the echoes of the *politiques* in Descartes's argument. The law, when it is not simply a matter of prevailing,[17] is understood as a social 'rule of the game', a rhetorical ploy and tactical manoeuvre. It too presupposes a social world devoid of human truth, a separate world made up of arbitrarily moved relations. The only guarantee is the formal value accorded to the respect for and application of the law.[18] Even when, in the last phase of his thought, Descartes attempts to provide new, more

15. For example, AT III 156 (for a question germane to the Stampioen–Waessenaer affair); AT III 158–9 (for the reference to Justinian). In general, for the juridical studies undertaken by Descartes, see H. Gouhier, *Essais*, pp. 253ff. On Descartes's juridical–philosophical thinking, the essential texts are Alessandro Levi, 'L'influence de l'esprit cartésien dans le droit. Ses avantages et ses limites', *Congrès Descartes, Études cartésiennes*, vol. III, pp. 49–54, and V. Giorgianni, 'Ripercussioni filosofico–giuridiche dello studio delle passioni in Cartesio' and 'Intuizioni giuspolitiche di Renato Descartes', *Sophia*, vol. 17, 1949, pp. 254–8, 334–50. These authors correctly downplay Descartes's contribution to juridical philosophy.
16. PWD I 113.
17. On law conceived as rules of the game, see AT IV 438. In the midst of the quarrel with Fermat there appears in Descartes's correspondence a series of juridical metaphors which are charged with considerable scepticism, see AT II 321, 335, PWD III 123. Following the popular manner, the techniques of lawyers, juridical promises, etc. – the law in other words – are considered not as an instrument of justice but as an instrument of confusion.
18. The *Lettre apologétique* (AT VIII B) is a monument to legalism. Among other things, it reveals a remarkably astute procedural and legal awareness in Descartes. For example, Descartes *cont'd over/*

humanly meaningful formulations,[19] one will always find the formal value of order, the negative guarantee required by the *politique* as the ultimate horizon of reference.

18. *cont'd*   continuously questions the lack of jurisdiction over him on the part of the Utrecht magistrates (214–15). He nevertheless frames his defence in terms belonging to the juridical science of his time: the reasons for the justice of his cause and the injustice of his enemies (202–3). He turns the accusation of libel against his adversary, since Voetius has demonstrated that he 'wanders in uncertainty' rather than showing, as the law prescribes, the 'certain crime' in Descartes, thereby leaving himself open to retort (255). He appeals to the international law protecting him (*passim*), and so on. There are passages, like the following – which is both a substantial and procedural moment and an incredibly refined lawyerly artifice – in which the priestly conscience and the tradition of the *robin* manifest themselves in an indubitable manner: 'In a situation where the presumptions are contrary to the proofs, there is good reason to be very circumspect before determining anything. But here the proofs are so clear and so certain . . . that one would be obliged to believe them, even if the presumptions were contrary. But in any case the presumptions entirely accord with the proofs . . .' (264). Another passage which reveals an elevated legal conscience is the following: 'Because the particulars have no right to demand the blood, honour, or possessions of their enemies; it is enough that they be put out of interest, as far as it is possible for the Judges: the rest does not concern them, but only the public' (225). Analogous remarks may be found in the *Epistula ad P. Dinet*, AT VII 602.

19. An explicit call to equity against the admittedly just rigour of royal justice may be found in a couple of letters from the end of 1646 and beginning of 1647, which Descartes sends to influential friends to plead for clemency with regard to a farmer accused of murder (AT V 262–7; AT X 613–17). See G. Cohen, *Ecrivains français*, pp. 589–90, and V. Giorgianni, 'Ripercussioni'. Having registered this preoccupation of Descartes regarding a substantial moment in the administration of justice it nevertheless seems frankly impossible to include Descartes within the current of natural law. As A. Levi has correctly noted against Bishara Tabbakh (*Du heurt à l'harmonie des droits*, Paris 1936, pp. 67–102), if there is a relationship between the Cartesian doctrine and the doctrine of natural law, it does not concern the a priori method as much as the individualist conception. In this regard, I think it suffices to add a single reference: 'I have never written or taken the view that the mind requires innate ideas which are something distinct from its own faculty of thinking' (*Notae in programma*, PWD I 303).

Insistence on order and the discourse of the *politique* – these are the two key elements. The *Discourse on the Method* thus contains a conception of the social horizon which is just as negative – privative, one might say, and derealized – as its vision of the natural world. So is the emergence of the I in the *Discourse* a metaphysical accident? Perhaps. But this accidental character must not lead us to view such an emergence as ineffectual, nor the situation as closed to further thematic investigation.[20] Quite the reverse, it is precisely from this point, which at first was perhaps psychologically irrelevant but is nonetheless essential, that an internal imbalance in Cartesian thought begins to spread – that imbalance whose problematization was the only possible source of new syntheses. The painful insufficiency of the bewitched world is increasingly felt; the juxtaposition of the I and the world seems static, incapable of providing any answers to the problem that has arisen ever since the moment of the crisis. The manifestation of this insufficiency is equally evident at the level of natural philosophy and of social philosophy. But for an exit from this impasse to be possible, it was necessary for Cartesian thought to return to that scientific research in which the dimension of derealized being showed itself with maximum intensity.

In 1638, Descartes is involved in a harsh polemic with Fermat and the circle of the new Parisian mathematicians.[21] The initial

20. Some have insisted, with different motivations but substantially analogous results, on the definitive character of this Cartesian position vis-à-vis the political world and the problems of society. See K. T. Budderberg, 'Descartes und der politische Absolutismus', *Archiv für Rechts- und Sozialphilosophie*, vol. 30, 1936, pp. 541ff. And L. G. Castella, *Las ideas politicas en Descartes*, in *Homenaje en el tercer centenario del Discurso de Método*, vol. III, Buenos Aires 1937, pp. 73–88.

21. Aside from Fermat, the other mathematicians are – to mention only the most famous names: Etienne Pascal, Mydorge, Hardy, Roberval, des Argues, the *abbé* Chambon, Petit . . . The mediator and inciter of the polemic is, of course, Mersenne. On the inception of the polemic, see AT I 354–63, 463–74. For the invariably malevolent attitude of Descartes toward his Parisian readers, see AT I 502: 'Besides, I fear there is still no one who has entirely grasped the meaning of the things I have written. However, I do not think this has   *cont'd over/*

argument revolves around the *Dioptrics* but soon the polemic encompasses the whole Cartesian foundation of mathematical knowledge of the natural world.[22] What the Parisian mathematicians fight – apart from questions of calculus and the many polemical pretexts whose identification Roberval particularly excels in (for Descartes, in any case, they are all 'spiteful characters whose aim is anything but the truth')[23] – is the metaphysical residuum of Cartesian geometrism, the Renaissance illusions and remembrances that continuously re-emerge within it. We have already seen how – precisely in order to respond to that need for philosophical mediation whose urgency is ever present – the rigour of Cartesian thought, which tends to lean towards geometrization, sometimes faltered, dissipating itself in the reprise of positions of heterogeneous provenance.[24] The criticisms now accentuate the need for a clarification, not so much a need for an elaboration of Cartesian geometrism, or for a fuller appropriation of the derealized figure of the world, but for a liberation of this figure from any reservation or alibi – all of which have become frankly unsustainable. And that is what happens. We could say that the polemic with the Parisian mathematicians is framed by a before and an after, which are precisely identified by this Cartesian exclamation: 'But to require me to give geometrical demonstrations on a topic that depends on physics is to ask me to do the impossible'.[25] Descartes still sees a physical horizon that is irreducible to mere geometricization, a horizon that for some of its features still rests on a metaphysical foundation. Is this position in contradiction

21. *cont'd*   happened on account of the obscurity of my words, but rather because they seemed quite easy, and no one stopped to consider everything they contain'.
22. The texts of the first polemic (i.e. the one that interests us here) are basically the following: AT II 1–33, 81–196, 307–43, 352–62, 406–7 and *passim.*
23. PWD III 89.
24. See above, chapter 2, section 3, about the physicist writings of the 1630s, and section 4 about the fifth part of the *Discours.*
25. AT II 142 (27 May 1638).

with the fundamental tendency of his thought? He is not slow to recognize that this is the case: 'my entire physics is nothing but geometry.'[26] This then is the result of the polemic with the Parisian mathematicians, a result which is of course due more to Descartes's impatience with criticisms than with the value of the latter (which, incidentally, are in some cases right on the mark). The outcome of the polemic is due more to the need of Descartes's thought to develop itself than to the presence of an adequate alternative as expressed by the Parisian mathematicians. But all of a sudden we see that the elimination of a host of equivocal elements still weighing down the geometrical conception of the world impedes any possibility of stasis for this thought and forces, by way of counterpoint, philosophical thought to face up to the demands and tendencies that shape it – no longer through shortcuts but rigorously. Only at this point, by appearing – under the pressure of its adversaries' polemic – in all its clarity, does the bewitched world of Cartesian geometrism enter the crisis in a subjective sense as well. The more the world is derealized, the more unbearable becomes the tension with regard to that sole point of reality that is the solitary emergence of the 'I think'. Not by chance, in the same letter in which Descartes declares the reduction of physics to geometry there appears the announcement of a new Latin treatise on the proofs for the existence of God:[27] the work on the *Meditations* has begun. The tension had become unbearable, and every alibi or defence against the need to face up to the gravity of the problem impossible. The crisis was so profound that it led to a final, necessary resolution: 'But please do not wait for anything from me in Geometry; for you know that for a long time I have remonstrated that I no longer wish to practice it,

26. AT II 268 (27 July 1638). On the same day, besides the letter to Mersenne, Descartes also sends off a formal letter of pacification to Fermat (AT II 280–2). But the declaration is not formal, so much so that it will be repeated to demonstrate an acquired awareness, on the part of Descartes, of the nature of his physics (see for example PWD III 135: '. . . although my entire physics is nothing but mechanics . . .').

27. AT II 267 (27 July 1638).

and I think I can honestly have done with it'.[28] Only metaphysics, only the elaboration of that moment that had hitherto seemed accidental, could allow the overcoming of this crisis. Perhaps it could even allow the establishment of a true relationship with the world.[29]

If, at the level of the inquiry into the natural world, the geometric image went into crisis – to the extent that it freed itself from any inhibition – and imposed the need to resolve the scission inherited from the *Discourse on the Method*, this awareness was no less present in Descartes's relationship to the world of politics. It did not take long for the historical concreteness of the problem behind the abstract formality of the issues to be revealed. Besides, was not the debate between Descartes and the Parisian mathematicians already in some way relevant for political experience? It suffices to consider – as Descartes himself remarks[30] –

28. AT II 361–2 (12 September 1638).
29. Perhaps we should downplay the opposition between, on the one hand, the theses of Alquié (as reiterated in Descartes's *Œuvres philosophiques*, vol. II, p. 7) on the centrality of metaphysical speculation in this phase from 1638 to 1640, and, on the other, those of Garin (*Opere*, vol. I, p. cxiv) on the primacy, in the same period, of physics – whereby Descartes elaborates his metaphysics 'almost as though to guarantee the orthodoxy, or at the very least the neutrality, of his physics'. The two disciplines play alternating roles in the clarification of the meaning of Descartes's investigation.
30. See AT II 28 on the high social standing of his interlocutors. On the life of the scientific societies of the 1600s, the Parisian ones in particular, and on the exceedingly high degree of political and state integration that may be observed in them, see R. Bray, *La formation de la doctrine classique en France*, Paris 1927; J. De Boer, 'Men's Literary Circles in Paris (1610–1660)', *Modern Language Association of America, Publications*, vol. 53, 1938, pp. 730–80; M. Ornstein, *The Role of the Scientific Societies in the Seventeenth Century*, Chicago 1938; H. Busson, *La religion des classiques (1660–1685)*, Paris 1948; P. Barrière, *La vie intellectuelle en France. Du XVIe siècle à l'époque contémporaine*, Paris 1961; as well as several interesting remarks in G. Bollème, J. Ehrard, F. Furet, D. Roche, J. Roger, *Livre et société dans la France du XVIIIe siècle*, Paris and The Hague 1965. We shall have several opportunities to return to this argument.

alongside the high social standing of his interlocutors, the public lineaments of the polemic, as it impinged on the public function of science and thus on the alternative between the political options that can be discerned within this public function. But, beyond these indirect references, there remains the fact that the bewitched world, hitherto depicted geometrically, exhibits an immediately significant political aspect. It expresses the most intense moment of the crisis between civil society and the state, the moment of maximum separation, of the starkest dualism. The absolute state is really a second nature, acting mechanically, a pure legality founded on the majestic inscrutability of the sovereign act. But what about civil society? What about the bourgeoisie that expressed itself within it, defeated but forced actively to affirm its own existence? It expressed nothing, save for its insuppressible existence and autonomy – of that we are certain. But for how long is this static duality, this closed juxtaposition, possible? The crisis of the geometric world, the process of the liberation of the I from the accidentality in which it was enclosed, could not but be felt here too. Here, as elsewhere, the articulation of the I–world relationship imposed itself. Perhaps it even did so with greater urgency, certainly with a desperate urge towards the definition of a human meaning for social life. The metaphysical accidentality of the I, left over from the *Discourse on the Method*, had to be overcome.

2

So there is in this phase of Descartes's work a need to overcome the separation of the I, to restore the relation between man and world, and to remove the accidentality of metaphysical emergence. But how can this requirement be fulfilled? How can the dissatisfaction and disquiet produced by the insufficiency of the existing frame of reference be assuaged?

We now confront a decisive turning point in the development of Descartes's thought: the spontaneity of the opposition of the I to the world must be organized, the weight of isolation – and insecurity – removed. However, Descartes lives in a world that has already given a general answer to the problems of the epoch, which, in the context of a comprehensive choice (negative, against naturalism and humanism; positive, for peace as a self-sufficient value), accepts radical dualism and organizes it into the scientific and political philosophy of mechanicism. This choice is not sensitive to the conditions for an overcoming, indeed it abhors the very idea. Descartes lives in this world of *robins* which, ever since he refused and fought the libertine alternative, fixed that dualism into its ideology. He even participates in it from afar, from his Dutch exile. He now seeks to positively force this world to bend to the demands of the material growth of the bourgeois stratum – not in order to break it, but to overcome and contest it. When the mechanicists attack the libertines it is not in order to regain a horizon for the free development of the class, but in order to compel everyone to the realistic awareness of the crisis and the hard, demanding advance into separate existence. 'The Politicians do not regard man in an abstraction of Metaphysics, but rather consider him in the offices of civic life . . .'[31]

Besides, the anti-libertine campaign that develops at the beginning of the 1620s, whose victims are Vanini and Théophile de Viau, and whose 'heroes' are the Jesuit Garasse and the Minim friar Mersenne, had goals that were far more political than apologetic. Indeed, the campaign developed, through the alliance between parliaments and royal power, in order to strengthen this historical bloc and to remove any possibility of a political alternative to the cultured bourgeois strata. It was a provocation that soon turned into a witch hunt,[32] using the martyrdom of Vanini

---

31. For the bibliography, allow me to refer the reader once again to my 'Problemi dello stato moderno: Francia 1610–1650'. The quoted sentence is from D. de Prierac, *Discours politiques*, 1652 (p. 59 in the 1666 edition).

32. Like every witch hunt it also has its moments of farce, as when, between 1623 and 1625, the rumour spreads of a Rosicrucian invasion of Paris. On this 'comic interlude' see R. Lenoble, *cont'd over/*

and Théophile to impose the wide-ranging awareness of the necessity of the established political order.[33] Its watchword was not only that of the elimination of the resistance to absolutism that was exercised in the name of humanism, but also that of active allegiance to the regime – championing it as the right and adequate regime for the epoch. First-generation libertinism, which was still vaguely naturalist and pantheist, was labelled a subversive ideology.[34] If libertinism still wished to exist, it would have to transform itself, as we have seen, into an attitude of evasion, becoming the concern of very restricted circles. Inversely, dualistic mechanicism turned into state ideology: it no longer represented a nostalgia for the revolutionary past of the bourgeois class, but the adherence to a situation of defeat, the structural conformity of absolutism to bourgeois separation and crisis. In short, there's no more use for the nostalgia of a good that has been destroyed, here we find instead the guarantee of peace, the positiveness of living in peace.

Does Descartes perhaps wish to contest this ideology, to counter it with a reformist hope, regaining a horizon in which separation is absent and the longing for a full, revolutionary life of the Renaissance bourgeoisie is thus renewed in its fundamental values? This question seems somewhat paradoxical if we recall the following statement by Descartes: 'I cannot approve of those meddlesome and restless characters who, called neither by birth nor by fortune to the management of public affairs, are yet forever thinking up some new reform'.[35] Moreover, this is a statement that reveals the influence of an incredibly weighty tradition. As

32. *cont'd*   *Mersenne*, pp. 30–1; it was already remarked in H. Busson, *De Charron à Pascal*, pp. 110–13. The confusion must indeed have been great if Mersenne himself was suspected of belonging to the sect!

33. J. S. Spink, *French Free-thought*, pp. 3–7, 43–7; A. Adam, *Les libertins*, pp. 7–31.

34. R. Lenoble, *Mersenne*, pp. 83–163, 168–99; T. Gregory, *Gassendi*, p. 52 and *passim* (showing in what way Gassendi was implicated by Mersenne in the polemic against Fludd: nevertheless, Lenoble does not seem entirely aware of the political problem underlying this polemic).

35. PWD I 118.

Montaigne had cautioned, particular defects cannot be cured with universal confusion. It is like curing patients with death.[36] And the *Tiers Etat*, in that last assembly of the French estates, quashing the hopes of renewal that some had entertained after the death of Henry IV, proclaimed:

> That to arrest the course of the pernicious doctrine introduced a few years ago against divinely established kings and sovereign powers by seditious spirits who only tend to trouble and subvert them, the king will be beseeched to establish in the Assembly of his Estates, by the fundamental law of the realm, which is inviolable and known to all, that there is no power whatsoever on earth, whether spiritual or temporal, which has any rights over his Kingdom to deprive it of the persons of our Kings, nor to dispense or absolve their subjects from the fidelity and obedience they owe to them, on the grounds of any cause or pretext. That all subjects, whatever their quality or condition, will hold this law to be sacred and true in conformity with the word of God.[37]

36. Montaigne, *Essais*, vol. III, ch. 9, in *Œuvres complètes*.
37. The text of the declaration of the *Tiers* may be found in Isambert, *Recueil général des anciennes lois françaises*, vol. XVI, Paris 1829, p. 54. On this famous declaration of the Third Estate, which represents a fundamental moment in the characterization of the political relations that found French absolutism, see P. Blet, 'L'article du Tiers aux Etats Généraux de 1614', *Revue d'histoire moderne et contemporaine*, vol. 10, 1955, pp. 81–106 (this is a superb example of Jesuitical historiography and historical blindness: the article of the *Tiers*, according to this interpretation, would be nothing but an episode in the anti-Jesuitical conspiracy of the bourgeoisie, and leading this conspiracy we would find, among others, Arnauld himself!); but especially S. Mastellone, *La reggenza di Maria de' Medici*, Messina and Florence 1962, pp. 169–70 (an excellent treatment) and R. Mousnier, *L'assassinat d'Henri IV, 14 mai 1610*, Paris 1964, pp. 246ff. In a more general vein, but still interesting over and above its apologetic attitude, A. Thierry, *Essai sur l'histoire de la formation et des progrès du Tiers Etat*, 3rd ed., vol. I, Paris 1856, ch. VII.

Guez de Balzac, long-time friend of Descartes and one of the advocates of the new sixteenth-century lifestyle, does not hesitate to exclaim (or to repeat?): 'when our young friend will have lived as long as we have, he will have no better opinion than we do of those who wish to reform the world. Let him read the Histories of all the Centuries, he will see that this reforming zeal has always given birth to new disorders rather than bringing an end to the old ones'.[38] Moreover, in the very same years that Descartes conceives his *Method*, Richelieu condenses the science of the *politiques* in a *Testament* which is also a pitiless condemnation of any Renaissance hope and an exaltation of the necessity and stability of the new political order.[39]

38. J. L. Guez de Balzac, *Œuvres*, vol. I, Paris 1665, pp. 762 and 218. See also the cited volumes by Sutcliffe and R. von Albertini. Naturally, there is an embarrassment of riches in Balzac when it comes to passages that move within this horizon of ideas.

39. Cardinal de Richelieu, *Testament politique*, ed. L. André, Paris 1947. Regarding the dating (beginning with 1634) and the authenticity, following a century-long polemic, of this text, the decisive contributions are those of R. Mousnier, 'Le testament politique de Richelieu', *Revue historique*, vol. 201, 1949, pp. 55–71, and E. Hassinger, 'Das politische Testament Richelieu', *Historische Zeitschrift*, vol. 173, 1952, pp. 485–503. Many voices have been raised against the old conceptions (W. Mommsen, 'Richelieu als Staatsman', *Historische Zeitschrift*, vol. 127, 1923, pp. 210–42; W. Andreas, *Kardinal Richelieu*, Göttingen 1958): see in particular, besides Hassinger, S. Skalweit, 'Richelieus Staatsidee', *Geschichte in Wissenschaft und Unterricht*, vol. 2, 1951, pp. 719–30, and especially the fundamental article by F. Dickmann, 'Rechtsgedanke und Machtpolitik bei Richelieu. Studien an neu entdecken Quellen', *Historische Zeitschrift*, vol. 196, 1963, pp. 265–319. These texts develop the idea – already present in the less metaphysical pages of Friedrich Meinecke's *Machiavellism: The Doctrine of Raison d'Etat and its Place in Modern History*, New Brunswick 1998 – that this was an effective, albeit desperate, attempt to rationalize the will and the power of the state, to render it juridical. Such a thesis singularly resonates with our own hypothesis: in effect this rationalization of power, even though it develops in an entirely negative manner, derives precisely from the new class equilibrium that the absolute state realizes – it is the substitute for freedom and truth where they cannot make the state their own. In this sense, it is something more, and especially something other, than the desperate, irrational and fleeting libertine conception of power.

That is the situation. So what is to be done? Descartes cannot and does not wish to accept all this. From the *Discourse*, from the labour and discussion that followed it, there emerges an ineluctable demand to find a terrain for overcoming the situation. It is certainly true that Descartes himself is placed within the structure of power,[40] within that new configuration of stability that had issued from the Renaissance crisis. He is placed within it for reasons to do with family tradition,[41] and because of intense political,[42] social,[43] and cultural[44] allegiances. It is not by chance

40. From this point of view, more than from any other, one should continue to reject pictures such as the one presented by M. Leroy in his *Philosophe au masque*, as well as in *Descartes social*, Paris 1931, where the figure of the conspirator is even joined by the one of the Saint-Simonian engineer. In truth, Descartes is a *robin*, a man of the 1600s, and nothing else besides.

41. See above, ch. 1, notes no. 166ff. We should keep in mind that Descartes's family, on both sides, includes Breton parliamentarians. Now, it is precisely the Parliament of Brittany that will become one of the strongholds of the Richelieu family, and, above all, of the Cardinal.

42. Simply to give a few examples: with Richelieu and his clan (AT I 500–1, II 151, III 388), with Séguier (AT I 364), etc. Furthermore, as his correspondence reveals, Descartes is quite informed about the political events of his time, despite the coolness he sometimes affects. See AT III 582, V 47–8, 183–4, PWD III 367–8. Especially in his last period of stay in Holland, thanks to the friendship of the diplomat Brasset, Descartes will be able to obtain more exhaustive information on political events. As for the rare judgements he gives, they nevertheless represent frequently banal, and invariably conformist, considerations.

43. Descartes's friendships in the milieus of the high bureaucracy *de robe* are innumerable. See, simply by way of example, AT IV 396. In the last period of Descartes's life these friendships will grow and deepen.

44. As regards Descartes's more specifically cultural friendships – if it is indeed possible to distinguish them from the others (which it is not, given the strong class character of the *robin* culture) – it is also true of them that they are extraordinarily wide-ranging. Balzac, Silhon, Huygens – to mention only some among the more significant 'men of culture', strictly speaking, of his time – are in more or less continuous contact with Descartes. But in the Sorbonne too Descartes is not without friends. See PWD III 169, just to pick an example. We should also keep in mind the relationship, continuous in spite of everything, with the Company of Jesus (some of whose representatives are linked to Descartes by kinship).

that his story will immediately be represented as part of the legend of the period: it is in La Rochelle, under the walls of the besieged city, that Descartes's vocation would have revealed itself to Bérulle![45] And mechanicism is the most congruous expression of the period, if not of its fable. It is the true public philosophy of constituted power. Despite all this, Descartes's thought cannot and does not wish to be reduced to mechanicism.

Of course, Descartes follows very closely the development of the natural philosophy of mechanicism. The long epistolary relationship with Mersenne is not only an isolated man's search for interlocutors; it also represents an encounter with a well-determined environment, that of the new official philosophy, that of the authors of mechanicism. Descartes can thus appreciate the response of mechanicism to some among the deepest demands of the century: the demand for method and the critique of the principle of authority; the critique of the qualitative physics of the Aristotelian school and the foundation of the new physics as a science of movement; the rigorous elaboration of the principle of the new physics in all fields, accompanied by an ample capacity for experimentation. But in what direction was all this going? Let us consider for example the set of writings that Mersenne published in 1634 and which constitute his own 'discourse on method'.[46] On the one hand, we find there the attack on the principle of authority, the denunciation (and positive distortion) of the *déception* to which the Scholastic tradition and naturalism had led science, the exaltation of the rational principle of proof as the exclusive criterion of science; on the other hand, the horizon within which is situated the methodical schema of the reconstruction of the real is entirely formal. Mathematics and science in general are sciences of the possible, wholly cut off from any metaphysical attachment, or even from being connected back to the schemata of a demonstrative physics: ideas, far from

---

45. The legend of Borel is recounted, as we have already seen, in AT X 35.
46. R. Lenoble, *Mersenne*, pp. 366ff. See also Lenoble's bibliography.

constituting just any universal horizon, are simple constitutive functions of experience. Mersenne's is really 'the discourse on method of empiricism', a flattening of essence onto existence.[47] The same can be said about the scientific project proposed by the other great mechanicist author, Gassendi: a *pars destruens* (which, in its use of sceptical motifs, finds the strength to develop itself with equal efficacy against Aristotle, against the naturalism of Fludd and the spiritualism of Cherbury) and a reconstructive part (a new theory of empiricism) follow one another in his thought. These two aspects are tightly held together and co-present in Gassendi, such that scepticism here really finds itself playing the role of father to the new science and empiricism appears as always regulated by the sceptical mistrust of any universalistic claim.[48] In truth, however, a profound instability constantly haunts the philosophy of mechanicism. It does so precisely to the extent that this philosophy is born in its articulation with scepticism and thereby presents itself as a moment of rupture, as a countervailing force to the erosion of Renaissance naturalism – which nevertheless remains the object of nostalgia inasmuch as it is experienced as the originary site of every modern problematic. Mechanicism both suffers this nostalgia and rejects it. It rejects it in so far as it suffers it. And it does so ostentatiously: in the works of the authors of mechanicism the critical and destructive part is by far greater than the reconstructive one, and their work

47. R. Lenoble, *Mersenne*, pp. 346–64. Against Lenoble, see E. Gilson, *Etudes*, pp. 40–6.
48. T. Gregory, *Gassendi, passim* in the first part of his book, but especially pp. 121–8 (to summarize, Gregory manages to define rather exhaustively the intrinsic communion between empiricism and scepticism in Gassendi's thought, showing how, compared with traditional erudite scepticism, Gassendi's scepticism succeeds in becoming a scientific problem), pp. 181–2 (on the function of scepticism with regard to empiricism, forbidding any positivistic metaphysical issue for the latter). But see also, on the topic of Gassendi's peculiar empiricism, R. Lenoble, *Mersenne*, pp. 328–9; J. S. Spink, *French Free-thought*, pp. 85–102; R. H. Popkin, *The History of Scepticism*, pp. 102–10, 143–9.

remains fundamentally a work of philosophical critique rather than a proposal for scientific research.[49] How they differ from the Renaissance authors who coupled the perspective of an often equivocal natural philosophy with a triumphal capacity for scientific experience! And from that very Baconian hope, to which mechanism often refers, of a unitary reorganization of science and experience!

Furthermore, the fact that mechanism is dominated by the sense of the defeat of humanist hope, that it conforms to the resulting situation of conscious acceptance of irredeemable separation, is demonstrated by the ethical and political theory of these authors. That process of mere transposition to the political level of the naturalist image, which we have already seen in Descartes – albeit in an unstable, ambiguous and above all subjectively insufficient way – is here fully operative. If moral laws exist in the social world in the same way that natural ones exist in their own domain, that is, as orders whose divine foundation is inscrutable ('Royal power is sacrosanct, commanded by Divinity, the principal work of His providence, the masterpiece of His hands, the living image of His sublime majesty, and proportionate to His immense greatness'), then it is not in any way possible to challenge or break them. Social order is comprehensively guaranteed by the divinity and this is straightaway translated into an apology for the existent order and a promise to act in its context. Such is the case with Mersenne.[50] And it is the same with Gassendi, for whom social order is already conceived as a transfer of rights from the individual to authority, and as a confirmation of

49. Popkin was not mistaken to underscore vigorously the sceptical component in the thinking of these authors. Neither did Spink err in underlining how many elements of Renaissance naturalism, both implicit and explicit, endure within their systems (regarding Gassendi, Spink speaks of a hylozoist conception of nature).

50. R. Lenoble, *Mersenne*, pp. 547–51. The passage cited above is from A. Duchesne, *Les Antiquitez et Recherches de la Grandeur et Majesté des Roys de France*, Paris 1609, p. 126.

those rights by that transfer, that renunciation.[51] It is important to insist on this point because it really represents the core of a diffuse and hegemonic conception, whose radicality is extremely significant. We could say that the social contract is confirmed by the contract of power, by the emergence of the priority of the values of order and authority vis-à-vis rights. It is another and more dynamic way of saying what the juridical conception of sovereignty already says: 'Sovereignty is no more divisible than the point in Geometry'.[52] Above all, it is a way of saying that the bourgeoisie has abandoned the claim to participate in sovereignty, and that as civil society it therefore expects the guarantee of its right from a transcendent and separate sovereignty.[53] The most extreme dualism thus intervenes in order to qualify the theoretical terrain on which the analysis is developed.

It is not worth recalling the original reasons of this whole attitude by returning to the crisis of the Renaissance experience: all of that should be clear by now. Better instead to emphasize that positive moment which these mechanicist philosophies manage to express despite the severe impact of the crisis. That is, the attempt to rationalize the form of the state, albeit in separation, and the propensity to see it as an efficiently operating machine, i.e. as mechanical.[54] We encounter here, acting implicitly, the awareness

51. Concerning Gassendi's political thought I refer the reader to the reflections and annotated bibliography in my 'Problemi dello stato moderno: Francia 1610–1650'.

52. Cardin Le Bret, *De la souveraineté du Roy*, Paris 1632, p. 71.

53. On the fundamental relationship between *Herrschaftsvertrag* and *Gesellschaftsvertrag*, see W. Näf, *Staat und Staatsgedanke. Vorträge zur neuren Geschichte*, Bern 1935. In general, on the political thought of the period, beyond the already cited and fundamental Albertini, see the modest (and often incorrect), albeit useful book by W. J. Stankiewicz, *Politics and Religion in Seventeenth-Century France: A Study of Political Ideas from the Monarchomachs to Bayle, as Reflected in the Toleration Controversy*, Berkeley and Los Angeles 1960.

54. For a general bibliography on the new form of the machine-state see my 'Problemi dello stato moderno: Francia 1610–1650' (especially regarding the fundamental theses by Chabod, Näf, *cont'd over/*

of a hegemony of the bourgeois form of social existence – at other times far more powerful, now forced into isolation but here, in defeat, nevertheless capable of imposing on the separate state the form of its own way of producing and existing.[55] The dramatic experience of crisis in the wars of religion that science had registered is now partly redeemed by the intuition of an insuppressible social role which, even in defeat, it is up to the

54. *cont'd*   Mousnier, Hartung, etc.). See also the writings collected by H. Lubasz, *The Development of the Modern State*, New York and London 1964. More directly, on the specific form of government in the period under consideration, see J. King, *Science and Rationalism in the Government of Louis XIV: 1661–1683*, Baltimore 1949; R. Mousnier, *Les Règlements du Conseil du Roi sous Louis XIII*, Paris 1949; O. A. Ranum, *Richelieu and the Councillors of Louis XIII: A Study of the Secretaries of State and Superintendents of Finance in the Ministry of Richelieu (1635–1642)*, Oxford 1963. R. Mousnier, *passim*, but especially in his essay 'Comment les Français voyaient la France au XVIIe siècle', *XVIIe Siècle*, vols 25–6, 1955, warns us against what he regards as excesses in the consideration of the rationalization of the state, which he thinks is far more limited than is commonly believed, and part of a far longer process of development. The work of King would exemplify the kind of errors that may be incurred in this field. Now, it is obvious that some measure is needed, but it is equally true that the kind of measure prescribed by Mousnier is itself excessive. In effect, as Ranum has stated, we are faced with a 'radical modification of institutions', and, as has been noted by R. Maspétiol ('Les deux aspects de la raison d'Etat et son apologie au début du XVIIe siècle', *Archives de Philosophie du Droit*, vol. 10, 1965, pp. 209–20), we are perhaps also confronted with an open awareness of this fact.

55. A good treatment of this question can be found in F. Borkenau, *Der Uebergang vom feudalen zum bürgerlichen Weltbild*, and R. Schnur, *Individualismus und Absolutismus, passim*. Regarding Schnur, it must be noted that his correct interpretation of the phase of bourgeois crisis nevertheless fails to identify the particular type of ideological productivity that the bourgeoisie manifests in the same period. Arguably, this limit is also shared by R. von Albertini, *Das politische Denken*, which nonetheless contains exemplary passages on the character and effects of the crisis. See p. 198: 'The bourgeoisie knows itself to be weak and asks above all for a strong state power to defend it both from the restlessness of the nobles and from revolts from below. This is required also for the state's support of manufacture and commerce'; p. 204: freedom has value only if it is integrated into the life of the state, 'not freedom but order is the decisive value'.

bourgeoisie to play. The reprise and renewal of Bodinian positions, so frequent in this part of the century,[56] and the acceptance,
for lack of alternatives, of absolutism, is thus accompanied by an
insistence on the class existence of the bourgeoisie as a socially
hegemonic force. Hegemonic, but separate. Hegemonic, but
hindered from reducing the gap between its own social existence
and political domination. That is the political lesson of mechanicism, which is as far from libertine evasions as it is incapable of
critically posing the problem of dualism. Mechanicism does not
see any alternatives to the twofold task it has taken on: to affirm an
autonomous conception of the world while being aware of the
absence of any prospect of a unitary reassumption of the universe.

Descartes opposes mechanicism on this ground: not because
Cartesian thought is at this point – at the end of the experience of
the *Discourse on the Method* – capable of indicating a viable path
for the reconstruction of the link between antagonistic moments
of reality; but because the tension suffered by the I–world relation
as defined in the *Discourse on the Method* calls for, demands, this
overcoming of mechanicism. Besides, what are the consequences
of the mechanicist stance? How long can one maintain this refusal

56. 'The importance of Bodin for the theoretical formation of French
    absolutism and therefore, in a wider sense, for the formation of state
    consciousness in the seventeenth century is extraordinary', we read in
    R. von Albertini, pp. 35–6. Note what the author adds on pp. 85–91:
    the desire for peace, at the beginning of the century, also turns against
    the right of resistance; Bodin (in the preface to his *Republic*) already
    prefers 'the strongest tyranny' to 'licentious anarchy', and this Bod-
    inian teaching is very widespread in the century. We should also keep
    in mind how in Bodin's thought the necessity of arriving at these
    results – the emptying out of the meaning of political value, its
    formalization – must pass through a nominalist type of logic which
    he inherits from the Ramist tradition. See K. D. McRae, 'Ramist
    Tendencies in the Thought of Jean Bodin', *Journal of the History of
    Ideas*, vol. 16, 1955, pp. 306–23. There is an analogous relation,
    despite the different cultural sources, between nominalism and scepti-
    cism, on the one hand, and scepticism and political relativism, on the
    other, among the mechanicists.

to relate to one another these two moments of reality which are so obviously dialectically defined? Descartes is keenly aware of the insufficiency of a dualism of the mechanicist type. Its ineluctable tendency to be dissolved either into a mere dogmatism of formal reason or into a blind empiricism unfolds before his eyes.

He sees his friend Silhon[57] as following the first path: a renewal of a mystically inclined Platonism, the hypostasis of dualism in the order of divinity – and authority. This is nothing but the suppression of the problem![58] And it is not in Silhon alone that this takes place. The attempt to eliminate the dramatic tenor of the I–world struggle, even if no longer as a problem of philosophical theodicy but as an ascetic, religious problem – the attempt to corroborate within history the search for a divinity (once the mediation of the ecclesiastical magisterium has disappeared), of reconstructing a path of personal salvation and quashing the anxiety left over from the humanist discovery of the individual character of the *salus Christiana* – that indeed seems to belong to the entire apologetic culture of the century. But all of a sudden we

57. It seems that Descartes's contacts with Jean de Silhon prior to the Dutch exile were frequent. Afterwards, the appearance of Silhon's name in the correspondence is increasingly sporadic: AT I 5–13, 132, 200, 352, II 97. But nothing leads us to believe that their relationship was interrupted. In the meantime, Silhon engages in a thriving political and cultural career: secretary to Richelieu, member of the Academy, councillor of State, dispenser of prizes, pensions and privileges . . .

58. The development of Silhon's thought takes place between 1626, the year of the publication of a volume entitled *Les deux vérités*, which is almost libertine and deist in tone, and 1634, the year of the joint publication of *De l'immortalité de l'âme* and *Le ministre d'Etat*, works which express, respectively, an extreme Platonizing mysticism and an apology for Richelieu's absolutism. On Silhon's thought, see H. Busson, *De Charron à Pascal*, pp. 55, 68, 92–4, 139, 141, 151, 221ff, 541–5; E. Gilson, *Etudes sur le rôle*, pp. 36–9. The influence exerted by Silhon's thought on that of Descartes seems to have been rather limited. Analogous to Silhon's, though far later, is the itinerary of Guez de Balzac, whose *Socrate chrétien* of 1651 reaches similar conclusions (according to H. Busson, p. 268, we are confronted with a 'radical and unalloyed fideism').

see that this tension wants to be placated again in the new fideistic dogmatism of the repose in truth, the renunciation of self in order to unite with the divine. The problem of salvation is no longer experienced as a kind of distress. It is entirely projected into faith, into the faithful abandonment to mystical experience.[59] If the awareness of the failure of the humanist experience demanded an anguished effort in order to resolve itself, if dualistic mechanicism had fixed this effort in an extreme manner, if all of this had reproposed itself in religious experience – now fideism dissolves everything. But the world is still fissured, consciousness is not placated, apologetics are not enough.[60]

59. P. Chaunu, 'Le XVIIe siècle religieux. Réflexions préalables', *Annales (ESC)*, vol. 22, 1967, pp. 279–302. We have relied heavily on this formidable article in respect of its approach and its capacity to synthesize the key issues. But we have serious doubts regarding the methodological aspect of Chaunu's investigation. He seems to regard the terrain of religious experience as self-sufficient for its own elucidation. A complete bibliography on *La vie religieuse en France de l'avènement de Henri IV à la mort de Louis XIV (1589–1715)* has been compiled by R. Tavenaux in the *Bulletin de la Société des Professeurs d'histoire et de géog. de gens. public*, vol. 200, 1960, pp. 119–30.

60. The religious crisis gives no hints of abating throughout the century, even in the extreme forms of mass atheism, though more often in those of indifferentism. The very activity of devotional groups, as culturally exuberant as it may be, remains essentially a minority pursuit. Beside the familiar H. Busson, pp. 5ff, 89ff, see R. Mandrou, 'Spiritualité et pratique catholique au XVII siècle', *Annales (ESC)*, vol. 16, 1961, pp. 136–46; G. Le Bras, *Etudes de sociologie religieuse*, vol. I, Paris 1955, pp. 39ff; Charles Chesneau (Julien-Eymard d'Angers), *Le père Yves de Paris et son temps (1590–1678)*, vol. I, Paris 1946. Note that the same decline, the same defeat, or at least the same contradictory development also takes place in the century's French Protestantism. This was noted by F. Strowski, *Pascal et son temps*, vol. I, Paris 1907, pp. 1ff; it is demonstrated with customary skilfulness by E. G. Léonard, 'Le protestantisme français au XVII siècle', *Revue historique*, vol. 72, 1948, pp. 153–79. This should cause no surprise. For if it is true, as P. Chaunu says, that 'Protestant reform and Catholic reform are inscribed on a continuum' and that 'they answer *cont'd over/*

On the other hand, mechanicist dualism can dissolve into mere empiricism or into sensism *tout court*. This is the more prudent path. Often, attitudes of acute mysticism serve as a cover – and are in turn bolstered by – this empiricist or sensist solution of dualism.[61] But the line of development is nevertheless different: it is a search for certainty within experience; it is trust in the senses as exclusive witnesses. This is true in both the theoretical and the ethical field: this sensist determination is affirmed everywhere, identifying Epicurus as its teacher.[62] Descartes sees in him the very symbol of sensism,[63] of its break with the precarious equilibrium of mechanicist dualism. As we have said with regard to the theoretical field, the attempt at a materialist reconstruction of the universe takes place – ambiguously albeit with determination – on the edges of the tradition of scholastic empiricism and of the new derealized mechanicist

---

60. *cont'd*   to selfsame preoccupations, partake in the same wealth, and are better understood side by side than in opposition' (p. 284), it is also true that this unity of theirs is the unity of a far deeper historical problem. Allow me a final remark. In general, the positions of religious renewal are, in politics, the most reactionary ones: Richelieu is often confronted by them. Is this not further proof that, with their flight towards a mystical kind of absolute, they fail to grasp the true problem of the epoch?

61. It is possible to observe an attitude of this sort in the *Second Objections* to the *Meditations* – in particular PWD II 87–8 and 89–90.

62. In this regard see the excellent analysis by A. Tenenti, 'La polemica sulla religione di Epicuro nella prima metà del Seicento', *Studi storici*, vol. 1, 1959–60, pp. 227–43, which grasps both the continuity, originating in the 1500s, of the process of rehabilitation of Epicurus, and its new specificity in the 1600s. On the Epicurean renaissance in the 1600s, see also H. Busson, *De Charron à Pascal*, pp. 418–27, and on the tradition originating in the 1500s, S. Fraisse, *L'influence de Lucrèce en France au seizième siècle*, Paris 1962; T. Gregory, *Gassendi*, pp. 239–42; as well as the now dated but still useful J. R. Charbonnel, *La pensée italienne au XVIe siècle et le courant libertin*, Paris 1919, pp. 714ff.

63. PWD I 182. Also AT IV 269, PWD III 261, AT IV 279–80; and PWD III 325.

image of the world.[64] But the empiricist attempt at a solution of dualism is exercised above all in the ethical domain. With what results? The renewal of libertine forms of appreciation of ethical experience, the elimination of the difference that mechanicism held on to so firmly. An ethics of mere existence, without hope for a substantial foundation; an ethics of decorum, of conformity, of convenience in a separation that, by definition, knows no overcoming.[65]

Of course, mechanicism, in its principal current, resists these antithetical solutions to dualism. Indeed, it must resist them, for mechanicism is the public philosophy of a society that is highly integrated into the constituted order and it sees, in these heteronomous effects of its own teaching, betrayals rather than

64. There is a commonly held view that the conception of nature in the 1600s, at least the one prevalent in the educated public, derives from a symbiosis of different elements: the last outcomes of Scholasticism, the posthumous effects of the naturalism of the 1500s, the new Epicurean atomism, mechanicism, and so on. This question is ably dealt with in J. S. Spink, *French Free-thought*, pp. 75–84, 108–9, 188–9 (the philosophy of Descartes, like that of Gassendi, is 'minoritarian': 'the majority' – in educated society, in the university – adheres to this eclectic amalgam of naturalist tendencies) and H. Kirkinen, *Les origines de la conception de l'homme machine. Le problème de l'âme en France à la fin du règne de Louis XIV (1670–1715)*, Helsinki 1960, pp. 27ff. Contributions to the definition of the phenomenon may be found in E. Gilson, *Etudes sur le rôle*, pp. 155–6; R. H. Popkin, *History of Scepticism*, pp. 121–31; T. Gregory, 'Studi sull'animismo del Seicento, I', *Giornale critico della filosofia italiana*, vol. 43, 1964, pp. 43–4.

65. Of paramount importance is the analysis by J. S. Spink (pp. 133ff) of the concept of *decorum*, as moral virtue (a dominant theme of Epicurean ethics), and consequently of 'conformity', 'convenience', all the way to 'justice' – three notions on the basis of which the idea of *decorum* coherently develops. A. Tenenti's remarks in 'Il libero pensiero francese del Seicento e la nascita dell'homme machine', *Rivista storica italiana*, vol. 74, 1962, pp. 562–71, aimed at further underscoring the symbiosis of the various currents of seventeenth-century thought, must therefore – at least as regards our own problematic – be handled with care.

philosophical errors. But it cannot fail to suffer from the severity of these attacks. In the attempt to resist and establish itself, the virile mechanicist awareness that the situation is this and no other, that it is devoid of alternatives, must, as it were, make itself attractive, it must depict in a more favourable manner the sad image of the present that it has come to define. Not wishing to take detours off the path it has chosen, it tries to leap ahead. At this point, we could insist on the functional role assumed in this endeavour by the mannerist and academic style of French high culture,[66] or on the specific character of classicism as literary theory and civic practice.[67] But this would be superfluous. Let us instead focus on the reaction of the figure who participated most directly in the mechanicist movement and who now, with the mounting criticisms and equivocal usages, recognizes its internal limit and fully endures its precariousness. In his interlocutor Mersenne, Descartes could make out a typical reaction. The ever more acute feeling that, on the plane of theodicy, it is impossible to restore the relationship between I and world through a positive mediation by the divinity is now ineluctably followed by a positivistic attitude that acclaims order and the conventional arrangements which alone can guarantee communication and survival in an otherwise corrupt world. And if that is not satisfactory, nevertheless the improvement of this formal horizon is the only thing we can rely on. Thus, it is to the utopia of a universal coexistence of sages,

66. R. Schnur, in *Individualismus und Absolutismus* (especially pp. 55–75), has insisted on this point with remarkable subtlety, reprising certain positions first put forward by G. R. Hocke, 'Das 17. Jahrhundert', in *Lukrez in Frankreich*, Cologne 1935, pp. 67ff. According to Schnur, mannerism (or rather the '*manieristische Ordnungsversuch*') is the 'internal' counterpart to the ideology of conventional, formal order which the crisis of the religious wars forced on most of seventeenth-century French culture, precisely in defence of a residual individualism. He reproduces, as an emblem of this thesis, a nice phrase of Valéry: 'doubt leads to form' (p. 67).

67. The reference is again to R. Bray, *La formation de la doctrine classique en France*, but we shall return to these themes.

nations and religions that Mersenne ultimately links the crisis of mechanicism.[68] This is the definitive pathetic relinquishment of the capacity to recognize the world, which results precisely from the opposition to the sterile daydreams of the libertines! In utopia, rational hope – the dissatisfaction of reason – is joined by irrational allegiance. Peace is a real desire that reason here demands over and above mechanicist dualism. The myth is that of the hero who will bring the world under his yoke and establish peace. It reveals unchained irrationality as the mystified need of reason, as the effective relinquishment of rationality.[69] Extreme dualism and the desperate awareness of the *corruption du siècle*, which imposes the tough discipline of the most consequent realism, do not suffice for men who, despite everything, had enjoyed the humanist imagination of a human realm. Thus it is not only the philosopher but also the *politique* who depends, at this limit of existential consciousness, on utopian hope.[70]

68. R. Lenoble, *Mersenne*, pp. 256ff, 547ff.
69. It matters little whether the hero one relies on is the *Gallic Hercules* of which the French chronicles spoke (C. Vivanti, *Lotta e pace religiosa*); or the German hero who will impose the *Golden Reich* (H. J. C. Grimmelhausen, *The Adventures of a Simpleton [Simplicissimus]*, London 1962; or simply the '*société savant*' on which the Minim friar Mersenne lays his hopes. See also K. von Raumer, *König Heinrich IV. Friedensidee und Machtpolitik im Kampf um die Erneuerung Frankreichs*, Iserloh 1947.
70. Two tendencies, or, if you prefer, two fields of application, must be kept in mind concerning the pacifism of the '*politiques*': irenism in the religious field, projects for a more or less perpetual peace in the political field. For religious irenism – whose problem is strictly connected to that of ecumenicism and tolerance – we must bear in mind above all Grotius's propaganda (J. Lecler, *Toleration and the Reformation*, vol. II, New York 1960; A Corsaro, *Grozio*, Bari 1948, pp. 224ff, 281ff; G. Ambrosetti, *I presupposti teologici e speculativi delle concezioni giuridiche di Grozio*, Bologna 1955, pp. 67 ff; as well as, in a more general vein, for the movement that goes under the name of 'Erastianism', R. Wesel-Roth, *Thomas Erastus. Ein Beitrag zur Geschichte der reformierten Kirche und zur Lehre des Staatssouveränität*, Lahr-Baden 1954). For the political utopia of perpetual peace we must consider above all the 'plans' of Sully and Crucé, recalling that *le père* Joseph and Richelieu himself were *cont'd over/*

That then is how the complete picture of the development and crisis of mechanicism unfolds before Descartes. Descartes glimpsed, in the bankrupt consequences of that standpoint, the form taken by the failure of his own philosophy, were it to have remained at the stage represented by the *Discourse on the Method*. This historical awareness permits us to explain the need to resolve the relationship between man and world. But in what sense? For, if it is indeed true that dualism decays with mechanicism, it is also clear that it is not possible to go back and coax the nostalgia of Renaissance universalism into producing something new. The path is a different one: to make dualism explode from the inside, conserving it whilst negating it. To move beyond the metaphysical accidentality of the I, which had been left over from the *Discourse on the Method*, not by once again planning its heroic possession of the world but by intensifying the metaphysical charge of the concept.

We shall see how this Cartesian path will progressively unfold. But let us ask right away: is all this not a way of avoiding the problem rather than resolving it? Maybe. The only sure thing is that Descartes refuses to retread the old path of the direct dialecticization of the I–world relation. He had seen it fail in the naturalist metaphysics of Aristotelianism, and in the end he had seen it undermined by the dualistic hypothesis of mechanicism. From this point of view, considering the intensity of the Cartesian refusal of contemporary experiences, he presents himself to us, in the context of his epoch, 'as the result of a biological mutation'![71]

Nothing is more mistaken, then, than accusing Descartes of

70. *cont'd*   not above entering into this discussion (R. v. Albertini, *Das politische Denken*, pp. 159–74; K. v. Raumer, 'Zur Problematik des werdenden Machtstaates' and 'Sully, Crucé und das Problem des allgemeinen Friedens', *Historische Zeitschrift*, vol. 174, 1952, pp. 71–9, and vol. 175, 1953, pp. 1–39.)

71. H. Kirkinen, *Les origines*, p. 45.

returning to the past. It is especially in the writings of Gassendi[72] that we find, as a kind of refrain, the accusation that Descartes lagged behind his own epoch.[73] The fact is that Descartes, having recognized the reasons behind mechanism, refuses to be held to them. He knows that if dualism cannot be suppressed, neither can the tension that pushes toward its overcoming. Are we to see a contradiction in the simultaneous affirmation of defeat and rebirth, dualism and the urge to overcome? Of course. Nevertheless, the specificity of Cartesian thought derives from this contradiction: the deeper the dualism, the more organized becomes this urge to overcome. Not in utopian daydreaming, which either forgets or wishes to obscure the intial situation of scission, but operationally, methodically: to control and possess the world, even in scission. Contradiction, but a real one!

Let us not forget that behind philosophy lies history, the history, in this case, of the bourgeoisie. This is the history of the bourgeoisie's humanist revolution, of its defeat in the 1500s; of the conjuncture of the twenties and the dramatic tone that it

72. 'Having reduced his polemic with Descartes to the schema of the scepticism–dogmatism opposition, Gassendi was led to place his adversary in the Aristotelian–scholastic metaphysical tradition', T. Gregory, *Gassendi*, p. 82, but see also pp. 93, 117–18. B. Rochot, 'Les vérités éternelles dans la querelle entre Descartes et Gassendi', *Revue philosophique de la France et de l'étranger*, vol. 141, 1951, pp. 288–98, moving on an analogous plane, even runs the risk of losing sight of the difference between Descartes and mechanicism. In fact, he imagines that Descartes's dualism is at least as rigorous as the mechanicist one and that the mechanicist interpretation of truth is not so narrow as to impede the formal affirmation of its absolute existence. Where then does the difference lie? It lies, in our view, in the fact that the problem is not that of defining reality in dualist terms, but rather that of determining the character of the extremes; and the spiritual extreme is for Descartes a productive, creative moment. That is what the mechanicist will never accept.

73. This refrain will later also resound in the 'democratic' tradition of historiography, which is entirely centred on the exaltation of mechanicism, of the new science as the progressive moment *tout court*. This is the case at least ever since Feuerbach's classic interpretation.

confers on the spirit of the epoch; of a social class which, though defeated and isolated from political power, nevertheless exists and grows, condemned to a war of position but aware of the ineluctable character of its own emergence. Looking closely, this situation can even be said to represent a fundamental element in the historical definition of the bourgeoisie as a class: a class forever separated from the capacity to be revolutionary, to possess the world, and stuck in an existence which nevertheless constitutes a perennial, indefinite attempt to regain unity. Descartes's thought establishes itself in this situation: its meaning and universality probably consists in this predicament.

3

The problem is concentrated in a metaphysical dyad: existence and essence. It is the problem of an (immediately emergent) essence that must confront and possess an existence. A continuous, historical existence, beyond separation. Essence had recognized itself in separation. Now it problematizes separation, it wants to find a relation with existence. What relation? And what form will it take?

Not a relation of identity, in any case. From this point of view, the *Meditations* really do follow the aim 'to clarify what I wrote in Part Four of the *Discourse on the Method*'.[74] The situation from which they take their cue is that of the metaphysical reality of separation, of separation appreciated in the full intensity of its conjunctural appearance. The only thing that changes is the order of treatment. In the *Discourse on the Method*, the problems were addressed 'not according to the order of truth of the thing, but according to the order of my thinking'.[75] The First Meditation (subtitled *What can be called into doubt*) will thus constitute a kind of recapitulation of the theme of separation, in which the order of

74. AT III 102: in a letter to Huygens of 31 July 1640.
75. PWD II 7. But also AT III 76.

individual memory will be replaced by the order of collective memory, the order of the historical thing. It will delve into and adhere to that body of historical, mnemonic experiences that constitute us qua genus and not qua individuals, in order to problematize this form of immediate existence.[76] The situation of crisis is thus restated against those who deny it; it is relived as a real situation and opposed in its consequences to those who do not understand it as such. It is opposed to those who renew the hope in the identity of I and world, the illusion and daydream of the immediate possession of truth in the world. Descartes is not that interested in the traditional motivations of the critique of sensible knowledge. What he criticizes is the whole world of sensibility as the general form of immediacy in the relation between subjectivity and objectivity.[77] This is a dream-world! Perhaps it was a revolutionary dream of possession, of perfect objective identity, but it is one that collapsed on itself and revealed itself to be a pure deception; just as it is a deception to maintain an unrealizable hope, to try to renew a defeated project. The harsh awareness of the urgency and imminence of the crisis nevertheless tends to be repressed and the critique stifled. Descartes repeats to himself that he must remember, that he must continue to remember:

76. Descartes takes the opportunity to elucidate this concept in the reply to Gassendi's objections to the first *Meditation* (PWD II 241–2). To Gassendi, who, from an Enlightenment standpoint, chides him for too many precautions and quibbles when confronting the thematic of doubt and critique (is pure reason not sufficient?), Descartes retorts: 'as if it were such an easy thing to free oneself from all the errors which we are imbued with ever since birth' (*Opere*, vol. I, p. 519). This historical density of reason, which is revealed by a focus on the question of memory, must always be kept in mind. See also the *Entretien avec Burman*, pp. 2–5, on the 'historical' concept of 'knowing through the senses'.

77. PWD II 12–13. It will not be difficult for Descartes, in replying to Hobbes's objection to the first *Meditation* (the reasons to doubt the senses are as old as Plato!), to say that the 'reasons to doubt' have been presented here 'in order to prepare the minds of the readers to consider intellectual things and distinguish them from corporeal ones' (PWD II 121).

this is an arduous undertaking, and a kind of laziness brings me back to normal life. I am like a prisoner who is enjoying an imaginary freedom while asleep; as he begins to suspect that he is asleep, he dreads being woken up, and goes along with the pleasant illusion as long as he can. In the same way, I happily slide back into my old opinions and dread being shaken out of them, for fear that my peaceful sleep may be followed by hard labour when I wake, and that I shall have to toil not in the light, but amid the inextricable darkness of the problems I have now raised.[78]

So the temptation of deception is opposed to the obligation of recognizing oneself instead in the situation. In the immediacy of the worldly relation there is no certainty, only the heteronomy of the development of freedom which turns against its author. I must free myself from deception, leave behind the Renaissance hope, reject 'the pleasant illusion' offered by the dream. I must free myself from the libertine temptation.[79]

But to what extent is the historically effective critique of libertinism – that is the mechanicist critique – valid? Having abandoned the dream of the immediacy of the I–world relation, what force of certainty can be derived from putting our trust in the procedure of the most perfect sciences? These are sciences that only treat of 'very general and very simple' things. If the world of the senses is not veracious, will it be different for this second, derealized world? The order of Descartes's reflection follows the historical order of the development of science, it grasps its origin in the response to the crisis of the naturalist conception of the cosmos. At the same time, it grasps its precariousness, the way

---

78. PWD II 15.
79. In the *Dedicatory Letter to the Sorbonne* that precedes them (PWD II 242), the *Meditations* are presented as a work whose aim is apologetic and essentially anti-libertine. This applies to the 'establishment', but as regards the libertines, as we have seen and shall see, Descartes's polemic is far more detailed.

it is tragically suspended over a void of being. The scientific project, as an abstract and formal project, does not possess reality. Its truth is a horizon. What guarantee is there that its content will be real? Sometimes deception is also active within a formal horizon. Will it not then be the case that 'some malicious demon of the utmost power and cunning has employed all his energies in order to deceive me'?[80] The paradox describes and attacks that actual world which refuses the immediate truth of sense but only at the price of making an insufficient hypothesis about the self-justification of science.[81] A world that does not justify itself, a critique of immediacy, a mediated relation. But what guarantee is there for the truth of mediation? Is it perhaps given over to the *deceptor* himself, to that Machiavellian prince in whose exclusive power lies the formation of the law? Does scission once again trick itself into thinking it can be placated in the political mediation of the crisis? Faced with illusion, with the new mechanicist illusion (which nevertheless presents itself as the critique of naturalism), for a moment Descartes embraces the reasons of the libertines. Against mechanicism, he re-enlists the full radicality of the libertine antithesis:

80. AT VII 22.
81. In the second part of the reply to Gassendi's objection to the first *Meditation* (PWD II 242), Descartes lays claim directly to the function of truth which is accorded to the procedure of fiction, paradox and '*falsa pro veris*' [TN: Descartes writes: 'it is often useful to assume falsehoods instead of truths in this way in order to shed light on the truth', PWD II 242]. The argument becomes deeper in the *French Letter Against Gassendi's Accusations* (especially AT IX 203–5), where the function of hypothesis and fiction is promoted over the empiricist and Enlightenment procedure of freeing oneself from prejudices through the correct use of reason. But, Descartes objects, how can this project be possible? Will it not fall prey to the bad infinite? The Enlightenment will risks being deprived of determination if it does not accept the preliminary, total detachment of the critical faculty, if it does not wrest the latter from the indefinite process of things that must be cast into doubt.

I will suppose therefore that not God, who is supremely good and the source of truth, but rather some malicious demon of the utmost power and cunning has employed all his energies in order to deceive me. I shall think that the sky, the air, the earth, colours, shapes, sounds and all external things are merely the delusions of dreams which he has devised to ensnare my judgement. I shall consider myself as not having hands or eyes, or flesh, or blood or senses, but as falsely believing that I have all these things. I shall stubbornly and firmly persist in this meditation; and, even if it is not in my power to know any truth, I shall at least do what is in my power, that is, resolutely guard against assenting to any falsehoods, so that the deceiver, however powerful and cunning he may be, will be unable to impose on me in the slightest degree.[82]

To oppose is necessary, even when the hope for victory (for bringing the subject back to reality) is lacking: 'obstinately', I will oppose the *deceptor*. Here Descartes's reasoning repeats the desperate genesis of the libertine opposition.

The First Meditation thus describes a situation and expresses a conviction. The situation is the one that had been left over after the *Discourse on the Method*: isolation, the self-absorption of the subject facing the world, the description of an absolute separation that involves mechanism as much as libertinism, a separation that marks the whole epoch. There is a conviction that the I–world relation will never be able to constitute a relation of identity. How then can one get out of this situation? 'So serious are the doubts into which I have been thrown as a result of yesterday's meditation that I can neither put them out of my mind nor see any way of resolving them. It feels as if I have fallen unexpectedly into a deep whirlpool which tumbles me around so that I can neither stand on the bottom nor swim to the top.'[83] But it is here, at the beginning

82. PWD II 15.
83. PWD II 16.

of the Second Meditation, when the whole of past experience is summarized and paradoxically radicalized, that the *Meditations* really begin. Here the demand for the relation with the world is positive. But we know, Descartes knows, that the relation cannot be one of identity. What path should be followed?

The entire affair of the composition of the text of the *Meditations*[84] is the story of this recurrent question. I find myself in a situation of irreparable dualism. In any case, the postulation of identity is not possible, so I am forced towards one pole of separate reality, into my separate subjectivity. I thus find myself as though obliged to aggravate the adherence to this autonomy of mine, to become habituated to this isolation. Descartes describes this path for us, once again thinking back to the *Discourse*:[85]

> Nothing exterior, then, is in our power except in so far as it is at the command of our soul, and nothing is absolutely in our power except our thoughts. But though this is very true, and no one could find it hard to accept when he thinks of it explicitly, yet I did say that it is a belief which one has to grow accustomed to, and that long practice and repeated meditation are necessary to do so. This is because our desires and passions are constantly telling us the opposite. We have so frequently experienced since childhood that by crying or commanding we could make our nurses obey us and get what we want, that we have gradually convinced ourselves that the world was made only for us, and that everything was our due. Those who are born to greatness are commonly seen to be the most impatient when they have to bear misfortune. It seems to me that there is no more fitting occupation for a philosopher than to accustom himself to

84. See H. Gouhier, 'Pour une histoire des *Méditations métaphysiques*', *Revue des sciences humaines*, vol. 61, 1951, pp. 5–29. But see also the *Avertissement* at AT VII, pp. i–xviii, as well as AT II 625, 629, PWD III 142; AT III 35, 126, 150ff; PWD II 157, 158, and PWD III 198.
85. PWD III 98 (in a letter from April or May 1638) in reply to objections to the *Discourse* (AT I 511–17).

believe what true reason tells him, and to beware of the false opinions which his natural appetites urge upon him.

In the following years the meditation deepens. It is then that we see – within the process of meditation, in the habit of meditation, there, inside the violent contact between self and self ('I am concerned only with that which I experience in myself')[86] – the process of internalization (offspring of defeat, product of the crisis, forced isolation) evince a possibility of positive contact with being. '*I am, I exist*, is necessarily true whenever it is put forward by me or conceived in my mind.'[87] This existential apprehension of the I cannot not be true. So the process of internalization is the offspring of defeat, the product of crisis. I agree. But the same cannot be said for the discovery of the existence of the I. That discovery is born in doubt but not from doubt, it precedes crisis and isolation. It is ontologically certain. It constitutes an irreducible emergence: the opposition to the malicious demon within a mechanism of doubt which encapsulates the crisis of an epoch. There is here a sectarian opposition that amounts to a refusal to let oneself be deceived to the extent that one exists, an opposition which is an affirmation of existence: 'In that case I too undoubtedly exist, if he is deceiving me; and let him deceive me as much as he can, he will never bring it about that I am nothing as long as I think I am something'.[88]

86. *Entretien avec Burman*, p. 6. The powerful call to exercise an accurate attention that isolates, in the flux of time, the full-bodied security of existential determination is also characteristic of the pages devoted to the second *Meditation* in the *Entretien avec Burman*, pp. 18–23. But in general motifs such as 'I will try to make myself little by little more known and familiar to myself' (PWD II 24) circulate throughout the *Meditations.*
87. PWD II 17.
88. PWD II 17. J. Maritain, 'Le conflit de l'essence et de l'existence dans la philosophie cartésienne', *Congrès Descartes. Études cartésiennes*, vol. I, pp. 38–45, has spoken, in this regard, of 'existential leaps': from a registering of essence we would move, in the absence *cont'd over/*

I doubt, I am: the link between these assertions is both a conjunction and a disjunction, a consequence and an opposition.[89] But especially an opposition. It is precisely whilst rethinking opposition that, in the Second Meditation, Descartes finally and directly indicates the basis for his attempt at a solution of the problem: the existent I is not only opposed to doubt but to everything that can be ravaged by doubt, to any possibility that the malicious demon may integrate itself into the world. The emergence of the *mens* over the body, which is determined through the use of doubt, is not only an operation of distinction but is directed against the body as the hope of the senses, as the possibility of imagination – it is an actual withdrawal from the general contact with the world. Thus, by delving into opposition the existence of the I qualifies itself – and in so doing is definitively given. The first qualitative definition of the existence of the I passes through the refusal. This delving into essence is the polemical negation of everything that is, or can be, against existence. 'Thinking? At last I have discovered it – thought; this alone is inseparable from me.'[90]

88. *cont'd*   of any proof, to the affirmation of existence. But here essence is existential opposition! Paraphrasing Maritain it would be better to say instead that we observe here an 'essential leap', that is to say, we witness an essence which reveals itself in opposition. Even less valid is the accusation – elsewhere raised by Maritain against Descartes's thought (in *Three Reformers: Luther, Descartes, Rousseau*, New York 1970) – of 'angelism'. On the contrary, here existential determination implicates essence entirely. There is no dream of perfection in the affirmation of essence. Rather, essence is continuously redefined in terms of existential determinateness.

89. Especially in the reply to the Second Objections to the Second Meditation (PWD II 93–6, 101–4), the qualification of the relation between essence and existence in terms of opposition is developed. In this way Descartes not only excavates a fundamental feature of his meditative process, but, in an effective and spirited way, he undermines the mechanicism/spiritualism alternative that governs these objections (see above, note 61 to this chapter) and shows how it is precisely out of the oppositions of mechanicism that the highest demand of spirituality emerges.

90. PWD II 18.

Only thought cannot be applied to the world like heated wax. Only thought can qualify in essential terms this existence that I have recovered. Every other sign of my existence is or can be conditioned by the prince ('malicious . . . of the utmost power and cunning'), only thought unconditionally qualifies my generic existence and posits it in its autonomy prior to any concretization that, historically or materially, may be impressed upon it, and may have to be accepted. Spirit is not distinct from the body by an abstraction of the intellect, but it is known as a distinct thing because that is what it in fact is.[91]

It is the passage from existence to essence, that second leap in the *Meditations*, which further qualifies the historical dimension. This passage reproposes the emergence of man as a thinking reality – with the whole humanistic resonance of thinking ('But what then am I? A thing that thinks. What is that? A thing that doubts, understands, affirms, denies, is willing, is unwilling, and also imagines and has sensory perceptions')[92] – and, thus, of man ('But what is a man?'),[93] in the full intensity of his humanist definition. Nostalgia is redeemed and the object of nostalgia becomes presence. Of course, the new foundation of man in being is still not operative. The definition is still given in separation and is reductive with regard to the whole horizon of being.[94] But if the general identity of essence and existence, of the I and the world, and the univocal universal predication of being are not possible, this new foundation of man nevertheless represents a solid starting point, a rich potential for development that is only

91. The affirmation of the spirit cannot be the outcome of an abstractive process, as Arnauld objects in the Fourth Objections. Descartes's reply (PWD II 154–62) is exemplary in its affirmation of the most strenous ontologism.
92. PWD II 19.
93. PWD II 17.
94. The justification of the reductive point of view maintained by Descartes in his treatment of the question is based on the need to follow the order of the subject-matter, not the exhaustive order of the thing. See AT II 263–6, 272.

awaiting to unfold. Because here, even in separation, being is touched upon and the intensity of the essential and existential emergence is infinite. In requiring nothing other than itself in order to exist, essence recognizes itself as substance; and as thinking substance, by definition, it shows itself as productive reality, as a tension turned toward the world but in itself already consolidated, stable and indestructible.[95]

Let us pause and ask: how much has Descartes's thought moved forward here with regard to the image of the I bequeathed by the *Discourse on the Method*? Is it only the order of treatment that has been modified, as Descartes wants to argue? It is beyond doubt that the order of treatment has changed; but a more profound mutation has also taken place, one that cannot in any case be underestimated. This is the new and potent tension that surges forth from the ontological emergence of the I. But, if that is true, if it is true that the marginality of the emergence of individuality has vanished here, we can say that a new frame of reference is offered by the *Meditations* when compared with the *Discourse*. In the first work, the I–world dualism did not allude to a mechanicist perspective (which was as unviable as it was rigorous) of a relation to the world. Here, in the persistence of the break with the Renaissance picture of identity, the subjective pole of dualism instead enjoys a kind of exaltation, overflowing the limits of its separation. The mechanicist horizon is overcome, sundered by the fierce re-emergence of humanist nostalgia. The world I see from this window is no longer a nothing – 'Yet do I see any more than hats and coats which could conceal automatons? I *judge* that they are men. And so something which I thought I was seeing with my eyes is in fact grasped solely by the faculty of judgement which is in my mind.'[96] Is this a new stage opened to the historical drama of individual existence? The fierce spontaneity and self-recognition –

95. The most ample demonstration of the productivity of being is to be found in the Fifth Objections to Gassendi. See PWD II 243–9 and AT IX 205–9.
96. PWD II 21.

even within separation – of the bourgeoisie as class? In the metaphysics the alternatives of bourgeois existence unfold, and here in the *Meditations* they are subjected to critical judgement.

Already in the Third Meditation the path begins to be defined more precisely. The I overflows, as we have said. But in what direction? The world is closed and dualism is an insuperable situation. Should we then circumvent this closure? Regain the world, not by throwing bridges toward it but by rising up so high within ourselves that we can look at it from above, as it were? The intensity with which individuality has understood its own onto-logical emergence demands that we follow this path, excluding every other one.[97] Having recognized one's own existence by separating oneself, it is only by acclaiming separation as an essential moment that individuality can move beyond itself. Having recognized itself as essence, it is only by stressing the internal productivity of thought that existence can project itself. The problem is formulated in terms of the evidence that I am not alone in the world but that there is something else that exists or, rather, that the existence of the world can be accredited in general and that knowledge of it can be veracious. We already know the road that we will need to follow to arrive at this proof of reality and veracity. Once again, it concerns advancing the inquiry into what it is to be an individual being. The reality and veracity of the world can only be the universal projection of the reality and veracity of the I. Even when the problem under consideration changes its name, turning into the traditional one of the proof of the existence of God, its substance is left untouched, and the path remains the same. Separation and productivity, in the nexus that binds them together, will then play a fundamental role in the demonstrative process – first, by way of contrast, then, by jointly sustaining the process of definition and characterizing it profoundly.

First and foremost by way of contrast, as we have said. The idea

97. This path is already indicated in the correspondence. See PWD II 129; AT III 181, 191–2, 212.

of perfection is in the individual; it is there as a component of his ontological apprehension. But it is also there as the painful awareness of the state of separation that every idea, in its individuality, endures. It is in this dialectical relation that the demand for a theological projection of the idea of perfection is established. That is because perfection, being an idea in the thinking subject, is productive being, incapable of limiting itself to individual existence. The already discovered essentiality of the affirmation of existence here gains in precision. First it reveals itself as innateness in subjectivity. It is as innate as it is qualifying, it is innate because it qualifies. Then it reveals itself as ideal complex, as articulation and determination of essence, of thought: ' "objective being" simply means being in the intellect in the way in which objects are normally there . . . "objective being in the intellect" does not mean "the determination of an act of the intellect by means of an object"; it signifies, instead, the object's being in the intellect in the way in which its objects are normally there.'[98] But precisely inasmuch as it reveals itself in this manner – as productive nucleus, as ontological thinking reality – existence sets in motion the process of overcoming. It cannot bear itself as limited. Perfection cannot bear its own imperfection: 'Now it is manifest by the natural light that there must be at least as much "reality" in the efficient and total cause as in the effect of that cause. For where, I ask, could the effect get its reality from, if not from the cause? And how could the cause give it to the effect unless it possessed it?'[99] If we compare it with the tradition, the rhythm of the causal process

98. PWD II 74, in the replies to the First Objections to the Third Meditation (PWD II 66–70, 74–8). Descartes's reply is entirely founded on the affirmation that while for Scholasticism causation is a kind of mirroring, for him causation is production. This derives from the fact that the idea itself is not a reflection but a production. The idea is to be understood as the organic and always mobile function of a life of the soul which never lets up in its productive expression. On this 'life of the soul' and productivity of truth, see PWD III 139–40, PWD III 183, 184–7, and AT III 474–9.

99. PWD II 28.

has been completely reversed. Here it is not a mechanical nexus but a productive nucleus. Are we dealing with the search for the foundation and for the guarantee of truth? Certainly, but only to the extent that truth is the productivity of the subject's unfolding. The existential hypostasis of perfection, that is, the affirmation of the existence of God as consolidated absolute perfection, is also the outcome of the contradiction that, given the requirement of unfolding, one finds between existence, which is certain but limited and separate, and essence, which is qualified as infinite productivity, idea, thinking nature.

> So from what has been said it must be concluded that God necessarily exists. It is true that I have the idea of substance in me in virtue of the fact that I am a substance; but this would not account for my having the idea of an infinite substance, when I am finite, unless this idea proceeded from some substance which really was infinite. And I must not think that, just as my conceptions of rest and darkness are arrived at by negating movement and light, so my perception of the infinite is arrived at not by means of a true idea but merely by negating the finite. On the contrary, I clearly understand that there is more reality in an infinite substance than in a finite one, and hence that my perception of the infinite, that is God, is in some way prior to my perception of the finite, that is myself. For how could I understand that I doubted or desired – that is, lacked something – and that I was not wholly perfect, unless there were in me some idea of a more perfect being which enabled me to recognize my own defects by comparison?[100]

But we have also said that, once the two conditions (existential and essential) that define the process have activated the proof of

100. PWD II 31. In the Fourth Objections and replies to the Third Meditation (PWD II 145–50, 162–72) the reversal of the entirety of negative theology into an internal articulation of the productivity of consciousness becomes a central moment in Descartes's thought.

the existence of God, they also contribute to defining the concept of God. What indeed is the God that the Third Meditation both discovers and defines? Whatever it may be, it is certainly a separate divinity. Descartes explicitly excludes the possibility of demonstrating divinity as a relation between potency and act, as a process of perfectibility that would realize individuality in the form of the absolute, i.e. in God: 'God . . . I take to be actually infinite, so that nothing can be added to his perfection. And finally, I perceive that the objective being of an idea cannot be produced merely by potential being, which strictly speaking is nothing, but only by actual or formal being.'[101] Descartes argues for this exclusion by identifying, in the separate emergence of individual being, the ontological insufficiency that prevents it from merging into the absolute: 'if I derived my existence from myself, then I should neither doubt nor want, nor lack anything at all; for I should have given myself all the perfections of which I have an idea, and thus should myself be God.'[102]

It would seem that separation, which we observed in the I–world relation, now unfolds and establishes itself in the I–God relation. This is because the situation of the I, the historical situation, is, in any case, definitively non-dialecticizable. This is the moment in which Cartesian thought attains its maximum specificity. In fact, God is the guarantor of my thoughts, of my existence as thought, not of my capacity of possessing the world:

> It only remains for me to examine how I received this idea from God. For I did not acquire it through the senses; it has never come to me unexpectedly, as usually happens with the ideas of things that are perceivable by the senses, when these things present themselves to the external sense organs – or seem to do so. And it was not invented by me either; for I am plainly unable either to take away anything from it or to add anything

101. PWD II 32.
102. PWD II 33.

to it. The only remaining alternative is that it is innate in me, just as the idea of myself is innate in me.[103]

God is therefore in me and not in the world, like 'the mark of the craftsman stamped on his work'. We have said this already: the overcoming of the metaphysical contingency of the I is not designed to overturn or remove the separation from the world. It cannot do this to the extent that the definition of the I is revealed to be the definition of a separate being. That overcoming is, instead, vertical; starting from the I it reaches God. But how does the I present this divinity? Precisely not as the possibility of science, of the productive possession of the world! The Cartesian divinity is the projection, the hope of perfection, that belongs to a separate individual.[104] This hope is a nostalgia, the correlate of an old but living experience. It is also burdened with an entire crisis. If not the possibility of science, then what?

'And now, from this contemplation of the true God . . . I think I can see a way forward to the knowledge of other things.'[105] Descartes's conclusion, which is no longer paradoxical, is that we will be led to knowledge of the world by the will. We will be led by the will because the divine guarantee relates to the truth of the existence of the I, to the projection of the myth of the I – not to the truth of the world. God renders explicit the 'natural lumin-

103. PWD II 35.
104. As we have seen, in J.-P. Sartre's 'Cartesian Freedom', this idea of God as a sign of liberated productivity, projected by the subject, is entirely clear. But according to Sartre all of this would only take place in the order of the will – will as productivity would be opposed to the will imprisoned by the Cartesian system of ideas. Only by freeing himself from ideal objectivism would Descartes attain the idea of God. To counter Sartre, it should be pointed out that the process of the projection of subjective freedom towards and within the divinity takes place just as much in the order of will as in that of the idea. This is demonstrated especially by Descartes's meditation on the idea of the infinite, as an idea of the 'freedom' of the idea, of its total productivity.
105. PWD II 37.

osity' of reason, of the truth of the I, and tells us that one can tread the path toward a knowledge of the world. But, at the same time, God declares the existentially determined character of the truth of the I – that is, its separation from the world. The divinity tells us nothing about the world, since the divinity is the horizon of man, not of the world. Therefore, the world will become a terrain on which to prove the truth of the I. The world is a problem of truth, of a truth which is not guaranteed but rather risked, experienced:

> I find that I possess not only a real and positive idea of God, of a being who is supremely perfect, but also what may be described as a negative idea of nothingness, or of that which is farthest from all perfection. I realize that I am, as it were, something intermediate between God and nothingness, or between supreme being and non-being: my nature is such that in so far as I was created by the supreme being, there is nothing in me to enable me to go wrong or lead me astray; but in so far as I am not myself the supreme being and am lacking in countless respects, it is no wonder that I make mistakes.[106]

The guaranteed truth is therefore only that of the I in its separation. The problem of the truth of the world is instead above all that of its falsity, of the tension between that which is owed to me as the possessor of the truth of the I and that which I do not have to the extent that I am separate from the world: 'For error is not a pure negation, but rather a privation or lack of some knowledge which somehow should be in me.'[107]

Having said that, we possess only negative conditions for the will to move toward the conquest of the knowledge of the world. The positive motivation of the project of the will – a motivation that can reside only in the will itself and serve as its direct causation – is not yet given, or rather, it is only alluded to. However, it is still

106. PWD II 38.
107. PWD II 38.

within the process of the I and its limitation that this positive causation of the I is founded. That is because the will is precisely still that selfsame tension between essence and existence, which is not restricted to the idea of a possible pacification, not directed to its teleological self-justification – but rather is open to the operative verification of the emergence of the subject onto the world.[108] Therefore, the will is a different figure through which to say God; its causation is once again that of the essential absoluteness of the I. The will is the divinity that puts the relation of perfection at risk by launching it onto the world:

> It is only the will, or freedom of choice, which I experience within me to be so great that the idea of any greater faculty is beyond my grasp; so much so that it is above all in virtue of the will that I understand myself to bear in some way the image and likeness of God. For although God's will is incomparably greater than mine, both in virtue of the knowledge and power that accompany it and make it more firm and efficacious, and also in virtue of its object, in that it ranges over a greater number of items, nevertheless it does not seem any greater than mine when considered as will in the essential and strict sense. This is because the will simply consists in our ability to do or not to do something (that is, to affirm or deny, to pursue or avoid); or rather, it consists simply in the fact that when the intellect puts something forward for affirmation or denial or for pursuit or avoidance, our inclinations are such that we do not feel we are determined by an external force.[109]

Here bourgeois existence, which had recognized and emancipated itself through the crisis, to the point of ideologically affirming its

---

108. PWD II 39. But in general, on the character of the will, we should bear in mind the following passages: AT II 628 [TN: partly in PWD III 141–2]; PWD III 160, 172, 179, AT III 378–82; PWD III 231ff; AT IV 632; and *Entretien avec Burman*, 48–51.
109. PWD II 40.

own absoluteness, once again confronts the world – with all its extraneousness, which it calls falsity. Through the will, it tries to realize ideology, to realize its own theological hypostasis. But the world is still dominated by the prince! Of course, the metaphysical deepening of the I has shown us the world as a possibility of conquest; the proof of the existence of God has allowed us to imagine it conquered; the will has fortified itself within this imagination. But the world is still dominated by the prince, we cannot forget that. To forget it would be to succumb to error – to the libertine error that does not make the will commensurate to the intellect, essence to existence, metaphysical emergence to separation. 'So what then is the source of my mistakes? It must be simply this: the scope of the will is wider than that of the intellect; but instead of restricting it within the same limits, I extend its use to matters which I do not understand. Since the will is indifferent in such cases, it easily turns aside from what is true and good, and this is the source of my error and sin.'[110] But despite this firm control on the will, the risk must be run. To avoid it would mean relapsing into the mechanicist impotence which is incapable of a correlation with the world[111] – because to run this risk is to prove the divinity of the world.

But proving does not mean reducing. If the Fourth Meditation established the extreme terms of the relation between subjectivity and world, in the Fifth Meditation thought once again retreats to the subject, it folds back once again, in a kind of disdainful jolt, onto the ontological reflection of the I. It almost seems as if this is done in order to remove any possible misunderstanding whereby that will which so humanistically partakes in both God and nothingness, which is so heroically launched onto the world, might really wish to find an operative efficacy within the world. No, the entire dignity of reason and will is to be seen entirely in

110. PWD II 40–1.
111. See (Gassendi's) Fifth Objections and the replies to the Fourth Meditation (PWD II 214–21 and 257–60).

itself, in its foundation. The world can be conquered only by mediating the project of its conquest through the process that leads from the I to God. The conquest of the world does not confer reality onto the world, it only expresses the reality of the I, and of the divinity as a projection of the I. The relation between I and world displays its consistency in the order of the idea, not in that of being, or better, in the order of being only because the latter is filtered through the order of the idea. It is a task, not a reality. If the world wants to have a certain reality, it must be entirely reconstructed by the subject. The world is not a reality of which we could gain possession, but a reality that must be produced. Possession comes before being in the perspective of the true will. The analysis in its entirety must be led back to the productivity of thought.

Therefore, the Fifth Meditation (subtitled *The essence of material things, and the existence of God considered a second time*) takes its cue once again from the problem of the existence of the material world, and dives straightaway into ontological demonstration – the most radical exemplification and at the same time the most rigorous excavation of the existential apprehension of the I, of its qualification as autonomous and productive essence: 'But if the mere fact that I can produce from my thought the idea of something entails that everything which I clearly and distinctly perceive to belong to that thing really does belong to it, is not this a possible basis for another argument to prove the existence of God?'[112] There is nothing more characteristic of Descartes than the fact that the discussion of the ontological proof is preceded, or even introduced, by the sketch of a discussion on the essence of material things. For the problem here is precisely that of once again signalling, after the will has ventured into the world, the essential condition which required that this be the case: i.e. that the productivity of thought be the substance of the subject. In this manner the Fifth Meditation anticipates the objection that the

112. PWD II 45.

Fourth Meditation could have elicited: if the will puts itself at risk in the world without possessing it, or possesses it only by reconstructing it in the I, does this procedure not determine either a totally unproductive cognitive process or a vicious circle in which thought turns on itself? To those who raise this objection[113] Descartes responds simply by reiterating the legitimacy of his examination of the ontological apprehension of the I and of the resolution of the world into this apprehension, thereby reproposing the model of the ontological apprehension of the divinity itself: the productivity of thought is in itself and for itself, it develops vertically. Thought is a complete and productive circuit of existence and essence. It is an infinite force which is pacified only, if at all, in its own perfection.

Let us pause here. By introducing the ontological proof,[114] Descartes has touched the limit of the metaphysical delineation of the I, of thinking substance, of its autonomy, and of the contents that all of this envelops. But let us never forget: this being is a separate being. It is the only possible apprehension. If Descartes finally ends up identifying a definitive figure of the identity of essence and existence and fixing it as the present and actual absolute in thought, if he thus replaces the indefinite order of the mechanicist horizon with the image of the productive infinite,[115] all of this nevertheless lives in the idea, in the horizon of ideology. The mechanicist indefinite concerns the I–world relation, the Cartesian infinite is linked instead to the I–God relation.[116] It spreads out like a myth,

---

113. See especially the Second Objections and replies to the Fifth Meditation: PWD II 89, 91, 100–1 and 106–7.
114. We should obviously underscore the difference between the causal proof (or proof of perfection) and this ontological proof (see PWD II 46–7). In effect, the first rests on the hypostasis of the subject, while the second is based on the internal analysis of thought and being. See *Entretien avec Burman*, pp. 26–9, 30–3; PWD II 231ff.
115. See the First Objections and replies to the Fifth Meditation (PWD II 68–73 and 81–6).
116. See the Fifth Objections and replies to the Third Meditation (PWD II 193–214 and 249–57).

like an ideal hope, over the reality of the external world whose truth must be operationally verified. The whole of the Sixth Meditation[117] takes its cue from this problem. The final non-resolution of the question of the unity (as well as the distinction) of soul and body demonstrates that the initial situation of scission cannot be resolved in terms of identity, but that nevertheless the intensity of the ontological relation is enough for the I to define a secure position for itself.[118]

4

Essence and existence come together in a unique encounter and a single point of fusion: the subject. The essential and existential form of subjectivity is projected into God; an infinite productive tension surges forth from being in general and, eminently, from God; the world is external, derealized, and can only be conquered by negating and reproducing it; the will is already engaged in this effort but it is restrained by the intellect. This is the picture offered by the *Meditations*, and its political meaning can be recognized at once: the active and independent subject is characterized by its confrontation with the bewitched world of absolutism; the productive form of this separate existence projects its own class essence in the shape of absolute autonomy; the impossibility of politically possessing the world, of remaking it as real from its current bewitched state, is registered, but it is accompanied by the hope – the unflagging albeit restrained conviction – that the productive, social and cultural hegemony of the bourgeois class will find in absolute mediation the capacity to rebuild the world.[119] We are presented with the productive autonomy of

---

117. PWD II 50ff.
118. See the Fifth Objections and replies to the Sixth Meditation (PWD II 228–40 and 264–7).
119. We have not said much about the emergence in the *Meditations* of hints relative to the definition of the character of bourgeois production and the social existence of the bourgeoisie. But we shall *cont'd over/*

the bourgeoisie – realistically aware of the limits of separation but certain of its class absoluteness – alongside the refusal of the vain, solitary libertine daydreaming, and of the resigned mechanicist acceptance of absolutism. Lastly, we may note Descartes's re-affirmation of the humanist tribute to the bourgeois revolution – a burning nostalgia which knows how to accommodate itself to the memory of defeat and which, in a long and indefinite process of bourgeois growth, establishes the possible expansion of the infinite potentiality of class.

If one knows how to read a text, one can see all of this in the *Meditations*. But to further elucidate the political impact of Descartes's oeuvre, we can turn to the important polemic, occurring in these very years, between Descartes and the greatest political author of mechanicism: Hobbes. This polemic represents a sort of counterpoint, and it sheds light on the fundamental contours of Cartesian discourse.

This is all the more so to the extent that this relationship is polemical and harshly critical from the very outset.[120] 'The Englishman' appears in Descartes's epistles in December 1640.[121] The polemic between the two starts right away. First a few mentions,[122] then the exchange of letters on

119. *cont'd*   return to them, above all when studying the redefinition of 'technical hope' in Descartes's thought. In any case, and without belabouring the point, we should keep in mind how the entirety of the I–world relation in the *Meditations* is characterized in a specifically bourgeois manner – take the geometric and manufacturing-based exemplification of the innate ideas about the world, or the example of the wax, a typical figure of the manipulative possibility of technical production, and so on. See F. Borkenau, *passim.*

120. In general, on the Descartes–Hobbes relation see C. E. Adam, 'Descartes et ses correspondants anglais', *Revue de littérature comparée*, vol. 17, 1937, pp. 437–60; J. Laird, 'L'influence de Descartes . . .'; R. Lenoble, *Mersenne.*

121. PWD III 167.

122. PWD III 169 (Descartes has seen Hobbes's text but does not wish to reply at length, not deeming it worthwhile. He sends a note to Mersenne so that the latter may make use of it as   *cont'd over/*

optics,[123] and finally objections and replies,[124] with the subsequent bitter and inimical break.[125] When in 1643 the *De Cive* ends up in Descartes's hands he responds to it with a heavy and venomous assessment, worthy of the Jesuit to which the letter is addressed:

> All I can say about the book *De Cive* is that I believe its author to be the person who wrote the Third Objections against my *Meditations*, and that I find him much more astute in moral philosophy than in metaphysics or physics. Not that I would approve in any way his principles or his maxims. They are extremely bad and quite dangerous in that he supposes all persons to be wicked, or gives them cause to be so. His whole aim is to write in favour of the monarchy; but one could do this more effectively and soundly by adopting maxims which are more virtuous and solid. And he writes with such vehemence against the Church and the Roman Catholic religion that I do not see how he can prevent his book from being censured, unless he is given special support from some very powerful quarter.[126]

---

122. *cont'd*   the circumstances require. But already at this point Descartes declares that there is nothing in common between him and Hobbes save for the fact that they both see nature in figures and movements, although Hobbes draws bad consequences from these good premises . . .); PWD III 171 and AT III 338 (more or less manifesting the same irritation).

123. AT III 287–92 [TN: partly in PWD III 170–1], AT III 300–13, 313–18, 320–7 [TN: partly in PWD III 173], 341–8, and PWD III 178–9.

124. In PWD II. But we should also keep in mind the following passage: 'I do not think I should have made my replies to the Englishman any longer, since his objections seemed so implausible to me that to answer them at greater length would have been giving them too much importance' (PWD III 180).

125. See for example AT III 633. We are in 1643: 'I am not curious to see the writings of the Englishman . . .'

126. PWD III 230–1.

For his part, Hobbes, a little later, notifies Sorbière, who is editing in Holland the second edition of *De Cive*, that: 'Furthermore, if he feels or suspects that this is being done so that my book (either this or another one) would be published, I know for certain that Descartes would hinder it if he could . . .'[127] We are thus faced with a sustained and bitter clash.[128] However, it was inaugurated and developed on themes which – in the gist of the disagreement – hardly justify such an intense engagement by the two interlocutors and such mutual bad blood. The fact is that, behind the contingent motivations of the polemic, both Descartes and Hobbes discern the progressive configuration of a profound philosophical and metaphysical separation[129] – a radical separation of viewpoints that implies substantial differences in both cultural and political sentiment. Thus, the later clarification concerning the themes of the naturalist polemic does nothing but open the possibility of an exacerbation of the philosophical polemic.

The fundamental catalyst of discussion in the letters that (via Mersenne) Descartes and Hobbes exchange between 1640 and

127. Quoted in F. Brandt, *Thomas Hobbes' Mechanical Conception of Nature*, Copenhagen and London 1928, p. 129.
128. It seems that in 1648 there was a pacifying encounter between Descartes, Hobbes and Gassendi. See H. Hervey, 'Hobbes and Descartes in the Light of Some Unpublished Letters of the Correspondence Between Sir C. Cavendish and Dr. J. Pell', *Osiris*, vol. 10, 1952, pp. 67–90. In this case Mersenne's attempts at recomposition and rapprochement (on which see R. Lenoble, p. 582) would have been successful. But this is doubtful. Even if a meeting really took place the pacification can only have been entirely formal. In December 1647, Elizabeth still considers Hobbes's objections to be the most unreasonable, even more than those of Gassendi. It is well known how much sympathy Descartes had for such a viewpoint (and vice versa).
129. F. Brandt, whose reading of the Hobbes–Descartes relationship is in many respects definitive, nevertheless considers the motives that underlie the polemic to be 'psychological'. In particular it appears to him that Descartes tends to consider Hobbes a 'plagiarist' (pp. 129–42).

1641[130] is rather paradoxical: Hobbes affirms (and Descartes denies) that the Hobbesian concept of *spiritus internus* belongs to the same family as the Cartesian concept of *materia subtilis.*[131] The paradox consists above all in the fact that the two authors are engaged in a bitter polemic regarding those aspects in terms of which these two concepts really are analogous, while they only mildly or marginally touch upon the sources of a real differentiation. The fact that the extension of the concepts is largely analogous can be easily recognized: both are predisposed to the determination of a continuous horizon in which movement can be presented in terms of pure mechanical contiguity. It really seems that, as far as this argument is concerned, the polemic really derives 'from will rather than from reason' as the irritated authors mutually accuse one another,[132] and thus seems worthy only of curiosity.[133] But soon the concepts part, in terms of their overall ramifications. This is so notwithstanding the fact that, in the two polemical rivals, the acknowledgement of this radical separation is at first only implicit or seems to stem more from animosity than from real awareness. However, the grounds of the separation are soon revealed by the discussion around the *Meditations.* The fact is that whilst Cartesian *materia subtilis* tends to dissolve into the geometric schema, into pure cognized extension (whence the Cartesian distinction between movement and the direction of movement, the theory of reflection and

130. The first (or perhaps the first two) of the letters to Hobbes has been lost. See the wide-ranging and very rich demonstration in F. Brandt, *Hobbes*, pp. 86–99.

131. The arguments follow one another: PWD III 170, AT III 301–3, 321–2, and PWD III 178.

132. For example, AT III 302 and 321–2.

133. For instance in J. Laird, p. 241. But F. Brandt has in any case demonstrated the extreme importance of this polemic with Descartes for the development of Hobbes's thinking. On the centrality of optics to Hobbes's development, see also F. Alessio, '*De Homine* e *A Minute* . . . di Th. Hobbes', *Rivista critica di storia della filosofia*, vol. 17, 1962, pp. 393–410.

impact, and so on),[134] the Hobbesian *spiritus internus* configures itself as the full-bodied and integral reality of movement – a physical rather than a geometric concept, formulated in terms of immediacy rather than as an abstract figure.[135] It is also the case that the general platforms of mechanicist and Cartesian dualism here reveal their deep-seated dissimilarity: the latter conceives of geometricized matter as a bewitched world to be defined in its precariousness, to be denounced in its instability, and to be overcome in the metaphysical nexus of individual and divinity (and yet this is demonstrated by the distinction between movement and the determination of movement, or *inclinatio*, which is – even in its contradictoriness – the registering of what is still a metaphysical aspect in the question of movement); the former instead is satisfied with this mechanical reality (or rather, it emphasizes it more and more, tending to transform, in what amounts to an extended interpretation of Galilean inertia,

---

134. See the beginning of part II of the *Dioptrics* (*The World and Other Writings*, pp. 76ff) and *The World* (*The World and Other Writings*, pp. 7–8) for the distinction between the power of movement and the power of the direction of movement. This entire question is very ably treated in F. Brandt, *Hobbes*, pp. 110–41.

135. A. Pacchi, 'Cinquant'anni di studi hobbesiani', *Rivista di filosofia*, vol. 57, 1966, pp. 306–35, and the note on p. 315: 'In our judgement Watkins [J. W. N. Watkins, *Hobbes' System of Ideas*, London 1965, pp. 45ff] grasps the nub of the question when he underlines that, as regards method, Hobbes, rather than projecting himself into the Bacon/Descartes alternative, goes back to the previous tradition, in other words that of Paduan Aristotelianism'. Perhaps it is worth adding that this is true not only with regard to method. From this point of view it seems that Hobbes's thought has noteworthy affinities with that naturalist–Epicurean–mechanicist syncretism which, as we have seen, constituted the dominant philosophy in the French schools of the time. For his part, F. Brandt, in his *Hobbes*, argues instead for the essential nature of the mechanicist motif in Hobbes's philosophy. Even if only in philosophical terms, Hobbes brings materialism to the edge of a mere motionalism: matter tends to disappear, the central point becomes mere movement.

mechanicism into mere kineticism), and if it opposes it with an antagonistic term, the divine absolute, it does so by establishing a definitive and insuperable difference between the elements of dualism. This relation is more mystical than logical – a separation which is basically accepted. Thus, beyond its contingent direct causes, there is an alternative implicit in this polemic that marks the whole epoch. We have already registered this alternative in the relationship between Descartes and his mechanicist friends – who, we should not forget, Hobbes was very close to during this period.[136] And how, in this environment, could Hobbes not appreciate a kind of polemic which, a little earlier, had been developed – almost in the same terms of an attack against the metaphysical residues in Descartes's thinking – by Fermat and his friends?

This scientific polemic is based on the implicit recognition of a distinction between general visions of the world:[137] would it be too much to draw from these considerations a radical differenti-

136. *Baillet*, vol. II, p. 120: 'The troubles in Great Britain having forced him to return to France toward the end of the year 1640, he found in Paris the rest and security he sought in order to cultivate his philosophy with leisure, and he linked himself more tightly than ever with Mersenne and Gassendi, who were the principal advisers and companions of his studies'. But see also F. Tönnies, *Hobbes, der Mann und der Denker*, Stuttgart 1912, p. 15, on the relation between Hobbes and the Dupuy circle; R. Lenoble, *Mersenne*, pp. xxviii, xxxviii, l–li, 308, 576–8 (containing copious information and bibliographical annotations regarding the fortunes and vicissitudes of Hobbes and his thought in France); finally, albeit in very general terms, R. Schnur, *Individualismus und Absolutismus*.

137. In general, for the reaffirmation of the close links between metaphysics and the new science (polemicizing, in other words, with all the conceptions that depict the birth of the new science as a polemic against metaphysics), and in particular with regard to the thought of Descartes and Hobbes, see E. A. Burtt, *The Metaphysical Foundations of Modern Science: A Historical and Critical Essay*, 3rd edn, New York 1954, especially chs IV and V. Burtt's book should be studied alongside A. Koyré, *From the Closed World to the Infinite Universe*, Baltimore and London 1957.

ation between these two authors with regard to political matters as well?[138]

This does not seem to be the case, however, at least as far as Hobbes is concerned. Precisely in the years of the polemical correspondence with Descartes, he is in fact principally busy with a study of political matters:[139] the *De Cive* is published in 1642. Thus the contestation of Cartesianism is in Hobbes inseparable from a rethinking of the political situation and of the political urgencies of the century. Hobbes is entirely aware of the implications that follow from a conception of the world, of the natural and physical world. After all, is his scientific philosophy not a kind of metaphor of his political thought?[140] Or at least, are his political thought and his mechanicist conception of nature not born and developed in the continuity of a single scientific design?[141] Even if

138. Some have thought that the philosophies of Hobbes and Descartes, 'save for the form', are absolutely analogous, and even claimed to demonstrate it. See C. Schmitt, 'Der Staat als Mechanismus bei Hobbes und Descartes', *Archiv für Rechts- und Sozialphilosophie*, vol. 30, 1936–7, pp. 622–32.

139. F. Brandt, *Hobbes*, p. 167; C. Robertson, *Hobbes*, London 1910, pp. 55–6.

140. This is the position put forward by Tönnies, Dilthey, Levi and Lubieski. See A. Pacchi, 'Cinquant'anni'. Considering natural and formal thinking to be fundamentally dissimilar, Robertson, Laird and Strauss polemicize against this approach.

141. Superb work in this vein is to be found in R. Polin, *Politique et philosophie chez Thomas Hobbes*, Paris 1953, and 'Justice et raison chez Thomas Hobbes', *Rivista critica di storia della filosofia*, vol. 17, 1962, pp. 450–69. In the latter article, Polin bitterly and successfully polemicizes against those interpreters who have sought to define political obligation in Hobbes as a separate and autonomous moment with regard to the overall process of Hobbesian philosophy. The polemic is especially aimed at H. Warrender, *The Political Philosophy of Hobbes: His Theory of Obligation*, Oxford 1957, and 'Hobbes's Conception of Morality', *Rivista critica di storia della filosofia*, vol. 17, 1962, pp. 434–49; and against M. Oakeshott, 'The Moral Life in the Writings of T. Hobbes', in *Rationalism in Politics*, London 1962, pp. 248–300. Polin strongly insists on the fact that obligation in Hobbes cannot be interpreted in Kantian terms. On the contrary, it is entirely internal to the philosophy of nature, developing coherently from that basis. See also N. Bobbio, 'Hobbes e il giusnaturalismo', *Rivista critica di storia della filosofia*, vol. 17, 1962, pp. 470–85.

we were to concede that mechanicism can have varied results once transferred onto the ethico-political plane, is it not still true that, already in the *Short Tract*, Hobbesian mechanicism had shown its own predisposition to be extended, in that determinate sense, to politics?[142] In truth, whatever the relation of dependence may be, the two branches of Hobbesian thought grow together, in reciprocal functionality – and they are certainly seen in this light in the French environment in which Hobbes lives and to which Descartes refers. Given the demand to salvage the competitive appetites from the catastrophe that their conflict would determine, it is precisely in the Hobbesian paradox – of a mechanical construction of individual, rational and equal elements which shift towards the concept of a power completely extraneous and superior to that same mechanicism – that the French mechanicists too find one of the most characteristic motifs in their conception of the world.[143]

142. This is aimed against Strauss's interpretation, which is violently targeted at disentangling natural philosophy from moral philosophy. A. Pacchi, 'Cinquant'anni', p. 318, correctly notes that in order to uphold his thesis Strauss is forced to ignore Hobbes's *Short Tract*, 'whose nascent mechanistic conception, through the deterministic conception of the "free agent", already presents a very close link with morality'. Perhaps the most balanced and comprehensive point of view within this polemic on the nexus of moral and natural philosophy in Hobbes is the one expressed by C. B. Macpherson, *The Political Theory of Possessive Individualism: Hobbes to Locke*, Oxford 1964, especially pp. 29–46. Without entering into the diatribe about the 'necessity' or otherwise of the relation between the two branches of Hobbesian thought, accepting instead the interpretation that sees it as a non-mechanical nexus (an 'other' element – psychological, ethical, theological – enters for sure into the configuration of Hobbes's political framework), Macpherson nonetheless insists on the effectiveness of this very nexus, which is sustained by and unfolds towards a determinate model of social and political constitution. The continuity of Hobbesian thought does not rest on an internal necessity but on a political necessity. This political necessity shows how Hobbesian thought has its roots in the culture of mechanicism and how it opts for absolutism.

143. As noted above, T. Gregory, *Gassendi*, pp. 236–7, has highlighted the importance of this passage in Gassendi's thinking, and noted the pervasiveness of the theme within the intellectual milieu.

The class essence of the bourgeoisie is rescued by the claim of the primacy of civil society and its inter-individual structure, through the insistence on the form of knowledge and the mode of producing – a form that the bourgeoisie wishes the state itself to assume, a form in which it wishes to see sovereignty organize itself. But at the same time, the weight of that terrible Renaissance defeat is not forgotten. On the contrary, the situation deriving from that defeat is assumed in all its weight.[144] Science can do nothing but describe this situation, subject itself to its weighty reality and transcribe it. What we are confronted with is a realism of nominal images which, in its fidelity to the world, bears within itself the memory of a historical tragedy from which a class does not know how to free itself. Here existence really does not know how to attain essence. Even granting that the form of bourgeois existence is imposed upon the state, that the state assumes its sovereign content – sovereignty remains different, other, it retains a mystical transcendent content. Class awareness cannot adequately perceive itself: it grasps itself as a lack of hope after having passed through the experience of crisis and undergone it as destruction.[145]

144. Note how Marx and Engels, in *The Holy Family*, Moscow 1975, underline the fading of the revolutionary import of materialism in Hobbes, introducing a comparison with Bacon. While in Bacon materialism is born with an enthusiastic sense of its own strength ('the senses are infallible and the source of all knowledge'; matter is not only quantitative essence, movement and mathematical structure but is also '*impulse*, a *vital spirit*': in Bacon 'matter, surrounded by a sensuous, poetic glamour, seems to attract man's whole entity by winning smiles'), in Hobbes instead the conception of matter is significantly disfigured: 'Knowledge based upon the senses loses its poetic blossom, it passes into the abstract experience of the *geometrician. Physical* motion is sacrificed to *mechanical* or *mathematical* motion; *geometry* is proclaimed as the queen of sciences. Materialism takes to *misanthropy*'.

145. Concerning both the conventionalist character that the concept of reason ends up assuming, and the destructive role in Hobbes of the annihilatory hypothesis (of doubt . . . ?), see *cont'd over/*

If the clash in matters of natural philosophy had not been enough to elicit in Descartes the possibility of a judgement on the global implications of Hobbesian thought, the polemic around the *Meditations* now enters the frame. Here the terms of the discussion are radically clarified and the alternative – which was implicit in the two philosophers' respective approaches to the physical world – is definitively established. The fact is that, putting aside all divergences concerning the mechanical conception of nature, the clash now revolves around general philosophical themes. And there is no possibility of mediation because – besides the specific objects of the polemic – from the very outset it is a clash of metaphysical perspectives. What is problematic for Descartes, what constitutes the horizon of his thinking – to wit, the dramatic tension between existence and essence – for Hobbes cannot even be an object of reflection: essence 'in so far as it is distinct from existence, is nothing more than a linking of terms by means of the verb "is". And hence essence without existence is a mental fiction.'[146] Nominalism versus conceptual realism?[147] But the break goes deeper, revealing that the reason for the contrast is ontological. Being is not given as radically problematic for Hobbes, but it is for Descartes. It suffices to see how Hobbes reacts to the theme of doubt: 'I would have liked this excellent author of novel speculations to have refrained from publishing such old things', these obvious doubts on the truth of sensible knowledge that philosophy has been repeating ever since Plato.[148] Hobbes does not even suspect that doubt here is not aimed at the

145. *cont'd*   A. Pacchi, *Convenzione e ipotesi nella filosofia naturale di Thomas Hobbes*, Firenze 1965, *passim* and pp. 70ff. From this standpoint we must therefore also amend the theses of R. H. Popkin on the reconstructive efficacy of scepticism in Hobbes. This whole question has been ably revisited in G. D. Neri, *Prassi e conoscenza*, pp. 34ff.
146. PWD II 136.
147. See in this regard the Third Objections and replies to the Second Meditation (PWD II 122–6).
148. PWD II 121.

single senses but in a radical way at the world itself, which it wants to grasp immediately, once again as naturing nature, as the triumph of the individual that wants and is able to possess it. Nevertheless, Hobbes too knew the crisis: but he accepted it without reacting, without suffering the necessary tension that from an essence which has become solitary relaunches us towards existence.

Hence, in order not to be a fiction, not to exhaust itself in a tension that seems mad to the mechanicist,[149] in order to be able to organize itself as real within the framework of Hobbesian science, the relation between essence and existence must be given, or rather can only be given, in the reductive terms bequeathed by the crisis. The Hobbesian exemplification of this predicament is both plastic and tragic: 'It seems, then, that there is no idea of God in us. A man born blind, who has often approached fire and felt hot; and when he hears that this is called "fire" concludes that fire exists. But he does not know what shape or colour fire has, and has absolutely no idea or image of fire that comes before his mind. The same applies to a man . . .'[150] In Descartes instead, the relation between essence and existence 'risks' being a fiction, but nevertheless wishes to be a project – which, without forgetting the actual determinacy of separation, can develop itself and reconstruct a meaningful horizon for man: 'I am taking the word "idea" to refer to whatever is immediately perceived by the mind.'[151]

We have perhaps reached the core of Descartes's thought and of its historical significance. We have said that the dynamic relation between essence and existence that Descartes projects onto the crisis of his time risks – or wants to risk – being a fiction. But what kind of fiction? What kind of relation? Not a relation that can somehow, beyond the initial fiction, resolve itself into an identity. If identity is given we are either on the plane of utopia, of

149. This is what justifies the mechanicist's bitter irony. See the Third Objections to the Fourth Meditation (PWD II 133).
150. PWD II 127.
151. PWD II 127.

enthusiastic naturalist identity and its disastrous effects, or on the plane of reduced being, of frustrated sensory identity, in a world devoid of human meaning.[152] The mechanicist world does not know how to provide an alternative for the crisis of the Renaissance world, because both see science as a reduction to identity. So what horizon opens up here? What relation? Once again, the *Meditations* provide a single, univocal reply. This relation is an exaltation of the I, of its determinate thinking existence, which projects itself and in so doing regains the world. The relation with the world can become science only to the extent that it is broken and resumed in the overflow of the metaphysical intensity of the exaltation of the I. Outside of this there is no science, there is only the mirroring of a futile situation, the betrayal of a human vocation that the Renaissance defeat reorganized as separation – but did not remove. But is this Cartesian science really science? If we hold to the terminology of the mechanicists we certainly cannot voice a positive answer: this Cartesian science is really a fiction.[153] But what kind of fiction? A fiction of the subject, rooted in his actual separation, which is no less real for that. The fiction that, from here, from this separation, a new world can disclose itself. We have been defeated – that is the humanist awareness of the 1600s. But in Descartes this awareness of defeat is accompanied by an insuppressible certainty: that all value, that all valuable being, now resides in that separate being. It is on the

152. See the Third Objections and replies to the Third Meditation (AT VII 179–89).

153. Positions such as those expressed by J. V. Schall, 'Cartesianism and Political Theory', *Review of Politics*, vol. 24, 1962, pp. 260–82, according to whom Descartes 'provided a new and revolutionary foundation for the political sciences' (p. 272) by proposing the use of the criteria of the exact sciences in the consideration of phenomena of power, seem frankly unsustainable. It is not mechanicist dualism but ideology – i.e. the 'fake' attempt to overcome dualism – which founds Cartesian politics. Note Schall's positive reference to the theses of L. Laberthonnière (*Œuvres de . . .*, vol. II, *Etudes sur Descartes*, Paris 1935, pp. 102–16) and especially of A. Del Noce.

basis of this separate being that the world is to be reconstructed. It is from it that the uncontrollable tension of overcoming derives. So is this Cartesian science not a science? It is not a science especially in its opening to the world of subjects, sociality, history. It is not the mirroring of reality. It is not the analytical reconstruction of a separate world. What is it then? It is a fiction, what today we would call an ideology. A reasonable ideology that spreads out over the space of the crisis of the world of the 1600s, over the mistrust and disequilibrium of the epoch. It is a hope for reconstruction. A humanist nostalgia is once again at work.[154]

Perhaps it was only the mechanicist antithesis that could give Descartes the strength to effectuate this radical break with the crisis of his time. Descartes's work thus represents both a break and a solitary undertaking.

But the historical significance of his thinking consists in the fact that, whilst Descartes broke with a general situation of crisis, after having recognized it and allowed it to operate in his thinking, he nonetheless grasped what was perhaps the most profound characteristic of the century's tendency. In the superimposition of the productivity of ideology onto the passivity of mechanicist[155] science,

---

154. From this point of view, Gueroult is doubtless right when he insists that Descartes's morality and politics are entirely outside the order of reasons of the bewitched world, the physical world (see below). But Gueroult does not even try positively to identify the position of politics, or better, the political figure of Descartes's thought. In the most recent interpretations from the German school (M. Bense, *Descartes und die Folgen. Ein aktueller Traktat*, 2nd edn, Krefeld 1955; G. Schmidt, *Aufklärung und Metaphysik. Die Neubegründung des Wissens durch Descartes*, Tübingen 1965), the sense of the un-resolved ambiguity – historically marked by crisis – that dominates Descartes's thought is often captured in a felicitous manner (even if the speculative results of these works are very questionable).

155. It is worth repeating that in Descartes the mechanicist scientific approach often possesses an 'ideological' character. Sometimes this has negative and mystifying consequences on the process of scientific explanation; sometimes instead it has positive consequences, which result from privileging the productive imagination;   *cont'd over/*

he succeeded in clearly revealing to the epoch its own specificity: a world in which the bourgeoisie, condemned to a separate existence, needed to salvage, develop and impose its own essence. But what path is possible besides hope? What hope if not in ideology? There is a bitterness in the acknowledgement that with the Renaissance defeat the bourgeoisie no longer possesses the world, or rather only possesses that reduced and bewitched part that its technical knowledge allows it. This bitterness is overturned in a metaphysical acknowledgement of necessity from which the dynamism of essence becoming existence takes off. Every other path obliterates the separate existence of bourgeois essence: mechanicism, as the true knowledge of the situation, fixes this essence, but without hope. Descartes knows how to rediscover hope. Is this the hope of reconstructing the mythical world of man that the Renaissance itself had hoped for? No. Only the hope to lead the world, the whole universe, back to the productive separation of bourgeois essence. It is not important to judge whether this is a lot or a little. What matters is recognizing that, perhaps, in this way a metaphysics was constituted through the conclusive definition of the bourgeois class.

155. *cont'd*   sometimes, finally, it has both positive and negative consequences. One example will suffice, on which E. Cassirer, in his *Das Erkenntnisproblem in der Philosophie und Wissenschaft der neueren Zeit*, has reflected with customary elegance and depth: the concept of 'work' in Descartes. Now, unlike what could be surmised from mechanicist science, which saw in work, in a non-mystified way, the capacity of an animated being to produce new effects, Descartes considers in a mystified way work as 'action', entirely contained within a self-sufficient system. What do we wish to highlight here? That Descartes's mystification, according to which 'the concept of work is an exclusive product of universal mathematics' (Cassirer refers to the *Traité de Mechanique*: AT I 435ff) corresponds to a real function of the bourgeois essence more than, or at least as much as, the correct mechanicist definition. Descartes's metaphysical definition in fact confers strength upon the bourgeoisie's illusion about the necessity of its own recovery, while the mechanicist scientific definition provides further confirmation of the situation of defeat. Can we thereby conclude that the Cartesian ideology corresponds to the class nature of the bourgeoisie more than mechanicist science?

5

The cycle of the reconstruction and foundation of the reasonable ideology is completed, around 1641, with *The Search for Truth (Recherche de la vérité)*.[156] In this dialogue we encounter the fundamental themes of the mature Descartes in their entirety: '. . . to lay down the foundations for a solid science, and to discover all the ways in which he can raise his knowledge to the highest level that it can possibly attain'. These things, Descartes declares 'I intend in this work to explain . . . I shall bring to light the true riches of our souls, opening up to each of us the means whereby we can find within ourselves, without any help from anyone else, all the knowledge we may need for the conduct of life, and the means of using it in order to acquire all the more abstruse items of knowledge that human knowledge is capable of possessing'.[157] The content of the *Meditations* is unravelled here in mundane form. It develops in the debate between Eudoxus ('a man of moderate intellect but possessing a

156. When was *The Search for Truth* written? We subscribe here to one of the 'conjectures' put forward by C. Adam (AT X 528–32): the dialogue was written during the summer of 1642 in Endegeest castle, following a series of discussions between Descartes (*Eudoxe*) and his friends Desbarreaux (*Poliandre*) and the *abbé* Picot (*Epistémon*) who were indeed staying there at the time. There are substantive reasons to opt for this, having to do with the analogy between this work and the *Meditations*. In the same vein, see F. Alquié's arguments in the note on his edition of Descartes's *Œuvres philosophiques*, vol. II, pp. 1101–4. Besides the elements of analogy with the *Meditations*, which we will point out as we go along ('the most necessary and illuminating comparison is the one between the *Search* and the *Meditations*', says Alquié) it is perhaps worth recalling the pages from the *Epistula ad Voetium* (AT VIII B 39–55 [TN: partly in PWD III 221–2]) where humanist wisdom and the search for truth in the world are opposed to Scholastic erudition. For other hypotheses regarding the dating of the *Search* see below in this section.
157. PWD II 400.

judgement which is not corrupted by any false beliefs and a reason which retains all the purity of its nature');[158] Episté-mon, the erudite one; Polyandrus, the man of the world; and the pure mind, the free man Polybius. It is precisely the form of the dialogue that allows Descartes to stress that reconstruc-tive point of view – laboriously investigated and recovered – which is constituted by the path within the I, within the full life of the soul. The tension vis-à-vis the world – which is not resolved, and cannot be resolved, into identity – devolves onto the subject. In the subject's separation, it becomes deeper and is articulated, inaugurating a project of universal comprehen-sion. Polyandrus – the bourgeois man, the *mercator* one might call him, who has had immediate knowledge of the great book of the world – is led by the hand, guided in the rediscovery of himself. He is led to see in himself, in the *cogito*, the basis for a new knowledge (and a new power) that nothing will be able to shatter.

That is as far as the text of the *Search* goes.[159]

Except that, besides this fundamental expository design, which follows the initial development of the *Meditations* (or rather furthers some of its arguments, accentuating the critique of the metaphysics of identity and, at the same time, the critique of the sceptical positions that the crisis of identity leads to), there appears a series of motifs that have provoked a wide-ranging debate around the *Search*. Stylistic motifs, but also and above all substantial ones, which have led some to place the *Search* in the youthful years of Descartes's activity.[160] Indeed, such is the intensity of the discussion concerning the spontaneity of the

158. PWD II 401.
159. The unfinished text of the *Search* is printed in PWD II 400–20. On the vicissitudes of the text and its editions, see AT X 491–4.
160. According to G. Cantecor, 'À quelle date Descartes a-t-il écrit la *Recherche de la vérite*?', *Revue d'histoire de la philosophie*, vol. 2, 1928, pp. 254–89, the work should be placed around 1628. Its style does in fact seem to demand this. In his introduction to the   *cont'd over/*

emergence of truth,[161] such is the insistence on the simplicity of the true and the immediacy of its appearance (for which simplicity is the medium),[162] such is therefore the sense of participation in the true, that the image of that Renaissance universe in which Descartes had actually lived – but from whose crisis his more mature philosophy had takent its cue – here seems to be both present and predominant. Further elements are added to the definition of that universe, among which of fundamental importance is the feeling of a universal metaphorical linkage: 'For the items of knowledge that lie within reach of the human mind are all linked together by a bond so marvellous, and can be derived from each other by means of inferences so necessary, that their discovery does not require much skill or intelligence – provided we begin with the simplest and know how to move stage by stage to the most sublime.'[163] Is this a paraphrase of *Regula IV*?[164] Perhaps rather than of a simple reference to that text, we should speak of a reappearance of the entire symbolic universe of humanist experience – the immediacy of the true, the

160. *cont'd*   *Opere* (vol. I, pp. cxxxiv–cxxxviii), E. Garin has adopted Cantecor's theses, insisting both on stylistic motivations (he discerns echoes of Silhon and Balzac) and substantive ones (we are within the framework of Descartes's first investigations, probably during his first Dutch sojourn: and the *recherche* might be a section of that *histoire* that his contemporaries were awaiting).

161. It suffices to recall the complete title of the dialogue: 'The Search for Truth by means of the Natural Light', which continues: 'This light alone, without any help from religion or philosophy, determines what opinions a good man should hold on any matter that may occupy his thoughts, and penetrates into the secrets of the most recondite sciences' (PWD II 400).

162. For, having been able to find truth, 'I shall not deserve any more glory for having made these discoveries than a passer-by would deserve for having accidentally stumbled upon some rich treasure for which many persons had previously conducted a diligent but unsuccessful search' (PWD II 401).

163. PWD II 400–401. But also PWD II 404 and *passim*.

164. But not just of the *Regulae*: there continuously emerge reminiscences of the *Preambula*, the *Discourse* . . .

happiness of its apprehension, the sense of plenitude in the universality of its possession: 'just as I think each land has enough fruits and rivers to satisfy the hunger and thirst of all its inhabitants, so too I think that enough truth can be known in each subject to satisfy amply the curiosity of orderly souls.'[165]

So is the placement of the *Search* in the early years legitimate? We do not think so.[166] Even if the emergence of these elements which, sometimes slowly, connect back to Descartes's early work is undeniable, the fundamental design of the *Search* remains that of the beginning of the *Meditations*: the discovery of the metaphysical tension of the I and its investigation, the collapse into the world of separation. Moreover, the critique of the alternatives to the direction outlined in the *Meditations*, developed by Descartes in his replies to his critics, here seems to be intensified: he violently turns towards all those who, sick with universality, nevertheless wish to possess the world;[167] and he reprises the

---

165. PWD II 402.
166. It also does not seem to be the case for H. Gouhier ('Sur la date de la *Recherche de la vérité* de Descartes', *Revue d'histoire de la philosophie*, vol. 3, 1929, pp. 296–320) and E. Cassirer ('La place de la *Recherche de la vérité par la lumière naturelle* dans l'œuvre de Descartes', *Revue philosophique de la France et de l'étranger*, vol. 127, 1939, pp. 261–300), who nevertheless tend to shift the date respectively to 1648 or even to the period of the Swedish sojourn. See also G. Rodis-Lewis, 'Cinquante ans d'études cartésiennes', *Revue philosophique de la France et de l'étranger*, vol. 141, 1951, p. 254 (attracted by Cassirer's dating, but persuaded by Gouhier's) and A. Vartanian, *Diderot and Descartes*. As far as I'm concerned, though I prefer Adam's and Alquié's hypothesis, nothing stops the *Search* from being considered a work written later than 1641: as long as the substance of the interest that moves the search is registered in the *Meditations*. To conclude these notes on the dating of the *Search* it is worth noting the view expressed in G. Sebba, *Bibliographia cartesiana*, pp. 77–8: 'Cantecor's thesis is a vigorous one, Gouhier's is solid, Cassirer's ingenious. All three suffer from the same incurable disease, the absence of facts'.
167. PWD II 402 and 404. Of course, at these points, as in others, there appear themes from the youthful polemic, in particular   *cont'd over/*

theme of doubt, of dream,[168] even more vivaciously. He does this, needless to say, in order to ground the subsequent reversal and, in so doing, he affirms the depth of the crisis he is living through. As in the *Meditations*: 'these are deep waters, where I think we may lose our footing.'[169] And from doubt the discourse reascends to being once again.[170]

But if that is the case, how are we to explain this paradoxical coexistence of the path taken by the *Meditations* and the humanist emphasis? That is the nub of the matter. We have said that the *Search* seems to represent the conclusive moment in Descartes's definition of the reasonable ideology. We must add that it represents it all the more in so far as it retrieves that happy paradoxicality. That is because through the *Search* we fully grasp the historical position and meaning of Cartesian thought: its humanist and bourgeois roots, the crisis, and finally the metaphysical overturning, the ideological reconstruction of that myth in which Descartes had rooted himself.[171] This takes place within the limits marked out by defeat. But within those limits the nostalgia for humanist man is alive and comes to be reconstructed. What is the reasonable ideology? It is certainty, essence, rediscovery of oneself, 'without any help from anyone else'.[172] In other

---

167. *cont'd*   where Epistémon requests information on the science of artifices, spectres and illusions (we are without doubt in the ambit of the problematic of a 'science of miracles'). There also returns – in the very subtitle, for instance – the expression 'curious sciences'. And we could go on. Yet it should be noted that these arguments operate as a polemic against universalism. They become particularly appealing if we bear in mind their genesis, which is at the very least ambiguous.

168. PWD II 407–9. These pages are full – it would seem – of quotes from the *Meditations*.

169. PWD II 408.

170. PWD II 412ff.

171. In the sense of a constant underscoring of the alternatives, the ambiguities, and the paradoxical rhythm of the search undertaken by this Descartes, I recommend the interpretive approach of G. Schmidt, *Aufklärüng und Metaphysik*.

172. PWD II 400.

words, it is the acceptance of separation. But in this separation truth is full: and the one who knows this 'enjoys the same tranquillity as would a king if his country were so isolated and cut off from others that he imagined there was nothing beyond his frontiers but infertile deserts and uninhabitable mountains'.[173] We might ask if there is a more adequate image for the drama of the bourgeoisie forced into separation but, having endured the crisis, showing itself capable of renewing within itself the full possession of its separate world. In this view, the bourgeoisie could express and enjoy a complete autonomy as the basis for a relaunching of itself onto the world, for a reconstruction, in itself, of the world. Such an image is also open onto the future. The autonomy of class, the autonomy of the I, is a productive, utopian nostalgia and a totalizing project. We will reconstruct our house; this separate truth of ours grows in us until we are able to project it onto the universe. The world has refused us: but here, in the I who produces himself, the world is thought. Thought today, reconstructed tomorrow. This was the first emergence of bourgeois man: a house constructed on insecure foundations. It was necessary to destroy it. The reconstruction would follow. These are the *a quo* and *a quem* terms of the reasonable ideology, which also specified itself in a tactical vein so as to gain currency in the present: 'Polyander, while engaged upon this work of demolition we can use the same method to dig the foundations which ought to serve our purpose, and to prepare the best and most solid materials which will be needed for building up these foundations.'[174] And further: 'For I do not wish to be one of those jobbing builders who devote themselves solely to refurbishing old buildings because they consider themselves incapable of undertaking the construction of new ones.'[175] One could say that the dramatic relation between the memory of the world of metaphor

173. PWD II 402.
174. PWD II 407.
175. PWD II 407.

and the experience of crisis, which we have seen unfold and from which we initially set off, is here finally placated. However, what we are interested in is the form this takes. Because even in mechanicism, even in libertinism, the immediate paralysing sensation of crisis had been overcome: in the elegance of a situation of longing, for the libertine; in the acceptance and fixation of the actual form of separation, for the mechanicist. In Descartes instead, the tension is alleviated by reproposing an operative horizon. And the renewed hope is accompanied by the certainty of the future realization of the ideal.

So, the 'search for truth' takes the form of a reconstruction of truth. We have seen the metaphysical conditions for this reconstruction and, in the course of our investigation, we have also had occasion to underline the cultural provenance of Descartes's discourse on the 'search for truth'. This was expressly linked to the movement of a certain, vivacious Catholic reform and, like it, was innervated by a strong reconstructive demand.[176] Not by chance Descartes sees in the oratorian Gibieuf, in particular, one who has always supported him 'in the search for truth'.[177] And he relies on Gibieuf for many of the culturally mediated aspects of his own discourse.[178] But that is not enough. Having reached this stage in its development, the Cartesian ideology in general wants to become operative, it wants to identify the practical conditions of its own vigorous exercise. It wants to prove itself within time. Where the vernal consciousness of humanism had failed, there Descartes's mature ideology once again forces thought to test itself. This confrontation with time characterizes this last stage of Cartesian thought, which renews – in the ambit of the new

176. See above, ch. 1, section 5; ch. 2, section 1; and *passim.*
177. AT III 472.
178. Besides what has already been said, see PWD III 89, AT II 97, 147; PWD III 153, 157–8, AT III 276, PWD III 179, AT III 386, 388, PWD III 201–4. Of particular importance were the steps taken in the Sorbonne, and Descartes's attempts to legitimate his own doctrine of freedom by referring to Gibieuf's *De Libertate.*

metaphysical conditions we have described – the old humanist demand of the renewal of the world.

Of course, when this operational horizon of ideology appears, it is still very formal: a declaration of principle, reliance on society (either generically defined or as a society of scholars) for the task of the search for truth: 'for the search for truth is so essential and so vast an undertaking as to need the united effort of many thousands; and there are so few people in the world who join it wholeheartedly that those who do should especially cherish each other and seek to help each other by sharing their observations and their thoughts.'[179] Of course, because of its formal and generic character, the demand risks being accused of utopianism: 'I complain that the world is too big, on account of the few honest people that may be found in it: I would like them all to be gathered in one city, and then I would be very pleased to leave my hermitage, to live with them, if they wished to welcome me into their company'.[180] The demand will therefore need to be confronted with the world and it must define its own positive contents through this confrontation. And in this confrontation many difficulties will emerge, many readjustments will be required.[181]

But all this should not make us forget the centrality and importance of this horizon which Descartes discovers for his epoch, for his class – even if, for now, the horizon is only formal. The excavation of the I that Descartes undertakes is an excavation that he undertakes into the social reality of his time. The projecting of the I onto the theological horizon and the subsequent confirmation of its universal essentiality are tasks that he sets the epoch. The reversal of the perception of the crisis into a new, conscious prospect of reconstruction is the urgent necessity to which Descartes responds. To this extent, the Cartesian reasonable

179. PWD III 143. Recall also the conclusion of the *Discourse* which, as Descartes himself underlines in his correspondence (AT I 339), is explicitly supported by this project.
180. AT IV 378.
181. We shall return at length to all these questions in ch. 4.

ideology discovers its importance as the political ideology of the epoch.

In so doing, and in these new general conditions of development, the reasonable ideology retreads, without paradox, the path already travelled by other thinkers who had participated in the crisis of humanism. Above all that of Machiavelli, who from the crisis of municipal freedom had managed to extract a hope of reconstruction, an even more radical hope than Descartes's, inasmuch as Machiavelli held in the highest regard the ambit of application of political action.[182] Of course, Descartes would never have recognized himself as a follower of Machiavellianism – and the history of the French reception of Machiavelli serves to tell us why: what triumphed there was indeed a Machiavelli 'reduced' to a defender of peace or to an ingenious and diabolical apologist for power, a libertine and *politique* Machiavelli – 'whose genius [is] sharp, subtle, and fiery'.[183] Descartes knows only this Machiavelli

182. This is the guiding thesis of F. Raab's interpretation (*The English Face of Machiavelli: A Changing Interpretation, 1500–1700*, London and Toronto 1964) of the influence of Machiavelli's thought in Europe, and particularly in England, which identifies the direct thread linking him to the bourgeois revolution of 1649 and the work of Harrington. We will have more to say about Raab's interpretation; an essential complement to it is to be found in the studies by G. Procacci, *Studi sulla fortuna di Machiavelli*, Roma 1965.

183. Justus Lipsius, *Politica*, ed. J. Waszink, Assen 2004, pp. 230–1. In any case, Machiavelli, at best, was taken up by French thought as a realist thinker in the manner of the *politiques*. This is a total misunderstanding. When he wasn't simply treated as a realist, he was regarded as the diabolical author of the wickedness of power (A. Cherel, *La pensée de Machiavel en France*, Paris 1935; R. De Mattei, 'Origini e fortuna della locuzione "ragion di stato"', *Rivista internazionale di filosofia del diritto*, vol. 26, 1949, pp. 187–202; H. Lutz, *Ragione di stato und christliche Staatsethik in 16. Jahrhundert*, Münster 1961; A. M. Battista, *Alle origini del pensiero politico libertino. Montaigne e Charron*, Milan 1966). A wide-ranging and persuasive explanation of the *politique* misunderstanding of Machiavelli's thinking in France is provided by G. Procacci (*Studi*, pp. 77–106), who sees it as originating in the cultural mediation that Machiavelli underwent *cont'd over/*

who 'makes one sad', he knows the author in whom the crisis of his time recognizes itself, not the one who recognizes and over-comes that crisis. Having said that, how much of the true Machiavelli there is in Descartes's reasonable ideology! Because in Descartes, as in Machiavelli, we encounter the generalization of the meaning of the end of the humanist revolution and of the necessary rescaling of bourgeois action in these new conditions. But the aim and the objective remain. What we encounter here is the recognition of the end and the (conditioned) relaunching of the humanist ideal. These are elements which become constitutive of the very definition of the bourgeoisie – a universal class, but one which does not know how (or is unable) to really ground its own universality, and which is forced into ideology because it has

183. *cont'd*   at the hands of Cardanus (and of his astrological pes-simism). It is nevertheless interesting to note how, once this operation had been carried out, Machiavelli became almost incomprehensible to the same *politiques* who wanted him thus interpreted. See the com-ments by E. Garin (*Giornale critico della filosofia italiana*, vol. 29, 1950, pp. 383–4), who reproduces a passage from the *Sorberiana, sive excerpta ex ore Samuelis Sorbière*: 'Machiavelli is spoken ill of in both Latin and French. In Latin it is declared that *The Prince* is a book which gains from not being read (*cujus libri minuit lectura famam*); in French the following parallel is made with Hobbes: "there is as much difference between the politics of Machiavelli and those of Hobbes, as there is between sugar placed in a marble mortar which has been rubbed with garlic and that which has been placed in another mortar which had been filled with amber. The reasoning of the first derives from a wild and inhuman spirit; those of the other from a tender, good, and benevolent soul. The latter, in his greater rigour, always feels like an honest man who only does harm regretfully, an able surgeon who regretfully cuts into the living flesh to separate it from its diseased part; the other feels like a bandit, cutting the throats of passers-by, an avenger, twisting the sword in the wound he has inflicted . . ."'. In general, still on the reception of Machiavelli by French culture, see H. Busson, *De Charron à Pascal*, pp. 520ff; R. Lenoble, *Mersenne*, pp. 176ff; F. Meinecke, *Machiavellism: The Doctrine of Raison d'État and its Place in Modern History*, Boulder 1984; and especially R. von Albertini, 'Das politische Denken' (pp. 175–95), who grasps the terms of the problem with his customary clarity.

burned, in its first contact with the world, any possibility of real possession. Essence and existence, forever separate. Anxiety, urgency, necessity, and the failure of the attempt to render absolute that which by now is, because of its nature and its history, already definitively separate. This is a paradox that renews itself with dramatic intensity each and every day in each and every situation. Descartes's reasonable ideology is the definitive response to this precariousness: an imperious demand to exist regardless, to develop itself regardless. And it is a fate – this fate that the reasonable ideology describes – which the bourgeoisie will experience in its entirety.

4

Time and Ideology

The last and greatest fruit of these principles is that they will enable those who develop them to discover many truths which I have not explained at all. Thus, moving little by little from one truth to the next, they may in time acquire a perfect knowledge of all philosophy, and reach the highest level of wisdom. One sees in all the arts that although they are at first rough and imperfect, nevertheless, because they contain some element of truth, the effect of which is revealed by experience, they are gradually perfected by practice. So it is in philosophy: when one has true principles and follows them, one cannot fail to come upon other truths from time to time.

PWD I 188–9

1

An interpretation of the historical consciousness of the bourgeoisie and a decision between the mnemonic contents that qualify the bourgeois existence of his time – this then seems to be Descartes's reasonable ideology. The motifs around which this ideology has taken shape seem to concern the epoch in its entirety, and the specific development of the bourgeois class in particular. Only at this point, once the immediacy of the relation with the world is found to be lacking, when the final, solemn conjuncture has made its effects felt, does the historical consciousness of the bourgeoisie emerge.[1] As we have also seen, the awareness of the revolutionary failure is so deep that from being an element of the current condition it soon turns into a trait of bourgeois consciousness as such. Nevertheless, there are still alternatives left: the reasonable ideology perhaps represents the most significant among these – in its complexity, in the positive ambiguity between the acceptance of defeat and the declaration of an inexorable bourgeois existence, and in the drive to realize in time, both within and beyond separation, the bourgeois essence.

The projection of the bourgeois essence in time must become real; that is, it must be articulated within history. Ideology must pass into politics. The project that had been presented, as we have seen, in entirely general and formal terms, now needed to be verified. The reference to time could not remain hypothetical, it had to become living experience. But is the reference to time legitimate? Can the positive recuperation of time from the essential project become real? The first of these questions is implicit in the very philosophical formality of the project, in the awareness of the difficulty that inheres in it and of the crisis that it registers. But within the philosophical horizon the demand of a solution to the problem, the legitimacy of a positive approach, had been recognized as indestructible. So it is in passing from the question of legitimacy to that of possibility, from the metaphysical to the historical terrain – that is, when we pass to the second of our questions – that the heart of the problem is grasped and infused with dramatic significance. All the more so inasmuch as the philosophical question is here not simply about history but in history; it is elicited, formulated and developed within a determinate series of events and a determinate debate. There are in fact

1. In this respect, the complaints about the lack of a national historiography repeated in *robin* circles are significant. On this question, see
   M. Yardeni, *La conception*, p. 109. In this respect, Descartes's own
   arguments about the uselessness of the study of pleasant historical
   fables seem to harbour the demand for a complete overhaul (see
   Discourse, AT VI 5; E. Gilson, *Commentaire*, p. 112).

noteworthy groups within the *robin* milieu itself who promote a dramatic negation, a radical opposition against every hope of a historical recovery of the bourgeoisie.

These groups dispute the possible relation between essence and world. They do not deny the emergence of the bourgeois essence, nor do they wish to ignore the irrepressible tension that derives from this emergence. Instead, they want to refute every pacification, every possibility thereof, every attempt, whether to alleviate in acceptance or to mystify in confident expectation the dramatic relation that has been registered. These *robin* groups radicalize the appreciation of the conjunctural crisis with the same intensity as the libertines – the defeat is definitive and the absolutist restructuring of the state is its sign.[2] Unlike the libertines, however, the

2. L. Goldmann (*The Hidden God: A Study of Tragic Vision in the* Pensées *of Pascal and the Tragedies of Racine*, London 1964) is the author who has done most to underline this dramatic Jansenist opposition to the political development of absolutism. And rightly so, since the fundamental character of this opposition must not be underestimated in any way. Goldmann has emphasized not only the general process that leads to this opposition but also the particular events that endow it with meaning and determinateness: 'As for Jansenism, its birth in 1637–38 is placed in the midst of the decisive wave of monarchic absolutism which succeeds in creating its own bureaucratic apparatus, indispensable for any absolute government . . . [furthermore] the years 1635–40 constitute, within this longer process, a critical period, a kind of limited but particularly acute crisis in the relationship between parliamentary milieus and central power . . .' But what are the reasons for the crisis? Let us recall what has been said by C. Vivanti, *Lotta politica e pace religiosa*, p. 355: '[The *robins*] needed to find themselves on the side of power at a moment characterized by the crystallization of the social organism, by the closure of those horizons that had permitted, throughout the 1500s, the rise of an entire class and the blossoming of an exceptional cultural period, but they were not capable of elaborating a political platform from which intellectually to stimulate and enrich the action of ruling groups. Rather than attaining this goal, they were obliged to renounce, be it within certain limits, the cultural and moral positions that had originally been linked to the *robins*' most advanced aspirations, submitting to the rigid political institutions which they had never been   *cont'd over/*

robins refuse isolation. They cannot fully endure the inexorable character of the situation, because they oppose to it the equal intensity of the humanist myth, renewed by memory. From the same standpoint, these *robin* groups, unlike the mechanicists, also refuse to make a virtue of necessity, to embellish defeat by justifying separation and absolutism in the name of the development of the social form of bourgeois existence. Moreover, they accuse Descartes of being a mystificator. Precisely inasmuch as

2. *cont'd*   capable of influencing. But beyond this there was only libertine evasion.' If one wished to save oneself, it was therefore necessary to accept the rules of sovereign power, which in the circumstances were those of the royal functionaries. The theoretician of this transformation of the function of the *robin* (from free bourgeois expression to function of the sovereign) recognizes it as follows: '. . . the power of the officers is nothing but a projection of the power of the prince . . .' (C. Loyseau, *Traité du droit des offices*, bk. II, ch. II, p. 621). How different this is from what was still being affirmed by Turquet de Mayerne: that the sovereign himself is a magistrate, that he himself is obliged to a pledge and to a contract vis-à-vis his subjects, and that, moreover, magistrate and '*officier*' are subordinated to the crown and not to the king. See R. Mousnier, 'Etat et Commissaire. Recherches sur la création des Intendants des Provinces (1634–1648)', in *Forschungen zu Staat und Verfassung. Festgabe für Fritz Hartung*, Berlin 1958, pp. 325–44. But also see, again by R. Mousnier, the 'Introduction' (pp. 7–192, vol. I) to *Lettres et mémoires adressés au Chancelier Séguier (1633–1649)*, Paris 1964 (here we should underline especially the original cultural elements determined by the new institution: a tendency to rationalism in the interpretation of the law and a universalistic conception of its validity); 'La participation des gouvernés aux activités des gouvernants dans la France du XVIIe et du XVIIIe siècle', *Etudes suisses d'histoire générale*, vol. 20, 1962–3, pp. 200–29; as well as the older and more comprehensive investigations: *La vénalité des offices sous Henri IV et Louis XIII*, Rouen 1945; *Le XVIe et XVIIe siècles*, Paris 1954. As for the specificity of the crisis in the last years of the 1630s, Goldmann has correctly underscored that it essentially consists in a further devaluation of the price of offices, such that the parliamentary bourgeoisie finds itself subjected to further competition. It is not only in the total dependence on its functions, but in the expansion of recruitment, that the parliamentary bourgeoisie is both controlled and defeated.

they themselves, with nostalgic love, exalt an unbridled individuality and feel its metaphysical absoluteness and centrality, time – in which the defeat was given and in which the struggle persists – cannot in any case be configured as a place of positive mediation. Instead, time is the place that has already been chosen as that of confrontation. The only thing that is renewed in it is the fall, the crisis at the end of a desperate opposition that was simultaneously hopeless, necessary, and called for.[3] In Descartes's reasonable project this time is combated by ideology. But, on the other hand, it is a time incapable of mediation, a place of perennial defeat for a revolutionary anxiety that nevertheless cannot be placated. These are the terms in which the very possibility of the reasonable Cartesian ideology is discussed.[4]

A debate thus arises aimed at clarifying the terms of the new opposition. As is so often the case, it emerges in roundabout

3. Following in Goldmann's footsteps, G. Namer (*L'abbé Roy et ses amis. Essai sur le jansénisme extrémiste intramondain*, Paris 1964) has furthered the analysis of the reactions by the parliamentary nobility to the crisis in which it was implicated. In this framework, Namer has identified a current – precisely called that of 'worldly extremism' – whose ideology and practice consist fundamentally in the recognition of the irrationality of the royal order and in the propaganda for resistance. Not in the hope of victory, but in the mystic confidence in the act of resistance as such. Namer speaks of a 'theology of defeat' as the feature of the extreme currents in Jansenism. To my mind such an ideology is the deep thread running through the whole of Jansenism: 'The world is the place of the eternal combat and eternal victory of God: God is present, of course, lived in his truth by those who proclaim him until their human defeat; his victory is hidden only to the eyes of those who do not partake in the combat . . .' A theology of testimony, therefore, which is tragic in its vocation and confident of its destination. The consideration of the existent balance of forces, which is decidedly unfavourable to an action of resistance, is transformed into an attitude of desperate demand for confrontation, which in any case produces positive theological effects. The devaluation of time as the place of defeat is the counterpart to the exaltation of defeat as significant for eternity.

4. See my 'Problemi dello stato moderno: Francia 1610–1650' for an in-depth treatment of the historiographical discussion around this theme.

fashion. What the opposition immediately contests is a (central) point of Cartesian physics: the conception of the full universe. This objection hits its mark and is furthermore endowed with an incomparable efficacy, since it concentrates on a theme with general implications for Cartesian physics. When, first through a personal encounter,[5] and then reading the *New Experiments Concerning the Void*,[6] Descartes grasps the underlying motives of Blaise Pascal, he infers at once that the latter wishes to fight 'my subtle matter'.[7] Nevertheless, he initially restrains the polemic, making out as if he is dealing with the same problems, offering benevolent advice and suggesting proposals for experiments.[8] Not for long though, since a little later Descartes shows his true colours: 'I am comfortable with the fact that the protectors of the void let their opinion be known in several places, and that they grow heated regarding this matter; for this will turn in their disfavour if the truth is discovered'.[9] He also observes, with a certain malicious pleasure, the intervention of Père Noël against

5. This encounter takes place during the trip to Paris of 1647. See AT V 68 and the notes at AT V 71–3.

6. Pascal, *Experiences nouvelles touchant le vide*, in *Œuvres complètes*, ed. Chevalier, pp. 362ff. Descartes's first judgement is from a letter dated 13 December 1647 (AT V 98–100). See the long comment in AT V 100–6, which tracks all the texts of importance for the polemic, and contains a strong affirmation of the originality of Pascal's discourse.

7. AT V 98. See L. Brunschvicg, 'Descartes et Pascal', in *Écrits philosophiques*, vol. I: *L'humanisme de l'occident. Descartes, Spinoza, Kant*, Paris 1951, p. 92, note: 'It is not a matter of establishing an abstract parallel between Descartes and Pascal. We are in the presence of two people who really met, and clashed.'

8. In effect, for some time already (since at least 1643) Descartes had been occupied with and interested in investigations on the void in particular, and on the physics of liquids in general, which had developed in the ambit of the Galilean school – namely at the hands of Torricelli. See AT III 617ff.

9. AT V 116 (from a letter dated 31 January 1648). See the note in AT V 117–18 on the works that continue to appear concerning this problem.

which Pascal will direct his polemic.[10] Finally, faced with the indisputable value of the experiments carried out by the partisans of the void, Descartes declares that all these are perfectly compatible and can be recuperated into his own system.[11] But the partisans of the void will not be persuaded. This is especially true of Pascal, who already 'tried to attack my subtle matter in a certain pamphlet of two or three pages', and who is led into the polemic by his friend Roberval – who has always been hostile to Descartes.[12]

Descartes's position in this debate can therefore be seen as a stark opposition or as an equivalent, albeit more ambiguous, attitude of recuperation, which attempts to neutralize the scope of the Pascalian discourse. The fact is that Descartes grasped in this

10. AT V 118–21. For Pascal's text against Père Noël, see *Œuvres complètes*, pp. 370ff (as well as the comment-complement at pp. 1438ff). In any case, it is worth reading the judgement of A. Koyré, 'Pascal savant', in *Etudes d'histoire de la pensée scientifique*, p. 347: 'Pascal has not given us the complete and exact story of the experiments he carried out or imagined; and this throws a singular light on his polemic with Père Noël and, moreover, significantly modifies the image of Pascal as a sagacious and prudent experimenter which the historical tradition opposes to the image of Descartes as an unapologetic apriorist. But Pascal is neither a faithful disciple of Bacon nor a first edition of Boyle'. Which, in any case, on the level on which we are moving, is rather irrelevant.

11. AT V 141–2 (from a letter dated 4 April 1648). See the notes in AT V 143–4.

12. AT V 366 (from a letter dated 11 June 1649). But see also AT V 370, PWD III 380, and – on the experiments concerning the problems of the void that Descartes continues to carry out even in Stockholm – the note in AT V 448–9. On the whole question of the experiments of Puy-de-Dôme in relation to Descartes's judgement, see C. Adam, *Vie et œuvres de Descartes*; 'Pascal et Descartes. Les expériences du vide (1646–1651)', *Revue philosophique de la France et de l'étranger*, 1887, pp. 612–24; 1888, pp. 65–90; C. De Waard, *L'expérience barométrique, ses antécedents et ses explications*, Thouars 1936; E. J. Dyksterhuis, 'Descartes, Pascal en de proef op de Puy-de-Dôme', *Euclides*, vol. 25, 1950, pp. 265–70; R. Dugas, *De Descartes à Newton par l'école anglaise*, Alençon 1953.

new affirmation of the void what in truth it contained: a radical attack against his physics. But also an attack on and an attempt to deny the very possibility of the reasonable ideology. As ever, in this phase, the scientific polemic functions as a metaphor of a debate that impinges on metaphysical positions and unfolds around the great themes of the time. This is soon noticed by Arnauld – the same author who, in an entirely coherent manner, had contributed with his objections to the Cartesian examination of the metaphysical themes of divinity, of that new productive hypostasis of individuality.[13] Arnauld in fact writes, intervening on Descartes's *Principles*: You assert that not only is there no void in nature but that no such thing even exists. But this seems clearly to detract from divine omnipotence. For what? Is God not capable of reducing wine contained in a jar to nothing, or of producing some other body in its place, or of allowing some other body to enter the jar? Although the latter is by no means necessary, since once the wine has been destroyed, no body can take its place without leaving another part void. Therefore either God must conserve all bodies or, if he is able to reduce something to nothing, he can also create a void.[14] So in Arnauld, and in the Jansenist faction, an acceptance of the void is above all viewed as a metaphysical sign, an index of divine omnipotence. This position recalls the Cartesian thesis of the creation of eternal truths, a thesis that introduces a radical precariousness into the world. But we have seen how Descartes, with difficulty but definitively, had extricated himself from that affirmation of precariousness and discontinuity in the world in a polemic against any and every humanist and naturalist extremism; how he passed from the metaphysical accidentality of the emergence of the subject to the ideological continuity between man and God – to the point of establishing an analogical identity of nature between divine and

13. In the Fourth Objection to the *Meditations*.
14. AT V 190. But see also, for the continuation of the discussion, PWD III 355, AT V 215, PWD III 358–9.

human freedom: 'The desire that everyone has to have all the perfections that he can conceive of, and consequently all those we believe to be in God, comes from the fact that God has given us a will devoid of boundaries. And it is principally because of this infinite will in us that one can say that he created us in his image;[15] an identity in which human nature, and especially consciousness, is appreciated in its entirety. The fact is that Descartes tries to reconstruct the continuous on the basis of the discontinuous, to project a new world – a separate world, as new as one wishes, but which is nevertheless real, constructed in its limited extension with intensity and truth undivided:

> The difficulty in recognizing the impossibility of a vacuum seems to arise primarily because we do not sufficiently consider that nothing can have no properties; otherwise, seeing that there is true extension in the space we call empty, and consequently all the properties necessary for the nature of body, we would not say that it was wholly empty, that is, mere nothingness. Secondly, it arises because we have recourse to the divine power: knowing this to be infinite, we attribute to it an effect without noticing that the effect involves a contradictory conception, that is, is inconceivable by us. But I do not think that we should ever say of anything that it cannot be brought about by God. For since every basis of truth and goodness depends on his omnipotence, I would not dare to say that God cannot make a mountain without a valley, or bring it about that 1 and 2 are not. I merely say that he has given me such a mind that I cannot conceive a mountain without a valley, or a sum of 1 and 2 which is not 3; such things involve a contradiction in my conception. I think the same should be said of space which is wholly empty, or of an extended piece of nothing, or of a

15. PWD III 141–2. As we have often recalled, J.-P. Sartre has insisted, with total and utter efficacy, on the centrality of the analogy between man (human freedom) and divinity (divine freedom).

limited universe; because no limit to the world can be imagined without its being understood that there is extension beyond it; and no barrel can be conceived to be so empty as to have inside it no extension, and therefore no body; for whatever extension is, there, of necessity, is body also.[16]

In contrast, the Jansenists use the declaration of divine omnipotence in order to extend the recognition of the precariousness of the human world, in order to consider it as the site of an unfulfilled tension, of a struggle that is never brought to a close: the crisis was never ended or placated; doubt, introducing us into metaphysical reality, does not show us horizons of mediation but only the abyssal depth of our own tragedy.[17]

From this standpoint, plenitude and void are thus opposed as completely heterogeneous models of the relation to the world. And if, in this phase of the development of the bourgeois consciousness of the world, the relation to the world also represents a judgement on the past and future of the bourgeois class, a temporally founded re-examination and forecast, we are now in a position to find some more determinate cues with respect to the Jansenist opposition to the Cartesian reformist project, to its hope of reconquering the world.

The void is above all an index of a particular mnemonic relation to the past. It marks a relation of rupture, it registers the Renaissance setback and represents the radical negation of every possibility of reconstructing the magical universe to which naturalism and theology had contributed. It constitutes an attack on humanism, signalling the awareness of the heteronomy of the

16. PWD III 358–9.
17. A. Gounelle has written a massively important introduction to the recent edition of the *Entretien de Pascal avec M. de Sacy*, Paris 1955, which sharply outlines a history of the significance of doubt from Montaigne to Descartes to Pascal. On this theme, see also K. Löwith, 'Descartes' vernünftiger Zweifel und Kierkegaards Leidenschaft des Verzweiflung', in *Congrès Descartes. Etudes cartésiennes*, vol. I, pp. 74–9.

effects issuing from its development – with the intensity that only the humanist character of Jansenist thought itself, only a polemic springing from an actual participation in humanism, can provoke.[18] Even Descartes can agree with this – as he effectively does in the lasting relationship he entertains with Arnauld.[19] But when we turn to what results from such a relation to the past, the spark of difference is lit. In Jansenism, the void is the sign of a break in development that implicates the very subject of this development: the temporality of defeat becomes a metaphysical temporality, the crisis of existence implicates essence. Defeat is experienced as humiliation, as a radical metaphysical precariousness: 'if the Jansenists condemn the pride that seeks to elevate reasoning to matters that transcend the human spirit, it is in order to humiliate the *raison imbécile*. And it is beyond doubt that Descartes's

18. The historiography on the genesis of Jansenism has strongly insisted on the humanist origins of the school. See in particular J. Dagens, *Bérulle*, p. 8; J. Orcibal, 'Le premier Port-Royal: Réforme ou Contre-Réforme', *La nouvelle Clio*, vols 1–2, 1949–50, pp. 238–80. In general, see the writings of J. Orcibal: *Les Origines du Jansénisme*, Paris 1948; *Louis XIV et les protestants*, Paris 1951; 'Néo-platonisme et jansénisme: du *De Libertate* de P. Gibieuf à l'Augustinus', in *Nuove ricerche storiche sul giansenismo*, Roma 1954, pp. 33ff; 'Les origines du jansénisme d'après les récentes publications du R. P. Lucien Ceyssens', *Revue d'histoire ecclésiastique*, vol. 53, 1958, pp. 336ff.

19. It should be clear that Descartes links to Arnauld in a manner that is positive, albeit partial: the agreement on the emergence of the I and its productivity is effective, even though in Arnauld it leads to different conclusions. I therefore dispute the truth of the argument in G. Rodis-Lewis, 'Augustinisme et cartésianisme à Port-Royal', in *Descartes et le cartésianisme hollandaise*, pp. 131–82, according to which the element that brings Cartesianism and Jansenism closest is above all a refusal of speculative theology ('the Jansenist diffidence with regard to any speculative theology is close to the Cartesian refusal to confuse natural and supernatural light', p. 136). On the other hand, it is not possible to exclude the effectiveness of the alternative proposed by Jansenism beyond the limits of the appreciation of the productivity and creativity of the subject. That is why an interpretation such as the one upheld by E. Bourdin, *Pascal et Descartes*, Neuchâtel 1946, whereby 'Pascal's error was his docility towards Port-Royal', is frankly absurd.

reservations on the limits of our understanding have a very different ring'.[20] Of course, the humanist nostalgia persists throughout the whole period. The 'I think', as the eminent sign of this nostalgia, traverses Jansenism like an indefeasible certainty. But the 'I think' cannot, or does not want to, free itself from the accidentality of its emergence. Having accepted the separation from the world and established the impossibility of a science that would amount to a possession of the world, Descartes had climbed up to God – and from here, from this productive hypostasis of bourgeois essence, he had looked again at the world, not in order to conquer it but to subsume it. The Jansenist type of relation to the past, the exasperated awareness of defeat, refuses the very possibility of this horizon: time as the void of humanity, as the sign of the defeat of man, stretches out not only between the individual and the world, but between the individual and God.[21] Every possible mediation is removed. The metaphysical accidentality of man, of his thinking emergence, is totalitarian. The void turns into vertigo, into the solitary and excessive affirmation of existence. The Cartesian awareness of the crisis remains far removed from this perspective! In Descartes, reason had risen up, freeing itself. With the Jansenists, reason seeks to debase itself. *Raison imbécile*! And while the Cartesian 'I think' had the force and the hope of a

20. G. Rodis-Lewis, 'Augustinisme et cartésianisme', p. 136. The motivations behind the void which we encounter in the mechanist school are therefore quite different: see the overall argument in P. Gassendi, *Opera omnia*, vol. I, Lyon 1658, pp. 185–216 (and the comment by B. Rochot concerning the problem of the void in Gassendi: 'P. Gassendi, le philosophe', in the collective volume *Gassendi*, ed. by the Centre International de Synthèse, Paris 1955, pp. 88–93). Against the Gassendian and mechanist conception of the void see in general the harsh critique in *Logique de Port-Royal*, pp. 251–3.

21. E. Garin (*Scienza e vita civile*, p. 168), with customary acuteness and subtlety, has remarked how the crisis of humanism, experienced as the reason for a 'direct', 'immediate', 'personal' defeat, determines the insurgency of the tragic. From this point of view, Galileo is close to Pascal.

'living man',[22] renewing (in separation) the constructivism of Renaissance man, here the humanist anxiety survives only as refusal, as a reliance on an isolated and subversive experience, in the vertigo of the break with the past.

The polemic shifts to scientific methodology. For it was precisely in that area that Cartesian constructivism was in the process of freeing itself completely, showing the deep motivation behind the theory of the plenum: 'Descartes. – We must say summarily: "This is made by figure and motion," for it is true. But to say what these are, and to compose the machine, is ridiculous. For it is useless, uncertain, and painful . . .'[23] To build the machine, developing the domination of the world on the basis of the principle of the I – for the Jansenists, this is ridiculous: 'And were it true, we do not think all Philosophy is worth one hour of pain'.[24] That is because for the Jansenists science too moves in a void and vertiginous space, which cannot be contained within the (necessary) rigidity of the Cartesian project.[25] Science is the metaphor and the operative conclusion of a situation of radical defeat: it cannot be otherwise, it must not be otherwise.[26] For his part, Descartes cannot even imagine a methodology that could configure scientific research as an adventure in the world – in an unsafe and alien world. His scientific horizon excludes sensible

---

22. Pascal, *Œuvres complètes*, p. 600. [Translations taken from W. F. Trotter's translation, New York 1958.] In this regard, see L. Brunschvicg, 'Descartes et Pascal', p. 94.
23. Pascal, *Œuvres complètes*, p. 1137.
24. Pascal, *Œuvres complètes*, p. 1137. But see also this other *pensée* (no. 76): 'To write against those who made too profound a study of science: Descartes' (p. 1137).
25. L. Brunschvicg, pp. 97ff, and A. Koyré, pp. 344ff, despite the disagreement between their respective approaches, nevertheless both equally underline this point.
26. The importance of the metaphysical presupposition in Pascal's thought, which even accords it primacy over the reasons of science, is identified by A. Koyré, pp. 344ff. On this question, see also J. Dagens, 'La sagesse, suivant Descartes et suivant Pascal', *Studia catholica*, vol. 1, 1924–5, pp. 225–40.

intuition and subordinates geometrical space to the law of algebraic proportions.[27] Any other possibility irritates him. When in 1640 he receives that first manifestation of Pascalian genius which is the *Essay on Conics* (in which many of the characteristics of the mature thought can already be discerned),[28] he reacts brusquely: I can happily elucidate problems concerning the conic section 'that a child of sixteen would struggle to untangle'.[29] This is the attitude that recurs in the following ten years, more or less restrained, but always present. It is true that for Descartes the elevation of reason goes so far as to affirm its productive infinity; it is true that the class essence manifests itself as infinite potentiality, ideologically organizing itself within the theological horizon; but it is also true that this relation – which is vertical, going from the individual to the divinity – refuses to lower itself into the real, to collide with the world.[30] Instead

27. J. Vuillemin, *Mathématiques et métaphysique chez Descartes*, though hampered by the limits we have already indicated, has grasped with extreme acuteness this algebraic determinateness of the Cartesian world. See in general pp. 29–35 and 139–40.
28. Pascal, *Œuvres complètes*, pp. 60–3.
29. AT II 628ff (in a letter dated 25 December 1639). But also AT III 40 and 47, where Descartes casts doubt on Pascal's originality. In Pascal's work Descartes sees above all the mark of his master Desargues. On this issue ('a genuine disciple of Desargues') also insist A. Koyré, pp. 329, and R. Taton, '*L'essai pour les coniques* de Pascal', *Revue d'histoire des sciences*, vol. 8, 1951, pp. 1–18, while the long note in AT III 53–9 insists on the originality of Pascal's essay.
30. In Gueroult's footsteps, J. Vuillemin (p. 140) has correctly underlined the gap between the Cartesian conception of the infinite and the analysis of the world: 'mathematicians have never accepted the limits imposed by Descartes on analytical geometry. Some will demand of a new intellectual principle, of continuity, that it legitimate the introduction of the infinite into the operations of the *je pense*. Others will turn this continuity into a property extraneous to our intellect and linked to our sensibility. This conflict, which reason finds unbearable, will be the motor of philosophical systems after Descartes . . . [but] Descartes remained extraneous to this conflict, save perhaps when, pressed by the need to legitimate the principle of causality which he uses in the causal proof, he will reply to Arnauld with *cont'd over/*

Descartes wants to reconstruct the world within himself, considering the separate existence of the I to be absolute.

Here then is Pascal's response: 'I cannot forgive Descartes. In all his philosophy he would have been quite willing to dispense with God. But he had to make Him give a fillip to set the world in motion; beyond this, he has no further need of God'.[31] Is this a false or unjust verdict? Certainly, if we wish to remain within the Cartesian universe. But what Pascal rejects is precisely the act of situating oneself in the completeness or plenitude of that universe. His God is infinite not only there, inside, in the separation of the I from the world; it is not productive only in the cognitive relation that springs from the individual. On the contrary: the productive infinity of the I, concentrated in the divinity, is the commitment to prove oneself in the world, to verify oneself in time. Is the world irredeemably separate? Is it the time of defeat? Of course. But it is a necessary world. The void, after having been the index of a mnemonic relation to the past, is the index of an operative relation to the future. Love is the sign of man's opening up to the future: son of *penìa*, suspended over the void: 'Man does not like to dwell with himself; nevertheless he loves; it is necessary then that he seek elsewhere something to love . . . Nevertheless, although man seeks wherewith to fill up the great void he makes in going out of himself, he cannot however be satisfied with every kind of object. His heart is too large . . .'[32] The void is the trait of the future in which defeat will be repeated, and therefore cannot be avoided. Rather, it is sought out, continuously demanded as the

30. *cont'd*   a passage to the limit. But even then Cartesian metaphysics has nothing to do with Leibnizian metaphysics. If in Descartes the infinite comes before the finite, it is qua idea and not method, qua presence not power. On this point Cartesianism is turned towards the past, not the future. The I discovers itself as a faculty of order without creative power . . .' But these conclusions are, as we have reiterated, entirely unacceptable.

31. Pascal, *Œuvres complètes*, p. 1137.

32. Pascal, *Œuvres complètes*, p. 539. But see also pp. 540–3.

truth of a lived vocation. Humanist nostalgia still presents itself as revolutionary anxiety – not in the impossible hope of success but in the deadly and theological obligation to testimony, to struggle.[33]

So is a positive reference to time possible? Descartes's reasonable ideology was radically disputed at this juncture. The alternative it pointed to – in the awareness of defeat, in the nostalgia for the ideal, in the attempt to mediate them reasonably – encountered the strongest opposition. In this opposition, the same elements (defeat and nostalgia) are at work, but rendered extreme, in any case considered as incapable of being reabsorbed and dialecticized in time. This is because Jansenist time is a place of defeat, a vocation of defeat. It is in the crucible of this opposition that Descartes's thought finds itself obliged to confront time in a more determined manner. What is the positive content of the reasonable ideology? How can it verify itself in the world? 'Descartes useless and uncertain'[34] – otherwise Pascal's exclamation could have been the century's verdict.

The problem is an immediately political one. In Pascal, as in his

33. Goldmann's and Namer's interpretations serve here as our guide. But see also the good introduction by R. Tavenaux to the following excellent collection of texts: *Jansénisme et politique*, Paris 1965 (in particular the two affirmations, amply demonstrated and fully analogous to the kind of considerations about Jansenism which we have put forward here: 'Jansenism appeared not only as a school of Augustinian theology but as a party of opposition', p. 16; 'all the forms of opposition harboured by Jansenism are connected in some way, through more or less direct paths, to bourgeois individualism', p. 19). Confronted with this new type of interpretation there is no doubt about the obsolete character of hypotheses such as the one proposed by P. Bénichou, *Morales du Grand Siècle*, pp. 77–130 (in particular p. 81: 'Port-Royal contributed to disaggregate the ideals inherited from the Middle Ages, throwing aristocratic idealism and religion into open conflict'). See also E. Auerbach, 'On the Political Theory of Pascal', in *Scenes from the Drama of European Literature*, Gloucester 1973, pp. 101–29.

34. Pascal, *Œuvres complètes*, p. 1137.

friend Arnauld, Descartes sees a party, a historically defined oppositional force.[35] He is unable to see them otherwise because the fabric of relations[36] and events[37] show them to be such. So the problem raised by the scientific and metaphysical polemic develops and expresses itself in an entirely explicit manner on the political terrain as well. As usual, the diagnosis is the same, the *robin* awareness is expressed in the same way, both the phenomenal separation and absolutism are registered in their plenitude – with critical adequacy, with the spirit of a *politique*:

The habit of seeing kings accompanied by guards, drums, officers, and all the paraphernalia which mechanically inspire respect and awe, makes their countenance, when sometimes seen alone without these accompaniments, impress respect and

35. *Jansénisme et politique*, pp. 15ff.
36. Mersenne in particular entertains a warm friendship with the Pascal family, especially the father, to whom he dedicates volume VI of the *Harmonie universelle*. See R. Lenoble, *Mersenne*, pp. 436–7. But it is not by tracking single bonds and connections that these arguments are to be proven: here we are in the very midst of the milieu of the *robins*, within the network of a social elite. Nor do we need to recall yet again the high bureaucratic standing of these interlocutors of Descartes – it is a characteristic repeated every time that we follow the pathways of French philosophical development during that period, whether our focus is libertine, mechanicist or Jansenist. Perhaps it would be worth saying that the Jansenists are those who are more closely linked to power, the highest *couche* of this elite, at least in the initial phase. It is enough to recall the story of the Arnauld brothers: they were Protestants and collaborators of Sully before converting around 1600 to Catholicism and becoming the pride of Jansenism. This is truly the fate of bureaucrats bound, for good and evil, to the vicissitudes of power!
37. Descartes is aware of the dramatic developments that the struggle against the intendants and royal policy determines in the milieu of the *robins*: he knows of the verdict against Arnauld (AT IV 103–4), later meeting him in Paris while Arnauld is in hiding (AT V). Already in 1638, he had seen Etienne Pascal's participation in the polemic of the Parisian mechanicist geometers suddenly interrupted by political events (did Pascal flee from Paris? – see AT II 114; *Baillet*, vol. I, p. 339).

awe on their subjects; because we cannot separate in thought their persons from the surroundings with which we see them usually joined. And the world, which knows not that this effect is the result of habit, believes that it arises by natural force . . .[38]

But the demand for an evaluation of the political moment of the worldly appearance of truth – against the extreme Pascalian view of society as a 'lunatic asylum'[39] – will stand revealed as a moment of contradiction and confrontation for Descartes. If Pascal sees it as tragically opposite and tragically implicated in the emergence and the crisis of the I, how will it be possible for Descartes to see it as a function of the reasonable ideology?

2

So the attempt to verify – which in this instance is the same as to ground – the reasonable ideology in time, to control its process of realization, becomes, must become, a characteristic and definitive element of Cartesian thought. The question springs from within the system, and, in its opening up to history, it is a theme that nevertheless remains theoretical, a passage endowed with necessity in the order of reasons, a link no less essential than the others in the 'chain of truths'. Moreover, it is the sign of the historical significance of Descartes's thought because it captures the effective problem of the century, that of giving form to that spontaneous emergence of individuality – more precisely: of realizing the pressing need of the bourgeois class to reconnect its existence to a project of development. The Renaissance defeat had separated the bourgeoisie, which had already appeared as socially hegemonic, from any participation in political power, that is from the capacity to consolidate the spontaneity of its own emergence in an organization that could assert, in a totalitarian manner, the

38. Pascal, *Œuvres complètes*, p. 1162–3.
39. Pascal, *Œuvres complètes*, p. 1163 (no. 31).

bourgeois form of the possession of the world. The problem, which had been confronted theoretically, is now recast by Descartes in practical terms. Having criticized the libertine and mechanicist solutions, to the extent that they fixed the break at its highest degree of intensity; and having encountered the Jansenist contestation of time as the place of realization of the historical mediation between bourgeois essence and bourgeois existence, Descartes had to show how the reasonable ideology could be a viable path. In Descartes, the spontaneity of bourgeois emergence had to seek out organizational nuclei.

The development of Descartes's thought in the 1640s shows how the identification of those men, milieus, groups and social forces that would form the points of reference for the realization of the reasonable ideology had become a profound requirement and an operation that would need to be continually repeated. Of course we are dealing with often contradictory attitudes, which not only show the ambiguity and uncertainty of Descartes's practical judgement but also reflect the far deeper ambiguities and uncertainties of the historical situation. But how indicative of his anxiety these attitudes are, and how organically bound to a single continuous design![40] As we said, these attitudes were contradictory. Indeed, Descartes presents himself to us – and is recognized by his contemporaries – in the most diverse of guises: '*iesuitastrum*' or 'avenger of Vanini'? Solitary 'mathematical physicist'? Or perhaps 'courtier'? To each of these appellations there corresponds a concrete referent in Descartes's development.

40. Once again we should fight against the image of the '*philosophe au masque*', which is all too often repeated – whether from Masonic or Catholic perspectives (just to mention the extremes). Not even in this phase of Descartes's thought – which is certainly the one in which he opens himself the most to the risks of political life – can anything justify seeing him as advancing masked. On the contrary, if he can be chided for anything, it is perhaps for his excessive candour, for a profound naïvety in how he confronts such problems. However, is it not precisely in this candour, in this naïvety, that there resides an irrepressible aggressiveness and – to the more expert politicians – an extremely ungracious one?

'*Iesuitastrum*'. This was how Descartes was commonly referred to by the Protestant priest Voetius:[41] 'born under the star of Ignatius of Loyola', the latter would add.[42] Descartes hesitates in responding to these allegations. Instead, he changes the subject: only the enemies of the King of France, he replies, could accuse me of being devoted to the Jesuits, to whom the selfsame King 'has the habit of communicating his innermost thoughts, by choosing them as Confessors'.[43] But to reply in this manner is already to admit to a relation. What relation? Certainly not that of mere discipleship, recalling Descartes's early studies at La Flèche.[44] Nor

41. AT VIII B 206.
42. AT VIII B 23.
43. AT VIII B 221. In any case, Descartes goes on to say, my devotion has not damaged my anxious search for truth: so much so that I have polemicized on scientific questions with P. Bourdin S.J. as bitterly as with Voetius.
44. This relationship is also evidenced with extreme frequency in both the correspondence and the works. See the selection of passages in E. Gilson, *Commentaire*, pp. 101–8, 117–19, 125–30 and *passim*. Furthermore, on La Flèche and the Jesuit culture of the time, see C. Daniel, *Les Jésuites instituteurs de la jeunesse française au XVIIe et au XVIIIe siècles*, Paris 1880; C. De Rochemonteix, *Un collège de Jésuites aux XVIIe et XVIIIe siècles: le collège Henri IV de la Flèche*, Le Mans 1889 (especially vol. IV, pp. 4ff); A. De Backer, *Bibliothèque de la Compagnie de Jésus*, Paris and Bruxelles 1890; A Schimberg, *L'éducation morale dans les collèges de la Compagnie de Jésus en France sous l'ancien régime*, Paris 1913; F. De Dainville, 'L'enseignement des mathématiques dans les collèges jésuites de France du XVIe au XVIIIe siècle', *Revue d'histoire des sciences*, vol. 7, 1954, pp. 6–21. Among the most significant recollections to be found in Descartes the following must be explicitly recalled: 'Now I am not of the opinion that all that is taught in philosophy is gospel truth; yet, since it is the key to other sciences, I think it is very useful to have taken the complete course in philosophy as it is given in the Jesuit schools before attempting to raise one's mind above the level of mere book learning and become a genuinely knowledgeable person. And to give my own teachers their due, I must say that nowhere on earth is philosophy taught better than at La Flèche' (PWD III 123–4). This passage should be borne in mind because it contains some political themes that we will see recur throughout the relation and polemic with the Jesuits. See also AT III 97ff, AT IV 139.

simply the relation solicited by the appreciation of the Jesuit society's culture and his friendship with some of its more influential members.[45] The essential fact is that, in some phases, Descartes looks to the Company of God for an effective support as regards the historical realization of his discourse.[46] On publication, Descartes presents the *Discourse on the Method* to the fathers at La Flèche 'like a fruit that belongs to you and whose first seeds you planted in my spirit, just as I also owe to those of your Order the little knowledge that I have of good Letters'.[47] He also insists on the congruence between his own teaching and theology ('the opinions, from my own reflection on natural causes, that seemed to me more true in physics were always those which are the most compatible with the mysteries of religion . . .'),[48] to the point of clearly expressing the hope that his own philosophy could become the official teaching of the Company. As he would later put it, not only is his philosophy true but it is also rigorous. If the goal of the Society is to safeguard the political and religious order, the methodical rigour of the new philosophy, by abolishing the litigiousness of Scholasticism, and impeding the heretical consequences of these conflicts, is in accord with that goal. Useful to the state, useful to theology, and the bearer of peace, the new philosophy thus hopes to enter into the schools.[49] And the hope seems to be confirmed after the publication of the *Meditations* and the *Principles*: 'I have received letters from Fathers Charlet, Dinet

45. See again Gilson, as well as the other authors cited. But also AT III 97ff, 591, 594; and especially the letters to Mesland in AT IV, up to the last one, in which he bids farewell to the friend departing for the Indies – a letter far more intimate and emotional than the others (PWD III 278–9).
46. H. Gouhier, *La pensée religieuse de Descartes*, pp. 114–37, has correctly insisted on this point.
47. AT I 383.
48. PWD III 75. But see also AT I 456–8, PWD III 77, AT I 508ff; PWD III 90, 118, AT II 345 and *passim*.
49. AT VII 574–82 (from the *Epistula ad P. Dinet*).

and Bourdin which make believe that the Society wants to take my side', Descartes even writes to the incredulous Picot.[50]

So, Descartes the Jesuit? Not just an expression of their school but someone who partakes in their politics? It does not seem so. The fact is that, if we examine matters more closely for a moment, Descartes's proposals are sustained above all by a practical–political judgement concerning the force and unity of the Company: Descartes is fascinated by this force and unity, by the magnificent disciplined articulation of the Jesuit body and its limbs, by the efficacy and potency of the Society.[51] Besides, as soon as Descartes perceives perplexity or even polemics and condemnations from the world of the Jesuits, his attitude reveals itself entirely. He accepts the polemic, and varies his tactic depending on the circumstances, always trying, on the one hand, to rebuff the attacks, on the other, to propose an alliance. He shifts from polemical threats[52] to the presentation of his own philosophy as an alternative to the Jesuit teaching;[53] he then retreats to refusing to attack the philosophy of the Jesuits, letting it be understood that he is not excluding the possibility of eventually joining hands.[54] Then, once again, Descartes enters into a phase of direct attack, threatening[55] and then refusing the confrontation.[56] In this sequence of positions one can always sense a judgement that is fundamentally of a practical kind.[57]

But does all this not lead to flattening out the problem of the relationship between Descartes and the Jesuits? Is not such a relationship far more profound and of a piece with the development of Cartesian philosophy? Will we not end up severely

50. AT IV 176. But also AT IV 156–61 [TN: partly in PWD III 240–1].
51. PWD III 89, AT II 50; and AT VII 563–6.
52. AT III 185, 255.
53. PWD III 167, 156–7, and AT III 269–71.
54. AT III 470, 480–1; AT IV 141. And again AT III 464–8, 564, 638–9.
55. AT III 523.
56. AT IV 225, 341, 498, 554.
57. AT IV 591: my philosophy aims to establish relations on the basis of its intrinsic force, without which it would be destroyed.

objectifying and denaturing the inner vicissitudes of the life and thought of Descartes?[58] This appears, in truth, to be a purely biographical and psychological type of presentation, which produces effects of interpretive distortion. That is because in this debate with the Jesuits – which we consider to be political through and through – Descartes tries instead not only to fix the conditions for a worldly success of his philosophy but above all, by attempting to elucidate its internal capacity to be historically significant, to identify the possibility for his philosophy to achieve logical completion. Logically completed because – as we have already largely seen – it is the very development of Descartes's thought that demands this positive relation to history. Whether the reasonable ideology is in force or not is absolutely determinant for the very progression of Cartesian thought, at its very core. The entrusting of philosophy to the world is for Descartes the proof of the interior validity of philosophy. And this essential character of the relation to the world is (subsequently and paradoxically) elucidated by the situation of crisis in which the whole of Descartes's thought ends up finding itself when the relationship with the Jesuits reveals its inefficacy. Descartes must then find new ways to realize the reasonable ideology. In searching for them he sometimes returns to doubt. The historical failure feeds back on and reproblematizes the internal trajectory of Cartesian thought. The reason for the historical failure needs to be investigated, identified and corrected within the system, within the ontological tension between man and world.[59]

Of course, we could regard Descartes's hope to influence the

58. F. Alquié, *La découverte métaphysique de l'homme*, has quoted in his bibliography to ch. I the opinions of those who hold this position. See especially, as regards the profound influence of Jesuitism in general, and the thinking of Ignatius in particular, what is said by L. Rivaille, *Les débuts de Corneille*, Paris 1936, pp. 465–559; it is also useful to consult O. Nadal, *Le sentiment de l'amour dans l'œuvre de Pierre Corneille*, Paris 1948.

59. See section 3 below.

cultural politics of the Jesuits as naïve, and thus be led to consider the interest of the polemic as marginal. Given the kind of relation we are dealing with, in order to dispel this perplexity it is therefore necessary to ask ourselves the reason for this relation, and what reasons Descartes may have had for setting himself this objective. As we have already remarked, there is the force and unity of the Society, which is certainly an essential motif. But there is more: Descartes sees in the Jesuit politics of the French 1600s an attempt to move in a reformist direction analogous to the one he himself had opted for. An optimistic morality, a supple doctrine of grace and a coherent development of some aspects of traditional humanism showed the eminence in Jesuit thought of themes that were reasonably predisposed to a strengthening of bourgeois positions.[60] Descartes concurred with this, and he intended to give these positions the support of the reasonable ideology. Having said that, in these features of Jesuitism we also find the reason for Descartes's ultimate failure, since, beyond the initial points of convergence, their respective finalities were not homogeneous and could not but ultimately clash. The Jesuits lacked any humanist nostalgia that did not amount to a renewal and exacerbation of the rhetorical tradition.[61] Their assumption of the themes of bourgeois reformism is simply opportunistic, representing an attempt at integration and blockage. It suffices once again to refer to the Jesuit and Cartesian polemics against the libertines and the Jansenists: how different they are! For Descartes, those positions are temptations, themselves dramatic fruits of the same humanist

60. G. Weise, *L'ideale eroico del rinascimento*, vol. II, *passim*, but especially on pp. 61, 82, 133, 177, has underlined the Jesuitic mediation of humanist and bourgeois feeling in the 1500s and 1600s. See also: R. Pintard, *Le libertinage*, p. 52; F. E. Sutcliffe, *Guez de Balzac*, p. 103; H. Brémond, *Histoire littéraire du sentiment religieux en France*, vol. I, Paris 1916, p. 15; F. De Dainville, 'Foyers de culture scientifique dans la France méditerranéenne du XVIe au XVIIIe siècle', *Revue d'histoire des sciences*, vol. 1, 1948, pp. 289–300.
61. E. Garin, *L'educazione in Europa*, pp. 212ff; E. Durkheim, *L'évolution pédagogique en France*, Paris 1938, pp. 69–133.

memory that nourished him. They are current alternatives. For the Jesuit the relation is instead entirely external, moderation and reasonableness are employed for the sake of integration and not in order to laud the ideological demands of the bourgeois world. Descartes had to discover, little by little, this basic discrepancy of aims and presuppositions. The history of the relation between Descartes and the Jesuits thus becomes the history of Descartes's discovery of the uselessness of that point of reference and realization for the reasonable ideology. The polemic against Father Bourdin, which represents a pivotal element in Descartes's experience of the application of the reasonable ideology,[62] concludes with the awareness of this impossibility of relation, with the reaffirmation of the reasonable ideology against any subordination to finalities other than those of bourgeois growth.

So is it to the bourgeoisie, to the revolutionary bourgeoisie of Descartes's time, that his reasonable ideology will address itself directly, in search of its own realization? There are contemporaries who accuse Descartes of seeking this goal, as the true follower, the true avenger of Vanini.[63] '[T]eaching Scepticism',[64] 'teaching and propagating Atheism',[65] 'smearing the poison of Atheism onto others deceitfully and in the utmost secrecy':[66] these are the 'extremely imprudent and atrocious slanders' that Descartes is subjected to on the basis of this new hypothesis for the realization of the reasonable

62. On the polemic with P. Bourdin, besides the objections by Bourdin to the *Meditations* and Descartes's replies, see the *Epistula ad P. Dinet* (AT VII, especially 566–74), as well as AT III 94–6, 103, 117, PWD III 149–50, AT III 160–2, 168–74, 178, 205–7, 221–8, 244, PWD III 210–11, AT III 575–7, and *passim*. See also the note in AT VII 21. In this instance we can verify once again how Descartes proceeds in his polemic against the Jesuits: with an alternating approach, passing from provocation to defence, articulating with extreme ability the progress of the polemic.

63. See *passim* in the *Pars Octava* to the *Epistula ad Voetium*, AT VIII B 136–68; and further 174, 207, 210, 254.

64. AT VIII B 170.

65. AT VIII B 173.

66. AT VIII B 174.

ideology. But why the accusations? Perhaps because in its theoretical propaganda Cartesianism really attains these kinds of assertions? Or rather because, in the context of a general ebb of the revolutionary movement of the bourgeoisie, his thinking appears such, notwithstanding the caution with which it is presented?

First of all, it is obvious that Descartes can dispel an accusation of this type, in its coarsest formulation, simply by suggesting that one read his entire philosophy – a philosophy that constitutes an explicit polemic against any demand of subversion proposed by humanist nostalgia. One could at most conditionally emphasize humanist themes, but as offered not so much by the extreme coherence of metaphysical nostalgia but by historical opportunity. This is the situation in which the polemic with Voetius unfolds, in the land of freedom, Holland. So, in order to give a correct response to those questions, we must observe how the attempted penetration of Cartesian philosophy into the Dutch universities is realized specifically – for it is here, in this citadel of reformed and bourgeois thought, that the clash takes place. Now it is fundamentally to Reneri,[67] Stampioen[68] and Regius that Descartes entrusts himself. Descartes's relationship with Reneri and Emilius, who back him, is, so to speak, a triumphal one. Here Cartesianism assumes a methodological inflection and praises reason 'in the freedom that God has accorded us in order to lead it in the search for truths (of which reason alone is the master)'. The humanist themes are emphatic and generic. The relationship with Stampioen is instead already of a critical type, and it displays the obstacles that the seventeenth century throws up against the penetration of Cartesian thought, against the proposal of an ideological reconstruction of the bourgeois standpoint. When, as is the case in the relation with Stampioen, the friendship develops around scien-

67. AT I 205–9, 300–2; AT II 306–7, 528–9; AT III 1–4.
68. On the friendship with Stampioen and the successive 'affair', see AT I 275–80; AT II 578, 581–2, 600–15, 616–17, 639, 642; AT III 5–7, 16–17, 69–70 and *passim*.

tific themes and excludes the possibility of attaining the global, metaphysical horizon of the Cartesian project, Descartes intuits – and sometimes dramatizes – the necessity to wholly win back the metaphysical terrain, even if only in the form of an occasion for a clash. So it is only by attending to the vicissitudes of his lengthy friendship and conflict with Regius that we can elucidate the historical framework of this second alternative within the project of the realization of the reasonable ideology. Therefore, in the relationship between Descartes and Regius we can see how Cartesian philosophy, in its entirety, impacts on the culture of the bourgeois universities and how it is articulated in three distinct phases, which can be accorded a general signification. A first phase of positive acceptance of the Cartesian project in its most extreme consequences, already in its metaphysical content. A second phase of debate and conflict which not only opposes Cartesianism to the official philosophies but also distils – in the debate – the positions of the Cartesians from those of Descartes himself. A third phase of ebbing, and thus a new need to verify Cartesianism. From acceptance to the excavation, therefore, not only of the scientific set-up but of the general metaphysical framework;[69] from the enthusiastic reception of a teaching that seems to adjust itself to the bourgeoisie's need for growth, to the extent of traversing and reconstructing its internal nexuses and

69. For the initial phase of the friendship between Descartes and Regius, see AT II 305–6, 334, 526–7, 548–9, 568–9 (first minor incident), 582–3, 616–17, 624–5. We should keep in mind that the Stampioen–Waessenaer polemic (as well as the preceding one with Fermat and the subsequent one with Bourdin, which also have specific repercussions) has weighty effects on Descartes's state of mind, predisposing him to an opening vis-à-vis Regius. In the course of the polemic on the Stampioen case Descartes in fact becomes convinced of the impossibility of usefully advancing the discussion on a purely scientific plane. The global project must instead develop by emancipating philosophy from science: scientific practice interprets the world, metaphysics makes proposals. And Regius is an interlocutor who seems ready for this task.

its most intimate nature; and here – once its meaning has been grasped – problematization, clash, identification of demands that the reasonable ideology seems unable to interpret. And finally refusal.

It is not by chance that the debate touches on the most important themes when Regius receives the manuscript of the *Meditations*:[70] these reveal the scope of the reasonable ideology, its positive ambivalence between a mechanistic stance in the interpretation of the world and a metaphysical perspective of transformation. After a first phase in which the relationship is dominated by a not altogether critical cordiality between Descartes and Regius and an enthusiastic proselytizing when it comes to third parties, it is thus at this point that the real debate is inaugurated. And the problems around which it revolves are those of the century, for which the metaphysical propositions serve simply as emblems. What meaning could the reasonable ideology have in the Dutch bourgeois world of Regius? Was there the possibility in Holland of posing the problem of the transformation of the world in the fundamentally radical (even if tactically moderate) terms of the Cartesian plan? Or did the historical appearance of revolutionary success in Holland instead block the possibility of the discourse? Did the solidity of the equilibria that had been attained impede its very comprehension? If there is something that must be immediately noted it is that the debate to which Regius subjects Cartesian thought is above all revelatory of his own incapacity to consider the situation as it stands to be even ambiguously open. Regius suffers the climate of the university, of the Dutch culture of the time, which considered the level reached by the revolution as definitive, which had mediated bourgeois demands and aristocratic tradition, and had expelled those forces that sought to make the movement permanent. The verdict against Dordrecht and the assassination of Oldenbarneveld represent for Regius, like for his contemporaries, irreversible

70. AT III 60–1.

conditions. Here too the *malin* shows his power![71] How different from the image that the young Guez and Descartes had communicated to each other when, in the footsteps of *robin* disquiet, they had begun to love Holland, the land of freedom![72] And if Descartes still responds with indignation when the academic senate of Utrecht 'passed a law in their Academy in which they explicitly prohibit the teaching of any philosophy other than Aristotle's',[73] Regius reacts

71. J. Lecler, in *Toleration and the Reformation*, vol. II, has correctly insisted on the fundamental crisis affecting civic and political development in the Low Countries in the years 1619–20, linking it to the repression of the Remonstration. Lecler's thesis is useful for demystifying the mythical images of the Dutch seventeenth century – so frequent in bourgeois apologetics, from which is not immune, for example, even J. Huizinga, *Dutch Civilization in the Seventeenth Century and Other Essays*, London 1968. Recently, E. H. Kosmann, *Politieke Theorie in het zeventiendeeuwse Nederland*, Amsterdam 1960, has insisted on the emergence in the first half of the century of a 'libertarian' current of thought, nevertheless recognizing (and we think, as we shall see, that his thesis is congruent with our own) that it is only in the second half of the century that this 'republicanism' will become significant at both scientific and political levels.

72. See above, ch. 1, section 5. And again: PWD I 126, AT V 25–6, AT VIII B 212 and 223. It is beyond doubt that from time to time, in Descartes's judgements on the Low Countries throughout his whole life, there reappears the strong image (but has it not become very rhetorical, literary?) of Dutch freedom.

73. AT III 251. P. Dibon, *La philosophie néerlandaise au siècle d'or*, vol. I: *L'enseignement philosophique dans les universités à l'époque précartésienne, 1575–1650*, Amsterdam 1954, still largely partakes of the apologetic judgement on the period. Dibon views Dutch university life as a citadel of bourgeois knowledge. This is true only in dialectical terms. In effect, Dibon is forced to recognize the almost total domination of peripatetic philosophy and the very strong influence of systematics in dialectical terms. We should also keep in mind that the first years of the seventeenth century see the ebb of humanism and peripatetic negation as a provisional, but no less massive, moment, repressive and heavy (in the second half of the century Cartesianism will instead forcefully assert itself). The first humanist vocation must pass through peripatetic negation to be reborn stronger. But it is precisely within this phase of defeat – all the heavier inasmuch as it represents a repressive reaction – that Descartes rehearses his reasonable ideology.

with far superior critical awareness. This is the situation, he seems to suggest with resigned realism. Once again, faced with the clash, the reasonable ideology does not know how to bend, and is rejected. It is in this situation that Regius cannot adhere to the basic pillars of Cartesianism. Paradoxically, the problematization of the *malin* in the historical structure of knowing and being is alien to him, because the feeling for the crisis – in this case the crisis of the development of the revolutionary movement – affects him too strongly. So, like many of his contemporaries, he represses this feeling. That is why we witness Regius continually breaking the positive function that ambiguity is endowed with in Descartes's discourse: in considering the relation between soul and body he alternates affirmations of a strict separation of the soul from the body[74] and positions of identification of the one with the other.[75] A rigid phenomenal dualism is the correlate of an entirely compact empiricist and sensualist monism: the flight from the world and its uncritical acceptance are equivalent. It is as though here, in the Dutch situation, the tempos of the century's crisis overlap. We thus find coexisting in Regius alternatives that have in common the acceptance of the crisis as an insurmountable condition, but which elsewhere had had different trajectories: libertinism and mechanicism stand together, notwithstanding that we are faced with an inability to prepare a terrain for reconstruction. Therefore, if, on the one hand, the soul is configured in such a way that man is *'ens per accidens'*,[76] on the other, it is only *'modum corporis'*.[77] What Regius is missing in both positions is the sense of the productive force of the soul, of the tension that radiates from spiritual being onto the world,

74. AT III 369–70, PWD III 181–3, AT III 440–2, 443–7, and PWD III 199 and *passim.*
75. PWD III 254–5, AT IV 254–6 and 256–8.
76. PWD III 200. E. Gilson, *Etudes sur le rôle* . . ., pp. 246ff, entirely consistent with his interpretation, declares that 'consequently deducing the premises of the Cartesian doctrine, Regius calmly affirms that man is an *ens per accidens*'.
77. PWD III 255.

he reasons 'as if the faculty of thinking cannot at all stand by itself' – but 'the name of this faculty itself refers to nothing other than power [*potentiam*]'. Cartesianism is interpreted by him in a register that does not allow him to grasp its true historical significance.[78]

Could it have been otherwise? Judging from the effects of such an interpretation, doubt cannot be sustained. In actual fact the priest Voetius – a man of power and the keeper of the stability of the bourgeois order in Holland – already sees in Cartesianism, even in its deformed state, a sign of subversion, a dangerous school of atheism. He therefore instigates a considerable persecution against both Regius and Descartes, who are brought together for the sake of the polemic. The cynical Huygens can thus remark: 'A reckless man once made the following comparison to me, saying that theologians resembled those pigs which, when you pull one by the tail, all cry out'.[79] Descartes's reaction is as dignified and firm as ever.[80] He

---

78. The preceding passage is from the *Notae in programma*, PWD I 303–4 and 305–6. G. Rodis-Lewis, in her 'Introduction' to the edition and translation of the *Lettres à Regius et Remarques sur l'explication de l'Esprit humain*, Paris 1959, has insisted very clearly on the mechanicist nature of Regius's thinking. For his part R. Specht, *Commercium mentis et corporis*, pp. 72–82, has stressed the other aspect of Regius's thinking, which I regard as complementary: the phenomenalist one. It is important to note that these speculative elements are present in Regius ever since the first phase of his relation with Descartes (see for example AT III 63–71). All of this raises the problem of why Descartes did not see them from the beginning. We begin to suspect that he did not wish to see them, preoccupied – and almost required – as he was to maintain in any case a friendly relation which allowed him an entrance, however preliminary, into the Dutch university.

79. AT III 678. Voetius succeeds in effect in eliciting '*troubles*' against the Cartesian philosophy: AT III 456–64 [TN: partly in PWD III 199–201], 485–520 [TN: partly in PWD III 205–9], 525–42 [TN: partly in PWD III 210], 557–74 [TN: partly in PWD III 213–14]. G. Cohen, *Ecrivains français*, pp. 535ff, accurately analyses the external and internal history of the polemic.

80. AT III 71–2, 202–4, PWD III 156, and AT III 365–9. Of course, see also the *Epistula ad Voetium* and the *Lettre apologétique aux Magistrats de la ville de Utrecht* (in AT VIII B), as well as the passages of the *Epistula ad P. Dinet* (AT VII) devoted to the affair.

proceeds to reaffirm the metaphysical dimension of the reasonable ideology and remains preoccupied with its clarification before friend and foe alike – even if the break with Regius is loyally and opportunely postponed.[81] Nevertheless – at the limit of the *querelle* – it finally arrives: it does so in the form of an impassioned affirmation of the power of the soul in opposition to phenomenalism and sensism.[82] Against any flattening of bourgeois existence, which occurs even where great hopes had been expressed from out of the happiness of popular war and the construction of a new state, Descartes passionately affirms the power of the soul, which is at the same time an affirmation of the productive essence of the bourgeoisie. The reasonable ideology must proclaim itself, even where the historical conditions prevent it from realizing itself.

In the obstinate certainty of the validity of his own discourse, what other paths can Descartes still tread? Very few, and they are all well travelled. As 'physicist', he once again turns to the Parisian society of scientists. With some insistence, he again proposes his model of the reasonable ideology. But he himself knows how illusory such an attempt is.[83] Such is in fact the severity of the crisis felt in the Parisian milieu, and such moreover is the force and integrative capacity of power, that ultimately this is only a cultivated milieu whose aim is to interpret 'the reason of state', to make itself into the channel for the monarchy's demands of cultural and political unification.[84] In this situation, the definitive triumph of mechanism is not disturbed in the slightest by the

81. AT IV 96–7, 123–6, 148–50, 235, 239–40, 241–2, PWD III 254–5, AT IV 254–6, 256–8; and PWD I 189.

82. The *Notae in programma* date from the end of 1647 (PWD I 294–311).

83. References to cultured Parisian society abound in Descartes's correspondence, and in this period they are particularly present due to the reprise of the (protracted) polemic with Roberval: AT III 362ff, 396ff, PWD III 207–9, 210–12, and so on.

84. This has been amply underscored by R. Bray, *La formation de la doctrine classique en France*, and P. Barrière, *La vie intellectuelle en France*.

impact of Cartesian thought. Rather, it is Jansenism that enjoys a certain role. But it does so for equivalent reasons, albeit of an inverse sign, to those that lie at the basis of the mechanicist option. Mainly because of an exacerbated sense of the crisis, which is to say for reasons that are completely incongruent with the Cartesian stance. As we have said, Descartes is aware of all this. Little by little his attitude with regard to the Parisian milieu and its political legitimism takes on tones of detachment and protest: 'His Excellency the Cardinal would have had to have left you two or three of his millions to carry out all the experiments necessary to discover the particular nature of each body; and I do not doubt that one could thus arrive at great results, which would be more useful to the public than all the victories that may be gained from waging war'.[85]

It is in this climate that Descartes's decision to go into (temporary) exile to the court of Christina comes to fruition.[86] Is this a final attempt, or at least hope, to find the path that would make it possible to apply the reasonable ideology? A 'courtly' hope? That is what some have generically argued.[87] It must be

85. AT III 610. But see also AT III 590, against the minute and riotous nobility. Finally, it is well known that Descartes refused to voice any judgement on the Parisian Fronde: frightened by the Parisian disorders he 'flees', disdaining any non-critical evaluation with regard to disorder as such (AT V 131, 183, 198, 232, 292, 293, PWD III 371, AT V 332, PWD III 375–6; and AT XII 473–5).

86. Therefore, this takes place in a climate of crisis: in France there is the Fronde; in Holland the bothersome and ever dangerous polemic with the theologians. This question has been ably dealt with both in Gouhier's *Essais* and in Cassirer's *Descartes, Corneille, Christine de Suède*, Paris 1942. However, other kinds of motivations also called Descartes to Stockholm. Among them, besides a friendship with Chanut, we think that the existence of a French community in Sweden and the consideration of the political and cultural situation were particularly important (see R. Pintard, *Le libertinage érudit*, vol. I, pp. 389ff).

87. In this vein see, for example, P. M. Schull, *Un souvenir cartésien*, and P. Dibon, 'Une lettre inédite de Descartes à Constantin Huygens', in *Descartes et le cartésianisme hollandais*, pp. 71–85.   *cont'd over/*

added that the situation of profound social, cultural and political upheaval experienced by the reign of Christina[88] could indeed fan such hopes. But nothing can positively establish that Descartes had effectively placed himself on this plane. The project for a Swedish academy,[89] on which he worked, can be seen as a first approximation to that plan, but it can just as easily represent a yielding to the political and cultural requirements of the monarchy. In truth, especially in the Swedish years, Descartes's activity seems to have adopted extremely sombre tonalities. He apparently accepted, albeit painfully, the fact that historical events seemed to reject the reasonable ideology.

To pass through nuclei of organization, to give positive form to the spontaneity in the emergence of the bourgeois class – this is the project. But all the groups to which Descartes turned rejected him. They were all committed to different alternatives, unable to understand the ambiguous but effectual parameters of the Cartesian ideology. What prevented this failure from implicating the

87. *cont'd*   It is undeniable that Descartes nurtures a sincere admiration for Christina. What is doubtful is that Descartes finds comfort in the court of the queen of Sweden. Incidentally, the judgement expressed in the *Prefatory Letter* to the *Principles* addressed to Elizabeth (PWD I 190–2), regarding the general lack of culture in the courts, seems never to have been sent by Descartes. In any case, on the vicissitudes of the Descartes–Chanut–Christina relation, see AT III 546; AT IV 144–5, 300, 318–20, 396; AT V 129–32, 182–4, 251–4, 289–93 [TN: partly in PWD III 368–9], PWD III 369–70 [AT V 293–4], AT V 295, 317–18, 322–9 [TN: partly in PWD III 370–1] and 351–2.

88. In other words, Sweden is no exception in having to suffer, in the middle of the seventeenth century, along with the other great European monarchies, the impact of the great European crisis in social growth. See M. Roberts, 'Queen Christina and the general Crisis of the seventeenth Century', in *Crisis in Europe*, pp. 195–221. In Sweden, this great social crisis, on which we have dwelt at such length, has a series of considerable and relevant effects on the very form of the constitutional and political regime. See N. Runeby, *Monarchia mixta*, Stockholm 1962.

89. AT XI 663–5.

very foundations of the Cartesian project, from affecting the internal structure of his philosophy itself? Descartes had dragged philosophy before the tribunal of time, entrusting to this tribunal the judgement on the validity of his thought. This is the key point: perhaps Descartes's philosophy never comes as close to making contact with the crisis as it does here.

3

In this situation of critical retreat Descartes tries yet another path toward the realization of the reasonable ideology. It is the final, extreme test. If specific points of organization are lacking, it should at least be possible to count on the intrinsic validity of the discourse! Thus the reasonable ideology entrusts the final possibility of its communication to its mere circulation among the public. Descartes sees in the public the final chance to effectively and comprehensively link ideology and time. What Jesuits and bourgeois, scientists and courtiers had failed to understand, the spirit of the epoch would clearly grasp, organizing itself around the Cartesian proposal, understood in terms of public literary renown. Thus, in the 1644 *Principles of Philosophy*[90] the Cartesian appeal to the public rings out with all the intensity it can muster. The form of the treatise is didactic, which is already an aspect of this appeal. But there is more: the systematic approach is restructured in terms of a project. This is the triumph of ideology as the reasonableness of a public discussion, as a relation that wishes to be persuasive, or a horizon which attempts to be exclusive. The fact that in Descartes's outlook the ideological horizon is now exclusive is proved, among other things, by a series of affirmations dating from the same period: 'I will no longer treat of any particular science', Descartes insists.[91] And

90. *Principia philosophiae*, 1644 Latin edition, now in PWD I, with *Avertissement*, AT VIII A XV–XVIII. 1647 French edition, now in PWD I 179–90, with *Avertissement*, AT IX B III–XX.
91. AT IV 527.

the few mathematical or physical *excerpta*[92] corroborate these statements.

We therefore observe a reordering of the systematic approach of the metaphysical discourse so as to ground and render possible an appeal to the public.[93] Of course, compared with the *Meditations*, the *Principles* only innovate in respect of the form of the argument, in the different emphasis that is given to the same themes. But to what effect! If in the *Meditations* the investigation developed inwardly, in the *Principles* it opens to the outside; if in the former it strives for the intensity of ontological contact, in the latter it verifies the capacity to communicate itself. Cartesian thought regains that progressive dimension that allows ideology to become real – a progressive, reformist dimension, which, as we have seen, the *Meditations* only alluded to when setting out its preconditions. The making explicit of the reasonable ideology through metaphysics thereby produces a series of extremely relevant effects, which bear some fundamental implications. First of all, in terms of the modified presentation of the argument, we encounter in the *Principles* a fundamental inversion of perspective: the infinite, *qua* productive motor, is placed as the support of the ideology's indefinite process of realization. Previously, the infinite derived from the unbearable tension of the indefinite. It issued from the contradiction between demand and determination, and was founded on the hypostasis of the limit. Now, instead, its foundation is internal to the metaphysical substance, it is entirely rooted in ontological completeness. It is no longer an external reference, a horizon, a task. Does not all this amount to saying that the ontological consistency of bourgeois fate is immediately revealed

92. AT XI 635–9; AT X 308–10.
93. The *Entretien avec Burman* which takes place at Egmond on 16 April 1648 is absolutely characteristic of the last phase of Descartes's thought. This is especially true for the pages of commentary on the *Principles* (in the edition by C. Adam, Paris 1937, pp. 78–115), where the reliance on technics and the appeal to the public are truly characteristic and expressed in an entirely disenchanted tone.

and does not wait for verification, that it instead waits for realization and poses this problem of realization with great urgency?

But in the *Principles* the affirmation that the infinite is the real support of the indefinite is not simply accorded a general meaning. It is proven through a series of arguments all of which have a particular prominence and indicate specific problematic tensions. First of all by privileging the ontological over the causal proof. In the first pages of the *Principles* we read the following:

> When thought closely reviews the different ideas and notions it has within itself, and it finds that of an omniscient, omnipotent and extremely perfect being, it easily judges, from what it perceives in this idea, that God, which is this extremely perfect being, is or exists. For, even if thought possesses distinct ideas of many other things, it does not observe in them anything that assures it as to the existence of their object; while in this one it perceives, not only, as in the others, a possible existence, but an absolutely necessary and eternal existence. And just as, by seeing necessarily contained in its idea of the triangle that its three angles are equal to two right angles it absolutely convinces itself that the triangle has three angles equal to two right angles, so it is that simply by seeing that necessary and eternal existence is contained in the idea that it has of the extremely perfect Being, it must conclude that this extremely perfect Being is or exists.[94]

With this passage the primacy of Cartesian ontologism, which previous works had often come close to, attains maximum prominence and the positive rootedness of the Cartesian discourse comes fully to light.

94. PWD I 197–9; IX B 31–4. [TN: given certain ambivalences between the Latin and French versions of the *Principles*, Negri opts for the Italian translation of Descartes from the *Opere*, vol. II, p. 32. We have accordingly decided to translate directly from the Italian.]

Of course, this privileging of the infinite, of the productivity stemming from the ontological foundation on which it rests – this projection of an indefinite process of realization onto the infinite productivity of the I – does not overstep the boundaries of the schema of separation that still remains fundamental to Descartes's discourse. The infinite is always placed in the separation – here it is posed as myth, as the exaltation of the content of bourgeois nostalgia. But the relation with the dimension of the indefinite process of the realization of essence in existence is not itself real: rather it is ideological, in the full sense of the term, as ideal project of realization. In the *Principles*, Descartes specifies the concept of the indefinite,[95] contrasting it to the plenitude of the infinite and using this plenitude to support the degree of certainty which is accorded to the indefinite process of science and consciousness. In so doing, he fixes what is perhaps the most adequate image of what the reasoned and ordered process of the realization of bourgeois essence must be: a certain tension towards foundation, a precarious tension towards realization. The point of view of ideology can, and must, present itself as absolutely grounded. It is accompanied by a tension which leads it to the limit of identifying with the infinite – knowing full well, however, that this limit of identification cannot be attained. The uncertainty of the process of knowledge cannot be removed. Here paradox is still possible: 'But as far as God is concerned perhaps he conceived of and understood certain limits in the world, number and quantity, and understood a greater world, number, etc.; and in this way things will have been finite for him'.[96]

We are therefore confronted with the metaphysical non-transcendability of the human condition of finitude, the existential impossibility of overstepping the limit posed by the Renaissance defeat to the emergence of the bourgeoisie. What a characteristic

95. AT VIII A 14–15; IX B 36–7.
96. *Entretien avec Burman*, pp. 82–3. But see also the famous letter to Mesland, in PWD III 231–6.

Cartesian affirmation this is. And yet how open it remains to the tension towards the infinite, how solidly rooted in it. In the centuries to follow, bourgeois thought, in search of the revolution, will exhaust itself precisely around this limit of identification. It will think it is becoming revolutionary by discovering the infinite in the indefinite, removing its separation. In so doing, it will believe itself to have gone beyond the parameters and the very character of Descartes's metaphysical framework.[97] But if we look more attentively, here, in these Cartesian *Principles* (as in some parts of the *Meditations*), the problem is not just posed – subtly, profoundly, and perhaps unawares, the path towards its resolution is also indicated. This path lies in the excavation of what founds the relationship between infinite and indefinite. It is the discovery of the urge towards the infinite already present within the subject. It is the liminal (but actual) identity of the infinite and the indefinite in substance. The Cartesian definition of substance in terms of 'ipseity' (*aseità*), which appears in the *Principles*, is an allusion to this path of recuperation and new foundation: 'By *substance* we can understand nothing other than a thing which exists in such a way as to depend on no other thing for its existence.'[98]

Have we left Descartes's proper horizon? Perhaps. After all, it cannot be said that Descartes builds much on this very pregnant concept of substance. But it is important to remark the appearance, the presence of this concept, because this is the extreme edge reached by the Cartesian hope to conquer, to dominate time. Having set himself the problem – how to make ideology become

97. From Spinoza to Leibniz, from Kant to Hegel, the investigation into the problem of the relation between the indefinite and the infinite will become a kind of central and decisive point within philosophical speculation. We are interested here in stressing that this problematic is posed by Descartes in an exhaustive manner. In this sense, Descartes is perhaps more explicit and more comprehensive of the possibilities and the difficulties within the development of rationalist philosophy than he might at first appear.

98. PWD I 210; AT IX B 46–7.

real and thereby move beyond it – Descartes could not fail to project this horizon. This definition of substance is therefore an absolutely significant point, moment or limit. For the first time, the aggravated sense of crisis which – ever since the 1620s – had invested and mobilized his thought, is alleviated and comes to rest. It is not by chance then that for the first time, and again in this text,[99] memory is regained: no longer just a sign of crisis and nostalgia for the ideal humanist experience, but also a positive function in the construction of science, providing a necessary contribution to its internal order. Memory is regained when the hiatus that separates it from metaphor is removed by the project. The originary hope can realize itself in time, it can materially define itself in time in the same way that the heroic emergence of humanism had managed to do.

But we should reiterate that this represents only a moment, which does not sunder the schema and fundamental characterization of Cartesian thought in its unity. Nor does it effectively renew its initial humanist revolutionary hope. On the contrary, the polemic against every form of the realist conception of the universe, against every metaphysical Prometheanism, is repeated incessantly. The polemical reference point – which had been defined in the first years of the conjunctural crisis, in the course of the specification of the project of the technical possession of nature – remains at the centre of Cartesian discourse. Over and over again the same criticism is renewed: 'it is not possible'. And even were it possible in thought, in the shape of an encyclopedic project aiming at dominion over the totality of knowledge, it would not be historically possible. This is what Descartes says about universal language: 'I maintain that such a language is possible and that the knowledge on which it depends can be discovered, thus enabling peasants to be better judges of the truth of things than philosophers are now. But I do not hope ever to see such a language in use. For that, the order of nature would have to

99. PWD I 218–22; AT X B 58–62.

change so that the world turned into a terrestrial paradise; and that is too much to suggest outside of fairyland.'[100] This old[101] reflection is unceasingly repeated by Descartes, every time that encyclopedic projects are proposed,[102] eventually defining, in terms particularly attuned to our own time – those of the opposition between 'history' and 'science' – the separation that his thought wishes to maintain: In more or less the same sense I customarily distinguish two aspects in Mathesis: history and science. Through History I understand what has already been discovered and is contained in books. But through Science I attain the skill to solve all problems and by the same measure the skill to discover by one's own efforts all that can be discovered by the human mind in that field; whoever has this skill does not desire very much else and is very rightly called ανταργηζ . . .[103]

But if we abide with these conditions – and if a point of metaphysical mediation can only be liminal, if the humanist nostalgia cannot and does not wish to shake off the feeling of defeat – what does the recuperation of time, which the public appeal of the *Principles* wishes to shape, amount to? To the establishment of a stronger foundation for the tension that inheres in the indefinite progression of ideology, in the awareness of the infinite possibility that came to light with the emergence of the bourgeois class. In any case, this tension is not resolved. The world is conquered only to the extent that it is reconstructed. So is the perspective an illusory one? A purely ideological perspective? Of course. But that does not make it any less effective. The fact is that this Cartesian project is really adequate to the public it is addressed to, more than any other historical project produced by his century. And it is adequate precisely to the extent that it is ambiguous, to the extent that it affirms the insuppressible class reality of the

100. PWD III 13 (in a letter from 1629).
101. See R. Lenoble, *Mersenne*, p. 518, n. 4.
102. See in particular Descartes's judgement on the work of Comenius (PWD III 119–20 and AT *Supplement* 97–102).
103. AT *Supplement* 2–3.

bourgeoisie, grasping its heavy destiny of defeat, and yet attempting a reconstruction within this very separation.

This ideological hope, with its appeal to the public, here turns into a technical hope. This technical hope has nothing in common with the first project of a possession of the world, because it now passes into the consciousness of separation. Despite opening onto an indefinite world, this hope is effective. The second part of the *Principles of Philosophy*[104] represents an argument that develops unceasingly within the atmosphere – at once rarefied and potent, separate and proud – of a technical urge to reconstruct the world. The principles of quantitative physics are now reproposed, no longer in the vain hope that they may harbour a description of the world, but simply in the name of their utility for the reconstruction of a world.[105] The metaphysical discovery of the (insoluble but real) relation between infinite and indefinite is put to use in this reconstructive sense.[106] And that urge really does configure a power. This power is separate, irreducible to science and its evidence, but nonetheless totally open to the future, positively unbalanced not in favour of a world to conquer but rather of an unknown land, a world that demands to be invented.[107]

Scientia inveniendi. That is what technics turns out to be. Memories, experiences, operative tensions – an entire life is now consolidated in the Cartesian project. This new horizon is shaped

104. AT VIII A 40–79 [TN: mostly in PWD I 223–47] and AT IX B 63–102.
105. PWD I 224 and AT IX B 64–5.
106. AT VIII A 52–78 [TN: mostly in PWD I 232–47] and AT IX B 75–101. G. Canguilhem ('Descartes et la technique', *Congrès Descartes*, vol. II, pp. 77ff) correctly remarks that 'some passages of the *Principia* even seem to suggest that the usefulness of Cartesian physics would obviate an interrogation of its objectivity'. More or less in the same vein, see R. Prévost, 'L'humanisme économique de Descartes', *Revue d'histoire économique et sociale*, vol. 29, no. 2, 1951, p. 134.
107. Clear statements in this direction may be found in G. Canguilhem and J. Segond, *La sagesse cartésienne et l'idéal de la science*, Paris 1932, *passim* ('Cartesian wisdom appears to us here as the antithesis of ancient wisdom').

in the passage from the tiring exchanges with Ferrier to the laborious exercises in lens-making,[108] from the correspondence with Villebrissieu – in which a social and historical conception of the technical function is already dimly expressed[109] – to the many vicissitudes and the necessary discontinuity that the crisis imposes on the technical project. And in the very act in which it is posed and reproposed, this technical horizon is specified and assumes specific connotations. A series of processes are closely superimposed and articulated in a development that increasingly reveals the present character of the Cartesian proposal: from the naturalist metaphor to the mechanical metaphor,[110] from the mechanical metaphor exposed in magical terms to the proper mechanical metaphor,[111] and finally from mechanism to constructivism.

108. AT I 14, 32–8, 38–52, 53–69, 170, 177, 183–7, 500–1, 504–5; AT II 373–6, 451–5; AT III 585; and *passim*. AT VI 82–3 [TN: partly in PWD I 152].

109. 'I advise you to put your ideas for the most part in the form of propositions, problems and theorems and to publish them so as to force somebody else to supply them with research and observations. That is what I would like everybody to do, so that many people's experience may help to discover the finest things in nature, and to build a physics which would be clear, certain, based on demonstrative proof, and more useful than that commonly taught' (AT I 216). But also the beautiful passages in AT III 598, AT IV 57 (as well as E. Gilson, *Commentaire*, p. 464).

110. The enchanted garden, the garden of marvellous games . . . This metaphor, which is closely related to the humanist one, nevertheless already represents a further passage vis-à-vis the latter, a discovery of more determinate technical meanings. See AT I 24; II 39–41; III 504–5; PWD I 139–40, AT VI 165, 343–4; PWD II 226–7; PWD I 3–5, AT X 231–2, PWD II 404; *The World and Other Writings*, p. 99, AT XI 669. And also PWD I 31, 33, 35; *The World and Other Writings*, pp. 99, 106–7, 139, 168–9, and AT XI 212–15.

111. This passage must be further underscored. From the image of the magic garden, Descartes's metaphorical thinking moves to a proper technical metaphor, which we should perhaps refer to as a technical exemplification. See PWD II 303–4; PWD I 141; PWD II 58–9; PWD I 288–9; AT X 229; *The World and Other Writings*, pp. 99, 169; III 504–5; PWD I 115, 139–40, 142–3, 150–1 (see also E. Gilson, *Commentaire*, pp. 145–6, 420–6); *The World and Other Writings*, pp. 171, 175 and 182.

This is how the definitive meaning of Descartes's discourse is crystallized in the *Principles*, as an appeal to the public in the name of technical hope.[112] It is therefore important to underline the nature of the conclusion which Descartes, faced with this tangle of themes, invariably reaches: it is the image of a thoroughly artificial world. We are tempted to add that this is a world of craft and industry.[113] Within this horizon, individuality indefinitely interprets its own infinite productive power.

We have already referred to this world as a power: a power that expands, reproduces itself, and which precisely constructs itself as a world.[114] Now we are in the position to say more about its characteristics. For this power is also a source of value.[115] If in fact technics, in its indefinite separation and its infinite possibility, constructs an autonomous world – with no real referent, in an efficacious hypothesis that through the world and thus justifies itself – then this world is nevertheless valuable, it is worth constructing. Its separate value must be sought in the human capacity to produce. In work? 'Thus workers are the primary and proximate causes of their work, whereas those who give them orders to do the work, who promise to pay for it, are accidental and remote causes, for the workers might not do the

112. See PWD I 35–6; PWD I 320, 333–5, 341; PWD II 17, 21–2, 35, 38, 58–9, 97 and 98–9.
113. The 'project of a school of arts and crafts' drafted in these years by Descartes (AT XI 659–60) is only an incredibly pale image of the artisanal, industrial interest and tonality from which originates Descartes's appeal to the public.
114. R. Prévost, L'humanisme économique, pp. 132–3: 'nothing remains of Aristotelian nature; and the unconscious art that it manifests is replaced by a conscious activity of fabrication. Descartes often compares nature and human art . . . That vast intelligible mechanism which is nature allows human action to insert itself within it with efficacy and without guilt, because no movement has in itself its own finality'.
115. R. Prévost, L'humanisme économique, p. 143; also E. Dolléans, 'A propos de Descartes: la technique soumise à la générosité', *Revue d'histoire économique et sociale*, vol. 29, no. 2, 1951, pp. 124–9.

work without instructions.'[116] Yes, in work. The bourgeois experience of work, of manufacture, is expressed here – despite the bombastic prose typical of the 1600s – with all the intensity it is capable of.[117] Once again a concept that had already been expressed in Descartes's youthful experience[118] – work as a product of universal mathematics – is disinterred, renewed and inverted: universal mathematics is a product of work. Are we dealing with the manufacture-bound essence of Descartes's thinking of technics? Writing to Descartes, Huygens acknowledges this, discovering – through the study of Descartes's mechanics – that he is ever more 'in love with the anatomy of things'.[119] But there's more. Here Cartesian thought tries to offer itself as the ideological moment of bourgeois growth by interpreting its essential form and, above all, its existential coordinates. The utopia of a liminal retrieval of a relation of identity between infinity and the indefiniteness of development, between bourgeois essence and existence, becomes fully political. The attempt to confer certainty upon bourgeois resistance and initiative in the open time of ideology positively connects to a determinate hope in bourgeois renewal. It finds in the 'public' its real support – and above all it carries within itself the axiological guarantee of the validity of the political project.

As we have noted, this appeal to the public is a last-ditch attempt to realize the reasonable ideology. We have now seen the features that mark the manner in which this attempt is proposed. We are left with the question: Does Descartes thereby overcome

116. PWD I 305.
117. The extent to which this idea is grounded in the Renaissance can be seen in the study by A. Sapori, 'Il pensiero sul lavoro dal mondo antico al cinquecento', in *Studi di storia economica*, vol. III, Florence 1967, pp. 487–514.
118. Recall the already cited *Traité de Méchanique*, AT I 435ff, and the elegant comment by E. Cassirer, *Das Erkenntnisproblem in der Philosophie und Wissenschaft der neueren Zeit*, Hamburg 2000.
119. AT IV 243. Once again we cannot but refer to F. Borkenau's classic work on this topic (and the commentary on it by L. Febvre).

the crisis of his reasonable ideology? Does he manage to answer the problem he has posed himself?

4

There is a moment, in the experience of the mature Descartes, in which the problem of the confrontation of ideology with time as a whole demands a solution. The problem had arisen autonomously, in the deepest recesses of Cartesian metaphysics, and its intensity was abhorrent, demanding as it did an impossible solution. It then grew deeper when confronted with the Jansenist riposte, which prohibited any recuperation of time, declaring it to be in thrall to malice. Finally, it unfolded by assuming a positive tension between the infinite and the indefinite, which were the terms within which the essence and existence of the I expanded as signs of the emergence of the bourgeois class. But was this kind of recuperation of time sufficient for that period? Or rather – and despite the insistence on liminal tensions, despite some passages that suggest an intuition that could resolve the scission, despite all this – is the scission not in the end so deep as to impede any possibility of redemption?

There is a moment – and defining it with precision is difficult, though perhaps it can be located in the subjective crisis provoked by the polemic with Voetius[120] – there is a moment in which Descartes's awareness of the insufficiency even of the final attempt at a temporal mediation of the reasonable ideology through the appeal to the public is revealed in all its gravity. That metaphysical scission that Descartes had dragged behind him ever since the conjuncture of the 1620s, when he felt duty-bound to recover its meaning, now appears wholly insuperable and psychologically unbearable. We are on the verge of a desperate awareness of its impact. Unless . . .

Unless one entrusts oneself to . . . Faith alone saves. Hope? No,

---

120. The severity of the case of Voetius and the overall vicissitudes of the polemic are perceivable in Descartes and can be registered in his writings. For example, AT V 1–15 [TN: partly in PWD III 316–17], PWD III 317–19, AT V 22–3, 24–7 and 41–5.

faith alone saves. Hope harbours some kind of verisimilitude. But what verisimilitude is possessed by this (entirely interrupted, only liminally possible and therefore utopian) relation between the indefinite and the finite? If the reasonable ideology wishes to resist it must put its trust in faith. This is a faith in the actuality of the potential, liminal identification of bourgeois essence and existence. Here Descartes's discourse really does become a meditation on the *preambula fidei*, even if the type of faith on offer is very modern and very different: the realization of the historical task of bourgeois essence. We are certainly not witnessing, despite the intensity of the reflection, an inversion of the Cartesian standpoint. We are still dealing with a further extension of the same thematic. Yes, putting trust in faith is in part an abandonment, but it also constitutes an accentuated contact with the ontological wealth given by individuality. Even so, we are at the centre of a new crisis imposed by the precariousness of the project of realization of the reasonable ideology.

In terms of the reasonable problematic of ideology the upshot and the sign of this Cartesian crisis is the return of ethics.[121] Some have chosen to see in this return the crowning moment, the definitive theoretical advance of Cartesian thought.[122] But

121. The texts on Descartes's vocation as the author of an ethics are contradictory and in themselves insufficient to explain the reason for his ethical interest. It is enough to compare PWD III 289, AT IV 473–4, and PWD III 326–7. See then, to make matters even more perplexing, what Descartes says about the '*morale par provision*' in the *Entretien avec Burman*, pp. 124–5: 'The author is not writing the Ethics of his own will but has been forced to add these rules to his writings by pedagogues and other similar types because otherwise they say that he is without religion and faith and that he wishes to overthrow these things with his Method'.

122. This thesis has been argued principally by H. Gouhier (see in particular the *Essais*, pp. 197–252), who believes that Cartesian ethics, over and above the author's particular assertions, reconstitutes that philosophy of concrete man, that thick ethical spiritualism, that defines 'all' of Descartes. Gouhier's interpretation must always be kept in mind because it is, perhaps, the most coherent example of the traditional interpretation of Cartesian thought. It is an attempt to maintain the 'old' at any price, scholastically arguing for it with the most 'modern' philological techniques.

nothing could be more inaccurate. Descartes had attempted the construction of an ethics subordinated to science,[123] which would draw from the latter the mechanical necessity of its consequences. Now, restoring autonomy to ethics, he recognizes the limits and the crisis of his thinking. What we are dealing with is therefore not an advance, but a critical reduction. The return to ethics is a recognition of the fact that discourse must return to spontaneity, since the search for nuclei of organization, together with the very appeal to the public, have turned out to be intractable paths. After the project of a collective bourgeois growth has revealed itself – for now – to be premature, what is required is the development of a discourse in close contact with individual experience.

This is not to say that the project disappears. Descartes still refers to this precarious morality as a 'provisional' fact. He always retains in the background the vivid image of the comprehensive, scientific project of a definitive ethics: 'the highest and most perfect moral system, which presupposes a complete knowledge of the other sciences and is the ultimate level of wisdom'.[124] But we are still dealing with something relegated to the background, which is at best a merely regulative and unattainable ideal. The fact is that the awareness of the impossibility of forging a definitive ethics, of being able to transcend the provisional one, makes more and more headway in Descartes's thought.

But in this situation it is the very character of provisional morality that changes. That is because its primitive propaedeutic sense – which makes it into an introduction to science – is progressively eroded.[125] The very foundation of the validity of ethical behaviour is thereby transformed. In the first phase, ethical

123. Not only in the *Regulae*, as we have often recalled, but also in that hint contained in the dedication of the *Discourse*, PWD I 111, where Descartes speaks of a morality 'derived from this method'.
124. PWD I 186.
125. For the definition of this character, see PWD I 122–5 (and E. Gilson, *Commentaire*, 229–64); PWD II 106; PWD I 194. Also in the *Preface Letter*, PWD I 185–6.

behaviour was only hypothetically valid but in substance tended towards the search for a new methodical foundation. Now instead the foundation is sought and found within the very process of historical ethicality, in its very determinacy. And it is here that, having lost the systematic reference, it is faith, faith in individual and bourgeois spontaneity, in the operative nature of modern man, that gains the greatest emphasis.[126]

The investigation follows two lines of inquiry: to make the provisional ethics definitive and to discover the source and value of action in individuality. In the epistolary exchange with Elisabeth[127] the path is clear, in both of its aspects. The princess's first

126. J. Laporte (*Le rationalisme de Descartes*, 2nd edn, Paris 1950) and G. Rodis-Lewis (*La morale de Descartes*, Paris 1957) are the authors who have better grasped and developed the internal nexus on the basis of which Descartes's ethics develops (materially and fideistically). This nexus is the offspring of all the internal contradictions of the system, especially the one between human and divine freedom. The paradoxical character of such an interpretation does not cancel out its capacity to adapt itself to the paradoxical reversal of Descartes's system which is evident in the final ethical period. If we put the theses of Laporte and Rodis-Lewis in the correct perspective of historical interpretation, they emerge enriched and their paradoxical nature is itself explained.

127. On the relationship between Descartes and Elisabeth, see AT III 351–3; G. Rodis-Lewis, *La morale de Descartes*, pp. 57–61; G. Cohen, *Ecrivains français*, pp. 603–36, 641–3; and especially M. Néel, *Descartes et la princesse Elisabeth*, Paris 1946 (Néel moves from an analysis of the relationship between Descartes and Elisabeth, which is truly conclusive albeit occasionally frivolous, to a very Laportian study of Cartesian ethics: overall, the essay is of fundamental importance for interpreting both the relationship and Descartes's final ethics). Let us recall that Descartes introduced himself, through his nobleman friend Pollot, to the court of the émigré princes of Bohemia in 1642 (PWD III 214). The first letter from Elisabeth is from May 1643 (AT III 660–2). The other texts are: AT IV 37–50, 131–8, 201, 207–13, 335–41, 449, 617–20, 624–31 [TN: partly in PWD III 314–15]; PWD III 317–19; AT V 46–50, 59–73 [TN: partly in PWD III 323–4], 89–92, 96–7, PWD III 328–30, AT V 194–202, 209–11, 224–7, 231–4, 280–9 [TN: partly in PWD III 367–8], 330–1, PWD III 378, 382–3 and 451–3.

demand is in fact that of 'a more specific definition of the soul than in your Metaphysics', through which to consider voluntary and ethical action in its real incarnation.[128] And Descartes's reply, in its apparent reticence, already reveals the general meaning of the new framework. In effect, Descartes denies the problem. The incarnation of the soul is a fact that cannot be decomposed but must instead be grasped and admired in its immediacy, in its spontaneity.[129] True, this is not explained by the previous metaphysical assumptions which, if anything, pushed in the direction of dualism[130] and its intensification. This unitary grasp of the soul constitutes an act that unsettles the Cartesian proposal as a whole, which up to this point had unfolded in accordance with an analytical rhythm:

> The things that belong to the union of soul and body are known only obscurely by the understanding alone, or even by the understanding aided by the imagination; but they can be known very clearly by sense . . . It is by relying only on life and ordinary conversations, abstaining from meditating upon and studying those things that exercise the imagination, that one learns to conceive the union of soul and body.[131]

The forcefulness of this affirmation is bewildering.[132] One might think it is obvious, but in truth it harbours an entire philosophy within it. After a long series of crises this primitive truth remains: the full-bodied and irremovable unity of individuality. Bourgeois existence as a given? This is the only possible

128. AT III 161.
129. PWD III 217–18.
130. AT III 685.
131. PWD III 226–7.
132. It is so disconcerting and conclusive that the dialogue with Elisabeth is itself interrupted between AT IV 1–3 and PWD III 249–50, AT IV 233–5. On this gap in the 1644 correspondence, see M. Néel, *Descartes et la princesse Elisabeth*, pp. 52–9.

retrieval of time for the sake of existence. This recognition is therefore an act of faith. All the attempts to positively articulate within time the relation between essence and existence have proven themselves vain. There remains the fundamental awareness of the immediate emergence and unity of essence and existence.

This recognition is accompanied by the most certain trust: 'I believe that since there is no good in the world beside good sense that can absolutely be called good, there is also no evil from which, possessing good sense, we cannot draw some advantage'.[133] In this reliance on good sense, Cartesian ethics is reconstructed. Now, in the precariousness which is essential to this ethics and which can no longer be overcome, it nevertheless finds a foundation. No longer 'provisional', but precarious! Because, within that dimension of trust, morality too is a description of the given, a concrescence in the tangle of passions that constitute man – a tangle that might be irrational but which faith, the rediscovery of this irremovable foundation, tells us is good.[134]

In its new scope, the Cartesian reconstruction of morality goes through various stages. Two of them are fundamental. In a first moment Descartes in fact limits himself to renewing the dicta of provisional morality,[135] concluding with a reasonable usage of the

133. PWD III 253.
134. See in this regard the striking letter to Pollot from mid-January 1641 (AT III 278–80). It is clear that here the supposed stoicism of Descartes's ethics is completely overturned. When faith – the immediate apperception of human unity and the human meaning of the nexus of the passions – becomes the centre of the ethical attitude, stoic asceticism is entirely sidelined (together with its Christian variant). This does not mean that, as we have emphasized, de facto Stoic positions are not present in the early Descartes. There faith means the acceptance of necessity, the repression of life, sacrifice. Stoic attitudes recur even in the mature Descartes. But they do so as mere cultural reminiscences, without modifying the new philosophical framework.
135. See above all PWD III 256–9, in the commentary to Seneca's *De vita beata*, which Descartes had been reading alongside Elisabeth. See also PWD III 255–6, AT IV 268–70, PWD III 259–62, 262–5, AT IV 287–90.

passions in accordance with the modalities of correct discernment, firmness in resolution, independence and autonomy: 'I am not at all of the opinion that one must entirely scorn the passions, nor that one should exempt oneself from having them; it suffices to render them subject to reason, and once they have been thus tamed, they are sometimes all the more useful inasmuch as they tend toward excess'.[136] But Descartes's argument is immediately deepened: it tries to grasp morality not as a precept but in its making; it attempts to relive it in the midst of that tangle it has entrusted itself to, growing with it. The *Treatise on the Passions* leads one directly into this situation.[137] The first impression is that of a work of excavation, of an indulgent contact with consciousness; of two paths – the metaphysico-deductive[138] and the physico-inductive[139] – which intersect, overlap. There is here a

136. PWD III 265.
137. The history of the composition of the *Treatise on the Passions* should be studied with special care and attention (alas, this is not the place to do so: perhaps we shall return to it at a later date) because it truly demonstrates how a recovered metaphysical demand – a profound and, so to speak, full-bodied humanism – can be reborn within Cartesian thought, unfolding itself and taking control of a very rich experimental material. In any case, we should bear in mind that a philological analysis shows that the *Treatise* is a consequence, both internal and external, of the correspondence and debate carried out with Elisabeth. Furthermore, we should also note the necessary interlude provided by the *Treatise on Animals* (PWD III 270), and the fact that the passage from the general physiological analysis to a particular ethical analysis is announced in PWD III 272. But the *Treatise* is not spoken of again, even though work on it proceeds. In November 1645 we discover that Descartes is at work on the number and order of the passions (PWD III 277). In March or April 1646 he gives to Elisabeth a first draft of the *Treatise*, which perhaps contained only Parts One and Two (AT IV 404). In May he promises that he will revise that draft for publication (PWD III 285) but in June, speaking with Chanut, he denies any intention of publishing it (PWD III 289). The publication of the text will take place in 1649. On the entire question see the notes in AT XI 293–300, *Avertissement* to the Adam–Tannery edition. The text is printed in AT XI 327–488.
138. PWD I 328ff, art. 1–30.
139. PWD I 328ff, art. 31–50.

density of the concept – preceded by a density of lived experience – that does not seek explanation, but rather expression. There is also a demonstrative approach which really amounts to a kind of coup, the conjunction of logically incongruent terms, a faith that unifies what is metaphysically condemned to a situation of insuppressible dualism. The will can direct the passions by utilizing their mechanics, and mechanics imposes itself on the will as a totalizing condition. The soul is reduced to the body, the body reassumed and dominated by the soul. A tangle, as we have said, seen through the eyes of logic;[140] but one that is absolute in its capacity to live,[141] expressing the overflowing, absolute emergence of individuality.[142]

The first passion is the movement of recognition, '*admiration*',[143] the contact of consciousness with the entire fullness of its content, an urge to exist and to grow. It is a passion that is at once spiritual,[144] incorporeal[145] and radical:[146] it moves between good sense[147] and memory . . .[148] *Admiration*: this then is the name of the actual, immediate, liminal unification of essence and existence. This is the name of the fully retrieved humanistic

---

140. This is precisely what Laporte and Rodis-Lewis do.
141. See again M. Néel and especially J. Russier, *Sagesse cartésienne et religion. Essai sur la connaissance de l'immortalité de l'âme selon Descartes*, Paris 1958.
142. P. Comarnesco, 'Les normes de la vie sociale chez Descartes', in *Congrès Descartes*, vol. II, pp. 86–94, has underlined with vigour this 'uncontainable' character of Cartesian individuality: the passage to ethical and social life takes place more in the name of this overabundance than in virtue of a normative continuity between individuality and sociality – a normative continuity that is nonetheless founded on and supported by the individual drive to the realization of the spiritual power of the subject.
143. PWD I 350, art. 53–5 [TN: '*admiration*' is in French in the original].
144. PWD I 353, art. 70.
145. PWD I 353, art. 71.
146. PWD I 353, art. 72.
147. PWD I 355, art. 77.
148. PWD I 354, art. 75.

nostalgia. In this memory time is positive. Here time is possessed, dominated. Finally that time around which the reasonable ideology had exhausted itself is regained. The cost is high: the reasonable ideology itself can no longer exist, at least as a discourse, as the articulation of the fundamental experience. The only real thing is the moment of the apperception of that fundamental content: faith. This is the immediate awareness that does not explain itself, and which moreover lives, as given, within separation and nevertheless against and before separation.

In *admiration* we thus encounter the real ontological foundation of Descartes's ethical discourse. After it there open up an articulation and a dialectic that are also significant but not as pregnant. Because, as we now know, beyond this moment of foundation there are at most hypotheses and lived experiences. But, to the extent that it detaches itself from *admiration*, every other passion is abstract. What the table of the *Treatise on the Passions* offers us is a rhythmical succession of abstractions.

Love and hate.[149] This is the first scission, still within the fundamental fabric of the primitive humanist experience. Love is the participation in the life of the whole, hope in the possession of the world.[150] Hate is separation. But both terms are abstract, just as memory is abstract, remote. Humanist nostalgia and the feeling of Renaissance defeat are the fundamental experiences. That being said, these terms do not yet concern time, that time which opens up before us, capacious and indefinite. *Admiration*, love and hate are still placed within the depth of potential consciousness.[151] They are real to the extent that they are liminal: that is the sign of the gigantic reversal that the reasonable ideology is forced to undergo – to portray as present what once was project, because the project failed, it could not but fail.

The second degree of abstraction, of distancing from the fullness of *admiration*, brings with it desire, joy and sadness.[152]

149. PWD I 350 and 356–7, arts 56, 79–85.
150. See the letter dated 1 February 1647, to Chanut, in AT IV 601–17.
151. PWD I 356, art. 80.
152. PWD I 358–62, art. 85–95. But see already arts 57–67.

It is the reflection which – whether immediate, triumphant or defeated – turns to the past to seek (finally) to dialecticize it in time. The only significant time is the one in which the past is relived as desire. This is a precarious situation. It is on the basis of desire that the reasonable ideology organizes itself: but then desire suffers the same affronts, the same defeats as the reasonable ideology. *Admiration*, transposed into time as desire, ends up inextricably caught between joy and sadness. This is the situation of the whole bourgeoisie, stuck between humanist nostalgia and defeat.[153]

So we have defined that moment in which the Cartesian discourse tackles the reasonable ideology. The failure of the immediate possibility of its historical realization, of the assumption of time, produces an incredibly profound modification of Descartes's discourse: it retrieves and exalts its humanist grounding and through it regains vigour. Once again the crisis relaunches Cartesian thought. On this basis, once again, everything is possible. It does not matter that the time has shown itself to be an irreducible sign of defeat, since we have before us the equally irreducible emergence of the I. The good is the possession of the I,[154] it is its production, the recognition of what one is. This is almost a return to the demands of the *Discourse*, a reappearance of that heroic naïveté. But with greater awareness, in an experience that has proven itself in time.

5

But the fact that the reasonable ideology does not realize itself in time, that it needs to return to its origins, to find comfort in the fullness of memory, does not mean that it does not represent a

---

153. These are the terms in which the Cartesian *Treatise* unfolds. What's more, the century's thematization of the passions, and of love in particular, moves within this alternative. See O. Nadal, *Le sentiment de l'amour*.
154. See for example PWD III 324.

valid hypothesis for Descartes. History might have rejected it by denying it the support of organized groups, the technical project might stretch out over the void of an insuppressible dualism – but the humanist demon continues to push from within: '. . . concerning the important actions of life, when they appear so doubtful that prudence cannot tell us what to do, it seems to me that there is great reason to follow the advice of one's demon [*génie*] . . .'[155] It even seems, as we have already recalled, that Descartes wrote a brief treatise on this extreme, substantive reference to interior subjectivity.[156] The Socratic genius or demon: perhaps no other image can better express this vigorous humanist retrieval which is the arrival point of Cartesian thought. This is precisely the outcome of the crisis of the relation between the reasonable ideology and time: the redemption of memory, as the basis or the condition for the relaunching (now untimely but nevertheless necessary) of the reasonable ideology. The final word of Cartesian philosophy is the claim concerning the utility and necessity of the reasonable ideology, the full redemption of its humanist basis – despite and against the conditions that have impeded its immediate historical efficacy.

Let us look at the *Preface Letter* to the French edition of the *Principles*.[157] We find there the expression of this Cartesian point of arrival in its maximum intensity. First of all, Descartes gathers

155. AT IV 530.
156. According to the testimony in *Baillet*, vol. II, p. 408: 'They still speak to us of another treatise of Descartes, entitled *De Deo Socratis*, where he examined what this "*esprit familier*" of Socrates could be, which has been the subject of such critical interest over the centuries. But it seems that this good was already alienated by the time that its author travelled to Sweden. So the text was not to be found among the others in the inventory made at Descartes's death. Perhaps it fell into different hands than those of Clerselier . . .'
157. Composed in 1647. Sent to Picot, the French translator of the *Principles*. See AT IV 147, 175, 181, 222; AT V 66, 78–9, PWD III 329. The full title is: 'Author's letter to the translator of the book which may here serve as a preface'. Now the letter is in PWD II 179–90.

together the fundamental elements of the reasonable ideology. This is a framework we are acquainted with: wisdom as the capacity to conduct oneself in life, to retain health and to proceed in *invenire* ('by "wisdom" is meant not only prudence in our everyday affairs but also a perfect knowledge of all things that mankind is capable of knowing, both for the conduct of life and for the preservation of health and the discovery of all manner of skills'),[158] the praise of good sense and spontaneity ('The conclusion that must be drawn from this is that among those who have studied whatever has been called philosophy up till now, those who have learnt the least are the most capable of learning true philosophy'),[159] the metaphysical and systematic conditions of knowledge ('These are all the principles that I make use of with regard to immaterial or metaphysical things, and from them I deduce very clearly the principles of corporeal or physical things . . .'; 'Then, when he has acquired some skill in finding the truth on these questions, he should begin to tackle true philosophy in earnest. The first part of philosophy is metaphysics, which contains the principles of knowledge, including the explanation of the principal attributes of God, the non-material nature of our souls and all the clear and distinct notions which are in us. The second part is physics, where, after discovering the true principles of material things, we examine the general composition of the entire universe and then, in particular, the nature of this earth and all the bodies which are most commonly found upon it, such as air, water, fire, magnetic ore and other minerals. Next we need to examine individually the nature of plants, of animals and, above all, of man, so that we may be capable later on of discovering the other sciences which are beneficial to man. Thus the whole of philosophy is like a tree. The roots are metaphysics, the trunk is physics, and the branches emerging from the trunk are all the other sciences, which may be reduced to three principal ones,

158. PWD II 179.
159. PWD II 183.

namely medicine, mechanics and morals. By "morals" I understand the highest and most perfect moral system, which presupposes a complete knowledge of the other sciences and is the ultimate level of wisdom').[160] Really, Descartes adds, at this point I could give my fellow citizens 'a body of philosophy that is quite complete'.[161]

Nevertheless, having reached this point, when the luminosity of the ideal of wisdom has become dazzling, we are faced with a sudden swerve: 'But this, I can see, would require great expense – too great for an individual like myself unless he were assisted by the public. And since I do not see that I can expect such assistance, I think that in future I should be content to study for my own private instruction and that future generations will forgive me if from now on I give up working on their behalf'.[162] But this does not mean an abandonment. Rather, it means putting one's trust in a future history that cannot be done away with because here, in philosophy, in the redemption of that elementary and inaugural patrimony of humanity, the basis is set. Trust is put in collective work, because the basis is given:

> The last and greatest fruit of these principles is that they will enable those who develop them to discover many truths which I have not explained at all. Thus, moving little by little from one truth to the next, they may in time acquire a perfect knowledge of all philosophy, and reach the highest level of wisdom. One sees in all the arts that although they are at first rough and imperfect, nevertheless, because they contain some element of truth, the effect of which is revealed by experience, they are gradually perfected by practice. So it is in philosophy: when one has true principles and follows them, one cannot fail to come upon other truths from time to time.[163]

160. PWD II 184 and 186.
161. PWD II 188.
162. PWD II 188.
163. PWD II 188.

But let us once again look at the writings originating in the milieu closest to Descartes, which together with the Cartesian replies function as the preface to the *Treatise on the Passions.*[164] We find there the same impetus, the same confidence. But when the invitation put to him by the unknown author of the *grande lettre* – asking him to place himself entirely 'at the service of the public' – seems to turn into a Baconian hope in a sympathetic and actual conquest of the world,[165] we observe Descartes responding with a sober and composed reflection: I am neither an orator nor a moral philosopher, but a physicist.[166] As if to say that the realization of the reasonable ideology is no longer entrusted to will, but to necessity.

This is an elaboration of the Cartesian thematic, which everything up to this point had prepared but which only now is explicitly elucidated. Ideology discovers itself as physics and physics sees itself as ideology. On the one hand, therefore, necessity is anything but mechanical: it is an ideal schema wherein the bourgeois emergence contemplates its own process of realization. But on the other, the reasonable ideology effectively harbours within itself its own necessity. Having fully undergone the drama of the bourgeois world, Descartes's discourse succeeds in conquering the vision required to re-launch its values, its comprehensive reality. Its overall historical meaning is thus elucidated to the very extent that ideology is aware of the necessity of this situation. That is because in this perspective ideology has dissolved the ideal into the real, because it has once again proposed the body as the basis of

---

164. AT XI 301–26 [TN: partly in PWD I 326–7]. We are dealing with two letters, and two replies by Descartes. The first letter, from an unknown source, and ironically passed into the history of Cartesian texts as the '*grande lettre*', is dated: Paris, 6 November 1648. Descartes's reply is from 4 December 1648. The second exchange of letters takes place between July and August 1649.
165. AT XI 301–21 *passim.*
166. PWD III 327.

ideology. This is the mnemonic dimension of that becoming body of the bourgeoisie, of its historical upsurge. Whence the consciousness of necessity, which will ground the bourgeois project of development and will even be able to support utopia. Whence the awareness that the failure of the single attempts at redemption might not be harmful, as long as the basis remains intact.[167] If the Cartesian philosophy had originated in the problematization (and in the partial rejection) of memory, it now concludes with the redefinition of memory as basis, as the radical support for the fortunes of ideology. It concludes with the integral redemption of memory. I say 'integral' because even the most problematic among the elements of the mnemonic experience are here redeemed; because it is in the continuous dialectic of nostalgia and the feeling of defeat that the internal articulation of Cartesian metaphysics comes to the fore. We encounter a positive dialectic, a necessity both vigorous and revolutionary – from which every passive historical submission is banished, even by means of a realistic practice of the evaluation of the world.[168] This is all the more bewildering for his contemporaries to the extent that what the

---

167. Many of Descartes's judgements on the political events of the time are subtended by just such an attitude of confidence in the future of bourgeois development, not disjoined, however, from a certain annoyance towards the more adventurous, properly seventeenth-century and baroque aspects of political events. Exemplary in this regard are the judgements on the Fronde. But in general see: PWD III 265–7, AT IV 301–4, PWD III 268–73, AT IV 324, 356–7, 405–6, PWD III 287–8, AT IV 485–94, 519–25, PWD III 297–8, AT IV 580; AT V 197–202, 231–4, 280–9 [TN: partly in PWD III 367–8].

168. In his *Descartes, Corneille, Christine de Suède*, E. Cassirer has strongly insisted on the evaluative realism and ethical activism that characterize Descartes's moral essays – thereby countering all those interpretations which see Cartesian ethics as flowing back into the tradition of Stoicism. Among the Stoicizing interpretations we should recall above all that of V. Brochard, 'Descartes stoicien', now in *Etudes de philosophie ancienne et de philosophie moderne*, Paris 1954, pp. 320–6 (but see also pp. 327–31).

situation of crisis led to was precisely historical passivity and a deficit of evaluative realism.[169]

The Cartesian alternative to the actual situation shines here in all its historical significance. It is not by chance therefore that posterity, going beyond the immediate appearance of the refusal of Cartesianism, founded the bourgeois philosophy of construction precisely on this articulation of the internal elements of Descartes's philosophy. From Leibniz to the thinkers of the Enlightenment and to Hegel we witness the problem progressively being defined, just as it had progressively established itself in Descartes, as the discovery of the liminal identity of the infinite and the indefinite.[170] Metaphysics continues to provide the metaphor for the emergence of the bourgeoisie as a class, the allusion to a project of reconquering a lived essence, of realizing a willed revolution. Metaphysics thus becomes more and more clearly the metaphor of the political demand to reconquer the world for the mode of production, to reconquer the state for society, to reconquer power for the bourgeoisie. This is always, in differing formulations, the Cartesian problem of the indefinite as the character of knowledge and action, which is placed before the actual infinite reality of the subject, of its

169. This is not the place to present the documentation on Stoicism's fortune in the 1600s (and already in the 1500s). Elsewhere we have dwelled on the studies by Gerhardt Oestreich and Julien Eymard d'Angers. It suffices here to recall once again the judgement of E. Cassirer (p. 26): 'Stoic morality, despite its teaching about autarchy and the autonomy of the will, in fact did not escape the circle of passivity. It taught how the sage could endure life, teaching him how to triumph over life. Modern stoicism reaffirmed this profound viewpoint: patience within suffering remained for it the supreme virtue'. Analogous observations should also be presented with regard to the other great intellectual current in this phase of the century, classicism. But in this case too I simply refer to the already amply discussed works of Georg Weise and René Bray.

170. As an introduction to the study of the fortunes of Descartes's thought, internal to the development of the great bourgeois philosophy of the modern age, one should certainly give privileged attention to Yvon Belaval, *Leibniz critique de Descartes*, Paris 1960.

power. Unification will desire to be ever more stringent, history will increasingly be made to unfold to the rhythm of ideology, in its pressing and reasonable necessity. It is impossible to read the history of bourgeois thought, beginning with Descartes, in any other perspective than this one. The relation between ideology and time, now mediated by Cartesian reason, will become, little by little, a relation historically dominated by the power of a hegemonic class. The political character of Cartesian thought thus becomes entirely evident, in its development as well as its genesis.

Of course in Descartes we do not find the totalitarian sense of the domination of reason over history which belongs to the last phase of triumphant bourgeois thought. On the contrary, in Descartes there is often an acute perception of scission, of defeat as a sign of the very quality of bourgeois existence. The burden of memory on life is a sign of this originary defeat. But is defeat a destiny? Does memory so deeply condition the bourgeois future as to eliminate any possibility of redemption? The Cartesian response is an ambiguous one. Descartes always juxtaposes the sense of transcendence, an irreducible dualism, to the position of the problem of the infinite as synthesis, act and overcoming of the indefinite. But is this enough to qualify, within the ambit of Cartesian thought, the destiny of the bourgeoisie as a dramatic destiny, the definition of the bourgeoisie as a non-revolutionary class? An 'ambiguous' Descartes: that is perhaps the best definition that can be given of a 'political' Descartes. In effect, the centrality of his role in the position of the bourgeois class problematic is situated in a period replete with incredibly profound contradictions. That is why, in spite of everything, the richness of his philosophy remains mysterious, but not any less attractive or open because of that. Perhaps already in Descartes it is possible to 'recognise reason as the rose in the cross of the present and thereby to enjoy the present, this is the rational insight which reconciles us to the actual . . .'[171] Or, perhaps, it begins to.

171. G. W. F. Hegel, *Hegel's Philosophy of Right*, trans. T. M. Knox, Oxford 1967, p. 12.

Postface to the English Edition

The first edition of this book is dated 1970. It was written for an academic qualification and submitted to the judgement of a committee of university colleagues. This was in the period immediately following 1968. I was known to be a professor who had sided with the student movement. Moreover, all my work of the '60s had been concerned with the analysis of the political movements of the workers and the critical excavation of Marxism. The book came as a surprise both to academics, for its choice of subject (what could a Marxist do with Descartes?), and to my comrades in the movement (why is Negri wasting his time on Descartes?). Today, to those who might wish to ask me why, after more than thirty years, I am allowing this book to be reissued, I can repeat the explanation I gave to both these groups.

The answer consists of three observations and a conclusion.

1) The first observation is that every metaphysics is in some way a political ontology – as has been clearly demonstrated by Machiavelli, Spinoza and Marx (and, after them, was the basis for the broad philosophical consensus that runs from Nietzsche to Foucault and Derrida). In the case in question, the study of Descartes's thought offered an extraordinary opportunity to demonstrate this thesis because, due to its originality and radicalism, Descartes's political thought stands, on the one hand, against the theological–political continuity of medieval philosophy and, on the other, against the mechanistic and Absolutist theories *à la* Hobbes. Moreover, it does so in that moment of historical and

political crisis that marked the birth of modernity. Descartes institutes not only a new political ontology but a different one. It is an *ontology* of mediation, not dialectical but *temporal*, progressive, aimed at building the hegemony of a social class. That is to say, it adds, to the constitutive reasons of modern politics (which presents itself in the form of the Absolutist state), an evolutionary project for cultural hegemony and the bourgeois domination of society.

2)   The second observation amounts to underlining that the continuity of a philosophical thought (and the fortune of Descartes's was long-lived) is linked to the power for the *implicit political dispositif* within its author's ontology. In this and only in this – to wit, in the endurance for the *dispositif* that the ontology comprehends – lies the reason of the historical efficacy, if any, of a given metaphysics. Faithfulness as well as betrayal, continuity as well as discontinuity, crises as well as transformations articulate a chain of ideas that is always commensurable to the being of its origin. The same can be said when the force of a thought is dispersed or vanishes. If a living archaeology nourishes creative genealogies, conversely new historical and political conditions can deceive us with defunct archaeologies. Cartesianism, in its French developments and its European offshoots, is a particularly efficient model for this historical figure of metaphysics. The critical and radically innovative features of the origins of Cartesianism are brought into relief by its theoretical duration and revolutionary continuity. Whence the usefulness of the study of Descartes's originary political ontology and of how it was formed and developed. It allows us to describe, through different *dispositifs*, articulated diagrams and constitutive blueprints, a few subsequent centuries in the history of thought and of the evolution of bourgeois and capitalist power – under the sign of hegemony.

3)   The third observation takes its cue from the recognition that the archaeological consideration of a philosophical stance can

be traversed by *different genealogies*. In other words, that a thought is (always) constituted and defined through choices and breaks, that it is all the more significant to the extent that it is able to control and subsume the different and, at times, contradictory historical articulations of a period, as well as the movement of subjects that in this period sought and/or constructed hegemony. To defend this methodological thesis, it suffices to consider the fundamental characteristics of the conflicts and alternatives that we defined (at the end of the 1960s) as lying at the basis of this analysis of Descartes's political thought. Beginning with an inventory of political thought in France in the first half of the 1600s, we attempted to demonstrate – harking back to the work of Borkenau and to some suggestions of Lucien Febvre – how the 'philosophy of manufacture' was anything but a unified bloc; and how, conversely, the structural elements of the productive trans-formation of the world, the revolutionary forces which – begin-ning in the 1300s in Italy and Flanders, and from the Renaissance onwards spreading throughout Europe – are set free, encounter, in the 1600s, in a definitive manner, a vast field of ideological alternatives, which is to say of different political possibilities.[1] It is in the face of these alternatives that Descartes's construction of a reasonable political order asserts itself – as a powerful attempt to represent a hegemonic development of the bourgeoisie within the formation of the Absolutist state.

4)   Finally, my conclusion is that a political ontology of the past (in this instance Descartes's) can be usefully contrasted with the current state of affairs, in order to understand or renew the image of the present. This is all the more evident to the extent that the present and the era in which Descartes's work was conceived

1. See my 'Problemi di storia dello stato moderno. Francia: 1610–1650', in *Rivista critica di storia della filosofia*, 1967, vol. II, pp. 182ff; 'Manifattura ed ideologia', in P. Schiera (ed.), *Manifattura, società borghese, ideologia* (with articles by F. Borkenau, H. Grossmann, A. Negri), Rome 1978; 'Prefazione' to C. B. Macpherson, *Libertà e proprietà alle origini del pensiero borghese*, Milan 1973.

resemble one another. There is no naïveté in saying this. The sense of the difference and the singularity of the thinking and the event is still very strong in us and our pedagogy in no way claims to produce that 'isomorphism' that is so dear to the champions of the base/superstructure relation. Rather, this stance calls for a bit of irony and a lot paradoxes. And yet . . .

To draw these methodological observations closer to reality, let us begin with the conclusion (see 4 above), that is by highlighting the similarities, if any, between yesterday and today. As we have already noted, Descartes developed his philosophy in the very midst of that period of social and political transition that forms *modernity*. Descartes's work is an attempt to measure up to this transition. Well, today we also find ourselves in the middle of a great transition that is forming *postmodernity*. The bourgeoisie then, and today the global proletariat (the multitude), confront power. But the similarities do not end here. The process that Descartes registers is given in the continuity of the alternatives that are experimented, one by one, either to be dissolved or to triumph. Disorientation and doubt trouble consciences. *In profundo gurgite* we are torn. Descartes depicts from within a process of crisis which bears many analogies to the one we are undergoing today. Today it is also the case that we are in an *interregnum* between the old forms of capitalist government and the new ones of a global governance, which are seeking an effective definition. That is, we are in the midst of a great social and political transition that opened up after 1968 and has yet to reach a definitive point of equilibrium. This transition has witnessed and still witnesses extremely strong political opposition to the movements of renewal. The historical period Descartes lived through is referred to as the epoch of the construction of the modern state, beginning with the crisis of the Renaissance and the first forms of bourgeois government and concluding with the definition of the Absolutist state. In that period, the revolutionary process of the bourgeoisie – like that of the global proletariat or the multitude today – underwent a grave crisis: the Thirty Years War lies at the basis of the Absolutist reaction against the bourgeois revolution, in the same way that 'pre-emptive war' lies at the basis of the capitalist reaction against the revolution of the global proletariat. Moreover, both of these periods are criss-crossed by processes of social and political reaction, of 'refeudalization' then, of 'privatization' of public goods now. In both periods we witness the collapse of the ideological model that had nourished the first revolutionary insurgencies, accompanied however by the persistence of the unstoppable and irreversible productive and social force of the new historical subjects: *whence the crisis.*

My problem, then (when I wrote *The Political Descartes*) as now, is that of interpreting the crisis from the standpoint of critical Marxism. Critical Marxism is anything but determinist. The clash between productive forces and capitalist relations of production, both in reality and in representation (theoretical and metaphysical, scientific and historiographical), is always linked to events, to relationships of forces, to the creative capacity of historical subjects. If today this is entirely clear, it was no less so in the great philosophical drama of modernity. Descartes and Hobbes, Spinoza and Leibniz, Kant and Hegel are not phantoms of thought (of a multifarious historical succession of ever-unresolved passions) but concrete alternatives within the reality of singular historical periods. That is why we love or hate them, why we consider them the very flesh of life or, conversely, skeletons that hinder our thinking. In other words, these alternatives mark the different virtualities that the power (*potenza*) of the historical process is capable of and consists in. The theoretical revolution within Marxism and the redefinition of its critical function that, in the 1960s, passed through Italian *operaismo* and French poststructuralism had, as a seal of its truth, the force of this living relation with philosophical thought in general and, consequently, possessed a privileged interpretative capacity *immanent* to the subjective becoming of modernity. This point of view is present in my *The Political Descartes.* The subjectivation of productive forces is not in fact a process that must await postmodernity, that is, the appearance of the *General Intellect*, so as to appear fully. Rather, it is implicit – virtually present and violently active – in the configuration of the ideological systems of power (*potere*); equally able to condition them and, if the opportunity arises, to put them in crisis. When one speaks of Descartes, one fully inhabits this machine.

But let us return to our work and ask ourselves the following question: How did Descartes react to the crisis that defines the genesis of modernity? Descartes proposed the hypothesis of the 'reasonable ideology'. It was a question for him, on the one hand, of confirming – from the metaphysical standpoint – the nascent power (*potenza*) of the bourgeoisie, the revolutionary potential of its action, the decision in favour of the autonomy of bourgeois reason: the '*I think*' is this determination. But on the other hand, it was a question of bending the absoluteness of the original position to the concreteness of a historically sustainable political project – here lies the reasonableness of his design. The idea of freedom, introduced by the humanist revolution, was threatened by the overpowering arrogance of the reigning aristocracies and the continuity of the patrimonial and charismatic monarchical order, but also, and above all, by the uprisings and revolutions of the new peasant and artisan multitudes. The latter represented the material basis and productive motor of that project of appropriation of value that the bourgeoisie was in the process of constructing. If the bourgeoisie presented itself as the hegemonic class, capable of constructing a new civilization, it was solely because it had recognized, as the foundation of such a civilization, a *new productive force* – that of labour. To hold back and exploit the new labour-power and, at the same time, to respond to the danger represented by the uprisings of the multitudes as well as to configure a space which, in the alliance with the *ancien régime* (since, without transcendence, it was impossible at the time to define authority), would allow the bourgeoisie to develop – this was Descartes's *reasonable project*. It was an open and *reformist* project that would allow the bourgeoisie to develop the idea of progress and, little by little, to broaden its hegemony within the new structures of the Absolutist state (and, consequently, to elaborate non-theological theories and material practices adequate to a new definition of authority). Moreover, it was a project that was closed and consciously *opportunistic*, because aware of the limits of bourgeois action, of the menace posed by the revolutions of the multitude and therefore in search of a temporality and forms of power (*potere*) adequate to the management of an effective project of reform of society and the state. Descartes's philosophy can be read in this light: as *ideology* (ideology in the true sense, 'partisan' representation of reality, that is, affirmation of the class truth of the hegemonic bourgeoisie) and as *reasonable* ideology, rooted in the awareness of the actual relationships of forces and the progressive possibilities that could potentially open up to that new social body and to that truth.

But as we have said, Descartes's hypothesis can be compared to an analogous situation today. That it is analogous is hard to deny. After 1968, after 1989; that is, after the insurrection of the *General Intellect*, of immaterial and intellectual, proletarian and exploited labour, and after the end of the Soviet-socialist strangulation of communism, the multitudes have reopened a hegemonic possibility and affirmed the project of the *liberation of work*. The response of the dominant classes has been repeated as counterrevolution and as social and political reaction. It constitutes a ferocious restoration, a repetition of the 1600s, a true baroque opening up under our very eyes. A crisis has erupted against the global development of the multitudes. In other words, the capitalist response has been a regressive stabilization. In this new situation of crisis, Descartes's hypothesis would today present itself *formally* as the proposal of a 'reasonable alliance' between new strata of multitudinous intellectual labour and old bourgeois forces of power (*potere*); that is, as a reformist hypothesis within the new postmodern framework. Nevertheless, it is impossible not to recognize, in the face of such a hypothesis, that if the situation is analogous, Descartes's conjecture is unrepeatable. Today, the state forms of capitalism and the living forms of 'collective capital' are no longer able to carry out the function of mediation that the old Absolutist state had effected, with some success, between bourgeois revolts, continuity of the monarchical–patrimonial state and the necessity of dominating proletarian uprisings and insurrections. Where, today, can one find a function of mediation? The dialectic, even the one depicted by Cartesianism as a long-term undertaking of *Aufhebung*, is, from the perspective of the metaphysical infinite, *untimely*: there is no longer a Third Estate, a body of '*robins*' or administrators rooted in the state's interest in the mediation of exploitation, which could create or manage the dialectic. More on this later.

On this basis, let us reconsider the observations we offered at the outset, in order to verify if the historiographical and philosophical literature produced *after 1970* requires us to modify, more or less substantially, our interpretive hypotheses. In reconsidering the debate over recent years, it appears to me, rather, that it reconfirms the theses presented at the time and further demonstrates their truth.

Let us begin with the observations contained in point 2, those concerning the continuity of Cartesian thought and the alternatives present within it. If we turn to the two texts that appear to constitute the definitive synthesis of recent studies,[2] we have a new demonstration of just how much Cartesianism, at a deep level, has profoundly woven together the threads and alternatives of French thought – certainly until the French Revolution. The extraordinary power (*potenza*) of Cartesian thought is studied (in these two works) in relation to the entirety of the social spectrum on which the effects of an innovative thinking can be brought to bear.

2. François Azouvi, *Descartes et la France: Histoire d'une passion nationale*, Paris, 2001, and Stéphane Van Damme, *Descartes: Essai d'histoire culturelle d'une grandeur philosophique*, Paris 2003.

Azouvi and Van Damme have very different approaches: on the one hand, we have a philosophical history that indicates the essential moments of the progressive transformation of Cartesianism into myth, together with the ideal and political conspiracy that lies behind it; on the other, a history that grasps the forms of cultural innovation and intellectual life that constitute, in the course of the seventeenth and eighteenth centuries, the 'great' figure of Descartes. Of course, all this is not enough. These are pieces of philosophical and cultural history that should be combined with the exploration of the most profound moments in social history. Nevertheless they clarify how Descartes's reasonable ideology extends from the classical age through the Enlightenment and up to the Revolution. The Revolution, as it were, completes its design. How this is done, how, on the one hand, history and the social relations that are modified within it work to remove the mystical–spiritualist elements (and the continuity of medieval Scholasticism) that lay at the basis of an earlier representation of modern philosophical rationality; and how, on the other, these tendencies were able to develop and become radicalized in the course of the Enlightenment has also been recently described by Jonathan Israel[3] and Erica Harth.[4] In this manner is set out how the continuity of Cartesianism becomes a network (able to enclose within its threads many of the century's spiritual expressions) and how the trajectory ends, as we have said, with the French Revolution.

Having said that, it is certain that 'reflection on the path travelled (from normalizing rationality), sets us on course for a history of France (and of the whole of modernity) which is very different from the "classical history" that Marx hoped to see'.[5] But

3. *Radical Enlightenment: Philosophy and the Making of Modernity, 1650–1750*, Oxford 2000.
4. *Cartesian Women: Versions and Subversions of Rational Discourse in the Old Regime*, Ithaca NY 1992.
5. M. Gauchet, in A. de Baecque (ed.), *Pour ou contre la révolution*, Paris 2002, p. vii.

this is only partly true, for in that *summa* of Furetian revisionism (which the de Baecque collection amounts to), one truly risks misunderstanding how Descartes's reasonable ideology could construct (and last as) a radical thought and, above all, as a radical subjectivity. Rather, we must recognize that these passages were not easy and that – while 'the seventeenth century suffers of man as of a sum contradictions ("*l'amas de contradictions*" that we are); it seeks to discover, order, excavate man – while the eighteenth century seeks to forget what is known of man's nature in order to assimilate him to its utopia'.[6] To say this is to recognize that those passages and those revolutions of the spirit took place with great force. Other historical revisionists add that the *dispositif* of the 'reasonable ideology' can develop into a utopia. Maybe so, but is it not then precisely on the basis of this awareness that we must recognize the historical process that underlies this transformation? In 1978 François Furet could write 'the French Revolution is over' but he could not thereby bring to a close the historical dialectic that the 'reasonable ideology' had, in its own way, interpreted; and if, precisely at that moment, one was forced to conclude that, in the metaphysical questioning of the fundamental principles of society, neither the political question concerning the nature and functioning of the systems of freedom, nor the social question about what kind of justice a community owes its members could be resolved in univocal terms, it was even more necessary to go deeper, that is to advance the analysis and thereby identify – precisely around these alternatives – the genesis of the revolutionary contradictions and presuppositions (which are the only *certain* products of the intellectual forces put to work by Descartes). That is what the study of Descartes's 'reasonable ideology' allows us to do. This is the dramatic basis for an archaeology of reason that a flexible and undetermined genealogy has bequeathed us.

Coming now to the third observation (point 3 above) and returning to the historical context in which – and in contrast to

6. Nietzsche, *The Will to Power*, New York 1968 §97, p. 61.

which – Descartes's political thought develops, it is clear that here too we will need to ask whether the great work of historical research on the nature of the modern Absolutist state, from 1970 to today, entails essential modifications that prevent us from continuing to defend our thesis of the 'reasonable ideology'. Indeed, there has been much *historical work on the origin of the modern state* in these last thirty years. Yet the advances made by interdisciplinary history, the broadening of sociological and economic analyses, as well as the cultural specializations put to work, have failed to modify the framework developed along the 'Max Weber to Otto Hintze' line of thought. In any case, the modern state, even if it is not precisely defined, as they would have wished, as 'enterprise-state' or 'machine-state', *becomes it*, representing in any case a *process* of unity and functional centralization. Paolo Prodi insists upon this historiographical continuity.[7] He notes how the conclusions reached by the historiography of the 1800s and 1900s continue to be fundamental with respect to the themes surrounding the genesis and development of the modern state. Of course, they need to be rearticulated and shaken up, but the three themes of structural (administrative) rationalization *à la* Maravell, laicization of power (*potere*) *à la* Kantorowicz and biopolitical specialization *à la* Foucault – these determinations do not change, if anything they advance along a continuous and consolidated line of historical interpretation.

The same is true if we observe the historiographical currents clustering around Braudel's positions.[8] We can observe here that the broadening and the 'de-economization' of the reading of the genesis of the modern state by many revisionist historians nonetheless leads to the 'surprise' of having to admit that the expansion and new intensity of hermeneutic techniques and figures (which in the 'new history' have, with much insistence, been deployed in the

7. *Introduzione allo studio della storia moderna*, Bologna 1999, pp. 68ff.
8. See, for example, *Early Modern History and the Social Sciences. Testing the Limits of Braudel's Mediterranean*, ed. John A. Marino, Kirksville 2002.

analysis of the linguistic, geographic, cultural and archival elements) do not cast doubt on the critical foundations of Braudelian economism; on the contrary, renewing analyses on the basis of these points of view, they confirm the *conflictual nature* of the ideology of the modern, uncovering and insisting upon other popular and class struggles that traverse the epoch. To sum up, the theme of the reasonable ideology can be entirely confirmed from a historiographical perspective. If anything, the contradictory content of the modern is emphasized and the intensity of the great crises that affect it is exacerbated. When, between the 1970s and 1980s, I once again traversed this era in my *The Savage Anomaly: The Power of Spinoza's Metaphysics and Politics,*[9] I too reached analogous conclusions.

Whence too some reservations – which I feel compelled to raise – concerning a number of interpretations of this philosophical period, which are linked, in the English-speaking world, to the so-called 'Popkin School'. Even recently, the observations of this great historian of modern scepticism have been repeated by some important works touching on Cartesian themes.[10] What is wrong in these readings and, more generally, in the presuppositions of the 'Popkin School'? I find these interpretations 'limp', so to speak. They spend much time studying the continuity of philosophical tendencies without, however, identifying their ideological function; they stretch over the historical horizontality of the processes without comprehending the nexus tying thought to events and to the materiality of the relations of power (*potere*) vertically, according to historically contingent and yet ideologically relevant relations. For example, they excavate late-medieval Scholasticism so as to discover within it linguistic continuities, but remain unable to indicate the *new* of the modern. They are unable to read the revolution that matures within the presuppositions of this epochal

9. Minneapolis 1991.
10. Tad M. Schmaltz, *Radical Cartesianism: The French Reception of Descartes*, Cambridge 2002; Richard A. Watson, *Cogito, Ergo, Sum: the Life of René Descartes*, Jaffrey, NH, 2002.

transformation of thought. They are unable to grasp the great alternatives and desperate progressive tensions that modern thought harbours within itself (from the beginning). For instance, the alternative Descartes/Spinoza/Pascal ends up being absorbed and mediated in the theoretical climate and metaphysical languages of the period – rather than being brought into relief, in its irreducibility, by reference to concrete historical differences. And yet Lucien Goldmann's excellent book on Jansenism[11] could, in this regard, have been conclusive. The problem is not that of connecting – in the Marxist, and therefore exclusive, manner – *philosophy and conjuncture*; nor that of binding base and superstructure (in the crude manner of a tradition of historiography that we hope is now exhausted). Rather, it is a problem of experiencing the history of philosophy within these relations, as it was lived by the philosophers and the historical subjects who, in each period, tried to produce thought, to affirm power (*potenza*) and hegemony. Political history takes on meaning when it is rooted in ontology and disentangles it. In this way, political philosophy articulated ontology.

Can we already begin to speak here of *biopolitics*?

To conclude let us note how, in these last years, the movement that focused on the renewal of historical studies on the genesis of the modern state reached its apex in the programme of the *Fondation Européenne de la Science* (under the general direction of Wim Blockmans and Jean-Philippe Genet). From the '80s onward it has developed with the aim of widening the consideration of the political history of the state through the examination of the sciences of culture, anthropology, history of art, political sciences, etc. It has reached the conclusion that the modern state is formed in the continuity of a historical process whose roots lie in the late Middle Ages; that the constitution of the modern rationality of the state represents a process that has nothing mechanical or voluntaristic about it; and that, finally, the forma-

11. L. Goldmann, *Le Dieu caché*, Paris 1970.

tion of the modern state occurs in patchwork fashion (differentially and, therefore, in a localized manner, revealing a great diversity in the conflicts that bind and separate state and Church, and in the forms of the *fiscal state*). All this, rather than restricting the grounds of conflict, actually extends them and, rather than confusing the function of the reasonable ideology, clarifies it. Denis Richet describes the historical context in which the 'reasonable ideology' develops in what is possibly the most articulate and exhaustive manner.[12] His irritation with the naïve or simplistic statements of liberal historiography leads him to forcefully illuminate the autonomy of many spheres of historical reality and to argue that they should not be referred to other elements which lie outside a (continuously open and recurrently closed) dynamic between society and state. The pleasure in historiography consists in the discovery of the singularities – individuals, families, social and religious groups, ruling classes – as well as in the discovery of the singularity of their trajectories. The history of Absolutism and of the birth of the Absolute state is constructed by articulating three lines of analysis: inquiry into the evolution of the *forms of dissidence* and of resistances; a *sociology of the actors* engaged in judicial and administrative institutions; and the study of the *political projects* formulated by the sovereigns and their councillors. These paths articulate and develop the traditional theme of the 'treachery of the bourgeoisie' . . . But what else is this 'treachery of the bourgeoisie' if not that realization on which Descartes's ideology is founded and in terms of which it develops? Is this ideology so potent as to be able to interpret, in its reasonableness, precisely that protracted lag, that spiritual, political and theoretical lethargy hindering the construction of the bourgeois revolution? Faced with these difficulties, Descartes tries to affirm a path that retains the freedom and autonomy of the nascent manufacturing bourgeoisie, which is close to being able to declare itself the hegemonic class, in the very midst of the process of construction of

12. *De la Réforme à la Révolution. Etudes sur la France moderne*, Paris 1991.

the modern state. And although a certain overly coherent and unbroken representation of the role of the mechanicism of the and in the Absolute state of modernity (as some Marxist theorists had described it) must undergo revision, by means of a comparison with the variety and diversity of the positions that appear in the course of history, all of this neither denies nor blunts the historical tendency, but rather confirms its force. Descartes and his 'reasonable ideology' sit better in this diversity and plurality of historical stances and episodes than in a more simplified framework. The historical analysis of modernity and of the genesis of the modern state that developed since the 1960s has enriched the scene of modernity without modifying its sense and significance.

At this point we can return to observation 1, that is, to the particular relationship that binds Descartes's metaphysics to a political ontology, and look at the impact of *philosophical critique* on Descartes's metaphysics over the last thirty years. Unfortunately, much has changed in this regard, which is to say that little has changed with respect to what a centuries-old tradition has handed down to us. In contrast to the great critical, structural and deconstructionist interpretations developed up to the 1960s,[13] philosophical analysis in recent decades has attempted, almost as a reaction, to drag Descartes's thought back to the tradition, that is, to normalize it on the terrain of speculative metaphysics – that is to destroy the very possibility of a Cartesian political ontology.

This interpretive line is represented most clearly in the work of Jean-Luc Marion. In a formidable trilogy,[14] Marion carries out a spiritualist renewal in the reading of Descartes, hybridizing the basic outlines of spiritualism with a Husserlian phenomenology and a

---

13. Particularly important was Martial Gueroult's synthesis (*The Soul and the Body: Descartes' Philosophy Interpreted According to the Order of Reason*, vols. 1 and 2, Minneapolis 1985).
14. *Sur l'ontologie grise de Descartes*, Paris 1993; *Sur le prisme métaphysique de Descartes*, Paris 1986; *Sur la théologique blanche de Descartes*, Paris 1981.

Heideggerian ontology. By taking this course, Marion removes all historical sense and any progressive tendency from Descartes's methodology, insisting instead on a decisive choice in favour of the neutralization of the world determined by the discovery of the Ego. Within Descartes's metaphysical perspective, the 'I' is given as a finite substance that is silhouetted against the horizon of a surplus being (*essere eccedente*) and yet is characterized by the absolute limits of the entity. Descartes's ontology is *grey*, the colour of a neutralized substance and of a finite excess. Marion effects a second operation, that of *theologically 'whitening'* Descartes's ontology. It is through the theory of the 'eternal truths' that every analogical residue of being (in the terms of the Scholastic theory of analogy and Renaissance pantheism), that is, every ontological relationship between divine infinity and human finitude, comes to be dissolved. At this point, the task of critique is that of eliminating (or of rendering liminally residual) any humanist attributions, any tendency of the Cartesian '*I think*' towards a univocally productive being and an autonomous ontological power (*potenza*). This process of evacuating the epistemological and constructive power (*potenza*) of the Cartesian *prise de conscience* occurs, according to Marion, in the passage from the *Rules* to the *Meditations*. From this stems an underestimation of the *Discourse on the Method*, in such a way that doubt is characterized simply as the manner of learning the finitude of being. On this interpretation, Descartes becomes the first agent in the progressive exhaustion of Western metaphysics; the first author of a finite conception of being that confers an absolute destiny upon the always excessive destitution of an entity. This path leads to an adherence to the Heideggerian interpretation of Nietzsche and of the genealogy of modern philosophy. The potential consequences of this interpretation for the analysis of Descartes's political ontology are clear. As Massimo Cacciari clearly perceived,[15] every attempt of this sort at an interpretation of Descartes ends up acknowledging the

15. 'Vita Cartesii est Simplicissima', review of *The Political Descartes*, in *Contropiano*, vol. 2, 1970, pp. 375ff.

insolubility of the problem of the modern metaphysics of the 'I' – which is the preamble to the political crisis of the nascent bourgeoisie. The modern is presented univocally as crisis, every internal alternative is withdrawn, there is no hope (and, in Cacciari's interpretation, no power (*potenza*) either).

However, against this – theological and pessimistic – apologetic reading of the *Krisis*; against the interpretation of Descartes's work by Marion and recent French phenomenology, there stands the impossibility of considering being (which emerges from Descartes's understanding of the 'I') as an emaciated index of finitude. Here (as Jocelyn Benoist notes in her superb article),[16] the significance of Descartes's intuition is removed and the *I think* is forced to admit the impossibility of going beyond its finite determination – i.e. as negatively saturated excess. Throughout Marion's interpretation, we discover, rooted in the ontological terrain, not only a desperate image of the crisis but the stark and determined reproposition of a mystical–theological stance. What we observe here is a sort of historical nemesis of the Cartesian Enlightenment: a narrow and irresolvable conservative direction, a re-emergence of reactionary thought that withdraws all progressive character from Descartes's philosophy, definitively confining it within theological dualism.

It is interesting to note how this interpretation (supported today by the prestige of the Sorbonne, as was already the case in the 1600s for the adversaries of Descartes) was – and still is – mocked by at least three different episodes in the development of contemporary philosophy. All three are subsequent to my work and are absolutely unrelated to the internal tensions that drove its development. Nonetheless, a biopolitical understanding of philosophy and an attention to the epochal shift from the modern to the postmodern afford me an easier grasp of deconstructionism, naturalist cognitivism and the feminist philosophy of difference – the three directions that govern the unfolding of the episodes

16. *Philosophie*, vol. 78, 2003.

that concern us. In some sense, then, they appear to converge in the *dispositif* of *The Political Descartes*. Here they are, in the order that I came across them.

First, the polemic between Foucault[17] and Derrida.[18] Foucault, interpreting the final pages of Descartes's First Meditation, underlined the force with which Descartes had insisted on the limit that opposed '*raison*' to '*déraison*'; finding there that mark of opposition that would characterize the definition of 'madness' in classical thought. Against this stance, Derrida insisted on the fact that the relationship between '*raison*' and '*déraison*' contains an implicit link, the same that is expressed by all the transcendental pairs proposed by Western metaphysics – and, as such, it should be subjected to a process of *radical deconstruction*. The departure from metaphysical continuity could take place only through a radical work of redefinition of the binary oppositions and the overcoming of dialectics implicit within it. There can be no homology within conceptual and/or real opposition. In truth, this contrast between Foucault and Derrida is much less marked than it at first appears, representing instead a difference of interpretation. Indeed, it is possible to positively integrate the two positions. Let us assume (as hermeneutic correctness demands) that Descartes's introduction of '*raison*', rather than constituting an oppositional *dispositif* (and so being defined dialectically), simply reveals a tension, a historical and metaphysical contrast between the autonomy of the 'I' and its fate. In this case, '*raison*' proposes a genealogical discourse that goes beyond all idealistic and theological readings of the experience. If this is true, Derrida is an interpreter rather than an opponent of Foucault. Both thinkers lead genealogical discourse back to a *critical* matrix that is *constructive* of a flux of being – precisely in so far as it is *deconstructive* of the antinomies of pre-modern reason. It confirms the power (*potenza*) of the entrance of *Raison* into history.[19] Here, an

17. *Histoire de la folie à l'age classique*, Paris 1972, pp. 56ff.
18. *L'écriture et la différence*, Paris 1967, pp. 51ff.
19. M. Foucault, *Dits et écrits*, vol. II, Paris 1994, pp. 245ff, 281ff.

ontology is posited and defined that is no longer white or grey but *red*. Descartes's thought is taken on by both thinkers as productive: the alternatives of *Raison* exist within the process of the realization of the '*I think*' (and of its antagonistic materialization). We rediscover them in the other episodes that concern us.

Second, there is the Damasio episode.[20] Here, in contrast to the theological or dualistic hypotheses, Descartes's natural philosophy in interpreted as an – *unsuccessful* – attempt to bring together, in a single process, soul and body. Following the historical development of Cartesianism, we cannot deny that this materialism, *implicit* in Descartes's mechanistic philosophy, becomes increasingly explicit. This is the basis of a naturalistic (and sometimes materialist) interpretation of Descartes's thought that enables us to reconstruct the alternatives that operate within the construction of modern science and in its link with a new practice of production. Thus, the recognition of Descartes's failed synthesis stands in relation to a considered project, to an affective and mental *dispositif* that will develop and realize itself. That failed synthesis is the springboard for the definition of a materialist physiology of the mind . . . and, naturally, of the body too.

However, the third, the least expected and most potent development is that which we find within the feminist political and theoretical debate.[21] Beginning with Luce Irigaray,[22] when she confronts the passions of the soul and – in particular – defines the notion of '*Admiration*', to Sara Heinämaa[23] and Lilli Alanen,[24] who take up and unfold these earlier interpretive suggestions, Descartes is revealed to us as the author of a singular incorporation

20. *Descartes' Error: Emotion, Reason, and the Human Brain*. London 2005.
21. *Feminist Interpretations of René Descartes*, ed. Susan Bordo, Philadelphia 1999.
22. *Éthique de la différence sexuelle*, Paris 1974, pp. 75–84.
23. 'Wonder and (Sexual) Difference: Cartesian Radicalism in Phenomenological Radicalism', *Acta Philosophica Fennica*, Helsinki 1999, pp. 277–96.
24. *Descartes' Concept of Mind*, Boston 2003.

of the mind into the body and of the consequent definition of a *difference* between subjects in relation to the gendered (*sessuata*) materiality of their existence. When the difference, revealed by 'Admiration', is posited as the fabric of every construction of singularity, we are so fully inserted into a biopolitical basis of being that it enables us to further the genealogical advancements of constitutive praxis and of the production of Self – in a materialist fashion. What formidable consistency is possessed by this materialist feminism of singularity and difference! It smiles at us as it lifts us out of stupor through the recognition of a loved thing or person. The difference revealed by singularity (and sexual difference in particular), the emotion provoked by the admiration for the loved singularity, place the body at the centre of the philosophical scene. Not only the individual body but the set of bodily relations that mark the gendered (*sessuati*) intersections and the articulations of difference. This feminist thought is a 'reasonable ideology' of difference, in the sense that it follows the event (the admiration for the loved thing, the difference of the singular standpoint) with the aim of constructing the bodily relation between desire and the desired thing. Difference is diluted (and simultaneously confirmed) in the always unresolved but always resolvable link between soul and body.

We thus rediscover, through these developments, that philosophical and critical terrain that constitutes the trace of Descartes's political ontology. I had presented analogous positions, at the end of the 1960s, in *The Political Descartes*, through the history of the modern state.[25] Descartes's *I think* was materialized in its figure and flung onto the world stage. The presupposition for this relationship to history consisted in the materialization of consciousness and in its becoming corporeal. It was a case at the time of advancing, enthusiastically, towards the requalification of the

25. A good synthesis of the Italian historical and philosophical studies of those years is presented by Pierangelo Schiera in *Lo Stato moderno. Origini e degenerazioni*, Bologna 2004.

Cartesian figure within the field of philosophical studies. Perhaps it would have been better to proceed more cautiously – as suggested by Spinoza, Descartes's pupil, not in the field of metaphysics, but in that of ethics and politics. It would have been better to insist, not only on the political nature of Descartes's ontology but also on his biological naturalism. However, neither biological naturalism itself, nor the feminist theory of the passions and the discovery of difference as the matrix of singularity, are able to draw on all the alternatives of ontology (by which we mean the determinate, that is to say political ones). However, it is necessary to note that this is the motif that the ontological interpretation of the world of the 1600s and the reading of the great transition to modernity usually represent in Descartes. Were I, today, to return to the study of Descartes, retaining (as we have seen) the historical framework more or less as it stands, I would certainly insist more on the question of the subject, on the character of Descartes's naturalism and on the movement of the passions – in the conviction that the new approaches, which we have indicated, enable us to sweep away, even more radically, any theological or simply metaphysical reading of Descartes's thought. Therefore, I do not think that the interpretive effort of the 1960s and 1970s can be surpassed. It can only be completed.

In the 1960s the fundamental problem, for those who operated within materialism and critically reinterpreted Marxism, was that of pitting historical materialism against the dialectic. The problem that is posed now, in the continuity of the battle, is to oppose the standpoint of absolute immanence to all transcendentalisms. The historiographical methodology that drives this effort is not merely adequate to the modern but constitutes the key to confronting the problems posed by postmodernity. That is why *The Political Descartes* is not only a book on Descartes but is a book on method. In my experience as a researcher, following this path and advancing this method, there then came *The Savage Anomaly, Insurgencies, Empire* and *Multitude*. In these works I hope to have demonstrated the effectiveness of this approach. In fact, grasping political ontology with the claws of philosophical anthropology and historiography still seems to be the only epistemological method that allows us to subdue all reactionary archaeology. This is all the more so today, as we live through the transition from the modern to the postmodern, which is so similar to the passage from the Middle Ages to bourgeois culture which Descartes experienced, endured and overcame.

Rome, April 2004

Index

Printed in the United States
by Baker & Taylor Publisher Services